nning Theory

Discussing some of the most vexing criticisms of communicative planning theory (CPT), this book goes on to suggest how theorists and planners can respond to it. CPT has become mainstream but is still criticized for emphasis on consensus building, underdeveloped techniques for dealing with stakeholder coercion, and facilitation of neo-liberal urban policies.

With these severe criticisms being raised against CPT, the need has arisen to systematically think through what responsibilities planning theorists might have for the end-uses of their theoretical work. This book extends the consideration into the responsibility for promoting inclusive dialogue, and, finally, theorists' responsibilities as educators. Much attention is given to the notion of responsibility because of its importance to the ethics of planners as well as planning theorists. Offering inventive proposals for amending the shortcomings of this widely adhered planning method, this book reflects on what communicative planning theorists and practitioners can and should do differently.

Looking at issues of power, politics and ethics in relation to planning, this book is important reading for critics and advocates of CPT, with lessons for both theorists and practising planners.

Tore Sager is a Professor in the Department of Civil and Transport Engineering at the Norwegian University of Science and Technology.

The RTPI Library Series

Editors: Sara Drake, RTPI, UK; Robert Upton, *Infrastructure Planning Commission in England*; Patsy Healey, *University of Newcastle, UK and Jill Grant, Dalhousie University, Canada.*

Published by Routledge in conjunction with The Royal Town Planning Institute, this series of leading-edge texts looks at all aspects of spatial planning theory and practice from a comparative and international perspective.

Planning in Postmodern Times
Philip Allmendinger

The Making of the European Spatial Development Perspective
Andreas Faludi and Bas Waterhout

Planning for Crime Prevention
Richard Schneider and Ted Kitchen

The Planning Polity
Mark Tewdwr-Jones

Shadows of Power
An Allegory of Prudence in Land-Use Planning
Jean Hillier

Urban Planning and Cultural Identity
William JV Neill

Place Identity, Participation and Planning
Edited by Cliff Hague and Paul Jenkins

Planning for Diversity
Dory Reeves

Planning the Good Community
New Urbanism in Theory and Practice
Jill Grant

Planning, Law and Economics
Barrie Needham

Indicators for Urban and Regional Planning
Cecilia Wong

Planning at the Landscape Scale
Paul Selman

Urban Structure Matters
Petter Naess

Urban Complexity and Spatial Strategies
Towards a Relational Planning for Our Times
Patsy Healey

The Visual Language of Spatial Planning
Exploring Cartographic Representations for Spatial Planning in Europe
Stefanie Dühr

Planning and Transformation
Learning from the Post-Apartheid Experience
Philip Harrison, Alison Todes and Vanessa Watson

Conceptions of Space and Place in Strategic Spatial Planning
Edited by Simin Davoudi and Ian Strange

Regional Planning for Open Space
Edited by Terry van Dijk and Arnold van der Valk

Crossing Borders
International Exchange and Planning Practices
Edited by Patsy Healey and Robert Upton

Effective Practice in Spatial Planning
Janice Morphet

Transport Matters
Angela Hull

Cohesion, Coherence, Co-operation
European Spatial Planning Coming of Age?
Andreas Faludi

Strategic Spatial Projects
Catalysts for Change
Edited by Stijn Oosterlynck, Jef Van den Broeck, Louis Albrechts, Frank Moulaert and
Ann Verhetsel

Implementing Sustainability
Caroline Miller

Land and Limits, second edition
Richard Cowell and Susan Owens

Insurgencies
Essays in Planning Theory
John Friedmann

An Anatomy of Sprawl
Planning and Politics in Britain
Nicholas A Phelps

English Regional Planning 2000–2010
Edited by Corinne Swain, Dr Tim Marshall and Tony Baden

Reviving Critical Planning Theory:

Dealing with pressure, neo-liberalism, and responsibility in communicative planning

Tore Sager

Routledge
Taylor & Francis Group

LONDON AND NEW YORK

First published 2013
by Routledge
711 Third Avenue, New York, NY 10017

Simultaneously published in the UK
by Routledge
2 Park Square, Milton Park, Abingdon, Oxon OX14 4RN

Routledge is an imprint of the Taylor & Francis Group, an informa business

British Library Cataloguing in Publication Data
A catalogue record for this book is available from the British Library

Library of Congress Cataloging-in-Publication Data
Sager, Tore.
Reviving critical planning theory : dealing with pressure, neo-liberalism, and responsibility in
communicative planning / Tore Sager.
p. cm.
Includes bibliographical references and index.
1. Communication in city planning. 2. City planning. 3. Regional planning. I. Title.
HT166.S21814 2012
307.1'216--dc23
2012006948

ISBN: 978-0-415-68667-9 (hbk)
ISBN: 978-0-415-68868-6 (pbk)
ISBN: 978-0-203-10418-7 (ebk)

Typeset in 10.5pt on 13pt Goudy Old Style
by Saxon Graphics Ltd, Derby

MIX
Paper from
responsible sources
FSC
www.fsc.org   FSC® C004839

Printed and bound in Great Britain by the MPG Books Group

Contents

List of Illustrations

Boxes

Tables

Figures

Preface

This book aims at the revival of critical planning theory. Communicative planning theory (CPT) was presented in early articles by John Forester as a critical theory inspired by pragmatism and Jürgen Habermas's theory of communicative action. The critical side of CPT was also accentuated in books from the early 1990s, such as Forester's *Critical Theory, Public Policy, and Planning Practice* (Forester 1993a) and Sager's *Communicative Planning Theory* (Sager 1994). CPT has since been criticized in such a way that – in so far as the arguments are valid and the planning theory is not modified – CPT will lose credibility as a critical theory. However, the present book shows that CPT can be reformed and enriched so as to take the sting out of the criticism and restore CPT as a plausible critical theory.

The book deals with some of the most vexing criticisms of communicative planning theory (CPT) and suggests how theorists and planners can respond to it. The suggestions are of different kinds, describing how to examine whether the criticism has merit, how to revise CPT to make it less vulnerable to the objections, and how to reflect on what to take responsibility for.

At the heart of the criticism is the alleged problem that CPT has no convincing strategy for countering repressive power in the planning process, and that – partly for that reason – CPT recommends a mode of planning that tends to facilitate a neo-liberal development of society. Questions of responsibility are sure to arise in the wake of such charges, so the last part of the book deals with the moral obligations of planning theorists.

The book addresses these core problems of mainstream planning theory (CPT), and therefore brings up central issues that are part of numerous planning courses. It is not a textbook that reiterates what has already been presented in the planning literature, however. Not only planners, but also graduate students, PhD candidates, and academics in the fields of planning, public administration, and policy-oriented urban geography will find new ideas of how to approach problems of communicative planning.

Planners will find a discussion of ways to legitimize communicative planning which have not received much attention previously. Practitioners will also benefit from the comprehensive account of models for withstanding non-deliberative stakeholder pressure by forging alliances between planners and activists who are external to the planning process. Furthermore, socially concerned professionals will appreciate the proposed strategy for examining whether an urban planning effort benefits neo-liberal social change or reflects the values of CPT. The new approaches are not heterodox whims leading the discussion of mainstream planning theory out on a sidetrack, but based on ideas from neighbouring disciplines that are potentially important to the future development of CPT.

Situating the book in current discourse on planning theory

It seems to be quite common that the literature on a new theory develops along a certain pattern, at least in the early phases of the theory's attention cycle. Initially, it is imperative for the originator of the theory and the small band of early followers that other academics open their eyes and minds to the new ideas. Early presentations of a theory typically give optimistic accounts of its potential and practical usefulness. Research evolves in a dialectic between creative invention, critique, defence, and modifications, however, and early tributes are bound to be scrutinized both theoretically and empirically. In the next stage, ameliorated and more nuanced versions of the theory are usually defended. Different branches of the theory are often distinguished, as it is realized that real world contingencies call for a range of specialized theoretical and practical tools. Painted with broad strokes, this gives a picture of where CPT stands around the year 2010. Three decades have passed since John Forester's (1980) first important articles on critical communicative planning theory.

The term 'communicative planning' as used throughout this book encompasses processes that are also called dialogical, deliberative, or collaborative. The terms are largely overlapping, although collaborative planning is sometimes consensus-seeking to such a high degree that little room is left for an approach that is critical of strongly biased power relations. In other words, communicative planning is not necessarily critical, and critical planning theory does not always emphasize deliberation or debate. The non-critical approaches to planning are more vulnerable to the charge of unintentionally facilitating neo-liberalism than the critical approaches that are always attentive to inclusion and representation in ways that immediately challenge neo-liberal theory and practice. In this book, 'collaborative planner' and 'critical pragmatist' denote planners that put, respectively, less and more emphasis on communicative planning as a critical and reformist endeavour. I sometimes use 'communicative planner' as a generic term, even if it is an odd phrase since all planners communicate.

Diverging approaches can be discerned from books on CPT that have been published since 2005. Harper and Stein (2006) prefer a theoretical and philosophical approach, aiming to situate CPT in relation to the modernism debate. They try to construct a robust platform for CPT by supplementing

Habermasian thinking with ideas from John Rawls, Donald Davidson, and Richard Rorty. Innes and Booher's (2010) introductory text on collaborative rationality draws on the authors' own experience as facilitators and mediators in a number of consensus building processes. The practical skills they acquired inform their theoretical sections on how to conduct communicative planning. Forester (2009a) takes on an even more empirical approach. He studies real confrontations, difficult mediation, and practical consensus building and brings valuable knowledge back to planning theory. Forester's book is a rich narrative analysis built on 'profiles of practitioners' created through case-focused interviews.

Major recent contributions to the literature on CPT successfully link mainstream planning theory to topical themes such as post-modernism, complexity, and 'organization of hope' in conflict situations (the books mentioned above), as well as to institutionalism (Verma 2007), networks (Albrechts and Mandelbaum 2005), and pragmatism. Books and survey articles on CPT (Healey 2009, 2011) have given more attention to these concepts than to other central themes, forming and being formed by current economic-political trends, such as sustainability, globalization, or web-based arenas of interchange. Notably, the nine-volume series *Classics in Planning* (published by Edward Elgar 2006–2008) contains no articles on planning and neo-liberalism. The same is true for the three-volume set on *Critical Essays in Planning Theory* (2008) edited by Jean Hillier and Patsy Healey.

The present book takes a step in the direction of politics by exploring the relationship between CPT and neo-liberalism (including its offspring, new public management). This focal part of the book situates CPT and its planning practice in relation to the most powerful economic-political ideology since the collapse of communism. This will hopefully meet a demand, as Lovering (2009:5) observes that very few planning textbooks have the word neo-liberalism even in their index. Allmendinger (2009) and Low (1991) are exceptions, but they do not comment on planning-related neo-liberal policies or on the relationship between neo-liberalism and CPT. The possibility that CPT might have the unintended consequence of facilitating neo-liberal policies makes the study of other key themes of the book – dealing with power and taking responsibility – particularly apposite.

The political side of planning is also brought out clearly in the analysis of the activist communicative planner role. Explication of that role fills two chapters and is not primarily about technical expertise or communication, but about strategies for coalition and participation. At the centre of the activist planner's strategy is the establishment of an informal coalition with an interest group or a social movement external to the official process. The political aim of the activist planners is to generate outside pressure that can help them to move the planning outcome towards fairness by inducing stakeholders to seek solutions in a deliberative manner.

Acknowledgements

The first material for this book was collected during a three months stay at Murdoch University in Western Australia in 2002. I am grateful to Dora Marinova, then chair of the Institute for Sustainability and Technology Policy, for providing facilities and an inspiring working environment. Thanks also to Jean Hillier, then at Curtin University of Technology in Perth, for stimulating chats on planning theory, and to both Jean and her planner husband Theo for bringing me along on excursions into the countryside. The lively debate in the Australian media at the time, about restructuring and commercializing the universities, triggered my interest in neo-liberalism.

Much later in the writing process, I had research stays in New Zealand and South Africa, two other countries that have experienced their fair share of neo-liberalization. During my three months in Auckland in 2007, I concentrated on responsibility issues. This is one of Michael Gunder's interests, and he read and commented on early versions of the texts for Part III of this book. I am grateful to him for that, and for making the arrangements for my fruitful sabbatical at his place of work, the School of Architecture and Planning at the University of Auckland.

Vanessa Watson kindly received me as a visiting professor to the University of Cape Town in 2008. Despite her busy days as acting head of the School of Architecture, Planning and Geomatics, she often came by my office for invigorating talks about planning theory in developing countries or the intriguing politics of her country. Vanessa and the people she introduced me to, especially Pieter Jolly, research associate with the Department of Archaeology, provided me with a very pleasant three months in Cape Town.

The help of peers in reading and commenting on research publications is invaluable, and thanks are due to those who have contributed to the various chapters in this way at different stages of completion. They are Nils Aarsæther, Ernest Alexander, John Forester, Michael Gunder, Jean Hillier, Judith Innes, Tore Langmyhr, Torill Nyseth, Matti Siemiatycki, John Sturzaker, and Rachel Weber. Patsy Healey read the whole manuscript thoroughly and came up with excellent advice for improvements. Furthermore, I appreciate the broad-mindedness and indulgence of my working place, the Department of Civil and Transport Engineering at the Norwegian University of Science and Technology (NTNU), and my colleagues' acceptance of the fact that I spend time on research that is only indirectly linked to transport planning. Careful checks of the language are indispensable, and I acknowledge the efforts of Nancy Lea Eik-Nes at NTNU in Trondheim, who has improved the English of the entire book.

Earlier versions of about half of the chapters have been published as journal articles or book chapters, and I value the constructive assistance of editors and anonymous referees. Chapter 1 uses material from the paper 'Collective action: balancing public and particularistic interests' which was written for the *Oxford Handbook of Urban Planning* edited by Rachel Weber and Randall Crane and scheduled to be published by Oxford University Press in 2012. The paper was significantly changed for inclusion in the present book and now focuses more on legitimation and less on the public interest. In 2006, Chapter 2 was published with the same title 'The logic of critical communicative planning: transaction cost alteration', in *Planning Theory* volume 5, issue 3, pages 223–54. This article won the AESOP Prize Paper Competition as the best article in European planning journals in 2006. Chapter 5 is an abridged and recast version of a comprehensive literature study with around 770 references, which was published as 'Neo-liberal urban planning policies: a literature survey 1990–2010' in *Progress in Planning* in 2011 (volume 76, issue 4, pages 147–99). Two different versions of Chapter 6 have already been published. The first appeared in *European Planning Studies* in 2009 (volume 17, issue 1, pages 65–84) with the title 'Planners' role: torn between dialogical ideals and neo-liberal realities'. A more theoretical version with the title 'Role conflict: planners torn between dialogical ideals and neo-liberal realities' appeared in 2010 in the book *Ashgate Research Companion to Planning Theory: Conceptual Challenges for Spatial Planning*, edited by Jean Hillier and Patsy Healey and published by Ashgate. The paper was revised once again for the present volume, and the classification of values is now given more attention. Earlier versions of Chapters 8, 9, and part of Chapter 10 were published together in 2009 as one long article in *Progress in Planning* (volume 72, issue 1, pages 1–51). The title was 'Responsibilities of theorists: the case of communicative planning theory'. The material for Chapter 8 has undergone thorough re-editing, and most of Chapter 10 is written anew. All previously published texts are reproduced here with the permission of the publishers.

Figure 7.1, showing the area Svartlamon, is used with the permission of the copyright holder, freelance journalist Bjørn Lønnum Andreassen. The seven other photographs are under the copyright of the author.

Introduction: Critiques and Evolutions of Communicative Planning Theory

For theorists and practitioners alike, it is necessary to know how the planning processes they work on can be justified. They should also know how to counter severe criticism of their favoured mode of planning or at least know how to determine the validity of grave objections. This book aims to convey such knowledge with relevance to communicative planning theory (CPT). In addition, much attention is given to the notion of responsibility, which is important in the ethics of planners as well as theorists. The book discusses the responsibilities of planning theorists, for example, regarding the consequences of practical applications of their theories.

The book has strong bearings on how to plan within a critical, communicative conceptual framework, although it is a contribution to planning theory. The discussion of combined activism and deliberation as a means to improve the empowering capacity of communicative planning in adverse conditions, and the increased emphasis on substantive values in order to prevent planners from unwittingly serving neo-liberal agendas, are both intended to have practical implications. Readers will hopefully find that CPT can be meaningfully reformed and pragmatically ameliorated in response to challenging criticism, and that there are interesting and helpful ways to reflect on the moral responsibility that planning theorists encounter – obligations which they might perceive as especially thought-provoking when faced with harsh disapproval.

Initial information is provided in three places. The preface stated the purpose of the book, identified its likely readership, and explained how the main themes of the book relate to the ongoing discourse on planning theory. Chapter 1 starts by acquainting readers with the essentials of CPT. This introduction tells what the book is about, why it is topical and important, and why planners as well as theorists will benefit from reading it. I also offer a brief account of the debates about CPT.

Reviving critical planning theory: dealing with pressure, neo-liberalism, and responsibility in communicative planning

From the outset, CPT was meant to provide a critical foundation for planning, as it was in some respects an adaptation of the critical theory of communicative action developed by Jürgen Habermas (Eriksen and Weigård 2003). The title of the book reflects my conviction that even contemporary planning theory should have a critical side to it that questions the political and economic processes of which urban planning is an integral part.

The overall argument

This book is about CPT, and especially the branch insisting that planning theory should take a critical view of society. This critical strand of CPT is here called critical pragmatism. From its critical perspective, problems of exclusion, inequity, discrimination, and private interests overshadowing the interests of the broader citizenry call for close probing. The basic assumption providing the motivation for the book is that CPT has been criticized in ways that can erode its credibility as a critical planning theory.

Two points of severe criticism have been raised against CPT. The first objection has been bothering planning theorists since the inception of communicative planning: The CPT mode of planning depends on the intellectual force of arguments; it has not devised an effective strategy for dealing with stakeholders who rely on their social position to dominate the planning process and ensure an outcome of their own liking. This objection is often followed up with the rhetorical question of what right planners have to drag ordinary people, protest groups, neighbourhood associations, etc., into co-opting and exhausting participation processes if there is no operational strategy for preventing (for example) real estate groups or strong commercial developers from getting the upper hand in the local negotiations.

A different but equally salient problem is how to keep CPT as a critical theory of planning, avoiding that it is intentionally – or especially unintentionally – used to justify policies that support the predominant economic-political ideology of the time. This problem was not often aired before the turn of the century, after many sections of society had been colonized by the neo-liberal ideology that hails entrepreneurialism, private business, market logic, economic efficiency, and materialistic lifestyle. Neo-liberalism is not only a programme of resolving problems of society by means of competitive markets, but also the latest institutional form of capitalism. The second point of criticism says that communicative planning and CPT serve neo-liberalism whether this is intended or not. It is a grave accusation, as many regimes with neo-liberal agendas have limited the tasks, resources, and mandates assigned to public planning, and because a considerable part of the public regards the policies often denoted neo-liberal as a threat to the living conditions of ordinary people.

The arguments put forward by the critics of CPT need to be scrutinized, but this is not my errand in the present book. I am neither out to take issue with the critics nor to write a defence of CPT. My approach is to take the core critical arguments seriously, even if the consequences of CPT outlined by the critics are very different from what communicative planning theorists intended. The aim is to investigate what can be done to revive CPT as a critical theory of planning, even in the eyes of those who consider the arguments of the critics to have theoretical appeal or empirical merit.

The purpose of the book, then, is to make CPT less vulnerable and more robust in the face of accusations that this planning theory serves other interests than intended. A convincing argument is needed, as critical pragmatism cannot claim to be a critical planning theory if it mainly serves the prevailing economic-political interests and sidetracks the opposition into exhausting processes that offer little substantive reward.

I start the strengthening of CPT by offering new arguments legitimizing this planning theory. Thereafter, I respond to the no-strategy-against-power critique by shaping an activist role compatible with CPT. The idea is that the planner builds an alliance with activist organizations external to the planning process and encourages them to put pressure on stakeholders that act too self-serving at the expense of broader interests. The serving neo-liberalism critique is addressed by identifying substantive criteria for good plans that are closely associated with the procedural values that CPT is promoting. When the outcomes of communicative planning satisfy these criteria, it will be unreasonable to describe the plans as serving neo-liberalism.

Some of the critics strike out at CPT indirectly by attacking the communicative planning theorists for being politically naïve and acting as if spellbound by their own good intentions. I provide a basis for assessing this critique by analyzing the theorists' responsibility for end-uses, and their responsibility for inclusion, which is a core aspiration of CPT. The analysis of responsibility ends in an account of the challenges of critical planning theorists as educators and scholars in an academia that seems to be ever more influenced by neo-liberal ideas. This outline does not clear communicative planning theorists of all suspicion of naïvely misjudging the effects of their own theoretical constructs, but at least clarifies what critical theorists are up against in many contemporary universities.

Critical planning theory

If one or both of the above points of criticism are valid, CPT will have applications and end-uses which promote a narrow set of economistic and market-oriented values, and will most likely give priority to segments of the population that are already well off. This is all very different from the original intentions of communicative planning theorists: to deepen democracy, 'to spread political responsibility, engagement, and action', and to take steps 'toward the renewal of structurally sensitive, practically engaged, ethically and politically critical planning theory and practice' (Forester 1989:162). This is a manifesto to which I subscribe.

Critical theory illuminates the ways in which people accept societies characterized by massive inequities and the systematic exploitation of the many by the few as normal. Critical theory reveals how bureaucratic rationality, hedonic individualist ethics, and the logic of dominant ideology push people into ways of living that perpetuate discrimination along economic, ethnic, cultural, and gender lines (Brookfield 2005). Brenner's characterization of critical urban theory is also valid for critical planning theory:

> Rather than affirming the current condition of cities as the expression of transhistorical laws of social organization, bureaucratic rationality or economic efficiency, critical urban theory emphasizes the politically and ideologically mediated, socially contested and therefore malleable character of urban space – that is, its continual (re)construction as a site, medium and outcome of historically specific relations of social power. (Brenner 2009:198)

Critical planning theory should examine the relationships between urban planning and the changing balance of social forces, power relations, socio-spatial inequalities and political-institutional arrangements that shape, and are in turn shaped by, the evolution of neo-liberal urbanization. Critical planning theory must reveal and question the ways in which planning contributes to the lubrication of the processes of taking unfairness for granted. Critical distancing from, and then oppositional re-engagement with, the ways and means of the dominant culture of planning are what critical planning theory is striving for. A critical theory of planning can be deemed effective to the extent that it keeps alive the hope that society can be changed by planned collective action to make it fairer and more compassionate despite the strong structures that favour the interests of the already well off.

The book is an effort to revive critical planning theory in the sense that:

- It aims to reinforce the legitimizing rationale for communicative planning which is based on autonomy (anti-paternalism), the improved quality of decisions made not by a single authority but by many people pondering the same question, and the appreciation of relational goods created in interactions between people working in concert.
- It tries to find new ways that communicative planners can resist pressure from predominant actors.
- It suggests that substantive criteria should be worked out so that it can be checked whether the elements of the plan are in line with the values guiding the process. When the values of CPT are brought out clearly in the plan as well as the process, it is easier to make sure that communicative planning does not run the errand of ideologies at odds with its own core values.

It is the task of planning theorists to respond to critique, sort out conditions in which the unfavourable assessment of CPT may be well-grounded, and consider ways to revise the theory and improve anticipated results of applications. The present book is an attempt to fulfill this felt obligation, and proposals for a revised critical CPT are offered in Chapter 4 on activist communicative planning and in Chapter 7 on the value approach to examining whose interests CPT is serving.

Takeaway for practice

The analysis in the central part of the book is explicitly based on the neo-liberal reality in which an increasing number of planners are working. Neo-liberal ideology is strongly market-oriented and commends transfer of authority from governments to the private sector. Even more than before, public planners must expect opposition from strong market actors who challenge any notion of public interest by pursuing private goals using power strategies that disrupt open and fair deliberation.

For example, the neo-liberal policy of privatizing large airports creates powerful private actors with whom planners in adjacent municipalities have to co-operate in order to produce city plans with a balanced geographical development of housing and employment, and land transport infrastructure with capacity for serving not only the aeronautical functions but also all activities in the airport city that are meant for a wider public than the air travellers. How can the planners marshal support if coordination to the benefit of the entire city seems to count for little with the airport corporation? Can alliances be built with external groups – perhaps activist organizations – to put pressure on the airport owners to act on goals beyond their own profit? Who is responsible for the congestion problems following the clustering of commercial activities on private airport land? Do neo-liberal theorists have any moral responsibility for the traffic jams and the faltering environmental amenities?

Another example: in many cases, public planners have been opposed to the neo-liberal policy of privatizing inner city land for shopping precincts, dining and entertainment. Planners and their allies in various just city movements sometimes succeed in negotiating wider access to such downtown areas than favoured by business interests. Planners inspired by communicative action theory might support open access on the principle of inclusion and out of the wish to preserve places of uncensored public interaction and verbal interchange. Are communicative planning theorists then morally responsible for greater visibility of winos, beggars and homeless people in places where most families want to shop, dine and relax undisturbed and unconcerned? The book analyzes problems that intemperate, self-absorbed stakeholders, neo-liberal policies, and moral responsibilities raise in communicative planning, with respect to working out practices that are both legitimate and effective in protecting public benefits.

The next three paragraphs outline, on a chapter-by-chapter basis, what the book provides for planners. It is embarrassing for professionals, whether practitioners or theorists, to reveal difficulties in explaining the usefulness of their preferred mode of planning. The purpose of the first two chapters is to facilitate such an explanation of the merits of communicative planning both in general and in cases where forceful egoism unsupported by reasoned arguments endangers the deliberation process. Planners engaged in participative and deliberative processes sometimes need to counter self-interested power strategies by exerting pressure of their own. Chapters 3 and 4 survey available models for activist planning and suggest how planners can respect the essentials of communicative planning while still mobilizing support from activist organizations external to the official planning process.

Activist modes of planning may grow in importance as growth-oriented, business-friendly urban regimes gain power in ever more cities around the world. Public planners will benefit from the systematic overview of neo-liberal policies for urban development featured in Chapter 5, and from the critical points made by other planners about the various aspects of neo-liberal urban policy. The trend in many countries is towards an increasing number of urban development plans being initiated by the private sector. Under neo-liberal regimes private profit tends more often to be privileged over public goods. The tendency reflects tensions between the values that are the foundations of CPT and the values of new public management; these are juxtaposed in Chapter 6. Planners in the many governmental agencies that have been broken up and partly privatized under neo-liberal rule will recognize the role conflict of adjusting to market forces on the one hand, and incorporating the viewpoints of the participating local public on the other. Planners can, of course, be for or against the neo-liberal ideology and the imprint it makes on urban development. What is worrying is the allegation that communicative planning is necessarily the handmaiden of neo-liberalism – whether intended or not. Especially because many planners are opposed to neo-liberal politics, it is imperative to devise a way to examine whether concrete communicative planning efforts have the alleged effect. This is the task of Chapter 7.

In times of serious criticism against communicative planning, it is to be expected that questions of responsibility are raised. Planners obviously play a crucial part in influencing the end-use of planning theories. Therefore, the analysis of theorists' responsibility for the consequences of theory application in Chapter 8 also concerns practitioners. This goes for the discussion in Chapter 9 as well, which is about the responsibility for inclusion in deliberation. Planners design the processes that are meant to be inclusive, although theorists provide the underlying ideology. Responsibility, dealt with in the final three chapters, is a key concept in the professional ethics of planners.

The relevance of the themes of the present book is strongly indicated by a comparison with the content of well-known books directly addressing planning practitioners. A few examples will make the point.

Patsy Healey's (2006) book on *Collaborative Planning* contains an account of the interface between spatial planning and the economy. This has several points of contact with the chapters on 'neo-liberalism' in the book at hand, although Healey usually prefers other terms. She is interested in planning as a form of local governance, and in how it can lose direction in encounters with social polarization, environmental carelessness, relational biases, and interests that see a market opportunity in corrupt practice. She sounds a warning against property markets without land-use regulation and against local economic development focusing on too narrow a range of stakeholders. Healey advocates a pro-active role for public planning.

Bent Flyvbjerg's (1998b) in-depth case study of city centre planning in Aalborg (northern Jutland, Denmark) is widely read by planners and planning theorists alike. Flyvbjerg demonstrates clearly the exertion of non-deliberative power in planning and the limited impetus of 'the better argument'. He concludes that many actors in the case again and again, for personal and group advantage, violated the principles of democratic behaviour they were supposed to honour as civil servants, politicians, and citizens (ibid.235). In the strategic struggles surrounding city plans, power defines which is the better argument, and the planners' need for building alliances with external supporters is evident. The Chamber of Industry and Commerce is the planners' main adversary, wanting no restrictions on the movement of automobiles in the city's downtown. Flyvbjerg's account confirms the pertinence of the chapters on power and activist communicative planning in the present book.

By far the most widely used textbook in US master's-level planning theory courses (according to Klosterman 2011) is Michael Brooks' (2002) *Planning Theory for Practitioners*. Many themes in the book at hand are considered so important by Brooks that he includes them among the topics he wants to teach practising planners. He briefly tells about the problems following the rise of neo-liberalism (p 201) and the problem of power in communicative planning (p 129). Planners' refusal to deal with power is mentioned as a major source of professional failure. Brooks devotes a chapter to values and ethics. Planning is seen as so intertwined with politics that the planner must have a well-developed system of values not to be led astray, and the responsibilities and obligations of planners are listed (p 74). This theme of value links to Chapters 6 and 7 in the present book. Brooks tells practitioners that 'communicative action theorists have made an important contribution to the profession's value system, and all planners should be encouraged to incorporate these values into their own practice' (p 131). Finally, it is worth noting the weight that Brooks places on drawing practitioners' attention to the rationales for public planning. Planners should know and reflect upon why what they are doing is worth the effort. This justification theme is followed up here in Chapter 1 on legitimation and in Chapter 2 on the logic of critical communicative planning.

The central subjects of this book have wide relevance geographically. Volume 3 of the globally circulated *Dialogues in Urban and Regional Planning* (Harper et al. 2008:xiv) lists the 'forces shaping cities and the urbanization process (and planning responses to them)' as a major theme. The present book deals with one of these forces – neo-liberalism – which has an impact on cities worldwide by privileging pro-growth private business coalitions and entrepreneurial government (new public management). This book is also about one planning response to neo-liberalism, as planning-oriented neo-liberal policies are identified and the values of communicative planning are contrasted with those of neo-liberalism.

In general terms, the takeaway for practitioners is well expressed by Brooks (2002). Addressing planners, he credits planning theory for guiding us 'through a continuous self-examination of what it is we are doing, how we are doing it, why, for whom, and with what results' (ibid.21). In his view, '(t)heory places our feet firmly on the ground; properly conceived, it provides ethical and behavioral frameworks for the definition of professional planning practice' (ibid.22). I concur with the conviction of Michael Brooks that planning theory is important to the profession's sense of identity and purpose.

Why bring together these essays on power, neo-liberalism, and responsibility?

Part I of the book on power (stakeholder pressure) and Part II on politics (neo-liberalism) are not independent of each other. On the contrary, the criticism of CPT for leading up to neo-liberal urban policies is coupled to suspicion of the outcomes of local negotiations conducted in a way that is relatively unconstrained by statutory provisions and general guidelines. This scepticism is nourished by the belief that strong pro-growth business coalitions will usually have their way in communicative planning, even when the majority of local people would be better served by conservation or less commercial development. In so far as the criticism of local communicative planning for yielding to industrious stakeholders is valid, it therefore reinforces the criticism of CPT for buttressing neo-liberalism.

Power is a core concept in planning discourse, and public planning can itself be seen as a power strategy:

(I) believe planning to be a modern strategy for wielding power, not over space but over time, not over yourself but over others. I believe planning to be a political and bureaucratic phallus symbol whereby the present penetrates the future. I believe that to plan is to preserve what now is by ensuring that current intentions are turned into the stones of physical and institutional structures. The values of the strong today are thereby ontologically metamorphosed into the facts for the weak of tomorrow. (Olsson 1984:76)

The main concepts of this book all have solid ties to the notion of power, and this helps to bring the parts of the book together. Part I starts with a discussion of legitimation, which is the set of strategies used for making authorities and institutions accepted by the populace. The processes of legitimation thus legitimize power. Public planning systems need legitimacy, or else they risk being eroded by constituencies choosing alternative ways of solving their common problems, for example through markets and clubs. Empowerment of local communities is often an aim of communicative planning. This is much the same as increasing the autonomy of the local citizenry, or again, enhancing its power to improve local living conditions. The other chapters in Part I address the communicative planners' problem of how to counteract coercion by stakeholders who rely on non-deliberative strategies instead of on the intellectual force of arguments.

Politics is about the exercise of power. Neo-liberalism, discussed in Part II, is a set of ideas that change power relations by disseminating ideology, transforming institutions, and revising policies to put more emphasis on market solutions and less on social welfare politics. The analysis of neo-liberalism has become a key point of departure in critical urban studies and political geography. Academic engagement with the concept has diffused across a vast range of theoretical fields and approaches and across multiple empirical terrains, as shown in Part II of this book. Empirical evidence suggests that neo-liberalism has transferred power from local authorities and public hierarchies to the private sector and strong actors in the market. The timing and force of the changes vary among countries, but a quite typical observation is 'a significant weakening of planning powers and a corresponding increase in the power and assertiveness of development interests' (Griffiths 1986:3). There are attempts in many countries to revive the economy by simplifying and speeding up planning procedures, exhorting planners to adopt entrepreneurial attitudes, reducing public capital expenditures, and privatizing public space (ibid.5). While many can benefit from free markets, the winners, with respect to power as well as profit, are corporate businesses in the position to extract monopoly gains from their market transactions.

Part III analyzes responsibility, which links power to ethics. Those who have no choice can hardly be held responsible for their action. Responsibility arises with the power to do things differently, with having options. Power exercised by an individual implies a cause-effect relationship between the actions of that individual and the phenomenon he or she wants to influence. If my actions have no causal significance and thus cannot affect the phenomenon in question, I can have no responsibility for its development. The more things an individual can influence, and the more this individual can change the state of the world, the more responsibility the person has. Moral responsibility correlates positively with power.

This book can, accordingly, be read as part of the discourse on the relationship between planning and power, seeking answers to the questions of:

- How planning can be supplied with power through legitimation.
- How the power of planners can be undermined by stakeholders exerting non-deliberative pressure to steer the outcome of the planning process – and what can be done about it.
- How planners lose power through institutionalization of an ideology (neo-liberalism) that narrows its scope and imposes restraining economic-political conditions through new public management.
- How indications of the power of planning theorists can be obtained by analyzing their possibilities of influencing the end-uses of their work, and thus their responsibility.
- How planning theorists come up against other social values and powerful social institutions when they strive to realize the basic dialogical values of CPT.

Even seen from the perspective of neo-liberalism rather than power, the themes of this book fit together. Neo-liberalism displays a variety of power dimensions, ranging from the power of capital to determine the distribution of wealth to mechanisms for controlling individual conduct. Neo-liberal governance has, in practice, entailed an intensification of coercive and disciplinary forms of state intervention 'in order to *impose* versions of market rule and, subsequently, to manage the consequences and contradictions of such marketization initiatives' (Peck et al. 2009:51, emphasis in original). Neo-liberalism affects governmentality (Hiemstra 2010), surveillance (Monahan 2006), and disciplining of the subject (Gill 1995). The disciplined worker presents herself on the labour market physically fit (not obese) and with impeccable work ethic despite the combination – in some countries – of demonstrated greed at the corporate top level, and minimum wages that do not sustain decent living.

Instilling discipline in individuals is facilitated by indoctrination of personal responsibility. David Harvey explains the success of the neo-liberal appeal to personal responsibility in the US context:

> The strength of the neo-liberal ideology, on a popular level, is its emphasis on individual liberty, freedom and personal responsibility. Those have all been very important aspects of what you might call 'American ideology' since the very inception of what the U.S. has been about. What neo-liberalism did was to take the demand for that which was clearly there in the 1950s and the 1960s and say, 'We can satisfy this demand, but we are gonna do this a certain way, we are gonna do it through the market, and you can only achieve those goals through the market. We are gonna do it in such a way that you have to forget about the issues of social justice'. It seems to me that the movements of the 1960s were about combining individual liberty and social justice. What neo-liberalism did was say, 'we'll give you the individual liberty, you forget the social justice'. For that reason it has been very powerful in the United States as an ideology, because it can appeal to this long tradition of individual liberty and freedom. (Harvey 2010:103)

The neo-liberal twist is to accentuate individuals' responsibility for their own living conditions and de-emphasize individuals' responsibility for others. This lack of concern for social justice comes out clearly in neo-liberal welfare reforms affecting employment and housing assistance (Trudeau and Cope 2003) and in justice policies (Wacquant 2010). If there are 'level playing fields' and if universal access to these is assumed, then an individual's inability to maintain a steady job and household must be the result of personal shortcomings. In neo-liberal political settings, theoretical explanations of poverty and crime are swinging back towards those based on individual qualities rather than those concerned with structural inequalities of society. Moral uplift takes centre stage at the expense of politics and social planning.

I now return briefly to my intentions with the book. These essays on power, neo-liberalism and responsibility are not brought together to construct a defence of CPT, and the point is not to repudiate the criticism addressed in the first two parts. It may well be that strategies devised by planning theorists for handling dominant stakeholders in communicative processes are not effective enough to ensure fair planning outcomes. It may also be the case that communicative planning efforts sometimes work as preparation for neo-liberal urban development policies. These matters can most fruitfully be sorted out by empirical research, although years may go by before conclusive material is compiled.

The main purpose of the book is to discuss and come up with proposals of how to make CPT a more solid and critical basis for planning, even if the power-based or neoliberalism-based objections should turn out to be warranted in some circumstances. I reflect on what communicative planning theorists and practitioners can and should do differently if the scepticism to CPT is justified to a certain degree. My aim is to address basic points of criticism against the major branch of contemporary mainstream planning theory and provide theoretically underpinned suggestions of how CPT may be pragmatically revised to reveal its qualities more clearly as a critical planning theory.

Structure of the book

The book consists of three parts. Each is equipped with a preview, so the content of each part is just briefly outlined here. The first part revisits the old problem of 'planning in the face of power' which continuously follows planners and planning theorists and keeps appearing in books treating the subject in ever shifting conceptual frameworks (Hillier 2007:105–22). The other parts on neo-liberalism and responsibility deal with problems that have found their way into planning theory books more recently, see Allmendinger (2009:105–27) and Gunder and Hillier (2009:157–80), respectively.

When communicative planning is recommended, there should be convincing reasons why this sort of governance is thought to be legitimate, and there should be a clear logic behind what planners are trying to achieve. It should also be carefully considered that pragmatic adaptations making communicative planning work in practice might require that some principles and ideals have to be relaxed. Part I runs through this sequence of analyses. The emphasis is on concepts that until now have not been much discussed in

CPT: relational goods, the Condorcet jury theorem, and anti-paternalism as reasons for the legitimacy of communicative planning; alteration of political transaction costs as the logic of critical communicative planning; and the design of activist communicative planning modes that are dialogical-strategic hybrids with more lenient demands for communicative rationality.

In order to judge whether CPT unwittingly promotes neo-liberalism, it helps to have a clear idea of what neo-liberal urban policies look like; what characterizes neo-liberal values and processes in contrast to dialogical ones; and what criteria planning outcomes must fulfil in order to be in harmony with CPT process values instead of underpinning neo-liberal goals and policies. Part II clarifies the relationship between CPT and neo-liberalism by drawing on an extensive survey of planning-related academic literature on neo-liberal urban development policies over the last two decades (around 770 references from the period 1990–2010). The survey's function in the book is to support judgement of whether measures proposed in specific plans point in the direction of neo-liberalism. Also in Part II, value conflicts are mapped by juxtaposing the ideas of CPT and new public management. Furthermore, a strategy for addressing the criticism against CPT for being the handmaiden of neo-liberalism is worked out. The idea at the heart of the strategy is to sharpen and reinforce the requirement that outcomes of communicative planning efforts should carry the mark of substantive quality criteria that closely mirror the procedural values of CPT.

It makes sense to outline the charges against communicative planning theorists before discussing whether they have met their moral obligations. Once it is cleared up what planning theorists are accused of – what is allegedly wrong with CPT – questions of responsibility can be addressed. Lovering (2009:3) asserts that 'planning and planners have been complicit with the neoliberal disaster'; if this is so, planning theorists are also likely to have been involved somehow. Nevertheless, the text is not about attribution of blame; the intention is to give planners and theorists ideas about how to reflect on their moral responsibilities. If there is to be any point of doing planning theory at all, theory must have consequences for real people in real situations. Theorists make a difference through the end-uses of their work, through decisions they make (on stimulating inclusion, for example), and through their daily work in universities. These are the aspects of planning theorists' work analyzed in Part III, and the ideas of Emmanuel Levinas and Jacques Derrida come to good use in the last two chapters.

PART I
COUNTERACTING NON-DELIBERATIVE STAKEHOLDER PRESSURE

The first part of this book includes the four chapters that deal directly with power, starting with an account of how to legitimize CPT. Legitimation is about the justification of power. In a democracy, public planning needs legitimacy in order to build and retain the authority required to implement plans. Solid anchoring of this authority in democratic institutions is of paramount importance to planners who are trying to restrain those particularistic interests that rely on force to fight solutions that would serve the great majority.

The three other chapters in this part of the book contribute to the debate on how the communicative rationality of ideal Habermasian dialogue can be modified by an infusion of instrumental motivation and action in such ways that the resulting hybrids still deserve the name 'communicative planning'. I argue that amalgams of strategic and communicative action are required to deal effectively with stakeholders and groups using non-deliberative force to pursue goals that are reasonable only within their own frame of reference.

Chapter 1 explores important motivations for CPT. Emphasis is put on legitimizing features that have received little attention elsewhere, but are nevertheless closely associated with the main attractions of CPT: its epistemological, empowering, and relation-building potentials. More concretely, the legitimizing functions of the Condorcet jury theorem, anti-paternalism, and relational goods are discussed. The jury theorem states that as the number of reasonably informed decision-makers increases, the likelihood of a right decision approaches one. Arguments for public planning can spring from qualities of the process leading up to the plan or from qualities of the substance of the plan itself. Communicative planning as part of deliberative democracy is discussed as a process argument, while 'the public interest' is discussed as an outcome-related legitimizing argument.

Communicative planners are often criticized for lacking a credible strategy for dealing with problems of biased power relations. The purpose of Chapter 2 is to make it evident that critical communicative planning has a strategy for handling the problems. To achieve this, the logic of critical communicative planning

(John Forester's 'critical pragmatism') is reformulated in terms of transaction cost politics. In Habermasian parlance, the critical planner counteracts systematically distorted communication to promote plans that are not marked by repressive power relations. It is argued here that this is done by augmenting the transaction costs of those trying to influence the planned solution by leaning on their power base instead of on the force of the better argument. Also, the critical planner aims to diminish the political transaction costs of groups standing to lose from the results of power-based argumentation. The idea is to make it relatively more difficult to pursue particularistic interests by means of repressive or manipulative strategies. Hence, the rationality of critical pragmatism rests on power management by deliberate alteration of political transaction costs. Analysis of 'network power' shows that the same chain of reasoning is not well fitted to strongly consensus-seeking collaborative planning.

The planner who wishes to raise the political transaction costs of actors trying to exploit the weakness of others for their own gain, can do so by building an alliance with an organization outside the official planning process and make this external actor exert pressure. In order to understand how this kind of co-operation can be established and used for transaction cost alteration, it is helpful to survey the activist modes of planning described in the literature. The purpose of Chapter 3 is to offer such a systematic overview. The various models are displayed in two tables, one grouping the unconcealed and recognized modes of activist planning, and another classifying the concealed or unrecognized modes. Important lines of communication are severed when the planning effort is concealed or unrecognized. Planning modes suffering from such loss of interactive capacity are appropriate primarily in authoritarian societies and in conditions of severe repression.

By deliberately manipulating political transaction costs in an attempt to assist one group at the expense of others, planners are themselves playing power games. This can be justified under undemocratic local conditions. In non-ideal circumstances, trying to achieve ideal ethical action is not an optimal strategy. Communicative planning theorists must nevertheless discuss how the political transaction costs of disadvantaged or marginalized groups, whose living conditions the planners want to improve, can be effectively reduced relative to those of other groups without leaving the domain of communicative planning. The purpose of Chapter 4 is to give content to the role of the activist communicative planner and analyze hybrids of communicative and strategic action that are invariably embedded in activist communicative planning. The best situation for the activist communicative planner is when contact is established with an external activist organization that believes in dialogue in principle, but also acts on the belief that the current economic-political structures of society call for non-deliberative measures in order to redress threatening or repressive social practices.

1
Legitimizing Communicative Planning

Legitimation is chosen as the opening theme, because I consider it easier to argue for the revival of critical CPT (communicative planning theory) when it is convincingly shown that CPT is justified, that it has several desirable qualities and affects knowledge, power, and collective action in favourable ways.

Approaching planning from the angle of justification provides the opportunity to highlight essentials of CPT without reiterating too much basic textbook material. The last few sections bring to the fore some legitimizing features of communicative planning that have for the most part gone unrecognized. Communicative planning has a solid epistemological foundation and is likely to produce certain rewarding interpersonal relationships more effectively than other planning modes. Being the practice of a would-be *critical* planning theory, it is also crucial that communicative planning affects autonomy so as to empower local publics. Throughout the chapter, legitimation is linked with power, which is the unifying key word in Part I of the book.

The extensive discussion of trust in relation to legitimation is largely left out, although admittedly relevant (Grimes 2006, Warren 1999). Even though 'trust' is a factor granting 'legitimacy' to governments and political institutions, the concepts hold different contents. Legitimacy stands for someone's conviction that the institution conforms to the moral principles of that person, her sense of what is right or proper. Trust, however, reflects someone's belief that the institution performs in accordance with her normative expectations.

Introduction: legitimacy and planning

This introduction starts by explaining some main features of communicative planning and then goes on to define legitimacy and legitimation. These concepts are first dealt with in relation to planning in general, while their meaning and use in communicative planning are taken up in later sections. A plan is broadly seen as a suggestion of how to manage our co-existence in shared spaces (Healey 2006:3).

Various theoretical frameworks for conceptualizing planning as an idea and an activity have been tried in different places and periods, including synoptic (rationalistic) planning, disjointed incremental planning, advocacy planning, and communicative (collaborative) planning (Forester 1989, Sager 1994). These models all purport to enrich democracy in various ways, and thus serve broad interests by improving procedures that lead towards that widely recognized goal. Synoptic planning aims to enhance democracy by using experts and scientific method to enrich the knowledge base of majority decisions. Disjointed incrementalism serves democracy by arranging for every important interest or value to have its watchdog (Lindblom 1959:85). Furthermore:

> It reduces the stakes in each political controversy, thus encouraging losers to bear their losses without disrupting the political system. It helps maintain the vague general consensus on basic values (because no specific policy issue ever centrally poses a challenge to them) that many people believe is necessary for widespread voluntary acceptance of democratic government. (Lindblom 1979:520)

Incremental planning avoids bringing democratically made decisions into disrepute by shunning any policies 'whose scope is such that if they miscarry, the evils will exceed the remedial power of existing institutions' (Braybrooke and Lindblom 1963:239). Advocacy planning makes local popular government less discriminatory by giving voice to marginalized groups whose interests would not otherwise be conveyed to political decision-makers. The democratic aims of communicative planning are outlined below.

Communicative planning

Communicative planning as an approach aims to advance deliberative democracy by exploring the potential for broad workable agreement on planning matters, in any case making deliberation inclusive and thorough before a planning issue is somehow decided upon. This mode of planning also helps democracy produce fair outcomes by striving to reduce the influence of systematically biased power relations on the dialogically determined recommendations. The hope is that a change towards more participative approaches will help to develop social capital and community cohesion, improve service delivery to meet local needs, restore information flows and accountability, and give voice to those most directly affected by public policy (Yetano et al. 2010:784).

While attempts have been made to found CPT on the ideas of John Rawls and other scholars of liberal democracy (Harper and Stein 2006), the variant adhered to here leans more on Habermas's (1999) theory of communicative action. Several theorists combine this approach with notions from pragmatism (Healey 2009, Hoch 2007, Wagenaar 2011). Communicative planning demands more than talking with stakeholders and an involvement process merely informing the public. This planning mode is commended as a respectful, interpersonal discursive practice adapted to the needs of liberal and pluralist societies that prevent one social group from legitimately forcing its preferred solutions to collective problems on other groups. The aim is to promote the deliberative aspect of democracy and create and protect the conditions for deep and genuine civic discourse.

Communicative planning is seen here as an open and participatory enterprise involving a broad range of affected groups in socially oriented and fairness-seeking developments of land, infrastructure, or public services. It is guided by a process exploring the potential for co-operative ways of settling planning disputes and designed to approach the principles of discourse ethics. The process of communicative planning is open in the sense of being inclusive and transparent; the public can gain knowledge of what is going on. Development efforts are socially oriented when they aim to further the interests of large segments of society rather than the interests of a few stakeholders only. Development is fairness-seeking when it aims to improve the living conditions of deprived groups, and when its substantive results observe the rights of all groups. The principles of discourse ethics state that the communicative process should be open, undistorted, truth-seeking, and empathic[1] – in line with (A)–(D) below (compare Allmendinger 2009 and Innes and Booher 1999a:419):

(A) Openness as formulated by Habermas (1990:89):
  1. Every subject with the competence to speak and act is allowed to take part in a discourse.
  2a. Everyone is allowed to question any assertion whatever.
  b. Everyone is allowed to introduce any assertion whatever into the discourse.
  c. Everyone is allowed to express his attitudes, desires, and needs.
  3. No speaker may be prevented, by internal or external coercion, from exercising his rights as laid down in (1) and (2).
(B) The communication between participants should satisfy the four validity claims of being comprehensible, factually true, sincere, and appropriate within the normative context of public planning.
(C) Nothing should coerce a participant except the force of the better argument.
(D) Participants should be committed to reaching mutual understanding in dialogue free from strategic action.

Dialogue is defined here as conversation with the characteristics (B)–(D), and a planning process with all the above features is communicatively rational. The basic moral principle of discourse ethics – the Universalization principle – states that every valid norm has to fulfil the following condition:

> *All* affected can accept the consequences and the side effects its *general* observance can be anticipated to have for the satisfaction of *everyone's* interests (and these consequences are preferred to those of known alternative possibilities for regulation). (Habermas 1990:65, emphasis in original)

The Habermasian 'ideal speech situation' satisfies improbable conditions: 'openness to the public, inclusiveness, equal rights to participation, immunization against external or inherent compulsion, as well as the participants' orientation toward reaching understanding (that is, the sincere expression of utterances)' (Habermas 1999:367).

The idea is that, with communication approaching the principles of discourse ethics, participation would more likely be empowering, and decision-making would be deliberative and democratic. The ideal of deliberative democracy is to reach a decision through debate rather than voting, although practice calls for both modes of making decisions, most often with careful exploratory debate preceding voting (Bohman and Rehg 1997). Inclusion and the giving of reasons are central to the deliberative process, and some empirical results indicate that these characteristics make it more likely that participants will change their positions (Schneiderhan and Khan 2008).

Habermasian dialogue as outlined here has been an important ideal in CPT. It should nevertheless be noted that deliberative democrats are moving away from judging the legitimacy of deliberation only by the standard of the 'ideal speech situation'. There is increased 'appreciation for what different forms of deliberation in diverse contexts can contribute to the democratic system as a whole' (Karpowitz et al. 2009:602). A number of prominent scholars on deliberative democracy 'contend that self-interest, suitably constrained, ought to be part of the deliberation that eventuates in a democratic decision' (Mansbridge et al. 2010:64). They include negotiation involving appropriately constrained self-interest in the regulative standard to which real deliberations should aspire. This turn in the thinking about dialogue-like conversation makes deliberative democracy more realistic and can provide CPT with a mooring that is less reliant on Habermas's theory of communicative action. The hybrids of dialogue and strategy that are explored in Chapter 4 reflect the new acceptance of 'complementarity rather than antagonistic relation of deliberation to many democratic mechanisms that are not themselves deliberative' (ibid.64).

Dialogue has strong democratic properties, although it does not count votes or bow to preferences. Democratic planning means, for example, that planning proposals should not be put forward in a dictatorial manner, and that there should be no censorship on the expression of preferences. Dialogue also fosters truthfulness and sincerity, so manipulation (strategic action), like misleading people about one's motives, false revelation of preferences, and setting the agenda to fit one's own interests, is no part of the desired dialogue. It follows that references to 'dialogue' throughout the book refer to a communication process that is both democratic and free from manipulation. Dialogue is only a part of the interchange between participants in communicative planning. Debate and negotiation are also inevitable elements in the processes and practices of this planning mode, as underscored by Forester (2009a).

The 'critical pragmatism' strand of communicative planning aims to reveal unnecessary and systematic distortions of communication and thus promote equal opportunities and build support for reasonably effective and fair decisions (Forester 1989, 1993a, Sager 1994). This is a critical planning theory. Wagenaar (2011:297) states that 'Forester's critical pragmatism rests on two pillars: a theory of communicative rationality that should help planners redirect attention toward a more inclusive form of debate and practice, and tactics of communication and mediation that help actors overcome debilitating conflict'. Planners who follow this up and put weight on social critique in their communicative planning practice are named 'critical pragmatists' in this book, while other practitioners of communicative planning are called 'collaborative planners'. 'Communicative planner' is sometimes used as a generic term.

Excellent books with comprehensive explanations of what CPT is have been written by Forester (1989), Healey (2006), and Innes and Booher (2010). The brief presentation here is rather narrowly focused. Even so, the above outline comprises the characteristics of CPT that are needed for the analyses throughout the book. While the need to equalize power in planning discussions and to counteract distortions of the deliberation has a distinct position in this brief introductory account of communicative planning, I do not want to give the impression that this is all that CPT is about.

Over the last three decades, CPT has given attention to a wide range of subjects. It is in the nature of the case that a number of communicative practices have been studied, such as listening, storytelling, rhetoric, and mediation. A rich literature links CPT to descriptions of the communicative aspects of a planner's day and to a variety of planning tasks, for example, conflict resolution, network building, creative thinking, envisioning, public goods provision, children's participation, dealing with traumatized people, and making collective decisions. Finally, the relationships between CPT and various methods, philosophies, and epistemological themes are analyzed in the literature: cost-benefit analysis, transformative learning in small groups, pragmatism, postmodernism, institutionalism, and phenomenology, just to mention a few of the topics. It should be clear from this selective list of very different phenomena that CPT is a broad discourse in the field of planning, going far beyond consensus building and the striving for dialogue.

Legitimation

Sustainable systems for collective action – such as communicative planning – need legitimacy. The discussion is structured around three ways to address the legitimation issue. First, it is argued that legitimacy of planning is largely derived from the legitimacy of the political system it serves. Second, there is a special need to legitimize the power of planners to influence the decision-making system to which they render assistance. Third, the role of technocratic legitimation is noted.

Legitimation is the process of explaining and justifying the validity of an institutional order or an organizational system (Ansell 2004:8706). Legitimacy is primarily attributed to sources of political authority, such as decision-making bodies, governments, and regimes. When the approval of decisions or actions is concerned, I use the term justification instead of legitimation. Even if policies, priorities, or the allocation of resources are decided in a legitimate planning system, some of the decisions may still be morally wrong or illegal (by overstepping the mandate of the authority). Political legitimacy refers to the moral and normative principles by which governing bodies justify their right to demand compliance, obedience, or allegiance. 'In a rule-governed social order we cannot separate power from legitimacy, since both occur simultaneously; in acquiring power according to the rules a person also acquires the right to exercise it' (Beetham 1991:65). Institutions (rules) and organizations (actors) define power relations. It is therefore meaningful to talk about the legitimacy of power relations. When deployed in the public sphere, power can be said to be legitimate to the extent that it conforms to established rules that can be justified by reference to beliefs shared by both dominant and subordinate, and there is evidence of consent by the subordinate to the particular power relation (ibid.15–16).

Rules that build the legitimacy of power relations should be based upon a generally accepted principle of normative differentiation between dominant and subordinate (for example, qualified and unqualified). The rules should also serve some social purpose in which the subordinate have a concern (ibid.70). Rules of power must stem from an authoritative source. Deliberation in democratic political bodies is important for furnishing them with moral persuasiveness. Enhanced order, stability, and effectiveness are advantages that accrue to society as a result of obligations upon subordinates derived from a legitimate system of power relations, including public planning.

Power relationships do not necessarily collapse when their legitimacy is eroded. Obedience can be maintained by the incentives and sanctions that are usually installed to support power. However, when incentives are unchanged, coercion must be more extensive as legitimacy falters. The system of commands, controls, and enforcements that becomes indispensable raises the costs of economic and political transactions. Legitimacy is no longer present to make political processes efficient by reducing the costs of enforcing compliance.

Public planning is legitimate only when planners can invoke sources of authority beyond and above themselves. A planning agency enjoys legitimacy when acceptance of its authority is general among people in its area of jurisdiction and those people consider their obedience as a just commitment. In this line of reasoning, the legitimacy of planning does not rest directly on any notion of the public interest. A decision is justified if made by the right legitimate authority, and if the procedural rules of this authority were observed. Building the authority of public planning usually requires that no special interest is allowed to leave its distinct mark on the plan and make it biased in particularist ways. This is the problem addressed in Chapters 2, 3, and 4.

Legitimation as dealt with here is both about planners' justification of their professional domain and about politicians' use of planning to raise acceptance of decisions. These aspects of legitimation are mutually dependent, as the legitimacy of planning increases with democratically elected politicians' demand for planning, and as the ability of politicians to justify decisions by invoking skilful preparation and expert advice increases with the authority of the planning profession.

Public planning can help justify political decisions when formal preparation is an integral part of the procedural rules of the political body, or when decisions are considered more approvable if ex ante input was received from experts. Preparing for the decisions to be made by democratically elected politicians has both substantive and procedural aspects. On the substantive side it means to provide information on plausible options for place-making and their consequences. On the procedural side it means, among other things, organizing the planning process in such a way that all interested parties feel they have been listened to. The political decision about a plan is more readily justified the more inclusive and deliberative the process, and the more comprehensive the search for options and the impact assessment – that is, the better the preparation. Politicians can then credibly assert that the knowledge required for taking rational action was available to them at the time of deciding.

Most important decisions on public plans are made by politicians on the basis of analysis and recommendation from planners. This suggests that planning gains legitimacy by producing useful professional input to the political decisions to be made by a legitimate democratic system. It would be too simplistic to think that the main task of providing analyses and recommendations to political principals leaves the planners powerless. In fact, planners have agenda-setting power that in many cases can affect the final outcome (Hammond 1986). This leverage follows from option seeking, impact assessment, and comparative evaluation of plans. In addition, planners have the power to form the planning process; broad agreement on the outcome of an inclusive process will put considerable pressure on the decision-making politicians to follow suit. The legitimacy of the power generated by those activities cannot come from the democratic system of representation and voting. The impact assessment and the other agenda-forming planning tasks are an external influence on this democratic system and must tap legitimacy from another source. This is an important reason why the public interest concept is still used by many planning theorists despite its weaknesses. Appeal to the public interest helps legitimize the aspects of planning that are not only passively serving but also actively influencing democratic decision-making.

The procedural aspects of planning give room for participation and sharing of information, while the substantive aspects cater for place-making, that is, the tangible production side of planning which balances expert proposals for physical design with bureaucratic and political considerations of urban development. The legitimacy of planning therefore results from a mixture of technocratic and democratic underpinnings. 'Legitimacy is particularly important in democracies since a democracy's survival is ultimately dependent on the support of a majority of its citizens' (Dogan 2004:111). When the population endorses democracy, the planning system gains legitimacy if it is believed to further the higher principles of a democratic society, for example, self-determination, freedom of speech, and governmental accountability to the people.

Under a wide variety of political systems and planning processes, planners prepare for the building of roads, management of traffic, protection of the natural environment, construction of attractive and safe residential areas, well-functioning city centres, etc. In terms of deliberative ethics, the legitimacy of expertise is derived from the discursively determined ends of the people at large, and is not internal to expertise itself (Parkinson 2003:183). The production side of planning contributes to the economy by preparing for public service delivery and collective goods provision (Lowry 1994:102). Economic growth is important to most politicians in societies where the neo-liberal influence is strong. It is a priority of theirs to fight alleged waste in the public sector in order to keep taxes down and increase private purchasing power. However, strategies pursuing efficiency can create democratic problems. For example, early agreements reached in closed negotiations between municipal planners and private developers undermine transparency and challenge legitimacy and accountability (Falleth et al. 2010).

In many societies with mixed-market economies there is a neo-liberal pressure to shift from planned solutions drawn up in bureaucratic hierarchies to solutions implemented in competitive or contested markets. Politicians risk losing decision areas to the market when democratic legitimacy is weak. They therefore explore every source of legitimacy, including public planning (Sager and Sørensen 2011), vacillating between restricting its mandate and exploiting its capacity for underpinning political decisions. Dialogical values can help to produce public goods in a democratic and efficient manner (Sager 2007); later sections of this chapter nevertheless draw attention to other reasons for communicative planning.

Six sections follow, of which the first deals with the public interest, as this is the concept most often used to legitimize planning. Attention is thereafter directed to communicative planning and its legitimation as part of deliberative democracy. The three ensuing sections explain how legitimation of communicative planning is advanced through epistemological advantages (the Condorcet jury theorem), anti-paternalism, and relational goods. Finally, the legitimation theme is linked to empowerment.

The next section's discussion of social conflict or harmony – strife or consensus – takes the reader into the contemporary planning debate concerning the public interest and related themes. Attitudes towards the notion of common goods correlate with conceptions of conflict or harmony as the natural state of society. The main positions are surveyed, and extensive dialogue is identified as CPT's solution to the problem of public interest.

Strife, consensus, and the public interest

This section discusses the most important concept that planners appeal to when justifying recommendations. One purpose of this discussion is to take the sting out of some misconceived critique of the public interest concept by showing that it can be given a meaningful content without assuming consensus.

Communicative planning theory is criticized for its alleged bracketing of power and exaggerated reliance on consensus building. Nevertheless, most advocates of communicative planning assume a pluralist and diverse society in terms of values and interests, which means planning against a background of all sorts of conflict. But their (often Foucauldian) critics insist that consensus building can only work when an underlying harmony is assumed. The main arguments against consensus building as a generic and central planning practice are listed below. No attempt is made here to distinguish between more and less substantiated claims; see Dryzek and Niemeyer (2006) for an attempt to reconcile consensus and pluralism as political ideals.

- Consensus is always shallow and does not respect difference (Hillier 2003:43, McGuirk 2001:213, Pløger 2004:87).
- Consensus is a threat to freedom (Flyvbjerg 1998a:229, Tewdwr-Jones and Allmendinger 1998:1979). The privilege to engage in conflict is part of freedom, and therefore attempts to vanquish conflict suppress freedom.
- Consensual discourse necessarily involves the exclusion of some voices and the foreclosure of certain possibilities; it might silence rather than give voice (Hillier 2003:53, Pløger 2004:87, Tewdwr-Jones and Allmendinger 1998:1979).
- Consensus is utopian: 'In such a heavily politicised arena as planning, consensus is completely utopian – there will always be winners and losers – and it will never be possible for all individuals to abandon their political positions and act neutrally' (Tewdwr-Jones and Allmendinger 1998:1982).

According to the critics, the consensual approach to planning cannot succeed as an emancipatory and empowering project. This view is to a large extent inspired by Foucault's (1980) thinking about power and Mouffe's (1999, 2000) theory of agonistic pluralism: The shallowness of consensus is due to language games and different community life forms causing participants hailing from different communities to talk at cross-purposes. 'Any agreement they come to would then be more the product of power politics or clever rhetoric than real consensus' (Kapoor 2002:464). Another main argument of Mouffe's (1999:755) is that '(p)olitics aims at the creation of unity in a context of conflict and diversity; it is always concerned with the creation of an "us" by the determination of a "them"'. Reaching the Habermasian 'ideal speech situation' is impossible in these circumstances; meaning can emerge only by advancing one point of view at the expense and exclusion of other viewpoints, rendering the establishment of any discourse authoritarian – or so the critics say. Most communicative planning theorists seem unmoved by this argument, as they see the ideal speech situation as an evaluative ideal, not as a 'destination' of politics and planning in practice. Mouffe's argument comes close to giving *any* real-life discussion an authoritarian stamp, not only the debates and deliberations of communicative planning.

Mouffe (1999:755) stresses the importance of 'distinguishing between two types of political relations: one of *antagonism* between enemies, and one of *agonism* between adversaries (italics in original) ... An adversary is a legitimate enemy, an enemy with whom we have in common a shared adhesion to the ethico-political principles of democracy'. Strife is the expressive form of agonism (Pløger 2004:75). Power, persuasion, and strategic behaviour are intrinsic to agonistic relations, and hence strife cannot be ended by appeals to mutual understanding and the force of the best argument. Instead, a pluralist democracy is one in which there are constant conflicts of interest and renegotiation of social identity, and – according to followers of Mouffe such as Hillier (2003) and Pløger (2004) – this is therefore the social condition that urban planning should be designed to deal with. Kapoor (2002) sees the Habermas–Mouffe debate 'as a stand-in for the modern-postmodern argument, with Habermas defending reason, legitimacy, justice, universality, Mouffe defending antagonism, pluralism, contingency' (ibid.466).

There would not be much need for a critical approach to planning theory if society were in harmony and agonism were rare. I see no contradiction between recognizing that society is criss-crossed by conflicts of interest, and believing in the potential of critical communicative planning. It is in conditions of agonism rather than harmony that the search for common ground is urgent, although deep-seated conflict also reveals the limitations of attempts to build agreement.

In general, the idea of a public interest holds a stronger position among those who believe that stable consensus solutions to difficult planning problems can often be figured out, than among those who argue on theoretical grounds that any consensus will necessarily be shallow and thus unstable. As a platform for the discussion of legitimation, the following paragraphs survey some problems and possibilities of employing the concept of public interest in urban planning.

The public interest as a buttress for public planning

From early on, the planning profession felt the need for a concept that can clearly describe what planners are aiming at. In the tradition of harmony theories, the 'public interest' has been such a concept. The AICP Code of Ethics and Professional Conduct (effective from 1 June 2005) states as a first principle for planners that 'our primary obligation is to serve the public interest' (APA 2005). The concept is held by Klosterman (1980) to provide a meaningful, empirically verifiable, and rationally defensible criterion for evaluating public policies. If the public interest does not exist, it becomes more difficult to argue against the pursuit of self-interest. Private profit may then be privileged over public good. It is not my concern to marshal support for Klosterman's view, but I take the position that the 'public interest' concept can be helpful if defined so as to not require everybody's agreement on a policy.

The concept of public interest is controversial, and the weaknesses of many definitions have been acknowledged for several decades (see Bozeman 2007 and references in Campbell and Marshall 2002:170). It is feared that articulation of a public interest masks difference and heterogeneity and therefore represents a potentially oppressive idea, similar to the critique of consensus. Moreover, the concept might mystify rather than clarify. 'For example, it is frequently used as a device to cast an aura of legitimacy over the final resolution of policy questions where there are still significant areas of disagreement' (Campbell and Marshall 2000:308). Conceptual weaknesses do not place the 'public interest' in a special position, though. There is hardly any concept or theory in the social sciences that cannot be meaningfully criticized from some relevant perspective. The disclosure of weaknesses in the definition of a concept should not necessarily lead to its rejection. For example, planning theorists never stopped using the concept of 'power' even though its content remains unclear and its definitions are legion. The same is true for the concept of 'planning'; already around 1970, enough definitions had been proposed to warrant a separate bibliography (McCloskey 1971).

Perhaps one reason for the strong wish in some camps (especially among those sceptical about consensus in planning matters) to abandon the public interest concept is the propensity to ascribe too much importance to it. Critics fear that once a project, plan or policy is found to be in the public interest, no objection will be taken seriously, and the proposal in question will be implemented. However, compatibility with the public interest does not provide the final answer regarding the desirability of a collective action. Contrasting views on social harmony and conflict make composite justification of plans imperative. Even proponents of the public interest concept agree to this, and Klosterman (1980:330) concedes that conformity with the public interest is not the only consideration that goes into deciding what to do: 'The collective interest of the community may conflict with, and on occasion be overridden by, the dictates of justice and individuals' legal and moral rights of free speech, due process, and equal protection'.

Surveys of the ideas of the public interest in planning are offered by Campbell and Marshall (2002) and Alexander (2002a). These authors choose substantive/procedural as the main distinction between different concepts of the public interest, and both differentiate subjective and objective points of view; these correspond to different assumptions about the way in which individual interests relate to the interests of everyone taken together. 'If an individual is considered to be the only judge of what is in his or her interest, this constitutes a subjective view … Under an objective idea of individual interest, on the other hand, it is quite possible to argue that a person can be wrong about what he or she defines as his or her interest' (Howe 1992: 233). The subjective/objective distinction is linked to paternalism later in this chapter.

Substantive definitions of the public interest assume the existence of a normative standard outside of the processes of politics and planning by which public policy is judged, and they are outcome-focused and thus make demands on the contents of the plan. This is in contrast to approaches relying on procedural norms and rules by which the public interest can somehow be discovered. Substantive definitions cannot require unanimity if they are to be useful in practice, as there will always be somebody disagreeing with planning proposals. The basic problem is that any limited consensus opens for the possibility that what is decided on is a plan that serves the particularistic interest of a very large majority. Is it possible to distinguish between a plan with 90 per cent support that is in the public interest, and another plan backed by 90 per cent that serves a particularistic interest? Benditt offers a line of reasoning that helps us get around this difficulty.

> (I)f a particular action or policy is in the public interest because it will provide enough to eat for anyone who meets its conditions, no one can claim that such a policy is not in the public interest on the ground that he himself, being rich, is unlikely to benefit from it. Its being in the public interest has nothing to do with whether everyone will actually get some of the results of it. It has to do with whether having enough to eat is an interest of everyone's and with whether the serving of this interest is social in nature. (Benditt 1973:300)

Benditt's example 'enough to eat' is a likely candidate for a generalizable interest, since in a public debate it would be hard to insist that others should starve because the debater in question would not benefit from the arrangements catering for them. Planning-related examples are nevertheless needed in order to check whether Benditt's reasoning is relevant to planning practice. Consider 'risk reduction' as a candidate for a public interest. In Western countries, people are expected to protect themselves against certain sorts of risk by private insurance contracts. A plan protecting people against the risk of loss due to bicycle theft, for example, is therefore not likely to be in the public interest. The risk of flooded residential areas, avalanches hitting public roads and landslides undermining railway tracks is a different matter. It is in the interest of everyone to be protected against accidents brought about by these forces, and in most places such protection is defined as a public task. The fulfilment of these two criteria – being in everyone's interest, and defined as a public task – is what makes plans to secure roads against rocks and snow candidates for being in the public interest. This conclusion is not changed by protests from a road user who will soon be moving to another part of the country and thus will not receive any safety gain from the planned measures. His support is not needed for the plan to be in the public interest.

The basis of the public interest concept is the belief that indicators of the collective will can be constructed that are broader and more integral to a community or society than any particularistic interest. If there is no entity with a will of its own above the individual, then individual interests must be aggregated in order to express the public interest. It is not always possible to do this in a consistent and logical manner when preferences are strongly diverging

(Sager 2002). One way to create a wider range of permissible preference aggregations is to apply public interest indicators that accept decreasing welfare for some people even when others gain (that is, to relax the Pareto condition). This is much like using definitions of the public interest that do not require unanimity.

Habermasian dialogue does not require acknowledgement of community or society as entities with interests of their own that are separate from individual interests. The demand for inclusive dialogue upholds the requirement that the judgement of each individual is to count when sorting out the best arguments and thus in the articulation of the public interest. The result does not emerge by formal aggregation and calculation but instead by deliberation and debate. This does not solve all logical problems (Sager 2002, 2005), although the possibilities of identifying a consistent collective will are improved (Dryzek and List 2003).

What seems to be worth doing together, according to communicative planning theorists, is determined by what the parties can agree on in a dialogical process. Hence, collective action should not be determined by an 'objective' notion of the public interest that is independent of the outcome of dialogue. Quite to the contrary, with the very demanding requirements that have to be fulfilled by a communicative process in order for it to be dialogical in the Habermasian sense adopted by most communicative planning theorists, it might not be unreasonable to *define* the consensual outcome of dialogue as being in the public interest. After all, everyone concerned should take part, freely and equally, in the co-operative search for truth, where nothing coerces anyone except the force of the better argument (Pellizzoni 2001). In ideal conditions, then, the public interest can be discovered discursively through participatory practice.

The debate on the public interest concept continues also in the literature on public administration (Box 2007). A potentially fruitful use of the concept is to apply the 'public interest' as a utopian standard in critical analysis, much like Habermas's (1999:367–68) 'ideal speech situation' or Rawls's (1972:136–42) fairness as conceived by individuals behind a veil of ignorance. As Cooper (1998:77) asserts, the public interest should stand 'as a kind of question mark before all official decisions and conduct'. The pursuit of the public interest leads planners to 'broaden the discussion, the time frame, and the roster of participants; public interest is a process – an exploration – rather than an immutable or even identifiable conclusion' (Lewis 2006:699). The hope is that devotion to a purpose that is more general than any particularistic interest will lead planners towards a democratic and fair practice, regardless of whether or not there are planning-related objectives shared by all.

Although planners can do without the exact terms 'the public interest', 'the common good', or Habermas's 'universalizable interest' (Finlayson

2000), many planners find it hard to discard the idea that public planners should serve 'society', defined so as to reflect their felt commitment beyond any particularistic interest. Healey (2006), for example, often avoids the controversial public interest phrase, while articulating its content in alternative terms. She writes about 'an aggregate interest', 'our shared interests', and our 'common concern, though immensely various in its forms' (ibid.124–25). The widespread reluctance to let go of the underlying idea is due to the usefulness of the public interest in legitimizing public planning, and politicians' need to call on impartial planning input when attempting to justify their decisions.

A critique of institutions that are meant to serve society impartially is implicit in the attack on the idea of the public interest. It is hard to see how science, analytic methods, laws, norms, and social organizations – such as NGOs (Kamat 2004) – can be neutral if the public interest is a chimera. If every interest is particularistic, any mental or physical construct serves such an interest, and institutions and organizations that are claimed to serve interests that we all have need to be unmasked and stripped of the authority gained by pretending to serve us all. To the extent that this happens, purportedly common institutions, like urban planning, lose legitimacy. The legitimation of communicative planning is analyzed in the remaining sections.

Legitimizing communicative planning: deliberative democracy

Public communicative planning is an integral part of deliberative democracy. This section explains how to draw on this close bond in order to legitimize communicative planning. Deliberation is said to be a process of careful and informed reflection on facts and opinions, generally leading to a judgement on the matter at hand (King 2003:25). However, this rudimentary and austere definition says little about process qualities, and it is quite restrictive concerning the mode of speaking. Even if 'dialogue' in the citation below is broadly interpreted as conversation in conditions that do not fully satisfy the requirements of a Habermasian ideal speech situation, the following definition is well in line with the ambitions of CPT:

> Public deliberation is a combination of careful problem analysis and an egalitarian process in which participants have adequate speaking opportunities and engage in attentive listening or dialogue that bridges divergent ways of speaking and knowing. (Burkhalter et al. 2002:398)

Deliberative democracy means that the affairs of an association are governed by the public deliberation of its members (Cohen 1989:17). Communicative planning aims for extensive deliberation through inclusive dialogue and thus supports deliberative democracy where the association is a municipality or another political-administrative unit responsible for public planning. The communicative mode can make use of several techniques for organizing small-group deliberation in mini-publics composed of ordinary citizens, such as citizen's panels and consensus conferences (Goodin and Dryzek 2006). Empirical evidence supports the hypothesis that deliberative discussion of political issues can increase the sophistication of individuals' political judgements (Gastil and Dillard 1999) and enhance rationality (Willson et al. 2003).

Very different approaches are available for making collective decisions. They may be, for example, formal aggregation of individual preferences, voting systems, interest-based negotiation, and consensus-building public deliberation. The essential political act of deliberation – 'the giving, weighing, acceptance or rejection of reasons – is a public act, as opposed to the purely private act of voting' (Parkinson 2003:180). List (2006) distinguishes between two (extreme) types of deliberation, focusing on *what* choices should be made and *why* those choices should be made, respectively. The 'minimal liberal' account of how to make decisions responds to the *what* question. This approach holds that 'collective decisions should be made only on practical actions or policies and that the reasons (or justifications) underlying those decisions should be kept private' (ibid.362–63). The 'comprehensive deliberative' account answers the *why* question. This approach emphasizes 'the importance of giving reasons for collective decisions, where those reasons should themselves be collectively decided' (ibid.363). The second of these approaches to collective decision-making has a higher legitimation potential than the first one.

Several distinguished scholars studying deliberative democracy link the public interest, legitimation, and deliberation. Cohen (1989), for example, holds that 'the interests, aims, and ideals that comprise the common good are those that survive deliberation, interests that, on public reflection, we think it legitimate to appeal to in making claims on social resources' (ibid.25). Bohman (1998) maintains that all forms of deliberative democracy must refer to the ideal of public reason, 'to the requirement that legitimate decisions be ones that "everyone could accept" or at least "not reasonably reject"' (ibid.402). Benhabib (1996:69) sees legitimacy itself as a common good that can be produced only if the institutions of the polity 'are so arranged that what is considered in the common interest of all results from processes of collective deliberation…'.

In the political sphere, unanimity engenders legitimacy but is most often unrealistic, as it requires communicative rationality beyond what people are capable of. 'The criterion of communicative rationality is that we pursue our goals *to the extent this receives qualified acceptance from others*, in other words, the maximising of interests is subordinated to and conditioned by a communicatively obtained agreement' (Eriksen and Weigård 2003:45, italics in original). Moreover, as Dryzek (2001) and Manin (1987:341) observe, most democratic theories are concerned not only with legitimacy, but also with efficiency. These are two reasons why deliberative democracy settles for decision-making procedures that combine communicative and instrumental rationality (introducing, for example, majority voting and negotiation). The need to relinquish 'the ideal speech situation' and instead combine modified Habermasian dialogue with means-ends thinking is equally pressing in communicative planning. Misuse of power that engenders systematic communicative distortion cannot be effectively opposed unless planners act strategically as well as communicatively, as argued in the next three chapters.

The scope of strategic-communicative hybrid models has recently been explored by communication theorists (Black 2008, White 2008). One aim is to study how types of strategic communication (discussion, purposeful storytelling) can facilitate non-interested dialogue. Another aim is to construct a theoretical basis for legitimizing, at least partially, the useful institutions that are grounded in openly strategic action, for example, markets (White 2008:11). Less reliance on consensus is part of this pragmatic (re)orientation of communicative planning theory. For instance, discursive legitimacy should not require a comprehensive deliberative approach that necessitates full agreement on why a particular decision should be made. Workable agreement on public plans will have to do, making use of the insight that assent can be secured for courses of action for different reasons. This realization was used by Lindblom when designing disjointed incrementalism already half a century ago. Goal formulations were pragmatic and dependent on available means, in order not to distract from possible agreement on practical policy (Hirschman and Lindblom 1962:215–16).

By situating communicative planning as an integral part of deliberative democracy, we can hope to achieve more solid foundation of planned collective action. Public deliberation is vital because the planning decisions imposed by governments must be justified to those burdened by the plans, and justification must appeal to evidence and arguments acceptable to the citizens. Deliberative democracy is an ideal of popular sovereignty, according to which legitimacy is ultimately assessed in terms of the judgements of those who are governed and have access to the public deliberations. 'As political decisions are characteristically imposed on *all*, it seems reasonable to seek, as an essential condition for legitimacy, the deliberation of *all* or, more precisely, the right of all to participate in deliberation' (Manin 1987:352, emphasis in original). A justified decision does not represent the will of all, but results from the potentiality of the deliberation of all. If participation is not inclusive, and if the representative system leaves much to be desired, suspicion will linger that the conclusions from deliberation serve particularistic rather than public interests.

Parkinson (2003:181) starts out from the difficulties of deliberating with more than a few people at a time when pinpointing the central problems of deliberative democracy. '(B)ringing more than a few people in would quickly turn the event into speech-making, not deliberation'. Those left outside the forum might not see the procedure as legitimate or the decisions as justified. Moreover, participants to the forum must observe rules of reciprocity and willingness to set aside strategic concerns. 'And yet, people's pre-formed preferences, interests and goals are an essential part of what motivates them to enter political arenas in the first place' (ibid.181).

Communicative planning is a practical mode of preparing for (and thus influencing) collective decisions. Its normative legitimacy increases with the degree to which it approaches the dialogical ideals on which it is based (outlined in the introduction to this chapter). The coming sections highlight three particular characteristics of communicative planning that facilitate its legitimation as a social technology serving democracy: pooling information and judgements from many different participants, fighting forms of power that undermine their autonomy, and stimulating the production and consumption of relational goods that serve participants in ways that in turn invigorate democracy itself. It will be shown how these features help communicative planning resist particularistic interests and improve the basis for place-making forms of collective action. Issues of cost and public expense are ignored here in order to concentrate on legitimizing aspects of the planning mode.

Attention is directed to three key terms, one for each of the elements in the knowledge-power-action nexus:[2] the Condorcet jury theorem, paternalism, and relational goods, respectively. The argument is that communicative planning is a legitimate way of defining what is in the interest of the public for the following three reasons:

- Many people representing all interests affected by the planning are drawn into dialogue, thus increasing the likelihood that decisions are right and fair.
- The expressed preferences of one interest group cannot be set aside by another group for paternalistic reasons.
- Social capital networks brought into being by communicative planning generate relational goods such as social approval, confirmation of identity, and community attachment.

The key terms of the succeeding sections have previously been little used for clarifying the legitimizing features above. The listed features come in addition to the legitimizing characteristics already discussed in this chapter: (1) the ability of the communicative process to help identify public goods that are worth producing, and (2) ensuring that votes, when they are required, follow arguments put forward in inclusive deliberation where efforts are made to level power differentials.

Knowledge: epistemological benefits as revealed by the Condorcet jury theorem

Theorists of democracy (Somin 1998) and communicative action (Habermas 2006a) worry that citizen ignorance and disinterest in political matters might mess up the governing potential of public dialogue. This section brings forward the Condorcet jury theorem which gives reason for optimism. Deliberative democracy has a complex epistemic value derived both from deliberation itself and from Condorcet's theorem applied to democratic forums enlightened by deliberative processes (Martí 2006:39). The message that can be drawn from the theorem is in harmony with topical ideas about knowledge aggregation via the Internet, for example, the 'wiki' realization that lots of different people knowing many small things can result in great advantages for everyone. Thoughts about exploiting 'the wisdom of the crowd' through web technology are currently making their appearance in planning theory (Brabham 2009).

Assume that there are questions in planning matters that have right and wrong answers, for example: Is traffic safety likely to be more improved by a roundabout than by an unregulated intersection at a specific location? Is it cheaper to use electricity or a central heating plant to keep a particular new residential area warm? Can a city terminal covering X acres be built with sufficient capacity to serve the number of future public transit passengers expected by the city council? The correct answer to these – and many other – technical-economic questions has been established by research and professional experience external to the single planning process. In such cases, the criterion for what is right should be independent of the process itself. It should also be inter-subjective, which is to say at least partly independent of the preferences and beliefs of any individual participant. Planning alternatives with potential for being in the public interest in the substantive sense have to be based on the correct technical-economic answers, and the question is whether deliberation among lay people is likely to identify the best solutions. This is a timely question as most people are unfamiliar with planning matters and cannot be expected to hold clear ideas of causal relationships between means and ends in public planning.

According to the Condorcet jury theorem, it is nevertheless likely ($p > 0.9$) that an assemblage of, say, fifty imperfectly informed lay participants (each with 0.6 probability of being right) will collectively opt for the best of two alternatives (List and Goodin 2001). The theorem states that majorities are more likely than any single individual to select the better of two alternatives when there is uncertainty about which of the two best serves the purpose. More accurately, the Condorcet jury theorem (McLean and Hewitt 1994) says that if each individual is somewhat more likely than not to make the better choice between some pair of alternatives, and each individual has the same probability of being correct in this choice, then (with each voter voting independently and sincerely) the probability of the group majority being correct increases as the number of individuals increases, towards a limiting value of 1.

The demand for independent votes is interesting from the perspective of communicative planning. It would be devastating to the applicability of the Condorcet jury theorem, were independence to require total absence of communication between deliberators. 'Communication is obviously inevitable in politics, and then, interference among voters is unavoidable' (Martí 2006:40). However, communication itself may not be the problem; what would undermine the results of the theorem is some people voting under pressure, force, threat, logrolling and so on, because this nullifies the aggregated value of such a vote (Estlund 1994).

There is a classical debate over the question of whether we want political outcomes to be right or whether we want them to be fair (List and Goodin 2001). The outcomes of communicative planning are expected to be fair when dialogue observes the Universalization principle, explained in the introduction to this chapter. However, it will presumably be much easier to convince political decision-makers that communicative planning is a practice worth supporting, if it can also be effectively argued that local dialogical forums have a high probability of selecting the right option according to generally accepted standards external to the process. For example, that such forums are likely to identify and select the plan with the most stimulating economic impacts on society when it is agreed that this is the superior goal. These are the conditions in which the Condorcet jury theorem is helpful.

Condorcet's theorem has been generalized in several directions and proved to be valid in decision-making conditions that are quite realistic for communicative planning. For example, a jury theorem still holds even if individuals have varying competence, that is, 'not every member of the jury has exactly the same probability of choosing the correct outcome: all that is required is that the mean probability of being right across the jury be above one-half' (List and Goodin 2001:283). Furthermore, a similar theorem is valid when plurality voting over many options takes place instead of majority voting over two options (List and Goodin 2001), and Miller (1986) shows that a straightforward extension of the Condorcet jury theorem can be applied to cases in which individual interests conflict. Finally, it has been demonstrated that Condorcet's basic insight is robust to strategic behaviour; that is, certain sorts of interdependencies between the judgements of different electors (Austen-Smith and Feddersen 2009, Coughlan 2000). However, to the best of my knowledge, it has not yet been shown how well the mechanism behind the theorem works with the kind of information exchange that is realistic in deliberative processes.

It must be conceded that more comprehensive inclusion is not an epistemic advantage under all circumstances. The probability of the majority decision being wrong increases with the number of voters when people are less likely to vote for the right than for the wrong action. There is usually little to go on when conjecturing about the epistemic competence of participants in communicative planning. Martí suggests the following intuitive reason why Condorcet's jury theorem will work, although he does not find conclusive evidence:

> (I)f someone, being a member of a Jury, is going to decide about the culpability or innocence of someone else by tossing a coin, with no rational deliberation at all, the probability of making the right decision is exactly 0.5. Then, it seems reasonable to suppose that if such a person examines the information available and deliberates with herself, that is, if this person introduces rationality in decision-making, the probability should be higher than 0.5. (Martí 2006:41)

'Best' or 'right' planning solutions must often yield to alternatives that are technically or economically merely 'good enough', but considered superior for political reasons. It may nevertheless be advantageous to use a participatory planning approach that has a high probability of recognizing the 'best' option and selecting it when political criteria are also satisfied. The literature on the jury theorem suggests that 'policy choices made by majority rule tend to be far more accurate than one would expect based on survey evidence of voter knowledge' (Congleton 2007:208). The statistical mechanism behind the Condorcet jury theorem – the law of large numbers – causes outcome quality to rise when the number of participants in planning dialogue increases, and the mechanism works more effectively when the competence of the interlocutors is enhanced (Gabel and Shipan 2004). The exchange of arguments in inclusive debate free from repression educates the interlocutors and makes it more likely that each of them identifies the best alternative. The conclusion is that the Condorcet jury theorem offers a strong argument for democratic practices such as communicative planning, and there are procedures embedded in that mode of planning which in turn further solidifies the argument.

Power: anti-paternalism

Paternalism denotes a certain type of power relationship, and the section heading signals that communicative planning theorists are critical to this form of power relations. This section is concerned with political paternalism towards adults who have not been declared incapable of managing their own affairs, and who are not pathologically addicted or ill so as to have lost the capacity of taking care of themselves.

In a paternalistic power relationship the subordinate is regarded as incapable of recognizing and defending his or her own interests, and the paternalist therefore defines and manages these interests on behalf of the less competent individual (Beetham 1991:88). Paternalism can be defined as the interference of an individual or a collective actor with another person, against his or her will, and justified by a claim that the person interfered with will be better off or protected from harm (Dworkin 2005:1). The subordinate can be mistaken about what her interests are or about what best serves her interests; she can be seen as mistaken about either her ends or her means, or both (Rostbøll 2005:383). Exertion of power in the form of paternalism raises the question of what the trade-off is between regard for the welfare of others and respect for their right to make their own decisions.[3]

Planning theorists have worried about too much paternalism in planning (Arnstein 1969:217, Silva 2005:313) and even too little (Fainstein 2000:457). Paternalistic interference is premised on the idea of an objective individual interest and the conviction that people are not – or not always – the best judge of their own interests. Paternalism is common, for example, in emergency preparedness planning (Jennings 2008). Such disaster planning often forces some people to protect themselves in ways of which they do not approve today, in order to make them better off in the future, should an anticipated type of emergency occur. For example, people can be prohibited from building new houses on land prone to flooding, and housing cooperatives can be forced to construct air-raid shelters even when they would prefer not to. Veer (1986) offers an extensive analysis of paternalism in policies for safety and health.

Clichés such as 'the white man's burden' from the ideology of colonialism reveal paternalism, and some authors think it still lingers on in the 'partnerships' of development planning (Eriksson Baaz 2005). There are very few in-depth studies of paternalism in other fields of planning, except for the industrial paternalism of company towns (Alanen and Peltin 1978, Oberdeck 2000). Neither these mainly historical studies nor Susskind and Elliott's (1983) discussion of paternalism and citizen participation define paternalistic acts as being against the will of the 'beneficiary'.

Note that the standpoints against building on flood-prone land and in favour of air-raid shelters are not necessarily discreditable in themselves. The building can be advised against for the reason that it wastes the resources of society, and the shelters may be recommended because they are long-term facilities which many others than the present residents might take advantage of. What would be blameworthy is not the planners coming to a different conclusion than the local citizens on these matters, but the use of paternalistic arguments to ground the decision.

Paternalistic policies are sometimes confused with collective action adjusting for the weakness of will. Consider, for example, the assignment of smoking areas and restrictions on where to place slot machines for gambling. For our purpose we can distinguish between two kinds of users in both cases: those who have become addicted to smoking or gambling and really want to quit, and those who see these activities as pleasure and entertainment that they wish to enjoy even in the future. Restrictive policies towards the last group can be built on paternalistic arguments (even if the negative external effects of smoking open other possibilities). The same policies would be adjustments for the weakness of will as far as the first group is concerned. This is not paternalism, as the addicted and the regulator have the same goal. For this group, the regulations do not imply imposition of someone else's judgement on the smokers and gamblers. Policies towards split clienteles such as the above are problematic, as actions to help people who badly need it and ask for assistance will often lead to paternalistic interference with the lives of people who would have liked to be left alone (Rostbøll 2005:384).[4]

Much paternalism in planning springs from the belief that identifying the public interest or the common good requires a special knowledge, and that those who have attained this knowledge – the planners – are thereby entitled to make policy on behalf of those who have not. This belief is a challenge to communicative planning in particular, as the credence questions the ability of local citizens to make rational choices concerning public goods. In contrast, the planning profession has a tradition for claiming rationality in some sense. So the debate on paternalism in planning raises the question of how members of the self-proclaimed rational elite should be allowed to treat people they consider to be endowed with less rational intellects. How should persons be treated when assumed to be less than fully rational? Can they demand autonomy in planning matters? Is paternalistic action okay as long as those interfered with subsequently come to approve of it (Kasachkoff 1994)? Who decides whether an opponent is rational when, after all, everybody deviates from the behaviour of the rational agent devised by rational choice theorists (Kahneman 1994, Sen 1977). In the discourse on environmentalism, Meyer (2008:221) recognizes the attitude that: '*We* – the informed, engaged, public spirited – wish to protect *you* the uninformed, apathetic, or egoistic – from the consequences of your environmentally destructive ways' (italics in original). This attitude is not linked to any mode of planning in particular.

Intrinsic to all paternalistic power relations is the problem that subordinates' attempts to articulate their own interests conflict with the paternalist's conviction, and will be repressed. In denying the subordinates all independent means of expressing and defending their interests, there is nothing to stop paternalism with a benevolent intent from degenerating into the exercise of power in the interest merely of the powerful (Beetham 1991:90). Communicative planning theory takes a clear stance against paternalism and tries to do what is necessary to fight it by advising that all affected parties be brought to the table and take part in deliberative decision-making.

> The only principle of government that is non-paternalist is one where the ultimate source of authority is located wholly in the people, because only here is the criterion for the public good to be found not in some special wisdom, revelation or expert knowledge, but in what the people, freely organised, determine it to be, whether directly or through their representatives. Only here are those subordinate to government recognised as the ultimate judge of what their interests are. (Beetham 1991:89)

Collaborative planners and critical pragmatists nevertheless have to be on guard to avoid especially one paternalistic conviction: *We know, even if you disagree, that it is in your best interest to be included in the planning process and participate in the debate on plans concerning your local community.* Thoughtful consideration of others' welfare on the one hand, and concern for their autonomy on the other, are easily brought out of balance when increased legitimacy is in demand, as planners and their principals may have a motive for paternalistically persuading even reluctant stakeholders and citizens to join deliberation. Planning processes are more useful for legitimation purposes when more people take part. Nevertheless, insisting, for example, that impulsive people listen to rational arguments for their own good amounts to paternalism (Dworkin 1983:107). It is not another's substantive judgement that is substituted for one's own in this case, rather another's preferred decision procedure (public deliberation) is substituted for one's own (Rostbøll 2005:386).

The principle of autonomy is that competent adults should be left free to make their own decisions about how to live their lives based on their own preferences, religious convictions, conceptions of justice and virtue, beliefs about honour and dignity, and views about what is prudentially best for them. Competent but annoying people should not merely be tolerated, as this might entail just a weaker sort of paternalism (see the section on toleration in Chapter 9). It is a basic purpose of critical pragmatists to promote the autonomy and empowerment of local citizens in planning matters. CPT assumes that in the course of dialogue on the issue at hand, people come to know what is in their own best interest. Planners might disagree with local citizens on what is to be done, but the critical pragmatist should not implement actions that overrule another's preferences with the main intention of making the recalcitrant participant better off.[5] The primary motive must be better living conditions for consenting persons. Paternalism is directly opposed to autonomy and self-determination, and CPT is about ways to remove this form of power from the planning process. The central problem of paternalism in democratic politics is 'that in a democracy all actions of the state have ultimately to be approved by the people, and yet one of the conditions of a paternalistic act is that it is not sanctioned by the individual whom the act is supposed to benefit at the time of the intervention' (New 1999:81).

> (T)he paternalist believes she knows what is good for others and feels herself justified in imposing her judgment on others, while the deliberative democrat believes that what is right must be justified and accepted in deliberation. A basic assumption underlying deliberative democracy...is that no one has privileged access to truth or to the true interests of others. (Rostbøll 2005:388)

Deliberative democrats and communicative planners find it objectionable that the paternalist is unwilling to go into an argument about her own view but wants to impose it on another person.

Action: relational goods

The planning process as well as the plan itself can be public goods. There is increasing understanding in economics and the various fields of planning that public goods are not only produced through market transactions, contracts and physical construction, but also through the building of interpersonal relations. Relational goods are public goods that are simultaneously produced and consumed in relationships between people who are not anonymous to each other.[6]

Examples of relational goods are social approval,[7] friendship, confirmation of identity, emotional support (encouragement and comfort), a sense of belonging, and solidarity (Uhlaner 1989:255). Gui (1996:261) exemplifies by mentioning the heritage of mutual acquaintance, consent and, possibly, intimacy a group of nearby tenants accumulates over time, which is bound to be dissolved when a landowner decides to redevelop an area. Relational proximity is viewed by some as a key resource for the development of trusting relationships (Murphy 2006:430).

The examples show that relational goods can have intrinsic as well as instrumental value. In both cases, they provide motive for collective action of the kind that requires relationship-building interaction. Voluntary work in political or humanitarian organizations (Prouteau and Wolff 2008), active membership in social movements (Diani and McAdam 2003), and participation in communicative planning processes (Rader Olsson 2009) are activities that belong to this category. Relational goods are important for the action element of the knowledge-power-action path to social change and afford incentives for communicative planning. The relation with CPT will be explored after first pointing out a few more characteristics of relational goods.

Relational goods can only be produced by people acting together; they are not conceivable as a sum of individual goods. Those who take part in the production of relational goods cannot be excluded from using them, as production and consumption are simultaneous and joint, and because such goods are non-divisible (Gui 1996). With most public goods, my enjoyment is not enhanced by yours. 'However, for a relational good, a person's utility increases both as his or her own consumption increases and as the consumption of some specific other person or member of a defined set of people increases' (Uhlaner 1989:254). Becchetti et al. (2008:346) denote relational goods 'anti-rival', as participation in their consumption creates positive communication externalities on other participants and contributes to the quality of the public good itself. Since people cannot enjoy a relational good without taking part in its production, such goods are not exposed to the free rider problem (Prouteau and Wolff 2004:436, Sager 2007).

The main thesis of this section is that communicative planning produces relational goods. Dialogue is conducive to empathy which in turn promotes pro-social behaviour (Stocks et al. 2009). In fact, a 'cycle of dialogical rewards' is at work, as relational goods in turn motivate more communicative planning. The cycle goes like this: Communicative planning → Interpersonal encounters → Social capital networks → Relational goods → Deeper and more extensive participation.

Several studies confirm the positive effect of relational goods on increasing participation, see Gächter and Fehr (1999), McLeod et al. (1999), and Ryan et al. (2005). We will take a brief look at the components of the causal circuit above that have not already been explained, and then examine how the cycle relates to other notions of significance to CPT.

In Habermasian communicative action theory it is assumed that the encounters most conducive to the production of relational goods are those that facilitate dialogue. Dialogue is seen as the most efficient vehicle for creating the positive communicative externalities that are inherent in relational goods and make them a type of public goods. Anticipation of relational goods can be one reason why people accept a moral obligation to reciprocate in dialogue.

The outcome of personal interaction between two or more agents depends, according to Gui (2000:156), on local information, mutual understanding among the interacting people, and the social climate of the encounter. The social climate is usually better the lower the ambitions for personal gain. And the mutual understanding developed through dialogue positively affects the production of relational goods. Encounters that come close to dialogue must also approach fulfilment of the validity claims mentioned in the introductory section, including sincerity. Relational goods cannot be bought or contracted, as that would raise doubts about companionship, social approval, solidarity, etc. (Becchetti et al. 2008:346). Hence, money is less important than time donations in the production of relational goods. But even more decisive is the generous endowment of attention, demonstrated, for example, by listening. Attention is a credible indicator of the sincerity required in relationships that produce relational goods.

In the cycle of dialogical rewards, the encounters of communicative planning generate networks of social relations in which social capital is embedded (Rader Olsson 2009:271, Torfing et al. 2009). The survey article by Adler and Kwon (2002:17) starts out by tentatively defining social capital as 'the goodwill that is engendered by the fabric of social relations and that can be mobilized to facilitate action'. Social capital is an input in the production of many individual goods as well as public goods, including relational goods. In planning-related literature, social capital is sometimes used synonymously with community building (Wilson 1997:745) and analyzed as a strategy for community involvement (Rydin and Pennington 2000).

Ostrom and Ahn (2009:20) distinguish between 'three types of social capital that are particularly important in the study of collective action: (1) trustworthiness, (2) networks and (3) formal and informal rules or institutions'. The award of possessing social capital is an augmented ability to transact with others at lower cost. An example of informal rules is the set of social norms, for example, generalized reciprocity, which is a precondition for dialogue. Trust and trustworthiness are integral elements of reciprocity. As such, they are also core links between social capital and communicative collective action. The cycle of dialogical rewards would not work without a certain level of trust. Enjoyment of many relational goods rests on trusting that the others are sincere. Mutual trust enhances participation in collective action and leads to a more optimal production of public goods. Communicative planning, in contrast to technocratic expert planning, produces both physical and relational goods.

Inclusiveness is a characteristic of communicative planning, and inclusion depends on relationships. A person cannot unilaterally include herself in a social group; she has to be accepted. There must be agreement on whether the person belongs or not. The identity of an individual is to a large extent formed by the sense of belonging to certain groups, and the development of an identity is greatly helped by inclusion. Confirmation of identity is a relational good offered by communicative planning and many other types of encounters and networks. Inclusion and tolerance towards different identities make the cycle of dialogical rewards operate more effectively and increase the legitimacy of the outcome of communicative planning. An effective cycle in turn makes the mechanism behind the Condorcet jury theorem work more forcefully, as it works better with increasing numbers of (epistemically competent) participants.

There is a connection between power and exclusion. Foreigners and subalterns can be excluded from possessing the resources, pursuing the activities or holding the positions that are bases of power. When someone is excluded from the participation and deliberation process, she is also excluded from consuming the relational goods that are produced in communicative planning. The exclusion in itself can seriously damage the relational public goods as conceived by those excluded; little might be left of the sense of belonging, the feeling of social approval, and the confirmation of identity.

Neo-liberalism threatens several of the relational goods to which communicative planning contributes, such as solidarity, community attachment, and social approval on a non-economic basis. Too great an emphasis on economic prosperity may enervate the sense of collective identity by intensifying competition among social groups. Becchetti et al. (2008:344) contend that 'the neglect of relatedness as a fundamental aspect of human life may severely limit economic analysis and curtail the validity of its policy prescriptions'. For instance, if growth-oriented urban planning is promoted at the expense of participatory processes engendering relational goods, the final outcome can have a negative effect on the wellbeing of the local people. It is well known that increasing income does not necessarily lead to more subjective happiness (ibid.344). A negative effect may reduce the local political consensus for growth-oriented policies and in turn discredit public planning.

Conclusion

Communicative planning achieves legitimacy by being an integral part of an attractive political system, namely deliberative democracy. The knowledge base and the likelihood of good decisions are augmented by pooling the information of many participants. Planners' transformation of *knowledge* into *action* is mediated by *power*. Communicative planning can improve practice in relation to each of these key words so as to enhance the legitimacy of governance. Communicative planning aims for (1) right decisions through the mechanism of the Condorcet jury theorem, (2) reduced misuse of power by encouraging anti-paternalism, and (3) a stronger motive for participatory collective action by producing relational goods. None of these legitimizing features requires that everyone agrees on the planning matter under discussion, and neither does the concept of public interest defended in this chapter. In fact, conflict should be anticipated between the building of a workable consensus and the ambition of being a critical corrective in matters of fairness.

Interchange of valid information is crucial in fulfilling the legitimizing potential of communicative planning. Well-informed people make the Condorcet jury theorem work more effectively. Moreover, the argument for anti-paternalism is stronger when individuals possess the knowledge needed to be competent judges of their own interests. Reliable information is important also for the working of the cycle of dialogical rewards. Communicative distortions that make information invalid – that is, untruth, insincerity, manipulation, and incomprehensibility – undermine the building of social capital necessary for producing relational goods. It is the task of critical communicative planning to counteract such distortions.

The legitimizing knowledge-power-action features of CPT intertwine and create a new opening for the public interest concept. Assume that inclusive and dialogue-like deliberation sometimes produces agreement in planning matters without offensive intimidation and pressure. This agreement is informed when even imperfectly knowledgeable participants are more likely to be right than wrong. Then the mechanism of the Condorcet jury theorem is functioning, and there is little reason to believe that a workable agreement would be due to misguided conception of facts. Neither is the agreement likely to be caused by alienated or misconceived views of some deliberators' place in society, when communicative processes have produced relational goods of identity, belonging, and solidarity. Planners cannot easily appeal paternalistically to the notion of 'false consciousness' (Augoustinos 1999) and contend that the agreement is due to lay people being ideologically duped, while they, the planners, see through the smokescreen and know what is really in the best interest of the participants. There will be cases, then, in which the agreed planning solution is best regarded as transcending particularistic interests and can reasonably be interpreted as being in the public interest.

Legitimation is linked to the power theme of Part I of the book in several ways, and is itself the process of justifying power. If communicative planners are incapable of handling and restricting power that is non-deliberatively exerted by actors in the planning process, the procedural system and the planning agency will lose legitimacy. The knowledge/power/action-related features of communicative planning that are analyzed in this chapter all have bearing on the discussion of power in planning: (1) knowledge aggregation (the Condorcet jury theorem) works more effectively when no small group of people dominates the preferences of other participants, (2) anti-paternalism implies taking a stance against a form of power declaring some party to the planning process incapable of managing its own affairs, and (3) production and consumption of relational goods are an important constituent of empowerment.

Critical pragmatists aim to empower the local communities where planning takes place. Empowerment follows both from increased knowledge, less dependence on the power of others, and more extensive social capital networks. The achievement of substantive goals as well as empowerment calls for a planning process motivating actors to strive for both instrumental and communicative rationality. If the deliberation and dialogue of the process empower the local community, higher social goals can realistically be fulfilled in the subsequent period. This is, in fact, equal to a definition of empowerment.

Empowerment inserts dynamism to the thought scheme associating communicative planning with social improvement. The results of empowerment are capability-increasing shifts in means-ends relationships in addition to personal growth (Sager 1994:31–34, Warren 1993). Experiencing that new and more ambitious goals can be attained is likely to reinforce the belief in win-win solutions and have a favourable effect on deliberation. It is at the core of the empowerment idea of CPT that participants should not only experience personal growth, but use their increased capabilities to improve living conditions through better substantive outcomes of public plans.

Notes

1.   'When empathy means to suffer with the needy person, helping can be considered rewarding, since the suffering of helpers ends with that of those who needed the help' (Montada 1998:85). Empathy can provide even utility-maximizing planners with a motive of working for fairness. However, it does not seem reasonable to expect a communicative planner to be both emphatic and rational like an 'economic man'. Justice motives have empirically been found to explain much more co-operative behaviour in community conflicts than self-interest (Müller et al. 2008).

2.   From one perspective, planning can be seen as a technology that systematizes knowledge in preparation for collective action and marshals the power required for implementation. As it was gradually realized that all affected parties posit some kind of valuable knowledge, forms of participatory and communicative planning emerged; for example, transactive planning championed by Friedmann (1973). Different ways to interpret and systematize knowledge, and different views on the relative importance of knowledge types, led to a range of more or less open and inclusive processes. Friedmann (1987) clearly thought that the concept of power deserves a prominent place in planning theory, but he did not explicitly introduce it in his overview of planning approaches. (This was done later, see Sager 1995.) Power is a prerequisite for the balancing of public and particularistic interests. It is needed for making private motives yield to interests that most people have in common – and vice versa.

3.   Forecasts are often used in planning and politics, and paternalism is sometimes part of the considerations about making them public. In the early phases of financial crises, the public is anxious and demands transparency, short-term economic forecasts, and information about recent developments in the housing market. However, top politicians are often reluctant to make the full picture of the downward spiralling of the economy clear to the public. They know that accurate predictions would induce even more pessimistic expectations and hence engender more rapid contraction of the economy. A faster track towards recession would hit everybody, and the unison cry for transparency might thus not be in the best interest of the citizens. Some leading politicians therefore think it morally right to act paternalistically when considering the publication of economic forecasts in such situations.

4.   This links up with the literature on the 'new paternalism' dealing with welfare policy under neo-liberalism (Jennings 2000). In addition to helping those in need, new paternalism recommends close supervision of the poor in order to change patterns of behaviour and counter welfare dependence (Keevers et al. 2008:467). The definition of paternalism is stretched in this literature, as it is rather obvious that the welfare policy is meant to serve society (the providers) as well as the receivers.

5.   Imagine, for example, a prisoner's dilemma situation in which two neighbouring landowners are played out against each other by a powerful developing company. The landowners could obtain a higher price if they coordinated their strategies before negotiating with the developer, but old animosity between the neighbours prevents them from doing so. The planner could paternalistically pressure the landowners to come together and help them design a bargaining strategy and find a way to share the gains for mutual benefit. Should this be done?

6.   Bruni (2010) argues that relational goods should be understood as a third category of goods, neither private nor public. This is because relational goods require something more than the non-rivalry of public goods:

> Two persons in a museum watching simultaneously the same picture are, for economic science, consuming a public good, because each act of consumption is independent from the other. The economic concept of 'public good' is basically individualistic: the key feature is the non-interference between the co-consumers who do not need to enter into a relationship among them, a relationship that is exactly what constitutes the nature of the relational good. (Bruni 2010:396-97)

7.   On the basis of public goods experiments, Gächter and Fehr conclude that:

> Social approval has a rather weak and insignificant positive effect on participation in collective actions if subjects are complete strangers. Yet, if the social distance between subjects is somewhat reduced by allowing the creation of a group identity and of forming weak social ties, approval incentives give rise to a large and significant reduction in free-riding. (Gächter and Fehr 1999:361–62)

2

The Logic of Critical Communicative Planning: Transaction Cost Alteration

I take criticism so seriously as to believe that, even in the very midst of a battle in which one is unmistakably on one side against another, there should be criticism, because there must be critical consciousness if there are to be issues, problems, values, even lives to be fought for ... (C)riticism must think of itself as life-enhancing and constitutively opposed to every form of tyranny, domination, and abuse; its social goals are noncoercive knowledge produced in the interests of human freedom.

(Said 1983:28–29)

Introduction

The opening quote from Edward Said serves to underline my position that there should be a critical aspect of public planning. Communicative planning has repeatedly been criticized for not providing an adequate response to unfair or destructive use of power in planning processes (Flyvbjerg and Richardson 2002, Mäntysalo 2002, McGuirk 2001). Some critics have even suggested that this mode of planning neither addresses the problem of power nor takes into account the possibility that participants act strategically (Tewdwr-Jones and Allmendinger 1998:1981–82, Woltjer 2000:62). Although I regard the last suggestions as misconceived, the misunderstanding indicates that it might be fruitful to state the approach of communicative planning to power in a new way, using terminology intended to highlight its strategy for managing power relations. Several proponents of communicative planning seem to have felt this need for restatement and have clarified their position on the power issue (Forester 2000, 2001, Healey 2003, Innes 2004).

The purpose of this chapter is to present the logic of critical communicative planning. The terminology of transaction cost theory is adopted from economics and applied to political transactions of information, arguments, ideas, and statements of values and preferences. I suggest that one task of critical pragmatists is to apply strategies raising the political transaction costs of agents in the planning process who wield power in ways that work against the public interest (as defined in Chapter 1), and to lower the political transaction costs of deprived groups whose interests are easily ignored. This is not to deny that those with considerable economic and political power may have something to contribute towards the public interest. They often have to be harnessed to this goal, though, as major economic interests tend to benefit at the expense of weaker social groups. Critical planners are alert to injustices brought on by biased power relations, and the aim here is to make explicit the strategy devised by critical pragmatists for dealing with the problem. Importantly, the transaction cost alteration logic does not give the planner *carte blanche* to increase the political transaction costs of stakeholders who disagree with her suggested solutions. The idea is to counteract confusing and manipulative argumentation, not to make it generally more difficult for opponents to speak in a persuasive way.

Transaction cost theory has gained a foothold in academic planning discourse, as witnessed by recent contributions (Buitelaar 2007, Musole 2009, Sager and Ravlum 2005, Webster and Lai 2003). The theory has been described by Williamson (1989), for example, and a general outline will not be given here. In accordance with North (1990a:27), transaction costs are defined very broadly as the costs of information, as well as 'measuring the valuable attributes of what is being exchanged and the costs of protecting rights and policing and enforcing agreements'. Transaction costs are not directly related to the technical production and consumption of what is being exchanged. The cost of constructing an argument is not a transaction cost. Transaction costs are incurred when the transacting parties are brought together for exchange of information and arguments, and when procedures are established to make them deal with each other according to informal agreement.

When several parties are involved, when no standard market procedure guides the transactions between them, when negotiations are required, and when sanctions against opportunistic behaviour are complicated, then high transaction costs are to be expected. This is the typical situation in public planning, for example, in land-use planning and development control (Alexander 2001a, 2001b, Dawkins 2000). I explain the choice of a particular type of planning process, critical communicative planning, by suggesting that this mode has a high likelihood of increasing the transaction costs of repressive groups to such a degree that the needs of all involved parties are accommodated. Repressive groups are those trying to influence the planned solution by using non-deliberative power strategies to make others accept their arguments. Such strategies can involve threats, manipulation, and withholding information, as exemplified in the next section.

It is a basic question whether it makes sense to graft the strategy of transaction cost alteration onto a practice aiming to move public planning in the direction of dialogue and communicative rationality. Dialogue in Habermas's sense is oriented towards reaching mutual understanding; dialogue is non-instrumental and not oriented towards success – for example, the goal of improving living conditions (Habermas 1999:118). A dialogically achieved agreement cannot be imposed by one party. Critical pragmatism does not confine the planner to the selfless behaviour required in Habermasian ideal speech situations, however. As announced on the cover of Forester's (1993a) book, he 'shows how policy analysis, planning, and public administration are thoroughly political communicative practices that subtly and selectively organize public attention'. In so far as the critical planner pragmatically modifies the pursuit of communicative rationality and acts strategically to the advantage of deprived groups, the tension between transaction cost alteration and critical pragmatism dissolves. This theme is revisited in the section introducing transaction cost politics.

The notion of public planning as an activity that has an inherent aspect of social critique is contested. The idea is that the planner (1) can tell what is a serious distortion of the debate between stakeholders and people affected by the plan, (2) can identify power relations that are biased to a degree that de-legitimizes the plan, and (3) can and should question contorted argumentation and power tactics in the planning process. Some planning theorists and planners see this as a very problematic perspective. The case for critical communicative planning is well stated elsewhere (Forester 1989, 1993a). It is nevertheless worth recalling that the planner does not *decide* what is right or wrong in the planning process. Potentially reprehensible distortions are identified in the interaction with other parties taking part in the planning process. By directing attention to dubious communicative practices and by questioning the stakeholders involved, it will become clear whether any power tactics need to be counteracted. There is little point in the planner pursuing the correction of misrepresentation, insincerity, etc. – unless other parties feel put off or deceived by the incidents observed.

The chapter is divided into sections according to the following line of reasoning. First, it is explained how critical communicative planning (critical pragmatism) is counteracting misrepresentation. Second, transaction cost politics is defined and seen in relation to modes of planning. The sources of transaction costs are identified in order to provide a theoretical basis for discussing the functions of transaction cost alteration in critical communicative planning. Third, the transaction cost politics rationale for critical pragmatism is outlined, and the transaction costs of informing, building mutual understanding, monitoring, and enforcing agreements are exemplified by a case study. Fourth, the question is raised as to whether the new logic is applicable to consensus-oriented collaborative planning. An analysis of 'network power' leads to a negative answer.

Counteracting misrepresentation

The role of dialogue in critical communicative planning was defined in the introduction to Chapter 1. This section exemplifies communicative distortions and sketches the planner's role in critical pragmatism – that is, the kind of critical communicative planning advocated by Forester (1989, 1993a). When manipulative power-based argumentation is observed, the critical pragmatist questions the non-deliberative behaviour and tries to manage the capacity of various participating groups or stakeholders for getting their message across.

The theoretical contributions to CPT (for example, Forester 1993a, Healey 2006, Innes 1995, Sager 1994) vary in the relative emphasis put on consensus building and the critical function of planning in society. I regard critical pragmatism as communicative planning giving a prominent place to social critique, while the term collaborative planning is here used to characterize more consensus-oriented communicative planning (Rydin 2003:30–37). The critical pragmatism of Forester uses questioning and shaping of attention in order to reveal and counteract argumentation in which the speaker depends on holding the controlling position in power relations.

Surely, the planner should recognize that every actor in the planning process uses some kind of power. The point here is that the planner should play an active part in separating the factual and substantive meaning of the arguments from connotations added by the social positions of the interlocutors, as far as this is feasible. When someone holds a power position with the authority to impose an interest unilaterally, the planner should try to involve this person in deliberation about the use of this power. Communicative planning is probably not the right choice of mode if such power-holders show no willingness to take part. However, if the authority rests on certain institutional claims that require legitimation, then community mobilization, legal complaint, or forms of organized political action may undermine this authority and give cause for those in positions of power to consider deliberation precisely because they can no longer act unilaterally with the certainty they previously enjoyed.

The rationality of the use of language oriented towards reaching understanding depends on whether the ongoing interchange of arguments is sufficiently comprehensible and acceptable. Forester (1989), Hillier (1995), and Sager (1994, 2002:Ch.9) discuss many examples of communicative distortions, most of them with politicians or developers as the active part. (See also the section on communicative features of activist planning modes in Chapter 4.) Both planners and other parties to the process can try to manipulate during the various phases of planning:

- Biased problem formulation, strategically directing attention to specific aspects of an alternative.
- False revelation of preferences, for example, insincere goal formulations.
- Agenda control with the tacit intention of supporting a particular alternative.
- Biased presentation of alternatives while pretending to be neutral.
- Strategic selection of participants; biased description of actors to affect trust, credibility, and the formation of alliances.
- Process design deliberately and tacitly serving partisan interests.
- Partisan implementation, while pretending to carry out the will of the decision-makers.

As an example of some of these practices, Flyvbjerg et al. (2002) have revealed the frequent cost overruns and demand shortfalls in transport infrastructure projects. They conclude that the unrealistic estimates are often due to deliberate misrepresentation in order to increase the likelihood of project acceptance.

The context of planning is often competition, conflict and discrimination. The argumentation of planners and stakeholders alike is affected by this. Forester suggests:

> a distinctively counterhegemonic or democratizing role for planning and administrative actors: the exposure of issues that political-economic structures otherwise would bury from public view, the opening and raising of questions that otherwise would be kept out of public discussion, the nurturance of hope rather than the perpetuation of a modern cynicism under conditions of great complexity and interdependence. (Forester 1993a:6)

From what I have said about the role of the critical pragmatist so far, it can be deduced that it comprises tasks related both to process and substance. It is in the planner's remit to advance plans that are fair and to the advantage of deprived groups, as well as to design a process based on open exchange of sincere and honest arguments. However, both deprived and powerful groups may sometimes distort the debate. Critical pragmatists should not be any less careful, or any less critically attentive, when hearing the claims of protest groups or community organizations than when listening to developers or public officials. '(I)f we're any less skeptical of the marginalized or "weaker" community members making claims of environmental injustice, for example, we risk ... being politically presumptuous and morally condescending' (Forester 2009a:12).

The wicked problem of the critical pragmatist is how to act on the distortions that her listening reveals. A degree of equal treatment is required to protect the mediator role and persuade all parties to continue deliberation and negotiation. The critical pragmatist might, therefore, sometimes have to criticize the argumentation of the same group that she wants the plan to cater for in a better way. On the other hand, there is likely to be some group needing 'deliberative affirmative action' (Fung 2005:407).

Unwillingness to confront a participating group that is acting unreasonably in the communicative process might easily create distrust and disrespect among the other participants. However, deliberate increase of the transaction costs for the same group that needs to be treated better by the plan would be a contradictory and untenable strategy. The critical pragmatist must find a way of getting around the dilemma. This can be done by assisting the group in developing an alternative line of argumentation in addition to criticizing the original one. The aim would be to formulate new arguments that are more likely to convince bureaucrats and decision-makers. Preferably, the net effect should be reduction of transaction costs for the groups most in need of having their living conditions improved by the plan. The planner's role is further explored in the comments to Table 2.1 in the next section.

What matters in critical pragmatism, says Forester (1993a:x), 'are the practical and institutional contingencies, the political vulnerabilities, of communicative action', amending the 'precariousness of our speaking and acting together', not the insistence on dialogical perfection. Forester's argument for critical pragmatism acknowledges that the various interests involved in planning try to make it difficult for their adversaries to get their message through. Moreover, institutional pressure is seen to work through bureaucratization and the media of power and money to pre-empt or encroach upon autonomous social action. Organizational and institutional contexts render 'making sense together' problematic and politically vulnerable. And the everyday claims of the planners themselves 'can have political effects upon community members, empowering or disempowering, educating or miseducating, organizing or disorganizing them' (ibid.4).

The above insights are a useful preamble to the next section on transaction cost politics, as they confirm the prevalence of this kind of politics in the planning process, although without using the transaction cost terminology.

Transaction cost politics

The purpose of this section is to introduce the concept of transaction cost as applied to the kinds of exchange relations found in politics and planning, thereby providing a theoretical backcloth to the logic of critical communicative planning. It is suggested that the notion of transaction or exchange helps to describe important characteristics of familiar planning modes. Transaction cost politics is defined and related to styles of planning via the idea of expert services and 'political' support being interchanged between planners and other important parties.

The political process is obviously a consideration, both in the production of public plans and other policy areas. It matters whether all those affected by the plan can be brought together, whether ownership rights to all valuable entities are assigned among the participants, and whether fully specified and fully binding agreements can be made at low costs. If these conditions are met, the outcome should be an efficient plan (Dixit 1996:37), and if not, plans may not be forthcoming. This is demonstrated by Sørensen (2006), who holds that local governments in Norway seldom make plans for merging small municipalities that are unable to provide adequate services. One reason is that local governments are unwilling to merge due to the lack of defined property rights to local revenues. Besides, central government is incapable of offering credible commitments regarding maintenance of the generous grants compensating for diseconomies of scale.

Transaction cost politics compares the consequences of alternative political processes when the conditions above are not met. It is the application of transaction cost theory to the analysis of the production of social outcomes which depend on the functioning of the 'political market' (see Epstein and O'Halloran (1999) for an introduction). In transaction cost politics, the transaction entails an informal agreement or understanding under which a policy, programme, or project is expected in return for votes, contributions, or other kinds of backing (North 1990b:362). This exchange of political support for the enactment of binding plans or the implementation of services, facilities, or infrastructure requiring political decisions constitutes a political market.[1] Political markets operate according to institutions (sets of rules) that make up an important part of the incentive structure of society, for instance, property rights, contracts, and credible commitments making the economy work smoothly (ibid.357). Political property rights are the rights to exercise public authority in certain policy areas (Moe 1990), and these are as important for well-working political markets as the ordinary right to ownership is in economic markets.[2]

Political markets of public planning

It is essential for the analysis of communicative planning to recognize that the exchange of arguments – in debate, dialogue, mediation, negotiation, etc. – entails transaction costs. Planning discussion may or may not end in agreement, but the cost of trying to reach it can in any case be substantial. The arguments are most often about features of the plan. The exchange of arguments is therefore mainly about the terms of transacting a certain plan design for enactment and implementation support. Many features and details of the plan are usually modified throughout the planning process in order to gain more backing for the plan. So there is an exchange of design elements for support. The exchange of arguments and the exchange of improved design qualities for increased support are the two most important political markets associated with communicative planning. Transaction costs in these markets are related to arguing, making viewpoints known, agreeing on a plan or its amendment, and monitoring and enforcing such agreements. Before turning to the sources of political transaction costs, I exemplify political markets by identifying crucial transactions in familiar modes of planning.

In the planning process, the political market exchanges the planner's professional design or amendment of a plan for other actors' provision of the information, resources, institutional framework, and political backing the planner depends on when arranging for a fair plan. Already a generation ago, Friedmann (1969:316) drew planners' attention to the transaction between local lay people and experts, exchanging local knowledge for processed knowledge: 'To be involved in action is to interact with others who contribute skills and knowledge that are different from those of planners...'. Citizens give support in the form of information and in return expect the professionals to put forward a plan catering to local needs. Public planning should be arranged so as to facilitate – that is, to lower the costs of – this transaction. The dialogical face-to-face process in which this exchange is the core Friedmann denoted by the term transactive planning (Friedmann 1973). This was a non-Habermasian forerunner to the CPT of today.

The main transaction in advocacy planning is that the client group agrees to participate in the planning process, and hence to rely less on direct and disruptive action, in exchange for the planner's unreserved loyalty and promise to use his or her expertise to further the group's interests when interacting with bureaucrats and decision-makers. Some critics doubt that poor and deprived groups stand to gain by this transaction. Piven (1970:35) holds that '(t)he absorbing and elaborate planning procedures ... are ineffective in compelling concessions, but may be very effective indeed in dampening any impulse toward disruptive action which has always been the main political recourse of the very poor'. (This point is spelled out in the section on critique of CPT in Chapter 8.) Hence, to give effective support, the advocate planner should be prepared to back partisan action unrelated to any aim of approaching dialogue and communicative rationality (Habermas 1999:315–17). Group loyalty, not communicative rationality, is the guiding light (Sager 2002:Ch.6).

To give an idea of what is meant by 'transaction' and 'political market' from the transaction cost politics perspective, the above characteristics of advocacy planning are displayed in Table 2.1 along with the central exchange relations of other familiar planning modes. Table 2.1 purports to show that public

Table 2.1: Main transactions in familiar styles of planning

Planning style	Transacting parties	Planner's contribution	Other party's contribution
Synoptic	Planner-politicians.	Expertise in transforming available policy instruments into planning alternatives with high goal achievement, i.e., knowledge-based and efficient solutions.	Mandates, goals, formal decisions, and the legal foundation of policy instruments, i.e., providing the legitimacy of the plan.
Incremental	Planner-stakeholders.	Disinterested arbitration and social experimentation, transforming competing input into tentative plans to be politically tested.	Development proposals, information, satisficing standards, and partisan assessment of tentative plans.
Advocacy	Planner-client group.	Unreserved loyalty to the client group, translation of client's arguments and preferences to the parlance of bureaucrats and politicians.	Commitment to the planning procedures, abstaining from disruptive action, lending a face to the social needs at the core of the planner's rhetoric.
Critical communicative	Planner-community.	Participation in public debate, conflict management, mediation with the primary aim of reaching fair solutions founded on arguments that are not power-based to an extent that intimidates other participants.	Preferences, local knowledge, empirically substantiated arguments, as well as an institutional context in which the planner can safely reveal and critique power relations and power-based argumentation (liberal democracy).

planning in general, and not only critical communicative planning, can be analyzed as an exchange relationship. When there is an understanding or agreement ('contract') about an exchange, it can be analyzed in terms of transaction cost theory.

The rows in Table 2.1 indicate the focus of each planning mode. The transaction indicated on each row is the one regarded as crucial by proponents of the respective planning style. For example, the transactions between planners and the local community are seen as important in communicative planning, but the other types of exchange displayed in the table will be present as well. That is, politicians, stakeholders, and possibly client groups would all be involved in the debates of communicative planning. With transactions of different kinds, a range of planner contributions will also be needed, as shown in Table 2.1. The role of the planner differs between the styles (see also Chapter 6), and she must address different segments of the public to elicit the input needed to play it well. This implies that the role of the planner comprises many tasks, of which public discussion, mediation and conflict management are given more attention in communicative planning than in the other styles.

Admittedly, the table is a bold simplification, as the planner is only one actor in a multi-party political market, in which a number of transactions of resources and commitments take place. Perhaps needless to say, the different styles reflect theoretical viewpoints adopted by planning analysts rather than mutually exclusive styles from which practitioners choose when they plan. It is convenient to present these 'ideal types' when studying what planners might think and do in different institutional settings.

The sources of political transaction costs

Political markets are characterized by bounded instrumental rationality and high transaction costs. Majone (2001:61) regards 'the lack of a technology of commitment' as 'the quintessential political transaction cost', hence underlining the incapacitation caused by opportunism. Twight (1994:190) holds that 'political transaction costs ... include information costs, organization costs, agency costs and other costs that exist in a political situation because of the fact that individuals strive to act collectively'. Information costs include the description and, if necessary, measuring of what is being exchanged. The costs of participation and acting collectively are affected by the discursive strategies used by the parties involved, as argued by Ostrom et al. (1994) and Rydin (2003). There may be both pecuniary and other transaction costs incurred in planning processes, and these are more closely examined in the ensuing sections. Here, attention is directed to the three main sources of transaction costs identified by Dixit (1996:54–8): asymmetric information, opportunism, and asset specificity.[3]

Asymmetric information gives informational advantage to one of the parties in the transaction. The strategic actions of this party might be unobservable while those of its rivals might be detectable. Assume that the planner regards protection of the natural environment as an integral part of the public interest. She might therefore cultivate close relationships with associations working for 'green' policies. (Compare with the activist relationships of Chapters 3 and 4.) Sustainable plans for protection of large beasts of prey are hypothetically set in a bad light by very high reported losses of domestic animals. Only the farmers have first-hand information about the circumstances under which the animals die. They have a motive to exaggerate the numbers allegedly killed by bears and wolves both to increase compensation paid by the state and to strengthen the argument for shooting some of the wild beasts. The planner has no possibility of controlling the farmers' information regarding single cases. The suspicion that farmers take advantage of the information asymmetry to serve their own interest makes it difficult to reach agreement between farmers, environmentalists, and government on which policy to adopt. Dealing with illegal hunting and demonstrations against lenient hunting regulation are parts of the transaction costs.

Opportunism is assumed in transaction cost theory (Williamson 1999). This means that the parties are supposed to be only boundedly rational, experiencing limits in formulating and solving complex problems. Manipulation, principal-agent problems (Laffont 2003), and betrayal of principles for short-term gains should be expected when both opportunism and asymmetric information are present. The municipal planning agency (the principal) cannot know for sure whether the planner (the agent) interprets and conveys official policy correctly in her dealings with conflicting parties. Perhaps she (the planner) is not to be trusted after all? In the case of planning for the large predators, the planner might have personal motives: She might hope to gain prestige by making politicians and local farmers assent to a solution favoured by her allies in the environmental associations. Or she might be tempted to let her proposals for a protection zone for the beasts of prey be influenced by the location of farms owned by her relatives. Suspicion of such opportunism might drive the principal into a costly monitoring scheme.

Asset specificity means that investment in the asset will only pay off in the relationship with one specific transacting party. It characterizes an irreversible investment making the investor vulnerable to demands of the other party to change the terms of transactions under the threat of dissolving the whole relationship. Actors in political markets invest in relationships, for instance, by giving favours to a special interest group. Time and effort invested by the planner in the relationship with environmental groups might not pay off in all processes. For example, being known as a 'green' planner could be counterproductive when the task is to come to an agreement with the farmers in drawing up a plan for how to deal with stock-killing bears and wolves.

All the above three sources of transaction costs create a need or justification for trust, as they contribute to uncertainty in exchange relationships. When one trusts, one accepts some risk of potential harm in exchange for the benefits of co-operation (Warren 1999:311). Planners make boundedly rational choices to trust others based on a desire to reduce the transaction costs involved in searching for information, screening potential allies, and monitoring compliance with agreements. Trust enables agents to conduct repeated transactions more efficiently despite there being incomplete information about the true intentions of others.

Without problems of the above types, one might imagine a utopian state of zero transaction cost and thus complete understanding or agreement between the parties in the planning process.[4] However, agreements are not complete and fully specified in planning, and the incompleteness of understandings and the salience of power relations are two closely related issues. Informal agreements guiding the transactions in the planning process (as shown in Table 2.1) are quite diffuse and imprecise. The process of negotiating the conditions of the transactions never really ends, as parties to an agreement will be continuously adjusting their actions in response to changing circumstances. Under these conditions, power relations matter exceedingly. The party in the planning process that can determine how to use economic and political assets when a gap in understanding becomes distressing, will have considerable influence over the planning agenda and thus the recommended plan.[5]

Having defined transaction cost politics and the critical pragmatist kind of communicative planning, it is time to revisit the question posed in the introductory section, and to ask whether the two can be meaningfully combined. The doubt here springs from the fact that 'cost' is a relevant concept only when trying to achieve something by means of scarce resources in a broad sense. This is the case in 'strategic action' but not in (strong) 'communicative action' oriented towards agreement emerging from dialogue (Habermas 1999:326, 334). Communicative action is not motivated by instrumental success, but is instead interchange 'where actors coordinate their plans of action with one another by way of linguistic processes of reaching understanding…' (ibid.326). However, the transaction cost altering rationale (logical basis) shortly to be presented does not require transaction costs to be linked directly with dialogue, rather with communication that is in some way distorted. 'Such communication pathologies can be conceived of as the result of a confusion between actions oriented toward reaching understanding and actions oriented toward success' (ibid.169). In practice, communicative rationality is entwined with the purposive rationality of actors in communicative planning processes, resulting in the complex behaviour just mentioned (and the strategies of activist communicative planners in Chapter 4).

Arguments are exchanged in all communicative planning processes. Efforts are made to convince others of the validity of the arguments, to explore the possibilities for consensus, and to monitor agreements based on the discussion. When deliberation is not purely dialogical, but instead couched in terms of means and ends, the above efforts can be measured in cost terms and analyzed as transaction costs. This will be the case in practical planning processes. Self-interested strategies will then be observed, and this provides a logical basis for the transaction cost altering rationale put forward in the next section.

The transaction cost politics rationale for critical pragmatism

The purpose of this section is to spell out the transaction cost alteration rationale for critical communicative planning. This logical basis fits with communicative planning where power relations between the involved parties are biased and subjected to critique. The fairness of the plan is seen as essential, and it is an important task of the planners to design the planning process as an easily accessible arena for open exchange of arguments in the pursuit of such an outcome. Hence, the rationale relates most closely to critical pragmatism (Forester 1993a), putting more emphasis on planning's critical function in society than on consensus building.

The new rationale

To start, a 'costless' utopia can be imagined, like the one sketched by Majone, who ignores the time costs of the interlocutors:

> (I)n a world of zero political transaction costs the institutions that make up a democratic polity would have neither substance nor purpose. Not only representative democracy but politics itself could be dispensed with, since people would debate and negotiate without cost until they found a solution benefiting all. (Majone 2001:75)

The existence of solutions benefiting all should not be taken for granted. In any case, however, as the gap widens between the Habermasian dialogical ideal and actual communication in the planning process, it becomes more costly to obtain trustworthy information, to build agreement among well-informed agents, and to induce rational participants to freely make the commitment required for implementation. These difficulties reflect the three sources of transaction costs explained in the previous section.

There is a connection between access to relational goods and the level of transaction costs. 'The value of relational rewards is their potential to reduce transaction costs in future collective actions' (Rader Olsson 2009:263). The political transaction costs of an actor can diminish if the planner brings the actor into a network that elevates the social standing of the actor and is conducive to increasing trust in that actor. Similarly, the political transaction costs of a stakeholder can increase if she is denied inclusion or deprived of relational goods, such as friendship and solidarity. It is often within the planner's realm of possibility to disseminate information about the stakeholder that makes the person or group lose sympathy and goodwill or raise certain people's distrust.

Threats, manipulation, incomprehensible statements, insincere suggestions, misinformation and so on tend to increase political transaction costs in the long run by eroding trust and complicating consensus building. While disinformants might gain in the short run, there is a positive connection between political transaction costs incurred by the other actors and the seriousness of the communicative distortions. The procedural aspects of real-life communicative planning can therefore be assessed on the basis of political transaction cost theory.

Transaction costs are pervasive and often substantial in practical planning. For this reason, collective choices in democracies are usually made by majority rule rather than by unanimity. When transaction costs are significant, the possibility of managing and controlling them becomes an issue both in politics and planning. The goals of any one party are more likely to be achieved when its opponents face augmented costs of informing, persuading, implementing, and litigating.[6] Thus, managing transaction costs is managing power relations. Part of the planner's role is that of the power-broker, as planning is 'a mediating process in which relations of power are continually renegotiated and reproduced' (Forester 1985:124).

However, it is unrealistic that planners are able to modify power relations among those involved in the planning process unless this process is to some extent separated and shielded from other social arenas where the stakeholders have their power bases. There must be laws, rules, and procedures that are observed by everyone involved in the planning process, no matter what power those individuals exert in other public settings. Only in these conditions can the planner hope for the protection and institutional backing to influence power relations in the planning process by altering political transaction costs. In order to encourage the construction of public space where resistance can be voiced against unacceptably biased power relations and thus ensure the feasibility of planning modes with a social consciousness, planners need to take an interest in the institutional design of the arenas in which they work.

According to the transaction cost alteration rationale for critical communicative planning, in order to attain a process that is likely to result in an outcome accommodating the interests of all involved parties, the planner must augment the political transaction costs of those who rely on non-deliberative power rather than reason as they argue for self-serving plans. The planner must also reduce the transaction costs of those arguing for fair plans without misrepresentation or the use of manipulatory stratagems. Intervention in the way power relations become manifest in the planning process is at the core of the critical pragmatist's working strategy. The point of reformulating the logic of critical communicative planning is to state this in a new and explicit manner. Transaction cost alteration lends cogency to critical communicative planning precisely because it interferes with power relations and is the way to counteract power-based communicative distortions in the planning process.

The broad applicability of the transaction cost alteration logic

'Transaction cost alteration' is a broad strategy that is incorporated into a range of critical social theories and practices, even though the term itself is not used. Alternative strategies include trying to eliminate the opponent, completely separating the contenders (by exclusion or withdrawal), or influencing the opponent's ideals or way of thinking. Furthermore, critical theories can be revolutionary with the aim of recasting the social structures within which transaction costs are generated, rather than altering the transaction costs themselves.

Critical communicative planning is a reformist practice developed to handle problems of a democratic society where the arguments of parties involved in planning can be freely scrutinized and criticized in public. The planner facilitates a juxtaposition of values and a meeting of minds of stakeholders and interests, encouraging mutual adjustment rather than the elimination and separation of ideas. The logic of transaction cost alteration is apposite even to critical social practices other than critical pragmatism. Examples of its use are found in planning based on the thinking of Foucault (Flyvbjerg 2002, Gunder and Mouat 2002), in feminist and gender planning (Leavitt 1986, Moser 1989), subtle or covert planning for empowerment and social transformation (Beard 2002, Scheyvens 1998), anti-ethnocratic planning (Bollens 1998, Yiftachel and Yacobi 2002), and in some radical and oppositional planning (Clavel 1983:Ch.6, Tuckett 1990).

The transaction cost altering planning practices emphasize different means of changing the relative costs of contending parties. Critical pragmatists seek to uncover distorted understandings and oppressive practices by questioning, shaping attention, and improving dialogue in the planning process. Activist planners explore the potential of mobilization of social movements and direct action such as protest rallies and other political demonstrations. Other critical planning practices might accentuate economic interventions or focus on the (urban) political economy rather than the single planning process.

A Norwegian case study exemplifying the alteration of various types of transaction costs is offered below. Such costs can be grouped in various ways, and the ensuing examples concern costs of information, building agreement, monitoring, and enforcement. The case deals with a process to curb urban sprawl, which is a problem in most countries. It would have been easy to choose an example where the critical pragmatist uncovers malpractice on the part of local authorities or powerful development corporations (Mäntysalo 2008), following 'the tradition in which planners search endlessly for a more glamorous way of presenting themselves' (Reade 1991:186). However, this would indicate too narrow and simplistic a role for the critical pragmatist. She will probably just as often have to deal with groups of ordinary people whose claims and arguments are mixtures of legitimate protection of private interests and the less laudable pursuit of personal gains at the expense of other groups. Admittedly, it may sometimes be difficult for the planner to make this distinction.

Case study: curbing urban sprawl in Trondheim, Norway

The main recreational area of the city is located on a peninsula, so land lost to urban sprawl cannot be compensated for by adding land farther from the city. Land use within the woodland recreational area is regulated by a legally binding plan from 1985, which prohibits further development of the properties. However, many dispensations have been given over the years, and monitoring of the plan has been very lax. A number of recreational cabins have been expanded and turned into permanent dwellings. Moreover, the owners have added outhouses, garages, and balconies, and also built many private access ways and a few new roads. Figures 2.1 to 2.4 give an impression of the area. The extent of the municipal negligence is such that it is now very problematic to bring the unauthorized development areas into harmony with the plan. It is also regarded as unsatisfactory to re-regulate the area and allow those who have been building illegally to reap the benefits. The city council has nevertheless passed a programme of action to clean up the political mess and give each property a legal status.[7]

The account which follows is openly non-neutral. I am writing as an external observer, siding with the planners working to keep the recreational woodland as a public good. Perhaps needless to say, a critical pragmatist involved in the case should not enter the process with predetermined ideas about the right

Figure 2.1 Cabin used for recreation during the summer

Figure 2.2 Modern single-family house in the woodland recreational area

Figure 2.3 A typical mixture of old, dilapidated cabins and houses of good standard; modern IT infrastructure is rapidly spreading

Figure 2.4 The Lian area attracts people enjoying the great outdoors, and several families keep packs of huskies for dog sled racing

outcome. This is essential, as minds made up at the outset of the process would make a sham of open dialogue and joint consultation. In the conflict-filled process of deciding which buildings should be allowed on each property in the area of unauthorized sprawl, the parties try to alter the political transaction costs of their adversaries.

The planner is critical in that there is more on her agenda than building a workable agreement between the home-owners and the city authorities. While trying to stimulate communication between the parties, she also questions the reasonableness of the arguments. Moreover, the planner continuously directs the attention of the general public to the essence of the matter, the unauthorized transformation of a public good to private use.

Information: the residents of the sprawl area eagerly propagate the message that their permanent presence on the recreational land is helpful rather than harmful. 'We who are living out here are not destroying the area. On the contrary, we are taking care of the woodland. We are not a hindrance; we love this place and want to make it as attractive as possible rather than ruining it' (representatives of the local residents' association interviewed in the local newspaper 1 July 2003). It is mentioned that the residents' association has arranged for cattle grazing on some open land to keep the scrub in check. In another interview, residents assert that they have done a favour to the district by moving there permanently: 'We have stopped the deterioration of this area. The attractiveness of the place is much improved since the cabins were renovated' (local newspaper 11 May 2000). Thus, residents see themselves as stewards of the land, not as intruders.

The critical pragmatist should acknowledge the precarious position of the owners of the illicit houses. Some of them might have acted in good faith, and they are all anxious to know whether they will be allowed to go on living in their current homes. The fairness of measures taken to reclaim the area for recreational use is important. However, the planner should question the residents' claim to be stewards of the woodland recreation area rather than intruders and not necessarily accept it. The woodland does not require their stewarding activities to serve as a public recreation area, while their activities as intruders (permanent residents) are devastating to it. Both planners and owners transact their partial problem descriptions with the general public, hoping for political backing in return. The planner should make it more costly for the residents to gain sympathy by invoking the image of 'nature wardens', and she can do this by redirecting attention to the main issue, viz that the residents are changing the character of a common good in an unwanted direction and privatizing chunks of it by hindering public access. The above arguments put forward by the house owners circumvent the ethical problem of excluding people from use of a public good by developing properties against democratically sanctioned regulations. By making this clear to the public, the planner raises the owners' political transaction costs.

Exploring the potential for agreement: it is in the interest of the inhabitants of the controversial sprawling area to nourish disagreement in the city council, as the long-lasting political consensus on protecting the recreational land surrounding the city works against them. Hence, they try to win the right wing political parties to their cause by transforming the issue from protection of a common good to protection of property rights. The populist-libertarian Progress Party has largely accepted this twist and supports the home-owners in the contested area. The residents see their case as the ordinary person's heroic fight against a faceless and insensitive bureaucratic system. Supporting such fights is in perfect harmony with the party's ideology, and it stands to gain votes if people accept this description of the conflict. However, the residents also need the backing of the Conservative Party, the closest neighbour to the Progress Party on the political left-right dimension. To the disappointment of the residents, the Conservative Party has taken a firm stand against re-regulating the area and against letting all those who have taken the law into their own hands off the hook. As the Conservatives are traditionally in favour of strong private property rights and want to preserve their clear image on this ideological issue, they are vulnerable to examples indicating the opposite. Accordingly, this is where residents of the contested area launch their attack, as shown by the heading 'The Conservatives in Trondheim – Communist Party in Sheep's Clothing' (local newspaper 6 October 2001). The unauthorized house owners and the Conservative Party transact ideological arguments affecting political support. Their arguments weakened, the Conservatives have to apply other means to build a broad city council majority on the protection of the contested recreational land, and hence their consensus-building costs are increased.

It is usually not the task of the planners to defend political parties. It is, however, their legitimate business to contribute to the public debate and contend that the transformation of the recreational issue into the question of communism or liberalism is a destortion in the sense that the original planning problem disappears from sight. There is nothing to indicate that liberal societies have less need for recreational land with public access than socialist societies. Nor do liberal countries have less need for protection against individuals breaking the law for personal gains. Most people would not be well served by transformation of this planning issue into a traditional left-right quarrel with the unauthorized residents in the role of the 'man in the street' fighting for freedom from bureaucratic oppression. The planner acts in the public interest by arguing to the effect that a majority prevails in the city council for keeping the location of the 'red line' marking the boundaries of the city's recreational woodlands unchanged on the map. Here, the planner increases the transaction costs of the property owners by questioning their transformation of the planning problem into a choice between broad political ideologies. To accomplish this, the owners attempt to recast their own role from that of active agents stretching the law for personal gains, to that of innocent victims of 'the system'.

Monitoring: the Planning and Building Department is the municipal agency responsible for the control of illegal construction and change of land use. Even in ordinary circumstances the monitoring section of the Department has a heavy work load, and for some years it was closed to the public two working days per week to speed up the handling of applications. The agency director applied for two new positions over a period of three years to get an overview of the illegalities in the contested woodland area. However, extra positions need to be politically approved, and years passed before they were accepted. It is a problem that the finances of the monitoring section depend on the number of applications handled. While application fees are an important source of income for the section, dealing with illegalities and the preparation of lawsuits generates little or no revenue. Hence, new positions mean shaving other parts of the municipal budget, and for several years politicians fearing the consequences were able to form majority coalitions against improved monitoring. On one occasion the conservative mayor sighed that 'this really threatens the credibility of the municipal government as well as the local democratic system' (local newspaper 15 December 2000). Indirectly and reluctantly, the majority of the local politicians sided with the residents of the controversial area for some years, in that they severely augmented the administration's costs of monitoring unauthorized land use. Ironically, this has caused a tremendous increase in the political costs of enforcement in the long term.

In spite of insufficient monitoring, new cases of illicit permanent houses, roads, etc. are brought to the attention of the Planning and Building Department time and again. Critical pragmatists ought to make the general public aware of such cases. They should present the single cases as parts of a broader picture and explain to the public what the accumulated private encroachments mean to the public's use of the woods for recreational purposes. The point is to put pressure on the bureaucracy and the politicians to follow up earlier decisions. The planner tries to reduce the political transaction costs of those objecting to the unauthorized land use by raising support for the monitoring agency uncovering the wrongdoings. In their transactions with the general public, the planners offer information on illegal land-use changes in anticipation of political pressure for extra staffing.

Enforcement: the lax monitoring and enforcement practice on the part of the municipal bureaucracy and local politicians aggravates the problem in several ways. Not only does a recent Supreme Court decision concerning a similar area confirm that the municipality cannot just close its eyes to violations of the law over a long period of time without eroding the basis of legal sanctions, there is also the change in property owners' expectations to consider. When neighbours have developed their plots and upgraded their cabins over a number of years without the authorities trying to stop them, it becomes easier for other owners to argue that they acted in good faith. As one resident said in an interview:

> Over the years we could see that the district grew more like a residential area than a recreational area with weekend cabins. A great optimism gradually filled us, in that we believed it would be possible to obtain housing status even for those of us living on properties with only cabin permits. We observed that neighbours got housing status, and we thought that would also apply to us. (Local newspaper 11 May 2000)

The spreading of such optimism makes enforcement costly, as it has to take place on a greater scale and deal with more disappointed and unruly owners. The number of perpetrators increases, and the municipality cannot prosecute only a few of them.

The planner should inform the property owners of what they are legally allowed to do and what they are not allowed to do with their plots. The planners must also make sure that they properly document that such information has been both provided and received. It might be helpful to arrange public meetings in the controversial area to receive the residents' points of view. The meetings would provide good occasions for explaining why upgrading to permanent dwellings is illegal and for alerting the property owners to the consequences that transformation of the cabins might have for them later on. In the case at hand, the critical pragmatist should do all this without acting as an advocate for the municipal administration, since the long-standing passivity and evasiveness of the local administrators and politicians in these matters is clearly deserving of criticism. In their transactions with the owners, the planners exchange advice and formal notification for an improved basis for taking legal action. In so doing, the critical planner reduces the enforcement costs of those trying to keep private opportunistic behaviour in check.

It is perfectly possible in a democracy that policies move in circles of strict regulation, lax monitoring, re-regulation with zealous enforcement, etc., while each of the political actors asserts that they have had the same goal all along (Sager 2002). Shifting majority coalitions must take part of the blame for this logical weakness in majority voting systems. Nevertheless, in the present process of stemming urban sprawl, it would be appropriate for the critical planner to pose tough questions about the long-lasting negligence of bureaucrats and the city council. Criticism of the municipal authorities' handling of the conflict between the protection of the common recreational good and the development of private properties would most likely lower the political transaction costs (of informing and building support) incurred by the property owners relative to the authorities.

What makes this example fit neatly into a critical CPT framework is the unmasking of communicative distortions. My somewhat one-sided exposition is due to the pedagogical need for clear and unambiguous examples. In practice, the critical pragmatist often has to strike out in several directions, not least against local politicians and administrations.

Current status: the new development plan for Lian passed by the city council in November 2008 does little to improve this part of the woods as a recreation area for the general public. It gave people the right to go on living in the contested area, even if they had been living in cottages without status as houses. While the residents' association was satisfied that nobody was forced to move, they were annoyed with the strict regulations that greatly limit what can be done with the buildings without formal application to the municipality, thus seriously reducing the market value of the properties. The winners in the new plan are the 110 families who were living legally or illegally in cabins that are now transformed to legal houses. The losers are the 23 cabin owners who followed the rules but did not maintain their buildings. Their cabins can not now become houses, and if they tear down dilapidated buildings, they will not be permitted to build new ones. Hence, when planners thought it was right to warn people not to take illegal action, this turned out to have some perverse consequences.

The case study above is meant to demonstrate how the logic of transaction cost alteration can be applied in critical pragmatism, and the next section examines whether it is also useful for strongly consensus-oriented collaborative planning.

Is the new logic applicable to consensus-oriented collaborative planning?

Power is actualized only where word and deed have not parted company, where words are not empty and deeds not brutal, where words are not used to veil intentions but to disclose realities, and deeds are not used to violate and destroy but to establish relations and create new realities. (Arendt 1958:200)

The term communicative planning spans quite different planning practices, and transaction cost alteration is not equally well suited to describe the rationale of them all. The primary purpose of this section is to argue that transaction cost alteration fits better as a logical basis for critical communicative planning than for strongly consensus-oriented collaborative planning. Booher and Innes's (2002) notion of 'network power' is used to build the argument.

Booher and Innes (2002) aim to develop a theory of network power where power is lodged in relations between people. This form of power emerges from consensus-building, collaborative planning and other self-organizing processes that link agents in interactive, communicative, and decentralized networks. Network power offers an alternative to the conventional idea that power is the ability of one actor to make another actor do something she would otherwise not do. The essence of network power is that it is a jointly held capacity embedded in the interaction and dependent on its qualities.

Booher and Innes do not explicitly acknowledge that a concept of power with this essential feature has been around at least since Hannah Arendt's examination of *The Human Condition* (1958). Arendt's concept of power was linked to the critical theory of communicative action by Habermas (1977). Her communicative interpretation of power was alluded to in some of John Forester's contributions throughout the 1980s, and its main features were outlined within the framework of communicative planning by Sager (1994: 65–66).[8]

For the sake of argument, it may be worthwhile to demonstrate the common ideas of network power and Arendt's communications concept of power. Once the network is able to act politically, power is present, just as – according to Arendt (1970:52) – power is 'inherent in the very existence of political communities'. As she sees it, 'power springs up whenever people get together and act in concert' (ibid p 52), while, in the parlance of Booher and Innes (2002:225), network power is present when the linked agents share the ability to 'alter their environment in ways advantageous to these agents individually and collectively'. Arendt regards power as 'the very condition enabling a group of people to think and act in terms of the means-end category' (1970:51). Hence, to her, power is not the means to an end, just as Booher and Innes's network power 'is not a weapon that an individual can hold and use at will' (p 225). Power, as defined by Arendt, 'is never the property of an individual; it belongs to a group and remains in existence only so long as the group keeps together' (1970:44). Analogically, Booher and Innes see network power as a shared ability of linked agents, 'a jointly held resource enabling networked agencies or individuals to accomplish things they could not otherwise' (p 225). Finally, Arendt's is a concept of power whose essence does not rely on the command-obedience relationship (1970:40). The same is true of Booher and Innes's network power, as there is no central or top-down control over individual behaviour in their ideal 'neural network' model.

Scrutinizing the concept of network power brings out more clearly the different foci of critical pragmatism and consensus-oriented collaborative planning.[9] The difference emanates from contrasting responses to the tension created by Booher and Innes's central assumptions of self-interested participants and authentic dialogue, as explained in the following paragraphs.

It is a distinctive feature of critical pragmatism to counteract systematic and politically motivated communicative distortions and to assess plans against the dialogical qualities of the process leading up to them. This is not the only evaluation criterion, but it nevertheless links critical pragmatism to the critical theory of communicative action (Habermas 1999). The emphasis on distortions follows from acknowledging that it is often not in the self-interest of all participants in the planning process to speak with sincerity, accuracy, comprehensibility, and full backing in rules and norms. Habermasian dialogue implies a different kind of reasoning than the strategic considerations of means-ends logic.

Even solutions to which none of the participants openly objects might sometimes have to be questioned. 'What comes about *manifestly* through gratification or threat, suggestion or deception, cannot count intersubjectively as an agreement' (ibid.222). Opportunistic interventions of this sort violate the conditions under which the bonding and binding forces of face-to-face dialogue arouse convictions and bring about the empowering connections of the network. Only in dialogue can 'the structural constraints of an intersubjectively shared language impel the actors ... to step out of the egocentricity of a purposive rational orientation toward their own respective success and to surrender themselves to the public criteria of communicative rationality' (ibid.233).

Hence, critical pragmatists' response to the tension between self-interest and dialogue is to check for opportunistic behaviour. They aim to rectify processes in which some stakeholders try to back their self-interest by unacceptable exertion of power, that is, by showing disrespect or violating the rights or integrity of others. Moreover, they question agreements suspected of resting on manipulation. The collaborative network, in contrast, has no central authority in questioning and shaping attention: 'It is not up to planners to challenge or to acquiesce' (Booher and Innes 2002:232). When there is a need to redistribute power, this problem should be addressed in advance, as the consensus-building process is not, in any case, the place for it (Innes 2004:12). The rules set for collaboration might well serve to bracket power inequalities during discussion, but changing the power relations between participants at the table is not the lodestar giving direction to the collaborative process. A collaborative process may nevertheless contribute to building a network with power to do things differently.

The collaborative style relies on a third characteristic of networks, the interdependence of diverse agents, to relieve the tension between self-interest and dialogue. Booher and Innes (2002) see diversity and interdependence as two independent variables which must coexist. It seems reasonable, nevertheless, that diversity tends to make the agents interdependent, as each of them has only some of the resources, experience, and information needed for achieving their goals. The agents come to realize that they need a solution supported by all parties in order to attain something they cannot achieve alone. It seems to be assumed that this mutual advantage, from a generally supported plan, will effectively discourage opportunistic behaviour.[10] Few of the benefits of diversity and interdependence can occur without approaching dialogue among the agents, so the assertion that 'self-interest and rational choice drive network power' (ibid.227) seems strangely biased. According to Habermasian reasoning, development of high levels of network power would require that the instrumental and goal-oriented thinking of self-interested and rationally choosing agents be suspended, and that this be accomplished in dialogue. However, Booher and Innes maintain that agents are and should always be motivated by self-interest. It is assumed that agents simply reframe their self-interest through dialogue and decide to work co-operatively because they stand to gain from it.

However, an extra carrot is needed to persuade self-interested agents to give priority to mutual understanding and partake in authentic dialogue, so the prospect of innovative solutions that serve everyone are held out to them. This is where creativity and processes of collective, intellectual bricolage and role-playing are given a crucial part in collaborative planning (Innes and Booher 1999b). 'Probably the most important aspect of network power is the ability of networked agents to improve the choices available to all of them as a result of collectively developed innovative ideas' (Booher and Innes 2002:226). Anticipation of such ideas serves to weaken the stakeholders' motivation to opportunistically exploit their power bases to sway group agreement towards their own preferred outcome. Furthermore, stronger elements of shared identity, a central outgrowth of dialogue and network power, lower the threshold for committing to new proposals serving the 'common good'. Hence, collaborative planners seek to ameliorate the tension between self-interest and authentic dialogue not so much by revealing and counteracting communicative misrepresentations, as by sensitizing stakeholders to their interdependence, demonstrating their need for co-operative accomplishment, and nurturing their hope for win–win solutions.

On the basis of the above characteristics of collaborative planning, I contend that alteration of the relative political transaction costs of the participants would not contribute significantly to solving problems in this planning style. One reason is that the even higher transaction costs incurred by stakeholders trying to promote their interests through alternative processes (such as litigation or political lobbying), provide a motive for co-operation and drive them towards the collaborative effort in the first place. Moreover, transaction cost alteration is not an efficient measure for stimulating the mechanisms that make consensus-oriented collaborative planning work despite internal stress and strain. The mutual understanding inspiring creativity, innovative thinking, and the sense of having something in common, thrives in processes that shun one-sided orientation towards means and ends, and the success of only the individual participant. The category of 'cost' is therefore not that relevant. Transaction cost alteration is also not an effective way to build trust or make participants feel comfortable and safe to express views and feelings, as is desirable in consensus building.

To sum up this section, the critical pragmatists rely upon critique of distorted communication to check that agreements on plans are not unduly forced, while collaborationists focus on procedures that foster consensus building. Alteration of transaction costs finds application in the former strategy because critical pragmatists do not presume that adversarial relations have been tamed by interdependencies so strong that pursuit of self-interest becomes pursuit of mutual interest.

Although increased capacity to act in concert is seen as valuable in all communicative planning, this ambition features most prominently in consensus-oriented collaborative planning. In the development of network power, the mode of thinking oriented towards mutual understanding is therefore of great importance. Consensus building is usually not promoted by critique of power relations or attempts to manage them by influencing the political costs of informing, negotiating, monitoring, and enforcing agreements. Hence, transaction cost alteration is not well suited as a rationale for consensus-oriented communicative planning.

Conclusion

The purpose of the chapter is not primarily to improve the planning practice of critical pragmatists, but to articulate the logic of critical communicative planning in a new way intended to enhance understanding of the strategy for dealing with power relations in this planning mode.

Some stakeholders exploit their strong position to distort the communicative planning process and promote outcomes catering first and foremost to their own needs. If the planner can use her guidance of the planning process to raise their cost of acting in a self-serving manner, she might improve the capacity of other involved parties to implement a plan that takes everyone's interests into account. Thus, process intervention – achieved through expert authority or the mandate of the planning bureaucracy – calls for transaction cost altering strategies whose effect is to raise the political transaction costs of stakeholders who are acting to achieve planning outcomes that unduly serve special interests (Twight 1994:194). Changing the relative transaction costs of participants in the planning process implies altering the power relations between them. The logic of critical communicative planning – critical pragmatism – is to alter political transaction costs by going against manipulative tactics and other deliberate perversion of communication whenever such intervention can promote the fairness of the plan. The planner can:

- Mediate discussion on values and preferences.
- Question assumptions, criteria, and the impartiality of arguments.
- Reveal motives and interests.
- Direct attention to contradictions, unfairness, and new possibilities.
- Confront actors launching unreasonable claims upsetting other participants.
- Facilitate the parties' learning about each others' needs and preferences.
- Convey rules and political signals curbing ambitions; each party must be led to understand that there are limits to what can realistically be hoped for.

In order to manage the planning process along these lines, the planner does not have to act as an 'elevated arbiter who objectively analyses and benignly controls the planning play from an Archimedean vantage point', as Brand and Gaffikin (2007:304) seem to believe. Neither the planner nor any particular stakeholder needs an Archimedean vantage point and objective analysis to alter the political transaction costs of another party to the planning process. This is true both in communicative planning and in other modes. In fact, if planners could not to some extent affect the cost of political transactions from their position within the process, they would be completely impotent, and their work would be of no social avail.

There are always fine balances to be struck in the design of a planning process, however. Even when intervening in order to manage transaction costs, the planner should be attentive and sensitive to the deliberative nature of the process. Furthermore, in the interest of a socially just plan, the critical pragmatist might choose not to make a fuss over an underprivileged group keeping secrets or applying other non-dialogical tactics to improve its position vis-à-vis a dominant adversary. This might be contrary to the 'paradigm' of Habermasian communicative planning (Innes 1995), but it is in line with the pragmatic ethos of critical pragmatism. In practice, the critical pragmatist will therefore neither be a purely dialogical planner-saint nor a power-wielding planner-prince (Alexander 2001c).

A change of emphasis in communicative planning, downgrading its critical function and upgrading the collaborative search for consensus, would make alteration of political transaction costs less urgent and give planners a weaker motive for affecting power relations. Provided that critical pragmatism is reasonably successful in altering transaction costs to the benefit of disadvantaged groups and persons, such a change of emphasis might shift power from 'the unorganized and vulnerable, and from the publicly-minded more generally, to the economically organized and influential' (Forester 1985:130).[11] However, the ability of critical pragmatists to alter political transaction costs to the advantage of the first-mentioned groups is still under discussion. So is the ability of consensus-oriented collaborative planners to generate win–win solutions that do not benefit the already well off much more than the less fortunate.

When planners are in a position to modify political transaction costs, they might to some extent be able to influence the processes leading to formal and informal agreements and rules – and thus institutional design. Among the issues of interest to planners are delegation (Epstein and O'Halloran 1999), public goods provision (Sager 2007, Webster and Lai 2003), budgeting procedures (Patashnik 1996), and deregulation (Choi 1999). In general, transaction costs have a bearing on the way problem areas are managed politically, and hence on the locus of the borderline between plan and market. The economism of the neo-liberal ideas dealt with in Part II of this book has widened the scope for market-based solutions. Before we turn to that issue, however, activist planning models which concretize transaction cost alteration are identified and analyzed in the next two chapters.

Notes

1. 'An efficient political market would be one in which constituents could accurately evaluate the policies pursued by competing candidates in terms of the net effect upon their well-being; only legislation (or regulation) that maximized the aggregate income of the affected parties to the exchange would be enacted; and compensation to those adversely affected would insure that no party was injured by the action.' (North 1990b: 360)

2. The right to exercise authority is of course part of what makes the public planner an attractive or even a mandatory contracting party in some processes. For instance, the client group in a potential advocacy relationship faces a choice similar to the make-or-buy problem analyzed in transaction cost economics (Walker and Weber 1984). The group can choose 'to go it alone' or demand the services of the advocate planner, that is, to produce a resistance strategy itself or pay somebody from outside to do it for them.

3. By and large, Dixit (1996) follows Oliver Williamson's outline of transaction costs. This means that opportunistic behaviour figures more prominently, and imperfect contracts less prominently, than if the outline were based on Steven Cheung's ideas. However, the focus on opportunism can lead to double counting of transaction costs (Cheung 2002). This does not matter much in the present chapter, as I am not seeking to build a refutable hypothesis to be tested empirically. I follow Dixit (and Williamson), as the idea of opportunistic behaviour is probably easier to grasp in relation to planning than the concept of imperfect contracts.

4. In transaction cost economics, the contract or the single transaction between two parties is the basic unit of analysis (Dixit 1996:48). Most often, however, understanding

or agreement better catch the informality of the 'contracts' between the parties in a planning process. Epstein and O'Halloran note that:

> In a world where contracts are complete, every provision that is or will be relevant to a transaction can be written down and bargained over by the contracting parties. Once the initial contract is signed, all that remains is a mechanical unfolding of its provisions over time ... In this world, the *ex post* division of power among parties has no meaning, since every action they take has been specified in the contract. (Epstein and O'Halloran 1999:37)

The diffuseness and informality of agreement correspond to the notion of incomplete contracts in transaction cost economics.

5. The question of who has 'residual rights of control' when an unanticipated eventuality occurs is thus important in transaction cost analysis of planning (Epstein and O'Halloran 1999:38). As seen from Table 2.1, the question concerns the relative power of the planner and the other parties setting the terms of the planning process. In critical communicative planning this power relation determines whether the planner can go on questioning and shaping attention; that is, pursue the critical pragmatist strategy for achieving a fair plan, even if important actors in the community feel threatened by it and want to withdraw from the main transaction. Critical pragmatism assumes agreements that are vague and not fully specified (incomplete contracts), as the consequences of biased power relations and their disclosure and counteraction are central in this planning mode.

6. The strategy of raising rivals' costs has been analyzed in economics (Salop and Scheffman 1983, 1987). Twight (1988, 1993) applies transaction cost augmentation to the analysis of government growth and ideological change. Choi (1999) shows how transaction costs may be manipulated in the contracting process of competitive tendering.

7. This case concerns the Lian district in the recreational woodland Bymarka in the vicinity of the city of Trondheim, Norway. A large part of the urban population is actively using Bymarka for hiking, skiing and other recreational activities, so the woodland is truly a common good where access is meant to be unhindered. Urban sprawl nevertheless occurs in several places, and transformation of cabins to houses is supposed to number about 100 cases in the Lian district alone. It should be emphasized that in Norway the great majority of people who choose to live at the edge of the city are not poor. Most houses in the contested area are of a similar standard to houses found in other parts of town. All citations in the case study are from the local newspaper *Adresseavisen*.

8. Arendt offered an elaboration of her communications concept of power in *On Violence* (1970). Habermas's 1977 article sparked off some clarifications of the differences between his and Arendt's notions of power (Canovan 1983, Luban 1979). Habermas (1983:171–187) revised his 1977 article under the heading of *Hannah Arendt: On the Concept of Power*. Reference to Arendt's concept of power is found in Forester (1981:200, 1989:218). In the new millennium, the communicative concept of power has received renewed attention in discussions of the forms of social control in democracies (Gordon 2001), and in comparisons of Arendt's and Foucault's thinking on agency and power (Allen 2002, Gordon 2002).

9. Planners working in less dialogical processes may in some conditions still be able to reap some advantages similar to those offered by network power. Consider the concept of 'planning doctrine' (Alexander and Faludi 1996). A planning doctrine for a territory is a master policy for the planning subject's and other stakeholders' discourse about

plans for spatial development (ibid.14). As planning doctrine is in the nature of a shared understanding in the relevant discourse community, there are similarities to an informal agreement creating 'a shared ability of linked agents to alter their environment' (Booher and Innes 2002:225). Moreover, a planning doctrine is not an instrument that one person can create to achieve her goals; it is the result of discourse centring on a suggestive metaphor. The doctrine is a manifestation of the communicatively produced power of common convictions.

10. Alexander (2001c) offers a broader discussion of interdependence. Moreover, even if all agents in the network support a plan, this does not imply that they have identical interests. As an analogue, it is a common interest of management and labour that a business firm makes a profit, yet there might still be conflict over the division of the earnings between the two groups. Being self-interested, why would agents not try to manipulate others in the network if they can get away with it? Self-interest and rational choice do not typically lead to authentic dialogue (Sager 2002:Ch. 12).

11. The quote is from Forester's description of the consequences of a general cutback in public planning. He is not dealing with a shift from critical pragmatism to more consensus-oriented planning. However, his description captures well the effects of a de-emphasis on critical planning: 'This reflects a shift in power that affects what citizens know, what their rights and entitlements are, what social roles they may play as members of the society in which they live, indeed even what issues they may recognize as pressing and worthy of attention in the first place' (Forester 1985:131).

3
Activist Modes of Planning:
A Systematic Overview

Introduction: planner/activist role combinations

This chapter offers a systematic overview of the kind of processes that usually, and rather intuitively, go by the name of activist planning. A scheme for classifying activist modes of planning is shown, and examples are given, while a more detailed analysis of the categories appears in Chapter 4. The present chapter is needed as a stepping stone to get from the rather abstract acknowledgement that political transaction cost alteration is required, to more concrete suggestions of how this alteration can be instigated by forming activist roles for critical pragmatists who rely on external allies to put pressure on the stakeholders who feather their own nest by using non-deliberative, coercive means. Planners with a critical agenda need to know how political transaction costs can actually be changed.

The aim is to provide a comprehensive survey of planning modes that are often mentioned in relation to activist planning. A couple of modes that are rarely used in practice are included to fill in the picture. Not all the planning modes catalogued here are well suited in liberal democracies, and they can be combined with CPT to varying degrees. These issues are discussed in the next chapter.

In nearly all of the examples recorded in this chapter, the planners have tried to strengthen their position by co-operating with partners outside the official planning process. This draws the planner closer to direct action. Humphrey (2006) argues that direct action, even against policies and institutions that are recognized as democratically legitimate, is easier to justify in the policy field of environmental issues, than in other areas. This is because the non-reversible element in significant areas of environmental change entails that environmentalists are forced to play a 'one-shot' political strategy.

This chapter's survey of candidate modes for activist planning should make it possible to assess which of the concomitant planner roles can be helpful in curbing destructive stakeholder games. It can subsequently be considered whether the activist roles that seem promising in this respect are likely to function within the CPT framework. Activist communicative planning includes hybrid strategies of communicative and instrumental rationality that show considerable dialogical traits in interchanges between involved parties, but nevertheless remain focused on the goal achievement of interest groups or social movements. This chapter is a preamble to the discussion of how dialogical characteristics can be modified and how instrumental components can be introduced within a procedural framework that still deserves to be called activist communicative planning.

Some activist 'planners' are not planning professionals, but bring their skills to the development process from outside the regulatory system of planning. This chapter starts the search for role models that can form the identity of professionals working as activist communicative planners. Predecessors and contemporary planning modes with a bent for activism are briefly investigated. We return to definitional problems of 'activist planning' after looking at the set of candidate modes that might deserve to be included under that term. Two delimitations can be made at once, however. The first is that a planner is not necessarily regarded as an activist planner even if he or she gives priority to groups such as women, children, indigenous people or immigrants, or to causes such as the natural environment, public transport, or eradication of racism. There has to be an activist style of working as well, which will be specified later.[1]

The second delimitation is that campus-based initiatives are given little attention. There is a grey area between activist planning, action research (Gibson-Graham and Cameron 2010, Silverman et al. 2008), and community outreach programmes (Hutchinson and Loukaitou-Sideris 2001, Reardon 1998, 2008). University academics are in a special position as activist planners, as they enjoy some academic freedom, regardless of whether they are affiliated with a public or a private university.

Several modes of planning have emerged from the struggle to find ways of combining the work of activist-minded public planners with the system-critical politics of social movements. Brief comments follow on advocacy planning, equity planning, radical/insurgent planning, as well as under-cover planning both inside and outside the government. Although these modes of planning overlap, it is convenient to keep them apart in order to obtain classification tables that facilitate the analysis in the next chapter.

The issues of concealment and recognition are combined in the classification schemes presented in the following sections. The reason is that the consequences of covert planning and unrecognized planning have important similarities from a communicative planning point of view. In the first case, potential reprisals from the government force civil society to camouflage its planning. In the second case, civil society organizations plan overtly but are ignored. In both cases, the communication channels are clogged, rendering impossible any deliberation on planning matters between core actors.

Three dichotomies are helpful in providing systematization. First, planning can be a clandestine or unrecognized activity (concealed planning or crypto-planning), or it can be an openly performed and recognized activity that the planners do not try to hide from anyone's attention (unconcealed or overt planning). Separate classification tables are presented for unconcealed/recognized and concealed/unrecognized activist planner roles. Second, the activist planner can work from a position in government (central or local) or from an organization belonging to civil society. Third, activist planners always have allegiance in some direction. They may be loyal to a particular group (community, organization) or committed to a general cause. Loyalty to a particular client (as shown in Table 3.1) means that the planner ranks policy alternatives in the same order as her client (Sager 2002:124). The types of allegiance can overlap, and the planner's general support of environmental protection, for example, may well lead to advocacy of a local community having its livelihood deteriorated by industrial pollution. The three dichotomies are chosen because the planner roles of the resulting table cells offer profoundly different communicative situations, which are spelled out in Chapter 4.

The eight cells generated by the classification schemes cover the great majority of activist planner roles dealt with in academic literature. Less used and alternative terms are put in parentheses in the tables. The wide range of activist roles has been explained by Krumholz and Clavel in the US setting:

> Perhaps alone among city hall employees, urban planners have much freedom to define activist roles for their agencies because planning practice is not uniform by law or tradition. To an extent, urban planning may be seen as an area of broad administrative discretion. Beyond the narrow powers and responsibilities mandated to planners by their city charters, the scope and content of the urban planning function to a large extent waits to be defined by the planners themselves. (Krumholz and Clavel 1994:231)

Planning forms from the 1960s and 1970s are over-represented in Tables 3.1 and 3.2 of the two following sections. The many engaging political controversies of that period engendered an unusual amount of activism. This is visible in the planning literature of many countries, not least in the US. Davidoff's (1965) article on advocacy and pluralism in planning inspired a number of progressive planners to experiment with their professional role, often stretching it towards activism. The planner roles are described in a sequence complying with the numbering of the cells of the tables.

The purpose of the overview of activist planning modes is to see what can be learned from earlier attempts to combine the roles of planner and activist.

The next section gives an outline of modes in which the planner's work is unconcealed and recognized. This is followed by a description of concealed or unrecognized activist planning. A separate section deals with activist mediation, which does not fit into the classification tables, mainly because the mediator is neither loyal to a group nor committed to a particular cause.

Unconcealed and recognized activist planning

The main forms of overt activist planning are displayed in Table 3.1 and described below. A few alternative terms are relegated to the endnotes. There is no well-established term for government planners that are loyal to a particular group (or community or organization). Such planners are dubbed 'official partisans' in Table 3.1.

Dilemmas are primarily associated with cells 1 and 2 in Table 3.1: government should serve the entire population rather than a particular group, and government has to pursue many causes, one reason being that social groups usually have diverging interests.

Watson (2011) points to self-enumeration and co-production as a strategy for improving public services in poor urban communities. Self-surveys and quantitative mapping of needs in informal settlements can document and specify the community's demand for land and services and increase its 'visibility' to the state (Hasan 2006). The mapping may lead to further engagement with the state, for example, in co-production – with the state and citizens working together – to secure political influence and access to resources and services (Mitlin 2008). This strategy can be used both by NGO-based and government-based planners in Table 3.1.

Table 3.1: Unconcealed and recognized activist planning implying open communication channels between planners and authorities

	Government planner	Civil society planner
Loyal to group	1 Official partisans.	3 Advocacy planners.
Committed to cause	2 Equity planners (inside non-directed advocacy planners, public democratization planners).	4 Radical planners (recognized insurgent and community-based planners, ideological advocacy planners, NGO-based democratization planners).

Official partisans

The actions of official partisans are ultimately determined by the preferences of the community or neighbourhood organizations that are their clients. Even if the planning agency and the official partisan agree that they should work to improve the living conditions of these clients, they might disagree on how this can best be done. Official partisans work in close contact with local people and may easily be frustrated by the gaps they observe between obvious needs and the resources granted. The planners are in a principal-agent situation in which the agent plays with exposed cards; that is, the principal (planning agency) knows about the disagreements and the actions of the planner. When the official partisan serves her client in her own way, the agency may judge the deviation from agency guidelines to be tolerable and let it slide. If the planner opts for more serious challenges to agency policy, she puts her job at stake.

An open activist planner role, defined by the combination of working in government and being loyal to a particular group in civil society, will most often be unsustainable in democracies. All groups would ideally be represented in the governing bodies, and other groups would be apt to protest against one group being strongly and systematically favoured by the government. The situation might be tolerable if different groups have different advocates within the public bureaucracy.

Harwood (2003) reports on a US case of neighbourhood planning (Santa Ana), where city planners worked as advocates for neighbourhood organizations. Some planners on the neighbourhood improvement programme took on the advocacy role for the lesser organized neighbourhoods, typically those with large low-income immigrant populations. Harwood does not report any serious problems for the planners as a consequence of their combined roles as activists and professionals.

In their account of the effects of the Law of Popular Participation in Bolivia, Kohl and Farthing (2008:73) write that 'in many areas, the local government was a community organization, whether a "traditional" *ayllu* or *capitania* or a "modern" *campesino* union that operated independent of local municipalities' (italics in original). In so far as planning took place in a local community, the planner would be an official partisan.

Olsson (2009) analyzes a Swedish case in which the inside activist co-operates with a partner that is not strictly external and is not an organization. The planner's alliance is with an informal network of ornithologists who are influencing local policy to the benefit of the natural environment. The network – to which the inside activist himself belongs – has members both inside and outside government. The inside activist is loyal to the network. This is, however, not a group that is entitled to extra service from local government, and Olsson's inside activist thus does not match perfectly with the role of the official partisan.

Equity planners

In his annotated bibliography on the theory and practice of equity planning, Metzger offers a useful definition of this planning mode:

> Equity planning is a framework in which urban planners working within government use their research, analytical, and organizing skills to influence opinion, mobilize underrepresented constituencies, and advance and perhaps implement policies and programs that redistribute public and private resources to the poor and working class. (Metzger 1996:112)

While advocacy planners' loyalty to external protest groups' point of view would hardly have been compatible with the obligations of government employees, 'some planners who pursued goals of social equity and redistribution sought to implement this new vision *within* government ... This became known as *equity planning*' (Metzger 1996:113, emphasis in original).[2] Hence, equity planning is seen by some as a variant of advocacy planning unobtrusively practised from inside government. This view ignores the difference between advocacy planners, who are loyal to a certain group or activist organization, and equity planners, who are free to express disagreement with any external group or organization in public (Sager 2002:124–42).

Co-operation with activists has not been a central theme in the literature on equity planning. Just like communicative planners, equity planners might also gain from allying with external activists, as pointed out by Davidoff:

> Planners in a city have an important role to play in establishing equity goals and in demonstrating effective means for achieving them; but unless they work in coordination with a political movement aimed at obtaining equity goals, the planners' victories will be sporadic. (Davidoff 1982:180)

Krumholz and Clavel (1994:242) found that all equity planners they interviewed had some connection with groups that were marginal to the decision-making process regarding the planning issues at hand. This was also the case with the equity planners in Cleveland (Krumholz and Forester 1990:247). Occasionally, the groups were not yet organized when the planners first needed an ally in the community. On several occasions, the equity planners took the initiative to form an activist organization that they could co-operate with (Krumholz and Clavel 1994:145, 163–64, 215–16). This indicates that community organizing can sometimes be an important part of the work of activist communicative planners. In the words of Alinsky (1965:45): 'The hell with charity – the only thing you get is what you're strong enough to get, and so you'd better organize'.

Krumholz explains what kind of backing the equity planners in Cleveland got from their external activist allies, in this case a group of 13 neighbourhood organizations:

(W)e respected their ability to follow through on issues, to consistently 'turn out the troops', and to capture substantial media coverage. We viewed them as allies because they provided a countervailing political force to the incessant demands by downtown interests for capital improvements and subsidies. We also thought their work might have a long-term beneficial impact on the efficient delivery of public services to the city's neighborhoods and the preservation of the decent, affordable housing stock. (Krumholz 1994:53–54)

Cleveland equity planners did not try to coax the activist organizations into official, expert-heavy planning exercises and away from their frequent confrontations with city hall, lenders, or other targets. Exhausting, long-range planning can often not deliver much in the way of the short-term benefits that are mostly the focus of activist organizations' operations (ibid.54).

Equity planners reject 'one of the informal rules of government bureaucracy, which is to keep down the level of interest-group activity – that is to say, demands on government' (Krumholz and Clavel 1994:229). One lesson learned is that coalition building with other members of the bureaucracy and lower-income interest groups can be central to success. Virtually all of Krumholz and Clavel's respondents talked about their extensive coalition-building efforts. Citizen participation and work with neighbourhood organizations have good effect because the organizations will presumably back the policies they have helped formulate (ibid.230). These experiences are also valid for the public activist planners in, for example, Kerala (India) and Porto Alegre (Brazil), where state campaigns or city initiatives for democratization have been successful.

Several planning theorists note that state planning is not always repressive (Beard 2003:16, Rangan 1999, Sandercock 1998b:196), and that it is sometimes necessary to keep in check intolerance, self-interest, and populist reactionary politics at the local level. Even clearly democratizing efforts are sometimes initiated by governments and spread across their territories in campaign-like fashion, which gives room for public activist planners. Examples are the People's Campaign for Decentralized Planning in Kerala and the participatory budgeting of Porto Alegre (Heller 2001). Attention is given to these cases below, as academics have commented on both of them from the perspective of public deliberation.

The People's Campaign for Decentralized Planning in Kerala

The People's Campaign comprises administrative and fiscal decentralization, as well as devolution of political power (Isaac and Franke 2002). Moreover, '(i)ts political and institutional design reflects its socially transformative ambition ... to compensate for the deficits of representative structures and bureaucratic decision-making' (Isaac and Heller 2003:78). The annual development plans of local governments take shape through a multi-stage process of iterated deliberation between elected representatives, local and higher-level government officials, civil society experts and activists, and ordinary citizens. The process begins in open local assemblies in which participants discuss and identify development priorities (ibid.79). The activist planners aim to significantly reduce the transaction costs of participation. '(T)he knowledge-capacity gap that has traditionally excluded ordinary citizens from playing an effective role in governance has been considerably narrowed by mass training programs, the active mobilization of civil society experts, and concerted efforts to empower historically marginalized groups – women, adivasis ('tribals'), and dalits ('untouchables')' (ibid.79).

It is of interest to activist communicative planning when Isaac and Heller assert that the participatory institutions of the People's Campaign 'are self-consciously deliberative – based on inclusive and reason-based decision-making – and directly empowered because they tie project choice and formulation to actual implementation' (ibid.79–80). A critical component of the People's Campaign was the elaborate training programme that became one of the largest non-formal education programmes ever undertaken in India. Each round of training focused on specific planning activities, such as designing projects, evaluating costs, managing finance, gathering data, and implementing programmes. In this way the public democratization planners educated thousands of elected representatives, officials, volunteers and trainees with whom they could later co-operate (Heller 2001:154).

Formation of expert committees helped to de-bureaucratize the project approval process. Members of the mass-based NGO Kerala People's Science Movement (KSSP) accounted for a majority of the campaign staff within the Planning Board as well as for the housing NGO Costford (Heller 2001:142). Without this extra-bureaucratic expertise, line departments (dealing with roads, water, sanitation, and electricity, for example) could well have 'paralyzed local planning through inertia and outright resistance' (Isaac and Heller 2003:95). Other difficulties encountered by the People's Campaign are described by Oommen (2005).

The planning process begins in open local assemblies, in which participants discuss and identify development priorities. These meetings are well attended, making them too large and unwieldy for meaningful deliberation. 'Middle-class participation has been low, and most participants have been from the lower classes that are the targeted beneficiaries of most development projects' (Isaac and Heller 2003:102–03). Neighbourhood groups have been formed in hundreds of villages to create smaller forums of 40 to 50 families, often initiated by KSSP activists. A possible model for organizing activist communicative planning is to use an NGO as intermediary between the publicly employed activist planner and the co-operating social movement. In this light, it is interesting that Heller (2001:154) regards the most significant contribution of KSSP (an NGO) to be the creation of a policy reform network that bridges the state and civil society and serves as the incubator of the People's Campaign.

The Participatory Budget in Porto Alegre

The Participatory Budget in Porto Alegre has been the model for similar democratic arrangements in numerous other places (Sintomer et al. 2008). The budget is well described by Santos, pointing to three major principles determining its structure and process of community participation:

   a. all citizens are entitled to participate, community organizations having no special status or prerogative in this regard;
   b. participation is governed by a combination of direct and representative democracy rules and takes place through regularly functioning institutions whose internal rules are decided upon by the participants;
   c. investment resources are allocated according to an objective method based on a combination of 'general criteria' – substantive criteria established by the participatory institutions to define priorities – and 'technical criteria' – criteria of technical or economic viability as defined by the executive and federal, state, or city legal norms – that are up to the executive to implement (Santos 1998:468).

The following comments on the Participatory Budget are adapted from Baiocchi (2001), as he studies this experiment from the perspective of deliberative democratic theory and therefore provides much useful information about the scope and effects of activist communicative planning. This kind of budgeting started in 1989 and now takes place in a two-tiered structure of forums where citizens participate as individuals and as representatives of various groups of civil society (neighbourhood associations, cultural groups, special interest groups). They deliberate and decide on needs in service provision, on projects for specific districts, and on municipal investment priorities for urban infrastructure. The citizen groups also monitor the outcome of these projects. Neighbourhood associations and groups elect their own delegates to the meetings and assemblies that are not open to everybody. In the first months of the budgeting cycle, delegates meet in each district on a weekly or bimonthly basis to acquaint themselves with the technical criteria involved in demanding a project as well as to deliberate about the district's needs (ibid.46).

The budgeting process creates direct deliberation between citizens at the local level and devolves a substantial amount of decision-making power to these local settings. Although vested with substantial decision-making power, the local bodies do not function completely autonomously from other units or from central monitoring units. Rather, central agencies offer supervision and support of local democratic bodies while respecting their decision-making power. The support comes from the administration in the form of regional agents who act as non-voting facilitators (ibid.48). In practice, forums at the local level also function as a space for community demands and for airing problems in general, for divulging information about the functioning of government, and as a regular meeting place for activists of a district. Baiocchi's own research showed that meetings were often 'taken over' by activists who make use of this regular forum to discuss issues beyond budgeting matters (ibid.69, note 13).

The higher tier of the participatory structures, the Municipal Council of the Budget, brings together representatives of each of the 16 districts as well as the thematic meetings which deal with sewers and drains, housing, social services, paving, water supply, education, street lighting, health, transport, sports and leisure areas, economic development, culture, and environmental improvement. The representatives deliberate on the rules of the process as a whole as well as on broad investment priorities. They also act as intermediaries between municipal government and regional activists, bringing the demands of the district to the government, and justifying government actions to regional activists (ibid.48).

The Participatory Budget has enjoyed increasing levels of participation over the years, and especially among the poor. Of the hundreds of projects approved, investment in the poorer residential districts of Porto Alegre has exceeded investment in wealthier areas. Despite significant inequalities among citizens, the didactic features of the experiment have succeeded in large part in offsetting the potential for domination by the wealthy and well educated. 'Once we consider only persons with a certain number of years of experience, we also find that there is no significant difference between men and women reporting participation, or between persons with or without formal schooling' (ibid.52). Baiocchi concludes that: 'Persons across all walks of life are effective problem solvers and discussants in their own affairs. The difficulty involves establishing a setting in which certain types of speech are not more valued than others, and in which learning is broadly available' (ibid.64).

Advocacy planners

The main goal of the advocate planner is often much the same as for the equity planner. Davidoff (1978:69–70) is adamant that '(i)f a planner is not working directly for the objective of eradicating poverty and racial and sexual discrimination, then she or he is counterproductive ... So long as poverty and racism exist in our society, there is an ethical imperative for a single direction in planning'. This single-mindedness is not entirely consistent with the belief in *general* advocacy which Davidoff professes elsewhere. He holds that 'planners should be able to engage in the political process as advocates of the interests both of government and of such other groups, organizations, or individuals who are concerned with proposing policies for the future development of the community' (Davidoff 1965:332).[3]

In his seminal article on advocacy and pluralism in planning, Davidoff states that '(t)he advocate planner would be responsible to his client and would seek to express his client's views. This does not mean that the planner could not seek to persuade his client' (ibid.333). In my interpretation, this persuasion is meant to take place before the preferences of the client are made known to the other stakeholders. Once the client group has made public its ranking of the planning alternatives, the planner feels bound by this ranking: '(T)he advocate's most important function would be to carry out the planning process for the organization and to argue persuasively in favor of its planning proposals' (ibid.333). Davidoff did not see this loyalty as a burden, because each planner would seek out a principal (client) with whom she or he shared common views about desired social conditions and the means towards their attainment.

Much of the advocate activists' role would be educational, according to Davidoff. They would inform other groups – including public agencies – of the conditions, problems, and outlook of the client organization. Attention would also be devoted to assisting clients in clarifying their ideas and expressing them. 'In order to make his client more powerful politically the advocate might also become engaged in expanding the size and scope of his client organization' (ibid.333). This indicates that, depending on the type of client, community organizing could sometimes be a task of advocacy planners, as it is for equity planners.

On a critical tone, Sandercock (1998a) notes that the planners set the agenda, conceptualized the problem and defined the terms in which a solution to the problem would be sought. Surely, advocacy planners would:

> think about and represent 'the poor' in the planning process – without, however, actually giving them a voice in that process. Instead, advocates became the ventriloquists for poor communities. *Advocacy planning*

expanded the role of professionals and left the structure of power intact, confident in the workings of plural democracy. (Sandercock 1998a:172, emphasis in original)

Heskin (1980:58) adds to this critique when referring to the experiences of some of Davidoff's advocacy organizations. Like other advocacy groups, he says, 'they found themselves working not with the poor but with the more organized upwardly mobile elements of a poor area'.

The idea of talking on behalf of deprived groups is problematic, as Sandercock (1998a) clearly perceives. Advocacy planners want to assist the underprivileged by translating their ideas into the technical jargon of planning, to make their arguments forceful in the policy arena. There is always the risk that ideas and opinions are misconstrued in the translation (Alcoff 1995). Davidoff was an ardent supporter of citizen participation, but was very critical of the way participation in US planning was organized in the mid-sixties. This can explain why advocacy planning and communicative planning recommend different solutions to the problem of 'talking on behalf of' someone. Advocacy planning keeps the risk of misunderstanding low by demanding loyalty from the planners: elicit the preferences of the clients and pass their ranking of planning alternatives on to the decision-makers. CPT, on the other hand, seeks to eliminate the translation problem by supporting participatory processes where each group presents its own point of view. In activist communicative planning, even this may be seen as problematic due to fear of co-optation. (See the section on critique of CPT in Chapter 8.) New co-operative techniques are currently sought, where planner loyalty and full activist inclusion in official processes are both shunned.

From his basis in communicative planning, Forester (1994b:156–57) perceived the challenge as extending advocacy planning in order to save it, 'for its formulation as "every community gets its lawyer" promises not improved but paralyzed plans, not democratic deliberation, education and learning, but rather raised expectations and adversarial drama that lack follow-through and real resolution'. With regard to the plural plans that Davidoff called for, Forester asked 'who was to play the roles of judge and jury? Who was to do the ongoing work of reconciling and actually refining these "plural plans" into anything more coherent when actual decisions had to be made?' (ibid.154). These problems point beyond advocacy to activist mediation and other roles that are less partisan than advocacy. Based on a critique with similarities to that of Forester, Marris (1994:144) finds that '(o)n close reading, the reconciliation of professionalism and political activism that made advocacy so appealing unravels in ambiguity'.

Radical planners

Radical planning and insurgent planning are often used interchangeably
(Beard 2003:14, Miraftab 2009, Sandercock 1998b). Both terms denote
counter-hegemonic practices that are most often performed by civil society
planners (professionals and lay people); this denotation is also assumed in the
present chapter. Insurgent planning is often about residents using 'their
ingenuity to create daily a world of adaptations, connections, and strategies
with which to inhabit modern metropolises on better terms than those imposed
by the powerful local and international forces that would have them segregated
and servile' (Holston 2009:249). Nearly all cases referred to as insurgent
planning in the academic literature describe overt practice (Miraftab and
Wills 2005, Shatkin 2002) and are considered part of radical planning here.
Covert cases are denoted crypto-planning in this survey and will be dealt with
in the next section.

State engagement in radical planning seems close to a contradiction in
terms (Friedmann 1987:407). In the conceptual scheme of this chapter,
radical planning is an oppositional but overt activity performed by planners
with their professional base in civil society and with strong commitment to
a cause. This definition gives room for planners belonging to very different
ideological camps. As an example, Roy (2009b) follows Saliba (2001) in
recognizing Hezbollah's intervention in the Elyssar project in the south-
western suburbs of Beirut as radical planning. Hezbollah succeeded in
replacing the private development company by a public one, and in making
the government consider the illegal settlers as an integral part of the
redevelopment of the area (Saliba 2001:7). Hezbollah is a faith-based
organization, and faith can lead to solidarity and mobilization for collective
action, in this example 'centrally elaborated but implemented via
decentralized institutions building on existing local participatory processes
(at least partially)' (Harb 2008:233).

The term radical planning is overwhelmingly associated with left-wing
political ideas in academic literature, and the present text follows suit. Even
with this delimitation, radical planning theory is a heterogeneous tradition
(Friedmann 1987, Sandercock 1998a). Some indigenous planning endeavours
are directed both at the advancement of the identity, rights, and living
conditions of a particular ethnic group, and to a special cause, such as
management of a national park which is also ancestral land (Hibbard and Lane
2004, Lane and Hibbard 2005). These cases are classified as radical planning,
and not as advocacy planning, as advocate planners are typically external to
the group they are acting on behalf of.

Planning theory based on Marxist political economy is given little attention
here, as that branch of theory has not said much about problems and possibilities

inherent in the combined role as activist and professional.[4] Its focus has been the relation between public urban planning on the one hand, and the state and the capitalist organization of the economy on the other. The present discussion therefore concentrates on John Friedmann's model of radical planning as social transformation (Friedmann 2011).[5]

Beard stresses the importance of Friedmann's idea of planning as the deliberate transfer of knowledge to action in the public domain for the purposes of moving towards a shared vision of the 'good society':

> (I)t expanded our realm of inquiry beyond the work of the professional planning practitioner working for the state. It justified the inclusion of community organizers, activists, and everyday citizens as 'planners' working either in collaboration with, opposition to, or completely beyond the purview of state-sanctioned, formal planning processes. (Beard 2003:15)

The knowledge-action ideas of Friedmann thus make it easier to imagine a wide range of combined activist/professional planner roles. He states that 'radical planning is action-oriented. It is allied with social movements ... and is inspired by the normative theories undergirding these movements' (Friedmann 2003:9). Although this brings radical planners close to the action and to the community they are working with, Friedmann does not follow the advocacy tradition of demanding planner loyalty to a client group. The planners must surely be committed to the immediate practice they are engaged in, but at the same time they 'must maintain a *critical distance* from the group's practice' (Friedmann 1987:404, emphasis in original).

In the radical planning model of Friedmann and Sandercock, the state is not always and only the adversary to empowered communities. It is acknowledged, moreover, that not only governments but also mobilized communities may have a potential for repression and exclusion. Sandercock (1998a:180) suggests that Friedmann's recommendation of a critical distance to activist groups, instead of loyalty or uncritical commitment, should be seen in this light. Another reason for critical distance is the mediation aspect of the planners' work; they often need the trust of mutually opposing groups to get results. The activist planner seeking co-operation with a social movement must balance the need for standing apart with the wish of being a part (Beard 2003:17). Friedmann's (1987) concept of the 'mediation' required by radical planners differs from Forester's notion of 'activist mediation', which is dealt with in a subsequent section. Friedmann underscores mediation between theory and practice rather than mediation between adversaries. His perspective implies a focus on the transaction of ideas, values, and opinions between professionals (experts, bureaucrats, elected politicians) and local lay people (activists). The mediation discussed by Friedmann is therefore a core task of radical planners

and activist communicative planners alike. Activists engaged in daily social
struggle (households, local communities, social movements) should be invited
into dialogue with planners and so become immersed in mediated processes of
social learning (ibid.394):

> (M)ediation suggests a role for radical planners that is Janus-faced: to shape
> transformative theory to the requirements of an oppositional practice in
> specific local settings, to create opportunities for the critical appropriation
> of transformative theory by groups organized for action, and to rework this
> theory in ways that will reflect firsthand experience gathered in the course
> of radical practice itself. In terms of social space, radical planners occupy a
> position tangential to radical practice at precisely the point where practice
> intersects theory. (Friedmann 1987:392)

Sandercock (1998a) comments on Friedmann's model of radical planning and
addresses head on the painful crossovers inherent in the planner/activist role
that is our concern here. On the one hand, the planners must allocate
enormous amounts of time 'hanging out' with activists in an attempt to gain
trust, while on the other hand they should be conveying expertise and analytic
skills to the mobilized community. The planners' processed, professional
knowledge must be balanced against the contextual and experiential knowledge
that those in the front line of local action bring to the issue at hand. Radical
planners will find themselves in opposition to state and corporate economy,
and thus distanced from the parts of society for whom the planners' knowledge
base was originally built. According to Sandercock, this requires nothing less
than a new professional identity (ibid.177).

One important point distinguishes Sandercock and Friedmann's radical
planning from both equity planning and advocacy planning. Sandercock
(1998a) is highly critical of the 'talking-on-behalf-of', which is implicit in the
two other modes. In contributing to community empowerment, the radical
planners must not target any activist group as their client, but instead see the
mobilizing community as an ally. In the new professional identity, the planner
is neither the key actor nor the driving force. The community initiates, and
the planner enables, assists, but never imposes her solutions; she offers advice
only when asked (ibid.178). A dilemma lies in the fact that not everyone –
and probably not even all groups – will feel up to the challenge of being active
participants in official planning processes. If no activist planner is willing to
risk being blamed for speaking on the groups' behalf, the interests of groups
that choose to avoid participation might be totally ignored.

In many countries there are non-governmental organizations (NGOs)
devoted to democratization (Kamat 2004). Some of these NGOs work to
empower local communities and are acting as advocacy intermediaries

between the government and the impoverished majority of the population (Rugendyke 2007). It is sometimes the task of planners working for these NGOs to facilitate the participation of local people in public planning processes (Apte 2007) or civil society initiatives (Horen 2002, Rao and Sheikh 2007). In other cases, their contribution is to bridge local knowledge and bureaucratic technical expertise (Phadke 2005). The planners find allies, for example, in grass-roots territorial organizations, trade unions, and women's movements. The line between radical planning and advocacy planning is sometimes blurred in the work of NGO-based democratization planners. For example, an NGO that is generally committed to the cause of rehabilitating squatter communities will tend to be the advocate of a particular group of squatters in each single resettlement process (Sengupta and Sharma 2009, Shatkin 2002).[6]

Concealed or unrecognized activist planning

This section surveys modes of planning collective action in settings where repressive mechanisms force planners to go underground or remain on the fringe of public discourse. Concealed or unrecognized planning is the result of serious conflict between the government (or sometimes other authorities) and part of civil society. The conflict may be manifest or potential (Sager 1994:148); that is, conflict at a personal level may or may not take place although the planners must feel a serious threat. Furthermore, the conflict may be formal or informal (ibid.148); it is informal if one or both parties do not recognize the other as a legitimate party to the conflict. Informal conflict usually lies behind unrecognized activist planning.[7]

Some of the planning strategies and initiatives dealt with in this section are subtle and difficult to detect. The planning may hardly catch the attention of authorities, as it can be clandestine or low-profile and non-confrontational. These are the nascent forms that politically charged planning takes when frontal assaults are precluded by the realities of power. It is common in concealed and unrecognized planning that the real intentions, the process, or the effects are in some way camouflaged. This is one reason the lines of communication between planners and government can be blocked. Another reason is that the authorities choose to ignore the planners' work, as this counter-planning is the endeavour of organizations they do not recognize.

Even if it is rather unusual in democratic, liberal societies that critical planners working for civil society organizations have to work in secret, the situation can be different for some government planners. This is especially so in cities where politicians and city officials have lost the confidence of broad strata of the population, who have become suspicious and hostile to public planners:

> The key problem for the community planner is that to be successful in his assignment of planning with citizen participation, he must develop rapport with the residents of his community. If the residents ignore or distrust him, he has failed in his own eyes and in the eyes of his administrative superiors ... To overcome [the] crippling 'city hall image', the planner must dissassociate his personal identity from that of the planning department. To be effective, he must demonstrate a credible transfer of allegiance from the city to his community. (Needleman and Needleman 1974:325)

The community planners' dilemma in cities with a serious confidence-deficit is, then, that to achieve what their department expects of them, they have to signal opposition to their department. And this is not all, for in cities where the planning department lacks direct control of resources and has no formal role in the programming of city services, the community planners' situation is even more untenable:

> Unable to deliver any positive benefits for his community ... the planner can only offer to aid the community in pressuring those who do administer city resources and services – the city's political officials and operating agencies. This pushes him into rejecting planning encapsulation in favor of aggressive expansionism. (Needleman and Needleman 1974:325)

In other words, problems are caused by the low status of the planning department relative to those departments where people may have some rights and thus be in a better position to oppose cutbacks, for example, departments responsible for drinking water, education, and health. Losing the budget battles motivates community planners to try activism in order to support badly served communities with every available means – whether inside or outside the planner's traditional toolbox. To carry out her assignment, the planner must engage in actions viewed as disruptive by her superiors (ibid.326), thus forcing her to conceal some of her work.

Planning theory has chiefly been developed in Western countries under democratic and liberal regimes. The need to conceal critical planning is less in these countries than in authoritarian societies, so there are fewer empirical accounts from Western countries in Table 3.2 than in Table 3.1 displaying overt planning. Nevertheless, the material on concealed or unrecognized activist planning related to Table 3.2 originates in the US, in Israel, and in Third World countries.

Table 3.2: Concealed or unrecognized activist planning implying closed communication channels between planners and authorities

	Government planner	Civil society planner
Loyal to group	1 Subversive planners as delivery agents.	3 Crypto-planners with community focus (covert planners, subtle planners).
Committed to cause	2 Subversive planners as change agents.	4 Crypto-planners with system focus (unrecognized insurgent planners).

Informal planning should be mentioned here because areas of insurgence and informality are intertwined. As pointed out by Briassoulis (1997:107), informal planning is 'often illegal, but not necessarily clandestine, as lack of coordination between state agencies, lax enforcement and other types of official connivance can permit informally run enterprises to flourish openly'. Roy (2009a) has developed the concept further. She finds informal planning to be a state of exception and ambiguity in which 'the ownership, use, and purpose of land cannot be fixed and mapped according to any prescribed set of regulations or the law' (ibid.80). Roy's account of informal planning differs from others in emphasizing that 'informality exists at the very heart of the state and is an integral part of the territorial practices of state power' (ibid.84). According to Roy (2009a, 2010), informality should be understood not as a grass-roots phenomenon, but rather as a mode of discipline, power, and regulation. Nevertheless, the link between informality and activism has been established for only civil society planners. In Table 3.2, informality is thus most readily associated with crypto-planners.

Subversive planners

Subversive planning corresponds to the kind of principal-agent problem in which the agent strives to fulfil a goal that deviates from the goal set up by the principal. Because of information asymmetries, the agents' private goals and some of their actions are unknown to the principal (Stiglitz 1987). This gives room for corruption and impropriety (Mäntysalo 2008) as well as worthy attempts to amend vicious effects of government policy. Principal-agent problems are common in the public sector, according to the public choice literature, but very few have studied covert activities of planners working for the government. It is in the nature of the matter that planning of this kind is likely to be seriously under-reported. I suspect that it is not unusual for politically engaged government planners to have private political goals that differ in some respects from those of their principals, while keeping these discrepancies and accompanying political-professional actions to themselves. Subversive planning is therefore allotted space here despite the lack of availability of empirical sources.

Connelly (2010) reports on the UN-backed *National Project for Preparing the Strategic Development Plans for Egyptian Villages*, which was a programme of the Egyptian government's General Organization of Physical Planning. For some planners who disagreed with the policy of including only participants that the government was happy with, the process had an element of subversive planning with a change agenda. The planners could not say openly that they were opposed to the list of participants in the village planning process that had been sanctioned by the government's local officials. Nevertheless, planners were able to overcome some constraints once the participative process started:

> Some exploited the local culture of social interaction to subvert the careful selection of participants, allowing meetings to become open to anyone who drifted in, since this is how village meetings traditionally 'have to be'. They could also be pro-active in this, bringing to the meetings people they met during their surveys of the villages, or at least recording their views and feeding these into the discussions. Planners were also able to influence whose voices were heard, with some interviewees speaking of moving meetings away from administrative offices or the 'big houses' in the villages to more neutral venues. One described reorganizing the stakeholder groups to 'empower the marginal, marginalise the powerful' by gathering dominant participants into a single group, and so allowing previously silent women and young people to voice their ideas in other groups. (Connelly 2010:345)[8]

Harvey (1999:275) suggests that 'the planner armed with resources from the utopian tradition can be a subversive agent, a fifth column inside of the system with one foot firmly planted in some alternative camp'. Eversley (1973:196, 219) holds that the role of 'bureaucratic guerrilla' sabotaging the system, is disloyal and will sooner or later be found out. The pivotal account of such planning is offered by Needleman and Needleman (1974), who write about the opening up of city planning to citizens who are encouraged to take a direct and active role in shaping the development of their own neighbourhoods. Subversive planners take on the following role:

> (T)hey respond to pressures from their communities' residents rather than the planning department and city government. However, since the city government that employs them defines the goals of the community planning program more conservatively, their advocate role is usually covert. They

become what might be called *administrative guerrillas*, working undercover for a specific client rather than the nebulous public interest they profess to serve as public city planners. (Needleman and Needleman 1974:120, emphasis in original)

The Needlemans question whether the planner is to accept the residents' own interpretation of what they need for community improvement. If she does, she will be working as the community's 'delivery agent'. Alternatively, she might impose a professional definition of community needs and act as a 'change agent', uncovering and bringing to the residents' attention community needs and problems they might otherwise misunderstand or fail to perceive (ibid.146). The subversive delivery agent is similar to the advocacy planner in being loyal and complying with the preferences of the clientele. Subversive planners are, however, different in that they are government employees and are working undercover. The subversive change agent reserves for herself the right to disagree with the client community organization, and is, in this, similar to equity planners. A planner working subversively could just as easily promote the interests of a powerful landowner as, say, an environmentalist organization. It is in the nature of subversive activity that it is difficult to check.

The Needlemans find another dilemma in successful activist planning (ibid.335). Once a critical amount of co-operation between planners and activist organizations is reached, the projects they are trying to press through inevitably provoke counterattacks from outside the planning department, particularly from the more technically oriented operating agencies. Ironically, it seems that through their very success, the subversive community planners create conditions increasing their likelihood of being reigned in due to external pressure on their parent bureaucracy. Because of its own marginal position in city government, the planning department that sponsors participatory community planning cannot resist a strong bureaucratic backlash indefinitely. Thus the activist planning efforts may be self-limiting in an organizational sense. This reasoning is based on the assumption of a vulnerable planning department, and this does not always fit with reality. However, neo-liberal ideology, with its front against agencies and policies that are suspected of controlling instead of facilitating economic growth through private investment, has weakened planning departments in many countries.

Crypto-planners

Crypto-planning is most likely to occur in authoritarian political contexts where residents engage in social transformation in an environment posing threats of violent repercussions for social activism (Beard 2002:15). It is a strategy for resistance and local initiatives by indigenous peoples, ethnic minorities, and other marginal groups in situations where overt challenge to dominant power structures is dangerous and ineffective. 'Crypto' carries the connotations of latent, unsuspected, and concealed as seen from a government perspective, and crypto-planning will often not be recognized (acknowledged) by the authorities. The planning efforts may sometimes seem like minor, insignificant acts, but they can nevertheless be incremental, incipient steps towards altering larger power relations. In such cases, covert planning precedes radical and openly insurgent planning.

Crypto-planners do not operate in spaces where they are invited in by the government, but rather in invented spaces of citizenship, where the grass-roots coping mechanisms can evolve in subtle ways. The subtle and clandestine local strategies are in opposition to formal planning and regulative frameworks and aim to address and redress unjust relations of power. When the state fails to deliver basic services, such as a minimum of protection against widespread and violent crime, insurgent collective action may be combined with vigilantism. This is illustrated by Meth (2010) in a study of women's insurgent practices in Durban, South Africa. Crypto-planners are based in civil society organizations, and their work is inherently activist. Their planning efforts challenge the hegemony of the idea of participatory planning solicited by the state in government-initiated projects.

For crypto-planning in particular, the authorities that compel the planners to go unrecognized or to go underground may not be the government. In some countries, paramilitary organizations or wealthy landowners with private bands of security guards may be the hostile authorities for crypto-planners with a system focus. Some covert and subtle planning addresses women's health problems, and may include family planning and issues of contraception and abortion. In such cases, authorities opposed to crypto-planning with a community focus may be clerics or male heads of family.

Table 3.2 distinguishes between crypto-planning with community focus and crypto-planning with system focus. Beard (2002) and Scheyvens (1998) have a community focus and provide examples of subtle strategies for small-scale, local social improvements. Beard's case is about residents of an informal settlement in Indonesia that is establishing and operating a community library. Scheyvens studies a team of development workers in the Solomon Islands that is trying to build up women's sense of dignity and self-esteem, so that they will have the confidence to speak out and make changes in their lives. The covert and subtle actions that Beard and Scheyvens describe are instances of surreptitious resistance analogous to the infrapolitics analyzed by Scott (1997). The logic of crypto-planning with community focus – as for infrapolitics – is to leave few traces in the wake of its passage (ibid.325). Infrapolitics is an unobtrusive realm of political struggle that is always pressing, testing, and probing the boundaries of the permissible, which is also the case with crypto-planning.

Cameron (2009) shows how infrapolitics that serve poor people's modest projects for improving their livelihood and sense of dignity can undermine the plans of government and NGOs for achieving local economic and social development. He explains how villagers in three South American countries use a local government planning tool – participatory budgeting similar to the arrangements in Porto Alegre (Santos 1998) – as a vehicle for furthering their own tacitly held ideas of what is modern and prestigious. The strategy of the villagers can be seen as a form of subtle planning with focus on the community.

Crypto-planning with a system focus is carried out by civil society organizations aiming to change the politico-economic characteristics of the social system. Planning in some societies is conducted by an elitist ethnic group. Those not in the elite are expected to obey, possibly after having been co-opted into the official planning and policy-making process. Recalcitrant non-elite voices presenting alternative plans (counter-planning) are ignored, and their plans go unrecognized (Laburn-Peart 1997). Examples here are the Bedouin's planning for unrecognized settlements in the Negev, Israel, and the counter-planning of the Zapatista movement in Chiapas, Mexico. In both cases, the crypto-planning aims to benefit entire populations and not only a local community, and its practitioners need to bring about changes in the planning system of the state in order to succeed.

Meir (2005) and Yiftachel (2009) study the Bedouin's long-term campaign for resisting state plans. The state plans are a government tool in the struggle for control over territorial resources, and aim for 'spatial grouping of the Bedouin population into a minimal number of settlement foci from which all services are provided' (Meir 2005:211). The planned concentration would give economy of scale but is not in accordance with the preferences, traditions, and lifestyle of the Bedouin. Their settlements are on land that is regarded by the Israeli government as state owned. Since the Bedouin refuse to evacuate their settlements, they are treated as illegal intruders on state land. Most of their 45 villages go unrecognized by the state and are denied public service and infrastructure and are excluded from all regional development plans. Service provision is contingent upon a completed land entitlement process, which the state has been refraining from finalizing. The major practical move in terms of crypto-planning was the preparation and submission in 1999 of *A Master Plan for Deployment of the Unrecognized Settlements in the Negev*. This was part of *A Plan for Developing a Municipal Authority for the Bedouin-Arab Unrecognized Villages in the Negev*. By bureaucratic logic, plans for unrecognized settlements are themselves not recognized. Trying to assess the effects of Bedouin counter-planning, Meir reports that in the year 2000 'for the first time the Bedouin are given access to the state planning authorities, albeit at a low level' (ibid.212). This indicates that the communication channels between the parties are no longer completely blocked. Meir (2009) reports that the alternative planning and the political campaigning of the Negev Bedouin have led to improvements. The state has established 12 more recognized settlements, and some villages have become eligible for services and infrastructure.

Zapatista counter-planning

The Zapatista Army of National Liberation (EZLN) has been in a partly armed conflict with the Mexican central government since 1994, and much of its planning must be done covertly. The low intensity war, repression and military surveillance in the Chiapas region remains in place despite demilitarization of the Zapatista movement. The strategy of EZLN now puts democracy and autonomy at the centre of the movement's political debates. By 2007 there were 38 Autonomous Rebel Zapatistas Councils, and these self-organized physical and political spaces cover almost 40 per cent of the Chiapas state.

In many respects, the Zapatistas value dialogue (Nash 1997). However, the *6th Declaration of the Selva Lacandona* from June 2005 conveys a vivid picture of the strained lines of communication between EZLN and the Chiapas and national governments, and the latter has failed to follow up the San Andrés Accords regarding the recognition of indigenous rights and culture:

> They were crooked, and they told lies that they would keep their word, but they did not. In other words, on that day, when the politicians ... approved a law that was no good, they killed dialogue once and for all, and they clearly stated that it did not matter what they had agreed to and signed, because they did not keep their word. And then we did not make any contacts with the federal branches. (EZLN 2005:Ch.I)

Since 2003, the Zapatistas have given priority to consolidating the Good Government Juntas in their autonomous municipalities. The Good Government bodies are democratically elected and expected to govern by obeying the grass roots. The process of learning how to govern includes learning to coordinate the work of autonomous municipalities, NGOs, and official authorities; learning to prepare and administer local projects; and allocating external resources (aid) to where it is most needed. Such planning skills are a significant part of the struggle for Good Government. However, much Zapatista planning is counter-planning, and EZLN protests to three government plans at different territorial levels are presented below. Most Zapatista planning goes unrecognized by the official authorities and is a case of crypto-planning with a system focus.

The Puebla-Panama Plan (Mesoamerican Integration and Development Project) is a multi-billion dollar development plan formally initiated in 2001, with the purpose of promoting regional integration of the nine southern states of Mexico (Chiapas among them) with all of Central America. The plan aimed to remedy the lack of investment and stimulate trade in the region by building and improving infrastructure, such as highways, airports, dams, and telecommunication grids. The counter-planning rhetoric of EZLN asserts that 'the plan threatens indigenous rights to territory, resources, and autonomy with hydroelectric dams, gas and oil pipelines, biological corridors, and free-trade zones' (Swords 2007:87). Network workshops and marches were organized to warn about the consequences of the plan and the corporate-backed bio-prospecting operations underway. People were mobilized, using a distinct anti-neoliberal rhetoric. Network participants 'shared information on proposed projects, expressed consistent opposition, insisted on true participation in planning and implementation, resisted government-led planning events, and promoted alternative local development strategies' (ibid.87).

An important local planning dispute centres on the area of protected land known as Montes Azules Biosphere Reserve in the Lacadon jungle (Crocker 2006). Central to the conflict is the large settler population within the reserve and the question of whether it is a threat to the jungle's viability. Environmental groups, such as Conservation International and the World Wildlife Fund, launched a conservationist campaign in the year 2000, demanding eviction of the settlers on environmental grounds (Harvey 2001, Stahler-Sholk 2007:59). The settlers are predominately Zapatistas, and EZLN is vehemently opposed to their eviction. However, some groups of Mayas outside the reserve support the eviction, and this is a problem to the Zapatistas who aim to cater to the interests of all indigenous peoples of Chiapas. Besides, EZLN sees the eviction as clearing the way for global capital and serving anti-Zapatista counter-insurgency, for example, by ensuring the completion of a strategic road connecting the Reserve to the San Quintin army base.

The last example of planning-related activity does not refer to one specific plan but rather to a set of co-opting government policies allegedly initiated to take the sting out of the Zapatista mobilization of indigenous people. For instance, in the second half of the 1990s, the federal Ministry of the Environment, Natural Resources and Fisheries promoted a new model for decentralization and local participation (Harvey 2001:1055). EZLN and some other organizations tried to counter this 'listening to the poor' offensive by demanding more meaningful participation in the design and implementation of conservation and rural development plans for their communities. Following the demilitarization of the Zapatista movement, a series of policies with co-opting intent, as seen by the Zapatistas, was launched and implemented by the government between 2006 and 2008. The Chiapas Solidarity Institute is a case in point: it aims at ministering civil society through state democratic planning. Indigenous communities are organized through neighbourhood assemblies which identify needs, demands, and priorities that are passed on to Committees for Regional Development (Dinerstein 2009). The programme *Sustainable Rural Cities* is another instructive case. It was launched to counteract exclusion via dispersion, referring to the lack of basic services in the multitude of very small settlements. The programme proposes to relocate and reorganize the population in eight new cities to maximize service provision (ibid.). The similarity with the Israeli plans for the Negev Bedouin is striking. To the Zapatistas, the plan for *Sustainable Rural Cities* matches the *Puebla-Panama Plan*. It allegedly entails a territorial reorganization where the relocation of the population will strategically vacate land for commercial use, tourism, and exploitation of natural resources by private investors (ibid.), and for this reason they fervently oppose it.

It is left to Chapter 4 to draw together the consequences to activist planning of all the above examples and discuss their communicative practices. In the section which follows, attention is shifted from planner roles that are general in that they do not focus on one specific kind of planning work, to a planner role that concentrates on the difficult task of mediation.

Activist mediation

Communicative planning is aiming for a deliberative process open to all groups and sectors of society that are affected by a particular issue. It is a process that explores the potential for agreement among people with conflicting interests, and the mediator role thus becomes important to the planners. The task comprises only part of the communicative repertoire; not facilitating dialogue or moderating debate, but mediating negotiation. Mediation – even of the activist kind – breaks with the structure of Tables 3.1 and 3.2, as the planner is neither loyal to a group nor committed to a cause in his or her role as mediator. Because of this, activist mediation is given separate treatment here.

In his influential book on how to plan in the face of power, Forester asks how local planning organizations can initiate effective negotiation and equitable, efficient mediation. 'How can mediated negotiation strategies empower the relatively powerless instead of reproducing existing inequalities of power?' (Forester 1989:83). Communicative planning theorists are still looking for good answers to that question, and this is also the purpose of Part I of the present book. The planner often has the administrative discretion to conduct mediated negotiation, and thus address power imbalances, although 'mediated negotiation ... will not solve problems of radically unbalanced power' (ibid.100).

Forester notes 'that power structures involve collective relationships and require collective strategies (e.g., social movements) if they are to be challenged' (ibid.102). Paraphrasing Forester, the question to be asked here is not 'can activist communicative planning change power structures?' (it cannot) but rather, 'can activist communicative planning support wider, collective efforts to change such structures?' (it can). The role of an active and interested planning mediator is dubbed 'activist mediation' in Forester and Stitzel (1989) and in Forester (1994a). The role as activist planner follows a showdown with the idea of planner neutrality:

> To be neutral in the face of inequalities of power promises not indifference to outcome, but acquiescence to the perpetuation of power imbalances, to the perpetuation of a status quo of power inequalities. Does it make sense, then, to recommend that planners play mediating roles when they are faced with conflicts characterized by severe imbalances of power at the same time that their very job descriptions mandate their concern with the quality of public participation? If planners play the role of 'neutrals' here, they become like referees in a boxing match in which one antagonist has a fist tied behind his or her back. (Forester and Stitzel 1989:254)

This argument for the activist planner role is fashioned in the same mould as more recent arguments for activism in liberal democracies (Fung 2005, Young 2001). Davidoff's (1965) argument for advocacy planning is also recognizable in the belief that '(t)he claim to neutrality is not simply wrong, it is ethically and morally deceptive, a self-serving and self-legitimating, but only semi-professional, falsehood' (Forester and Stitzel 1989:261). This account of Forester's position makes it clear that the idea in the present book of an activist communicative planning is not altogether new, but is partly a restatement of earlier CPT attempts to deal with the problem of very unevenly distributed stakeholder power. The recommendation that planners, when dealing with differences, should take the activist mediator position is by no means outmoded. On the contrary, activist mediation was recently given a full-length treatment by Forester (2009a).

Forester is influenced by the mediator Lawrence Susskind, and the role that Susskind sticks to is incompatible with strong commitment to a particular substantive planning agenda.[9] Susskind is concerned with power imbalances and unrepresented parties, and while he does not claim to be neutral with regard to the outcome, he nevertheless insists on being non-partisan (Forester 1994a). Activist mediators can offer services that benefit deprived groups disproportionally, but they do not take sides. What Susskind offers to one party, he offers to all within a specific mediation process: 'I will not side with any party, including the least powerful'.

Consequently, Susskind does not have an equity agenda, for example, but wants 'an outcome that maximizes mutual gain, that doesn't leave joint gains unclaimed' (ibid.329). Forester (2009a) adopts the approach of being sceptical and critical to all involved parties (as already noted in the introduction to Chapter 2).

The activism of this sort of mediator consists in:

- Helping groups to coalesce and name a representative to the negotiation table.
- Suggesting widening of narrow agendas.
- Providing skill-building training.
- Pushing the parties to consider their best alternatives to a negotiated agreement.
- Cross-examining the parties to help them understand whether and when they should agree or not agree to certain packages (Forester 1994a:326–30).

Mediators have responsibilities to all parties. The activist mediator role deviates from the activist planner roles of the previous sections in that these put less weight on mediation and thus have more scope for substantive planning agendas. Even so, Forester sees activist mediation as a strategy for planners who are aiming to be 'activist realists, not resigned cynics' (Forester 2009a:36).

Conclusion

Communicative planners should encourage conditions of coercive power's non-interference with the giving of reasons in the deliberation among the parties affected by a plan. In order to alleviate communicative distortions, it is sometimes necessary to put pressure on stakeholders who challenge the deliberative format of the planning process. The assumption here is that the critical pragmatist must seek the support of allies not involved in the official planning process to exert the pressure required, and that this brings the planner into co-operation with activists.

There is a rich and half a century old planning tradition to draw upon when looking for ways to conduct activist planning. However, some of the activist planning modes are tailor-made for political conditions that are so oppressive and authoritarian that public conversation has come to a halt. The planner role of these modes is not suited for communicative planning. Further analysis of which of the activist planning modes that give room for planner roles sufficiently in line with dialogical ideals, is left for Chapter 4.

This chapter has presented a systematization of the modes of planning that seem to be the frameworks for various types of planner-activist partnerships. The next chapter comments on the activist character of the planning modes and analyzes their potential for facilitating dialogue. The aim is to identify the planning modes that are applicable as a platform for activist communicative planners looking for external allies.

Notes

1. Activist planners have been a sub-group of the planning profession for several decades (Leavitt 1982). In the US, some of them were members of Planners for Equal Opportunity in the 1960s. In 1975, Chester Hartman created the Planners' Network, which also has members from outside the US (Hartman 2002:29–32). About 500 planners, academics, activists, and students belonged to the network in 2009.

2. A couple of side forms of equity planning are mentioned here. Kaplan's (1969a, 1969b) planning work in preparing the Oakland Model Cities application led him to identify 'non-directed advocacy', which has most of its important characteristics in common with equity planning. The professional planners are working within an official governmental setting where they develop programme proposals according to their perceptions of a constituency or the community's needs. No client directs the professional planner, who might aim at other goals in addition to equity, such as meaningful citizen participation. Corey (1972) names this activity 'inside non-directed advocacy planning'. According to Kaplan (1969a:97), the planner will be subject to criticism from 'constituents who want to directly participate in decision-making going on inside the organization and who feel the planner should not, or is not able to, represent them'. Those within the organization who question the planner's ability to mix a commitment to a constituency with loyalty to an employer will also be critical.

   Friedman et al. (1980) try to work out a role for the progressive planner employed in government, drawing on their experience from the US Department of Housing and Urban Development. They emphasize co-operation with external activist organizations: 'Strong alliances with the community provide the legitimacy and power necessary for effective action within the state. It is difficult for the state to ignore or repress alternatives that represent the view of a vocal and active constituency' (ibid.254). They also hold it to be essential that the activist planner supports community action with information and material about the actions, policies, and resources of the state, and about the objective conditions of the community. An important task is to encourage community organization around specific issues and contribute to the building of networks of different community groups.

   Elimination of health disparities is one issue that has created fertile ground for activist planners. From the US, Roe et al. (2005) report on community building through social planning and the method of empowering evaluation. The HIV prevention planning groups required equal opportunity for input and participation and an equal vote in decision-making among all members of the planning body.

3. A side form of advocacy planning is put forth by Clavel (1980). He wants opposition groups to consider moving from advocacy planning on a case-by-case basis to what he describes as opposition planning: 'a thoroughgoing region-scale program based on an opposition ideology. The purpose would be to combat and challenge the official agenda' (ibid.216). Opposition planning resists metropolitan penetration and class

domination, and is locally rooted (Clavel 1983:27). Clavel regards such planning as a useful strategy in conditions of hegemony; that is, a situation characterized by external domination through an alliance of central and local elites and by relatively undeveloped independent local political and administrative structures (ibid.189). He studies the cases of Wales and Appalachia. Successful opposition groups must connect specific issues with more general ones. This means broadening the opposition; for example by linking up the poor, the working class, and parts of the middle class in a territorially based coalition. The broader this coalition, the more the activist planner will have to turn from advocacy of a particular group to commitment to a cause.

4. Kraushaar (1988) is an exception, discussing the problems of progressive planners and radical reform. Holgersen and Haarstad (2009) offer a Marxist critique of communicative planning.

5. A side form is described by Grengs (2002), who gives an account of community-based planning which has much in common with equity planning. He defines community-based planners as professional planners who, like equity planners, pay particular attention to the needs of poor and vulnerable populations. Unlike most equity planners, however, his community-based planners contest government plans from a base of support outside government institutions (ibid.166). And unlike advocacy planners, the community-based planners are committed to a cause more than to a group within the community. This variety of activist planning responds to the fact that justice is sometimes best promoted by planners who take their skills to the grass-roots and oppose government plans. With their practice based in community institutions, these planners are not in a position where they can be accused by superiors of sabotaging the plans of their own organizations. Hence, they can co-operate with activist organizations without sparking off serious tension. It is worth mentioning that the role of 'ideological advocacy' was proposed by Davidoff et al. (1970, 1971) and has the same main characteristics as the above.

6. Bang (2005) describes what he calls a new political identity, namely the 'expert activist' who is a professional in voluntary associations. The description is quite fitting for the roles of activist planners who are working for civil society organizations, such as advocacy planners and radical planners including NGO-based democratization planners and many community planners. Bang finds that the work of expert activists is above all a matter of:
    *   having a wide conception of the political as a discursive construct;
    *   adopting a full-time, overlapping project identity as one's overall life style;
    *   possessing the necessary expertise for exercising influence in cooperation with other elites;
    *   placing negotiation and dialogue before antagonism and opposition;
    *   considering oneself a part of 'the system' rather than external to it. (Bang 2005:164)

    The goal of the expert activist, according to Bang, is no longer (as in many grass-roots movements) 'fighting the system as a "constitutive other", but rather gaining access to the bargaining processes which go on between public authorities and various experts from private and voluntary organisations' (ibid.165).

7. Concealed or unrecognized planning is given such wide definition by some authors that it becomes indistinguishable from oppositional political activity in general. One example is Sweet and Chakars (2010), who claim that 'Buryat women are ... active as insurgent planners, particularly in their roles as transmitters of culture' (ibid.206).

They then list spiritual activities, language promotion, and revival of previously taboo historical figures as forms of insurgent planning.

8. Karpowitz et al. (2009) study the practice of encouraging participation of disempowered groups by letting them deliberate in their own enclaves before entering the broader public sphere. They conclude that there are strong reasons to incorporate enclave deliberation among weak groups within civic forums.

9. See, for example, Susskind's contributions to the edited book Susskind and Crump (2008). Some formulations indicate that Susskind was more willing to risk his non-partisan image at an earlier stage of his career. Worrying about the situation of hard-to-represent interests, he held that 'the mediator might purposefully shape the mediation *process* in an effort to influence the *outcome*' (Susskind and Ozawa 1983:267, emphasis in original).

4

Activist Communicative Planning: Hybrids of Dialogue and Strategy

Introduction: a reason for activist planning

The general CPT strategy for dealing with stakeholders who are playing unreasonable power games was outlined in Chapter 2. The main idea is to increase their political transaction costs compared to the transaction costs of parties showing commitment to dialogical ideals – discussing the process and outcome of planning in a non-coercive fashion. Those actors who rely on good arguments, rather than those who exercise the right of the strong, will then be able to influence decisions. Studying the potential of activist communicative planning is primarily a continuation of the attempt in Chapter 2 at making it evident that CPT actually has an approach for dealing with power-based strategies on the part of stakeholders.

By deliberately manipulating political transaction costs in an attempt to help some groups at the expense of others, planners themselves are playing power games.[1] This is sometimes justified, as the theorists of second best solutions proved half a century ago that employing a single instrument as close to the ideal as possible, is not an optimal strategy in non-ideal circumstances (Lipsey and Lancaster 1956–57).

The position that it would not be desirable for public political deliberation to resemble Habermas's 'ideal speech situation', even if it were possible, is held by prominent theorists of deliberative democracy (Estlund 2006, Fung 2005, Young 2001). Some stakeholders might reject attempts to insulate the exchange of reasons from the distorting influence of coercive power. Striving for maximum resemblance to the ideal situation would often mean letting egotistic deviations by these stakeholders skew the results of the process. The problem of dealing with stakeholders' use of non-deliberative power, which is the theme of the present chapter, is recognized as important also in general theory of deliberative democracy:

> A ... seemingly discordant use of power consonant with deliberation arises in attempts to achieve balance when one party in a negotiation has more power

resources than the other party and intends to use those resources to achieve her ends against the other's interests or in other ways to depart from the deliberative ideal. In cases like these, it is morally acceptable for the other party also to exercise power or consonantly depart from the deliberative ideal. (Mansbridge et al. 2010:82)

For negotiations in the planning process to be fair, their procedures should provide all parties at the table with equal opportunities for pressure, that is, for influencing one another's standpoints during the actual transactions. Some marginalized groups need to build such pressure with support from external actors, and sometimes this can be achieved most effectively by planners forming alliances with activist organizations that can exert pressure from outside the official planning process.

Communicative planning theorists need to discuss how the political transaction costs of disadvantaged or marginalized groups, whose living conditions the planners want to improve, can be effectively reduced without leaving the value-sphere of communicative planning (as described, for example, by Forester 1989, Healey 1992b, Innes 1995, and Sager 1994). The border is transgressed when the planners tip the balance between communicative and instrumental rationality too much in favour of the latter, that is, towards strategic action.

The purpose of this chapter is to discuss the role of the activist communicative planner and analyze hybrids of communicative and strategic action that are invariably embedded in activist communicative planning. In conformity with Hillier (2002b:116), activism is seen here as being at home in 'agonistic' planning processes (see the section on the public interest in Chapter 1). The more the deliberating parties depart from dialogue and the more they fall back on non-deliberative and coercive means of negotiation, the less hope there is that a fair agreement will emerge. Activism is needed because the internal actions of the planners – that is, the means they can use within the confines of the official planning process – may fail to curb unduly power-wielding stakeholders and fail to bring about a participatory, democratic process and a fair planning outcome in cases where a more activist-oriented planner role could do so.

Sometimes, forces more compelling than the better argument are necessary to establish fair and inclusive deliberation or the conditions that support such deliberation. When circumstances justify the use of such force for deliberative democrats, they become deliberative activists. (Fung 2005:401–02)

The activist communicative planners would be among Fung's deliberative activists. Their role is not meant to be that of a revolutionary. Preferably, their activities should be in line with ethical guidelines for planners, so as to keep activist communicative planning as a branch of mainstream urban planning.[2] The power that is antithetical to dialogue and deliberation 'is not power in general, which could include the simple capacity to act, but coercive power, defined as the threat of sanction or the use of force against the others' interests' (Mansbridge et al. 2010:81).

The previous chapter identified nine modes of planning as candidate platforms for activist communicative planning practice. The two sections that follow analyze the activist and dialogical potential of the nine modes, respectively. A few possibilities and problems of combining dialogue and strategic action in planning processes are then discussed. This clears the ground for an outline of the principles for activist communicative planning. A separate section compares the modes of activist planning with regard to their compatibility with these principles.

Activist planners rely on external allies

The survey of activist planning modes presented in the previous chapter helps to identify planner/activist role combinations that mobilize activist organizations or other external allies for the purpose of pressuring strong stakeholders to take a broader set of interests into consideration. In other words, the aim is to single out activist planner roles that are helpful in curbing stakeholders trying to compel opponents by non-deliberative means.

Activism means vigorous practice or involvement as a means of achieving political or other goals. The activist advocates or opposes a cause or an issue through direct action. Direct action is politically motivated activity that takes place outside the institutionalized channels of political goal-achievement in the society where the individual acts in the capacity of being a citizen, and outside the normal channels for reporting problems in the organization in which the individual is employed, when he or she acts in the capacity of being a professional.

The list of possible types of direct action is a long one, containing, for example, picketing, pamphleteering, sit-ins, boycotts, large and loud street demonstrations, solemn processions, vigils, guerrilla theatre, graffiti, public meetings, rallies, petitions, statements to public media, blocking e-mail systems by a tsunami of messages, burning flags, banner-waving from symbolic landmarks, protest post-card campaigns, cyber attacks, throwing eggs/cakes/tomatoes/shoes at establishment decision-makers, and hurling stones at the police.

Such actions both restructure discourse and coercively alter the social relations in which discourse is situated. They are symbolic and expressive, but they do not prompt other parties to act solely through persuasion. Rather, they also threaten crucial interests, disrupt customary alliances and ordinary ways of doing things, and create crises. As a result, problems are made to seem more urgent, interlocutors are pressured to argue consistently, and parties are compelled to take actions and enter arenas of contention that they have avoided. (Medearis 2005:55)

Some direct action takes immense courage: The video clip of the single man trying to stop the tanks rolling into Chang'an Avenue in Beijing the day after the Tiananmen Square massacre in 1989 is iconic (Parviainen 2010). Activist stunts can be peaceful, or they can be disrespectful and violent to an extent that is hardly compatible with any form of communicative planning.

It seems reasonable in the present context to widen the range of activities that count as direct action. The concept should include some actions requiring the professional competence of planners. For example, conveying information to activists about what is going on in the official planning process, advising external allies of how to file complaints or submit formal proposals, and assisting activist organizations in writing expert statements. The activist planner might also take part in community organizing. Lobbying is routinely used by activist organizations, and is sometimes used by planners as well (Albrechts 1999, Hillier 2000, 2002a:120–30, 156–59, 232–35).

A prime course of action for planners wanting to increase the political transaction costs of particular stakeholders is to co-operate with an external organization in order to put pressure on the stakeholders. Preceding sections have already shown that this idea is far from new. For example, Friedmann (1969:316) enthusiastically declares that 'a new breed of action planners ... is moving forward', and states that '(w)here action and planning are fused, the role of the planner changes fundamentally'. Friedmann posits that being involved in action means that the planner interacts with external actors of various skills and roles, also representatives of interest groups (ibid.316–17). The problem of the activist planners seeking co-operation with activist organizations is that they are boundary-spanners trying simultaneously to be both inside and 'outside the whale' in the phrase of Kraushaar (1988) – the whale being the institutional and political structures that radical reformers target for change; that is, the structures that reinforce extant social power relations (ibid.93).

The building of close affiliations to organizations that are not involved in the planning process (external organizations) is at the centre of the criteria suggested below for defining an 'activist planner':

- The planner actively seeks and builds co-operation with an external ally that can be a community, an interest organization, a social movement, a public agency, or an informal network.
- The planner supports the external ally by politically motivated activity outside of normal professional channels and agency-sanctioned planning practice.
- The planner tries to make the external ally push towards a fair planning process or a plan that has much broader appeal than initiatives satisfying narrow stakeholder requirements (the public interest, see the definition in Chapter 1).

The planner may or may not be a member of the external activist organization. Informal networks that have members both inside and outside government blur the internal/external distinction (Olsson 2009). The state is a fragmented organization, and other branches of government may have opinions and preferences that differ from those of the agency administering the planning process in question. The choice of a government agency or a civil society organization as an external ally does thus not affect whether or not the planner is to be characterized as an activist planner.

The attention here is nevertheless directed to activist organizations (social movements or interest organizations) that fear co-optation. The external activists decline invitations to be fully integrated with the official planning process, wanting instead to uphold their practice of direct action. Relevant activist organizations fight against the interests of the stakeholders using unacceptable means to sway planning decisions to their own private advantage. The sporadic tension between non-coercion and democratic ideals mentioned in the introduction of this chapter resurfaces in the question of strategies for activist organizations. Social movements must often act coercively in order to be included on terms that do not co-opt (Medearis 2005).

Interest organizations are policy actors such as corporations, advocacy groups, experts, and professionals (Hendriks 2006:572). Social movements are defined broadly as 'collective forms of contentious politics activated for the purposes of achieving political goals through non-traditional means' (Nicholls 2008:841). Social movements are vehicles of large-group action for carrying out, resisting, or undoing a social change. They are a major instrument for engaging ordinary people in politics. Social movements are seen here as committed to universalist causes, while interest organizations pursue partisan causes.[3] The pursuit of a partisan cause usually makes the interest organization loyal to a group, which is not the case for social movements. The difference between interest organizations and social movements mirrors the categories 'loyal to group' and 'committed to cause' in Tables 3.1 and 3.2 of the previous chapter. (Compare also with the distinction between community focus and system focus for crypto-planners.)

North (2001:357) reminds planners that social movements 'can make policy work more effectively by pointing to what has been tried and failed in the vicinity, what local people want, and who might best make it work'. Much has been written lately about the way activist organizations use their websites and other net-based tools to build relationships with publics and facilitate intercommunion with and among followers (Stein 2009, Taylor et al. 2001, Wall 2007). Surveys suggest that the organizations are not utilizing the web to its full potential, and not yet fully engaging their adherents in two-way communication. Evans-Cowley (2010) found that the public using social networking primarily organizes to oppose development projects. However, '(w)hile the groups opposed to development projects or plans were often able to attract hundreds of people to join in their opposition, they were not successful in translating this into public action' (ibid.415).

External activists as envisaged here recommend that those eager to promote justice in cities should engage primarily in critical oppositional activity, rather than spending time and energy deliberating with opponents supporting and being supported by existing institutions and power structures.[4] Young (2001) describes the activists' position well. They usually believe that the decision-makers and their allies would have the power to unfairly steer the course of the discussion, also in communicative planning. Rather than risk being tied up in long-lasting debates with experts representing the interests of 'the system', activists provoke and challenge the establishment by conveying their criticism through means that could not have been used inside the more or less democratic system's official processes (Miraftab and Wills 2005).

Inclusion is a goal of communicative planning, and activist organizations that choose to remain outside the official process can still obtain a degree of inclusion by co-operating with an activist planner who can convey their viewpoints and bring them inside information. The purpose of the co-operation is both to help the activist organization achieve its goals, and to improve the official process by marshalling external pressure on stakeholders who use non-deliberative coercive means. Both the wide range of ideological leanings, and the gamut of measures from peaceful torchlight processions to downright violence against adverse groups and authorities, suggest that activist communicative planners should be careful in selecting their allies among social movements and interest organizations in a community. Krumholz and Clavel (1994:230) list under lessons learned that community empowerment can be a liberating force, but at times also a very conservative and racist force.

Although planning academics have had a predilection for portraying progressive social movements (Hager 2007, Miraftab 2009, Routledge 1997, Sites 2007), some have studied reactionary movements or simply protests and demands expressed by well-educated, articulate, professionally oriented middle-class people concerned by perceived threats and risks to their quality of life, acting, for example, on a not-in-my-back-yard agenda (Elliott and McClure 2009, Hillier 2002a:99–131, Zografos and Martinez-Alier 2009).

Planners need allies to put pressure on some stakeholders to be more involved in deliberation and rely less on their power base. I now comment on the planning modes classified in the preceding chapter in light of the 'activist planner' criteria above, in order to assess the activist potential of the planning modes and see if they suggest planner roles that are likely to result in co-operation with external activist organizations.

Official partisans: the planner does not choose freely which external group to support in this mode of planning. The government and planning agency decide which community needs organizing and which group is in need of planning assistance. By and large, the planner can work for her designated external group by following ordinary agency practice and employing the normal professional channels. Help goes one way only; the planner does not need backing from her clientele in return, as she works in understanding with her superiors, at least with respect to the goals. The activist planner criteria are only partly met, and this model is not particularly helpful in resolving the power problem of the critical pragmatist.

Equity planners: the three criteria for defining an activist planner are met by the equity planning model. The equity planners in Cleveland, for example, repeatedly needed external allies to put pressure on city government and corporate actors, and they built alliances with community organizations as well as oppositional employees in other government agencies. Planners' assistance to external allies was usually of a professional nature; their style was not high-profile direct action. The Cleveland planners were not collaborative planners or critical pragmatists and did not arrive at their plans through broad dialogue with all affected parties. But there is nothing, in principle, to prevent the external relationships and the allies of equity planners from being entrusted with the task of putting pressure on stakeholders in a communicative planning process.

Advocacy planners: advocacy planners pick their allies among civil society organizations. The advocate's activism does not usually entail participation in the direct actions of the activist organization (which is not the client group). Support is primarily professional, as in the relationship with the client group: organization building, technical assistance, and efforts to increase the impetus of the ally's opinions in the official planning process. The planner is usually not hampered by restrictive agency planning practice, as she is working for a non-governmental agency sympathetic to the idea of professional advocacy. The planner's self-imposed restrictions come instead from loyalty to the client group. The planner is typically in opposition to the city planning department which presents a different interpretation of a controversial plan to the city politicians. Advocacy planners need external support to fight the department's account. Were the client group strong enough to be effective in this respect, it would probably not need the services of the advocacy planner in the first place – or, at least, would not need the planner's full loyalty. Loyal advocacy locks the planner to the partisan views of one particular group and for that reason does not seem to be a promising model for solving the communicative planner's power problem.

Radical planners: the practice of the radical planner typically complies with all three criteria that characterize activist planners. As pointed out by Beard (2003), radical planning is not always conducted by professional planners, and some of them will therefore feel less pressure to work in normal professional channels and conform to agency-sanctioned practice. Radical planners may be, for example, scholars (Leavitt 1994), writers – like Jane Jacobs – (Klemek 2008), as well as professional planners (Wolf-Powers 2008, 2009). Judging by what is reported in academic literature, radical planners seem more willing to be involved in the direct actions of their external activist allies than planners choosing to work in other unconcealed planning modes.

Subversive planners: the need to work undercover seriously limits the manoeuvring of subversive planners. For example, participation in direct action in companionship with external activist organizations would threaten to ruin their camouflage. Besides, it can be questioned if it is at all possible to work in secret with one particular external organization in a transparent and inclusive public planning process, such as communicative planning.

Crypto-planners: when their planning goes unrecognized, crypto-planners are themselves external to any official planning process. It can nevertheless be their strategy to build alliances with other activist organizations, as in the case of the Zapatistas. Crypto-planners are often more activists than professionals in the planning field, and their choice of direct actions is not restricted by professional codes. They push towards a just plan from an outside position. Crypto-planners do not usually have insights from inside bureaucracy to offer other externals unless they have inside undercover sympathizers. Neither can they act effectively as moles and forward and reinforce pressure from external allies to sway stakeholders in the official process, as this would be likely to break their cover.

Activist mediators: activist mediation is a balancing act under the sharp gaze of each party at the negotiation table. Deviation from normal professional behaviour is likely to be looked at with suspicion, and will be condemned if it is discovered to be part of a strategy that treats one stakeholder differently from the others. Even though activist mediation can be seen as a role option for activist planners, it is unlikely to contribute much towards resolving the problem of stakeholders playing destructive power games in the communicative planning process. The reason is that non-partisanship is easily jeopardized by the planner's co-operation with an external activist organization.

Most of the planning modes dealt with here have activist potential. It can nevertheless be concluded that in the normal working conditions of collaborative planners and critical pragmatists, this potential is not readily realized for all modes. Reliance on covert or unrecognized work would, for example, seriously limit the activist possibilities of communicative planners. In contrast, equity planning and radical planning seem to give wide scope for activism in combination with communicative planning. The next section examines the communicative characteristics of each activist planning mode to assess whether this aspect of the modes strengthens the motive for using them in developing activist communicative planning.

Communicative features of activist planning modes

The general properties of communicative planning were outlined in Chapters 1 and 2. What is of interest in the present context is how, and to what degree, the activist extension of the critical pragmatist role makes it hard to live up to the values embedded in those general properties. The purpose of the section is to articulate claims about the process which seem reasonable in an activist setting, and to investigate how well the various activist modes of planning meet the claims.

Requests for dialogical perfectionism are even more futile in activist contexts than in ordinary deliberation processes (see Rienstra and Hook 2006 for an overview of critical points). As John Forester has repeatedly insisted, the essential condition of communicative planning 'is surely not ideal speech but rather the concept of communicative action phenomenologically understood as practically-situated, contingent and vulnerable, precariously intersubjective, meaning-making performance' (Forester 1990:51). If the standards for how to communicate and argue are set too high, the activist planner will not find worthy allies among the activist organizations. Social movements do politics with all that this implies by way of strategic action in a tough political climate. With a few exceptions (Schlosberg 1995), living up to the norms of discourse ethics is not among their primary goals. Alinsky (1971:25) was convinced that '(t)he means-and-ends moralists, constantly obsessed with the ethics of the means used by the Have-Nots against the Haves, should search themselves as to their real political position'. Although controversial for his uncompromising methods, he reminds us that in some situations where someone is very unfairly treated, 'the most unethical of all means is the non-use of any means' (ibid.26). The goal in activist communicative planning should nevertheless be that decline in dialogical quality of the process not be accepted unless overshadowed by increased fairness of the plan itself.

The communicative features of the activist modes of planning are informally judged on the basis of four claims on the dialogue and four claims on the overall planning process constituting the framework for deliberation. The first set consists of the validity claims listed by Habermas (1999:22–24) and explained in planning terms by Innes and Booher (2010:97–100): truth (accuracy), sincerity, comprehensibility, and justification. That is, communicative action is predicated on an orientation towards mutual understanding that motivates interlocutors to speak as if they might be asked to explain and justify implicit claims they make about the truth of what they say, their sincerity in saying it, its relevance to the issue at stake, and its moral appropriateness in the given context. One should check the justification of silence as well as utterances. There is no legitimacy in deliberation unless there is reciprocity. For example, it is not right to respond to a question by ignoring it, that is, by silence.

The second set, that is, the set of process claims, consists of inclusion, transparency, equal opportunities to present arguments and comment on the viewpoints of others, and proportionality in the use of non-deliberative means (Fung 2005:403). The last claim can be reformulated in more communicative terms as proportionality in deviation from communicative rationality. Transparency in deliberation and consensus building is accentuated by Susskind. In mediated negotiation:

> (T)he group's mandate, its agenda and ground rules, the list of participants and the groups or interests they are representing, the proposals they are considering, the decision rules they have adopted, their finances, and their final report should, at an appropriate time, be open to scrutiny by anyone affected by the group's recommendations. (Susskind 1999:45)

The following points concretize how activist communicative planners can try to satisfy the process claims:

- Planners critique any party that exploits power bias to repress others or exclude them from the communicative process.
- Planners draw attention to – and question the practice of – stakeholders trying to compel by employing tools outside the framework of democratic deliberation.
- Planners balance the procedural advantages of satisfying the validity claims and any potential substantive gains that might accrue from relaxing them.

- Planners are willing to discuss the process and the plan with affected parties whether inside or outside the official process, without imposing conditions concerning working methods or communicative style. They keep communication channels open to activist organizations choosing to remain outside the official process for fear of co-optation.
- Planners make communicative planning more inclusive by finding a way to give 'voice' to external organizations that do not want to be part of the official process.
- Planners are instrumental in making the viewpoints of activist organizations known in the official deliberation process and inform the general public about outcomes of the process.
- Planners compare the direct actions of their external allies with the power techniques of stakeholders participating in the official process. The communicative distortions caused by outside collaborators should not be more harmful than the power-based behaviour of stakeholders, the political transaction costs of whom the activists try to increase.

The communicative distortions mentioned in the last point are very seldom of a nature that links them conceptually to one particular mode of planning. This holds also for the following few instances of distortions drawn from activist planning practice, so they are presented here, before we turn to the communicative features of each activist planning mode.

Alinsky (1971:114–15) tells the story of a fight that was a cinch to win. It explains how Alinsky's Back of the Yard movement in Chicago made health service return to the run-down district by means of noisy protest and militant demands, although the same could easily have been achieved by simply asking the local authorities. As the peaceful option was kept secret from the members of the movement, activists were manipulated by their leaders. The point was to strengthen the activist organization by giving it a badly needed victory. This was done by making the members rally around an important goal (local health service) that seemed difficult to achieve, although the leaders knew that the risk of defeat was negligible in reality.

Needleman and Needleman (1974) explain a tactic allowing planners to borrow political muscle from the activists in their designated community. The tactic is to generate a 'gratitude trap':

> (T)he planner uses his influence with community residents to create a political problem for the councilman – for instance, a flood of letters from residents who would not have articulated or pressed their demands and questions without the community planner's guidance. Then the planner offers to assist the councilman in solving the problem. The councilman,

grateful for the rescue, will be more inclined to trust and consult the planner in the future. (Needleman and Needleman 1974:137)

A different tactic is used to create gratitude to the planner among the external activists. This tactic of relying on 'delivery windfalls' entails taking credit for any new capital improvement in the community even if the planner's influence in determining the location of the new facility was minimal (ibid.129).

A battery of power tactics was deployed by the Cleveland equity planners. Krumholz and Clavel (1994) offer a number of examples involving various forms of manipulation, for example, planting people at meetings (ibid.54) and deliberate provocation (ibid.55). They also provide a telling example of the well-known manipulative planning strategy of deliberately including controversial and unnecessary planning elements, later to be 'reluctantly' removed in order to demonstrate good will and soften the opponents while leaving the substance of the plan unchanged (ibid.53). Another strategy is secretly gleaning and dispensing information to people not entitled to receive it, going behind the back of superiors (ibid.144). Planners are often in positions that open for such manipulation, as they have inside knowledge. Krumholz gives a detailed account of how he used means of this sort when fighting the proposed Downtown People Mover in Cleveland (Krumholz and Forester 1990:Ch.9).

Krumholz and Forester also mention strategies that are well inside the ideological framework of communicative planning:

> 'The powerful' depend at times on benign public images, at other times on secrecy, here on public acquiescence, there on the control of information. Planners can at times affect those conditions. They might enable public scrutiny of a developer's inflated promises. They might help to publicize alternatives to a privately lucrative but publicly costly construction project. They might support equity-oriented coalitions. (Krumholz and Forester 1990:220)

This citation points to the practice of questioning and shaping attention which has been part of the critical pragmatist's toolkit since the inception of the communicative planning mode (Forester 1977) and contains a distinct element of instrumental and strategic thinking.

In their concluding chapter on ethics and evaluation of equity planning in Cleveland, Krumholz and Forester (1990) choose to steer clear of a direct defence of equity planners' pragmatic deviations from the dialogical validity claims listed earlier in this section. However, they offer an indirect defence by regarding machinations to gain profit, re-election or other advantages as normal games in politics and policy-making, and by insisting that activist planners 'must act with a political literacy' (ibid.260) in such a troubled environment. If activist planners subscribe to ideal speech that is blind to the real world of politics and pragmatism, they become the victims of an ethics asking them 'to be saints and martyrs, not planners' (ibid.253). It is tacitly understood that planners – like other players – will have to be activists and will have to manipulate.

> In a political world, time is short, conflict is rampant, agendas are long, and the powerful have the initiative and do not wait for the unorganized to organize and make their wishes felt. To fail to respond to the political structuring of public agendas means effectively to be silent. (Krumholz and Forester 1990:259)

> '(N)eutral' action in a world of severe inequality reproduces that inequality. When public resources can either be chaneled to serve the poor or be appropriated to enrich the already affluent, planning neutrality, even planners' silence, will help the strong take from the weak. (Krumholz and Forester 1990:257)

I take this to be Krumholz and Forester's central argument in favour of planners acknowledging their role as political; rather than withdrawing into silence in frustration that neutrality and ideal speech situations are nowhere to be found they accept the hybrids of communicative and strategic action that are inevitable in this role. Their argument is valid not only for equity planning, but for all activist planning aiming to help weak groups. Some communicative features of the various activist planning modes are highlighted below.

Official partisans: planners can argue openly and sincerely when it is generally accepted by the government that the group or community for which the partisan planner has responsibility, is entitled to extra service. It is an important task for the planner to prevent paternalism in the helping relation, and dialogue between the planner and the officially favoured group should be established to make sure that community preferences are clarified and transformed into physical projects that can be politically accepted. In some countries, such as Bolivia, indigenous planners try to assert the interests of their activist organizations within the apparatus of state planning, while retaining a critical stance as part of an oppositional movement (Goudsmit and Blackburn 2001). The dual role generates tensions that are bound to encourage strategic speech rather than dialogue.

Equity planners: writing about the Cleveland planners' relationship with neighbourhood organizations, Krumholz (1994:54) explains that they worked as technical people who were extensions of the organizations' own staff, and that the planners' 'work was low-key, behind-the-scenes'. The activist planners did not want to attract attention to their direct assistance to the neighbourhood organizations. Nevertheless, and despite the fact that the Cleveland planners went behind the back of the mayor in the case of the People Mover, equity planning is here regarded as a mainly unconcealed activist planning mode that is not intrinsically at odds with communicative planning.

Advocacy planners: both for official partisans and advocacy planners it can be argued that the subordination of their judgement to the preferences of the client group hampers the pursuit of practices based on communicative rationality. The loyalty requirement in itself undermines the free discussion that is supposed to provide a check on what is the best argument. Critical communicative planning is not compatible with letting another actor determine the public utterances of the planner. Another problem with advocacy planning as seen from the viewpoint of CPT, is its inherent practice of talking-on-behalf-of, as already mentioned. On the other hand, strong communicative aspects of advocacy planning are that its explicit abandoning of neutrality and objectivity might enhance sincerity, and that the translation of messages back and forth between the client group on one side, and bureaucrats and experts on the other, improves comprehensibility.

Radical planning: radical practice is the way of dialogue, according to Friedmann (1979:160). The mediation between theory and practice, between formal and experiential codes, involving the transaction of processed and local knowledge, is a core element of dialogue and of Friedmann's radical planning (Friedmann 1987:402–03). This is the sort of communicative practice 'content with the partial and fragmentary transformation of power in specific settings. So long as dialogue is possible, radical practice is possible' (Friedmann 1979:43). Friedmann is alert to the need for bracketing power in dialogical planning processes. If the institutional framework of planning does not arrange for shielded planning forums where intimidating tools of domination have to be handed in at the entrance, planning is not going to be transformative or radical, but will rather reinforce extant social structures.

> To set aside social roles and bracket the inherent differences in power means to refuse to use the other instrumentally, as a means to my ends, in an exploitative relation. (Friedmann 1979:106)

> If the power derived from the juxtaposition of these roles in their respective institutional settings is not bracketed, if it is not in some way overcome, I cannot trust you; and in the yawning gap between power, submission, and revolt, dialogue ceases. (Friedmann 1979:105)

It is worth stressing this point, as the planner's difficulty of bracketing power in communicative processes is exactly the problem prompting this chapter.

Dialogue is to Friedmann (1979:103), as to Habermas (1999:300), a non-instrumental, non-exploitative relation that finds its sole reason within itself. It is assumed in CPT that dialogue, in favourable circumstances, leads to decisions based on agreement produced through probing argument. It should be questioned, though, what motive the interlocutors have to make efforts to construct the intellectually best argument when dialogue has no end outside itself, that is, beyond addressing a specific problem of common interest to the deliberating parties. Why would participants not lapse into groupthink instead (Street 1997)? Why would they not give priority to making the dialogue a peaceful, harmonious event and put forward arguments that the others supposedly want to hear, as no other end is in sight (Tonn 2005:410)? There would be problems rather than an ideal situation in planning if the conversation were to be cleansed of all instrumental thinking. This does not happen, however, as planning communication in real life consists of debate and negotiation in addition to more dialogue-like deliberation. Participants have a stake they are concerned about.

Subversive planners: in some hostile political environments, public community planners, torn between community demands and government constraints, are driven into the role of administrative guerrillas. 'They go underground within the bureaucracy that employs them, responding covertly to pressures from the community while seeming to work within the limits of traditional planning' (Needleman and Needleman 1974:326). Subversive planners use distortion and breach of communication as escape strategies from a double bind dilemma: having moral responsibility and rule-based responsibility, respectively, to organizations with conflicting interests. In the relationship with their formal principal, who is both their employer and the implementer of the public interest as seen by elected politicians, subversive planners have to withhold information, keep secrets, manipulate or lie in order not to reveal their double game. These implications make it very difficult for critical pragmatists to adopt the subversive role and do their work undercover. This is the more so, as the secrecy inevitably also affects and limits the planner's communication with other parties for the sake of preventing leakages.

Crypto-planners: the chief characteristic of both crypto-planning and subversive planning is that vital communication channels are not functioning. Then there can be no dialogue between actors who – in normal conditions – would have been the leading interlocutors. Even in this situation, communication can run smoothly in some channels where trusting relationships are established, for example, between the activist planners and selected community organizations. Broadly inclusive processes cannot be kept secret, however, so participation in deliberation about planning must be severely restricted. Therefore, covert crypto-planning does not go well with the CPT goal of inclusion and open, transparent processes. Concealed action in the public sphere is so much at odds with dialogical values that the label communicative planning seems unsuitable for processes of subversive planning and covert crypto-planning.

Activist mediators: negotiation is marked by arguments between parties which, in this situation, think strategically. Activist mediators aim for trustful relationships in all directions, but communication between the planner and each negotiating party cannot be purely dialogical. Moments of communicative action might occur that give increased understanding and have no other goal, but each party will realize that the activist mediator is in the position to influence the negotiations. Parties can therefore be expected to express themselves to the planner with an eye to successful bargaining. The typical communication of activist mediators will consequently be strategic-dialogical hybrids. Communicative planners in this role would have to act instrumentally and strategically to succeed, albeit within the framework of CPT. The question is how strategy is introduced, and how the ideals of CPT must be relaxed to incorporate it.

The mediator role puts severe restrictions on what the planner can say, for example, about substantive issues. A key task for mediators is to help the parties find a way forward through a deadlock, but having viewpoints on the plan itself means taking sides. Chapter 7 argues that it is often necessary for collaborative planners and critical pragmatists to expose their preferences on planning outcomes, as purely procedural efforts can yield plans that are far from fair. Hence, the activist communicative planner role cannot be narrowed down to activist mediation only.

An overview has now been established showing what activist modes of planning have to offer by way of communicative processes. However, the ground is still not cleared for laying out the criteria for activist communicative planning. There is theoretical literature on possible hybrids of communicative and strategic action which has to be taken into account. Scanning this literature for ideas that can inform activist communicative planning is the task of the next section.

The place of strategy in communicative planning under adverse conditions

Cross-national studies show that democracies spend more money than authoritarian states on education and health, but the benefits seem to accrue to middle- and upper-income groups. Besides, democracy has little or no effect on infant and child mortality rates. Ross (2006:872) concludes that: 'Democracy unquestionably produces noneconomic benefits for people in poverty, endowing them with political rights and liberties. But for those in the bottom quintiles, these political rights produced few if any improvements in their material well-being'. The global trend towards decentralization has been accompanied in many countries by a process of democratization in the cities. 'But at city level, democratic processes are often dominated by local elites, with little accountability to local citizens' (Devas 2001:393). There are indications, then, that representative democracy needs to be supplemented with direct forms of political participation by dispossessed and marginalized sections of the population in order for them to reap material benefits from majority government. Both this chapter and the previous one are about how planners can be involved in this process.

By seeking co-operation with external activists, planners tread into foul political waters. Democracies must have their coercive as well as their deliberative moments in order to integrate the marginalized (Schudson 1997:308). However, recognizing 'that no coercion can be either incontestably fair or predictably just, democracies must find ways of fighting, while they use it, the very coercion that they need' (Mansbridge 1996:46). This is the reason why planners cultivating relationships with activist organizations should hold on to the ideal of dialogue despite several obvious reasons why it cannot be fully achieved (Rienstra and Hook 2006).

Communicatively rational agents must be heroic in their ability to identify, segregate and set aside self-interest. To the extent that they do not fully succeed, their actions will be guided by a mix of communicative and instrumental rationality. Rather than being a problem in practice, such blends resolve a dilemma. Because dialogue (as defined in Chapter 1) is empty of instrumental contents, it will easily function as a therapeutic substitute for the policy formation necessary to remedy social ills. In contrast, political deliberation comes with a clear instrumental purpose. Political dialogue is therefore a contradiction in terms. Habermasian dialogue must mix with other types of communication, such as debate, to be political. Compound conversation is an advantage also because pure dialogue can be democratic only in a procedural sense, not in any substantive sense, as it does not have any goal outside itself (Tonn 2005).

It is the purpose of this section to discuss arguments concerning compounds of dialogical and strategic thinking.[5] Activist forms of communicative planning must by necessity be built on a mixture of communicative and instrumental rationality (Dodge 2009). In the political context envisaged here – that is, communicative planning in unfavourable circumstances due to stakeholders' recalcitrance to the force of arguments recognizing interdependencies between interests – undistorted dialogue is not even offered as an ideal worth pursuing.

Iris Marion Young's maxim could well stand as a manifesto of activist communicative planning:

> To the extent that structural inequalities in the society operate effectively to restrict access to ... deliberative processes, their deliberations and conclusions are not legitimate. Responsible citizens should remain at least partially outside, protesting the process, agenda, and outcome of these proceedings and demonstrating against the underlying relations of privilege and disadvantage that condition them. They should aim to speak on behalf of those de facto excluded and attempt to use tactics such as strikes, boycotts, and disruptive demonstrations to pressure these bodies to act in ways that respond to the needs and interests of those effectively excluded. (Young 2001:680)

The aim here is not to recommend one particular hybrid as a prototype for activist communicative planning. This would be misguided, as the gamut of forced deviations from dialogue for mutual understanding is far too wide-ranging and heterogeneous to call for the same kind of planner response in all cases. What can be said generally is that arenas and institutions must be designed, which are flexible enough to tolerate passionate speech and emotional outbursts as well as detached argumentation and seminar-style deliberation as the context changes (Fung 2003). Proposed designs are, among other things, planning cells (Hendriks 2005), visioning workshops and design charrettes (Sokoloff et al. 2005), citizen juries and deliberative polling (Fishkin 2006), consensus conferences (Goldie et al. 2000), and consensus-based decision-making (Pellow 1999). Hendriks et al. (2007) compared partisan (stakeholders) and non-partisan forums and found that the latter were superior in terms of deliberative capacity.

These deliberative designs give some room both for amicable and problem-solving conversation. Commitment to ethical process, and debate as a means to the end of instituting improved governance are both catered for (Schudson 1997). The designs reflect the two contrasting perspectives on democratic deliberation that exist side-by-side in the scholarly literature. The one holds that dialogue springs from a 'longing for the other' that equates communication with communion and mutuality (White 2008), while the tension of constantly being confronted with disagreement is emphasized in the other perspective: '(U)ncomfortable settings predominate in the institutions of public discussion. Democracy is deeply uncomfortable' (Schudson 1997:304).

Activist organizations that do not want to be part of the official planning process will mainly rely on the effects they can produce through direct action. But they can seek extra influence in several ways:

- Participate in deliberative forums (such as the above) outside the official planning process.
- Spread their views by co-operating with NGOs external to the official process.
- Seek influence via planners who are engaged in the official process.

The interaction between the planner and the activist organization in this last case is at the centre of attention here.

The activists might be reluctant to join deliberative forums, as 'participation on their part requires exposing their arguments to public scrutiny, committing resources to a process with unknown outcomes, and accepting lay citizens into the policy arena' (Hendriks 2006:575). When activist organizations nevertheless partake in deliberative forums, it is not to reach mutual understanding or to discover the 'common good'. Their participation rests on strategic considerations about improving their public image, circulating what they consider right and true information, eliciting public opinion, and facilitating reform (ibid.580–84). Co-operation with an activist planner can give similar advantages, both providing inside information and disseminating their points of view to public officials and decision-makers. The activist communicative planner may in return receive help to put pressure on certain stakeholders.

White (2008) explains that an interlocutor's dilemma can complicate the transactions. It is not to be expected that the activist organization and the activist communicative planner are equally committed to dialogical ideals, so the planner faces a problem of the prisoner's dilemma type:

> (I)magine two interlocutors who each are faced with a choice of engaging with the other communicatively (i.e., dialogically) or strategically. If they both choose strategy, then neither is particularly advantaged nor disadvantaged: They make their trade or conclude their negotiations and ... each gives as good as he or she gets. If they both choose dialogue, however, then the transformative potential of dialogue is brought to bear and the fruits of collaboration and true cooperation are reaped by both ... (A) commitment to dialogue allows for challenges to taken-for-granted assumptions about the operation of the world and those in it, and thus lets interlocutors *really hear one another*, to their mutual benefit...
>
> But in cases where their choices do not match, then the one who was oriented toward communicative action suffers an instrumental disadvantage: Perhaps he or she reveals something embarrassing or gives away information that is subsequently used against him or her. (White 2008:12, italics in original)

The interlocutor's dilemma describes the risk of activism built on a professional basis, demanding that planners' priority be given to implementing agency policy and acting in line with the means-ends model of superiors. Activist communicative planners living by dialogical ideals to an extent unwarranted by real-world politics, and trusting their external activist partners more than their track record would seem to justify, are likely to lose out instead of receiving relational goods. Inside information may be used by activists in ways endangering the planner's position, and the protective support from outside might be disappointing. To the external activists, the growth and striking power of their social movement will count for more than the precarious situation of the planner.

The risk that activist communicative planners will be let down in interlocutor's dilemma situations correlates with their preceding efforts in building a relationship of mutual solidarity and cultivating reciprocal commitment to dialogical values. Success in the planners' strategic game, aiming to make stakeholders observe precepts of fair deliberation, depends on norms of discourse ethics being followed in the coordination with the external activist partner. That is, the benefits of strategy hinge on the level of communicative rationality. This realization makes White (2008:14) conclude that 'the valorization of communication and the demonization of strategy mask the extent to which they are in fact inextricably bound up with one another: The dichotomization of strategy and communication is ultimately not sustainable as a categorical antinomy'.

Several planning theorists have emphasized the potential of storytelling in building mutual understanding among the parties to a planning process (Forester 1993b, Throgmorton 1996). Communication theorists contend that storytelling helps deliberators to identify their own preferences, demonstrate their appreciation of competing preferences, advance unfamiliar views, and reach areas of unanticipated agreement (Polletta and Lee 2006). Stories can be chained, supplemented, and responded to. Hence, storytelling does not entail monologue and the breaking up of conversation but can be multi-vocal by presenting the experiences and perspectives of different participants.

Even if it is unrealistic to establish ideal speech conditions for an entire conversation, Black (2008) suggests that storytelling can bridge dialogue and debate. Storytelling can make interlocutors experience presence, openness, relational tension but also collateral kinship between self and other, and thus be an invitation to dialogical moments. These are momentary experiences of profound mutual awareness of the other person. The idea is that storytelling can make moments of dialogue occur in the midst of other kinds of interaction. 'Such moments ... can potentially have positive influences on deliberative discussion by helping group members participate in a sense of shared collective identity and seriously consider the views and values of their fellow group members' (ibid.109).

It is thought that the sympathy created by the glimpse of the other as deeply human and vulnerable will carry over to the non-dialogic phases of deliberation and reduce the risk of the planner and the external activist falling into the 'one wins/one loses' trap of the interlocutor's dilemma. However, Polletta sounds a warning that the story told does not always have the intended effect:

> Say that a member of a marginalized group recounts her life story to political decision makers in the hope that her experience will expose the inadequacy of a current policy. Her story may be misinterpreted or dismissed because it is heard against the backdrop of familiar stories about her group or her experience, stories that make her story ring untrue, idiosyncratic, or no different from the stories that are already known. (Polletta 2006:172)

Polletta finds that storytelling is more effective and more often used when it comes to issues of culture and memory than in discussions of policy and finance. In her cases, stories were less often narrated in policy deliberation on transport, housing, and economic development than in discussions of a planned memorial and broad themes in rebuilding after 9/11. Polletta (2006:176) surmises that this may make it more difficult for groups who are traditionally excluded from the policy elites' decision-making to register their preferences on typical planning matters, even as they are invited to do just that.

Stories are told by all parties, for very different purposes, and with widely varying effect. Endorsing storytelling in the public deliberation of planning matters is no guarantee that the needs of marginalized groups will be given more consideration. There should nevertheless be room for narratives and passionate speech in deliberation open to lay people, as many groups have a better command of emotional expression and narrating concrete events than systematically presenting abstract arguments to back up their opinions (Hall 2007). 'Discouraging storytelling in policy-oriented discussions in a public deliberative forum casts such discussions as more properly the purview of experts than the public' (Polletta 2006:177).

Preceding sections clarified the activist potential of the most relevant candidate modes for activist communicative planning, and discussed their communicative features. An activist communicative planning mode is necessarily an amalgamation of instrumental and dialogical elements, and the present section has analyzed arguments and tools for putting together such combinations as well as the problems of making them work. The foundation is now in place for laying out the principles of activist communicative planning.

Principles of activist communicative planning

This section starts out from Fung's (2005) four principles of deliberative activism. They pertain to a setting where all parties are in principle equal participants in the deliberation. The role of somebody – for example, a planner – responsible for the process is not explicitly dealt with in Fung's article; neither is co-operation with a partner outside the deliberative process. Special attention is here given to the principle of proportionality, stating that activist communicative planners can use non-deliberative means deviating from dialogical norms to an extent proportional to that of other actors in the planning process. This principle is clarified and supplemented in the following. The purpose is to offer guidance on how activist communicative planners can encourage and protect deliberation while still acting with political savvy in environments unfavourable to dialogue.

Fung's deliberative activism perspective is based on his belief that 'the most sensible stance for a deliberative democrat who lives and acts in circumstances characterized by inequality is to advance deliberation through persuasion when possible, but not to limit his means to persuasion only' (ibid.399). A position for activist planners has to be forged between the loser strategy of unilaterally restricting oneself to (dialogue-like) deliberative action, and the cynical strategy of choosing freely among power-based contrivances as long as others do not observe the norms of discourse ethics. These two extreme options will both get communicative planning into disrepute, as the first gives the impression of an impotent planning approach, and the second reveals an approach empty of political ethics. An intermediate position is displayed in Box 4.1.

Activist communicative planners should subscribe to the four principles in Box 4.1. Charity and exhaustion tell the activist planner how to act as long as the other parties are willing to comply with the norm of reciprocity, while fidelity and proportionality guide activist planners' non-deliberative actions. Fidelity implies that non-deliberative power employed by stakeholders should not make the activist communicative planner adopt revolutionary strategies. Even when the planner is faced with aggressive self-interested strategies, she should keep looking for possibilities of taking small steps back to deliberative problem-solving. There might well be short-run tension between this commitment and the principle of proportionality which guides action when two-way communication is coming to a halt. However, the idea is that coercive adversaries might consider moving towards deliberation when experiencing that power strategies are not for free, as the activist communicative planners work to raise the political transaction costs of such adversaries proportionally to the extent they apply coercion instead of reason (compare Chapter 2).

Box 4.1: Archon Fung's principles for deliberative activism

Fung's (2005) principles for the intermediate position of deliberative activism:

- *Fidelity* states the commitments of the deliberative activist to the method of deliberation and to the integrity of liberal society. Deliberative activists view institutions and political practices of liberal societies as flawed but improvable and aim 'not at institutional rupture but at incremental improvement in a deliberative direction' (ibid.403).
- *Charity* requires deliberative activists to act as if their 'would-be interlocutors are willing to engage in good faith deliberation, until they prove themselves unwilling to comply with the norm of reciprocity' (ibid.403).
- *Exhaustion* explains how charity is to be applied. Deliberative activists should refrain from using non-communicative forms of power 'until reasonable efforts to persuade and institute fair, open, and inclusive deliberations fail' – that is, until deliberative means are exhausted (ibid.403).
- *Proportionality* governs the range of non-deliberative instruments that follow when communicative actions have been exhausted. The means chosen by deliberative activists 'should be scaled according to the extent to which political adversaries and opponents reject the procedural norms of deliberation and the substantive values that ground it' (ibid.403).

The following paragraphs concentrate on the principle of proportionality, which is criticized on three points:

- It is not clear what proportionality means in this context or to whom the principle is directed.
- The basis for judging suitable proportional responses should not be purely procedural.
- The proportionality principle is only about how much to deviate from dialogical ideals, not about the right way to digress.

The principle of proportionality is problematic because there are several aspects of deliberation (compare the four validity claims), and deviation from the acceptable standard might differ greatly between the aspects. There might, for example, be ample opportunity to talk, but no willingness to listen; truth might be spoken, while serious threats are put forward; a stakeholder might organize an inclusive deliberative meeting just to present downright lies when 'information' is exchanged. What counts as a proportional response on the part of the activist planner must take all aspects of democratic and fair deliberation into account and has to rely on the judgement of the planner.

When the behaviour of one stakeholder implies coercive power's interference with the giving of reasons, this does not mean that every other party to the planning process can invoke the proportionality principle. Estlund (2006:85) suggests that dispensation from the norms of dialogue be 'given selectively to those whose viewpoints are being denied their due hearing by an imbalance of power'. The role of the activist communicative planner elaborated in this chapter requires that the right to respond according to the proportionality principle is extended to the planner(s) responsible for the process.

There are arguments both for and against extending the permission to respond with proportional non-deliberative means to a wider circle of participants. Proponents of CPT have often professed that dialogue promotes mutual understanding, empathy, and solidarity. As this is a central tenet, it seems unreasonable that companion stakeholders in a communicative planning process should not be allowed to show solidarity with an ally suffering from somebody else's coercive action by responding to the coercive party with proportional, non-deliberative sanctions. Such a front would help the planner put pressure on a stakeholder straying off the deliberative course, but the risk is that the targeted stakeholder chooses to withdraw from the deliberation altogether.

Procedure and substance are linked; stakeholders depart from dialogical norms in pursuit of substantive gains – a plan that better serves their interests. One party's digression from fair deliberation is likely to make some other participating group worse off. Deviation from dialogue gives a purely procedural basis for deciding on a proportional sanction. However, as emphasized especially in Chapter 7, communicative planning should not neglect the substantive outcome. The reaction of activist communicative planners to manifest disrespect for fair deliberation should therefore reflect the substantive consequences of breaking with procedural norms. If somebody stands to lose much as a result of one stakeholder's improper behaviour, then much should also be done by the planner to prevent the stakeholder from causing the harm. This suggests that the greater the expected negative effects of the stakeholder's rejection of dialogical norms, the more the activist communicative planner is at liberty to conduct politics by non-communicative means. In other words, when searching for response in accordance with the proportionality principle, the activist planner's interpretation of proportionality should take into account substantive consequences of the stakeholder's deviation from appropriate procedure. There is probably no general answer to the question of how much substantive effects should count in the determination of proportionality, as it is a goal to make the parties resume deliberation. The planner must consider how stakeholders will react to a proportionality principle based on substantive consequences. Another difficulty follows from the activist planner's co-operation with an external activist organization. The planner would most often not be in the position to control how the activist organization exerts pressure on the non-deliberative stakeholder. External activists might not feel any obligation to act in line with the proportionality principle.

In what ways are activist planners allowed to use non-deliberative strategies in response to stakeholders' break with dialogical values? Relevant strategies must enable the planner to target one particular stakeholder; advising the planner to accentuate more instrumentally oriented behaviour in general will not do. If the political transaction costs of the opponent can be increased in alternative ways, what criteria should the activist planner choose by? Revenge or punishment motives should not drive the planner's strategic response; 'there would be no apparent justification for such extreme suppression of a message that it disappears from public awareness altogether' (Estlund 2006:85). '(T)he object of these efforts is always to advance deliberation by ultimately persuading adversaries or by raising the costs of rejecting reason' (Fung 2005:403). Whatever action the planner takes, it should not create antagonism towards the deliberative process or resentment against other actors at the table. This is one reason why it may be convenient for the critical pragmatist to make an external ally put pressure on the stakeholder digressing from dialogical norms, and tone down his or her own strategic action.

The goal of not jeopardizing future deliberation is top-ranked. This is analogous to the superiority of 'political rationality' (Diesing 1962), designating a mode of reasoning directed to the maintenance of the capacity for making collective decisions. Nothing is basically solved until the political decision-making problems of an organization or society are solved. The reason is that without a well-functioning decision-making structure the system is unable to deal with its other problems in a perpetual fashion. So also in the present context: Regarding instrumental and communicative rationality as equiprimordial opens for the inferior choice combinations in the interlocutor's dilemma. However, 'if the strategic and the communicative are equally rational modes of social action, then choosing between them requires some form of "meta-rationality" that specifies when one or the other is operative' (White 2008:11). Here, this is the political rationality of acting so as to maximize the capacity for public deliberation.

This section has analyzed and elaborated on a set of principles that activist communicative planning practice can be measured against. It remains to compare the different activist planning modes with regard to conformance with these principles.

Comparing the modes of activist planning

This section examines which modes of activist planning can be subsumed under communicative planning without creating significant conceptual and practical problems. The activist planner criteria and the characterization of activist communicative planners from preceding sections, as well as the principles of deliberative activism from the present section, are used to argue that some modes (in Tables 3.1 and 3.2 of the previous chapter) have higher communicative planning potential than others.

Activist communicative planners have two ambitions. The critical ambition follows already from the basic reason for activist planning in general: reforms are needed in many countries because the availability of resources and power are biased to an extent that makes even well-intended dialogical processes fortify current social injustices. The deliberative ambition springs from the conviction that a political ethics is needed in public planning, and the belief that – despite the reason for the critical ambition – discourse ethics offers the best foundation. The two ambitions reveal that 'activist communicative planning' is a concept with inner tensions and a set of practices with inescapable, frustrating compromises.

Suitable hybrids of communicative and activist planning must be developed from practices that can ameliorate stakeholders' non-deliberative strategies, while in themselves causing the least possible conflict with dialogical values. The deliberative ambition gives precedence to the overt modes, and the critical ambition requires an independent planner role in which the planner's standpoints do not follow from the preferences of others – that is, uninduced planner judgement. In liberal societies with a commitment to democracy that reaches beyond periodical elections, this points in the direction of equity planning and radical planning as platforms for activist communicative planning. Further reasons for this tentative supposition are given in the ensuing paragraphs.

The activist potential and the dialogical potential of each activist planning mode were studied in preceding sections. For equity planning and radical planning there turned out to be no significant discord between (1) activist planner behaviour serving to mobilize external pressure, and (2) upholding the possibility of operating inside a CPT framework. Those modes of activist planning are promising in both respects, as they require neither the loyalty nor the secrecy that makes it harder to realize the combined activist and dialogical potentials of several other planning modes.

The ideal in CPT is that collective decisions should be reached through the force of the argument that is 'better' according to inter-subjective criteria, however difficult the application of such criteria might be (Pellizzoni 2001). Loyalty, in the strict sense assumed here, implies that the standpoints of the activist planner are dictated by the preferences of his or her allied external activists. Loyalty can clash with the force of the best argument, and disregarding the argument that seems to be best according to agreed criteria can undermine the planner's attempt to make stakeholders who are opposed to the favourite activist organization, resume deliberative practice. It is probably easier to persuade sceptical stakeholders to take incremental steps towards deliberation if the process up to that point has not systematically favoured a particular clientele.

Loyalty can be turned into a form of false play when practised in a process where dialogical ideals are observed in other respects. The planner should make it clear to the other parties that she is loyal to a particular group, and explain the implications of this. If not, the activist planner *pretends* to use her own judgement to identify the best argument and act in harmony with it, while she is in fact letting her acts be steered by one particular group. This amounts to a way of manipulating the other parties in the planning process. In so far as loyalty is interpreted simply as having sympathy with a certain group, without any felt obligation to act in agreement with the policy proposals of that group, official partisanship and advocacy planning will be less objectionable as forms of communicative planning.

Secrecy and its concomitant misleading manoeuvring often give rise to serious departure from open dialogue. By referring to the proportionality principle, stakeholders might then find an excuse to apply more coercive non-deliberative means. Subversive planners, for example, manipulate in an important relationship, namely that between the planner and her superiors. Manipulation is inherent in their planner role, and subversive planning can be justified only if the activist planner experiences even more coercive strategies on the part of her employer.

Whether or not the covert activities are actually disclosed, undercover planning is an emergency strategy, as the continuous need to protect one's cover limits the set of actions available to the activist planner and therefore reduces her effectiveness. Assume now that the undercover activities of the activist planner are indeed revealed. The secret co-operation with an activist organization in order to put pressure on one particular stakeholder is likely to be regarded as differential treatment and result in a breach of trust which may ruin that stakeholder's motivation for further deliberation.

When the activist planning is unrecognized, this implies that the other party (the authorities) is using severe non-deliberative means. The planner may then likewise resort to stern non-deliberative measures, but must consider whether this is compatible with an incrementalist strategy for re-establishing the conversation about the plan in question. At any rate, important communication channels are blocked when planning efforts are not recognized, and this seriously restricts the scope for communicative planning.

Activist mediation is well designed for fulfilling the deliberative ambition of activist communicative planning. But the non-partisan obligation which is typical for this planning mode is not consistent with the substantive part of the proportionality considerations. The mediator role can thwart the activist planner in her attempts to pursue the critical ambition.

Equity planning and radical planning seem to be the modes that are most readily combined with the role of activist communicative planners, especially when this role is to include a range of tasks that comprises much more than mediation. Activist communicative planning can thus be practised by public as well as civil society planners.

In some activist planning modes, problems are created for the critical pragmatist both by loyalty and secrecy. Subversive planners working as delivery agents, and covert crypto-planners with community focus, jeopardize development towards deliberation both through the manipulation embedded in loyalty and the potential loss of trust resulting from secrecy. This is not to say that these modes of activist planning are of little value. The political conditions might well be such that any variant of communicative planning would be doomed to failure, so that working subversively or following covert crypto-strategies with community focus is the best the planner can do.

Equity planning and radical planning do not generally require that the activist communicative planners digress from dialogical ideals in ways that complicate future deliberation. These modes do not contradict the political rationality of deliberative democracy. It is also helpful that the substantive proportionality consideration in equity planning and radical planning has its basis primarily in commitment to a cause rather than a particular group, as this poses a lesser threat to independent planner judgement.

Recall the difference between interest organizations and social movements; the first is committed to a group, while the goal of social movements is related to a cause – as for equity planning and radical planning. Hence, the outside support that activist communicative planners can count on when working in these modes will probably be stronger if they choose social movements as external allies. The activist planner and her external partner would then fight for the same cause instead of the one fighting for a cause and the other for a group. Matching interests increase the likelihood that the activist communicative planners can be effective while observing the proportionality principle.

Conclusion

Activist communicative planning combines the deliberative principles and the activist planner criteria listed in this chapter within the procedural and ideological framework of planning modes that are open to dialogue – for example, Friedmann's radical planning and non-technocratic equity planning. The best situation for the activist communicative planner is when there are external activist organizations that believe in dialogue in principle, although their leaders are also convinced that the current economic-political structures of society call for non-deliberative measures in order to redress threatening or repressive social practices.

> The activist remains suspicious of the deliberative democrat's exhortation to engage in reasoned and critical discussion with people he disagrees with, even on the supposition that the public where he engages in such discussion really includes the diversity of interests and perspectives potentially affected by policies. That is because he perceives that existing social and economic structures have set unacceptable constraints on the terms of deliberation and its agenda. (Young 2001:682)

A dilemma will sometimes arise, because activist planners lose credibility when trying to entrench deliberation in the planning process by co-operating with activist organizations that are more hostile to dialogue than the stakeholders they are trying to impel. Activist communicative planners cannot simultaneously preach the blessings of dialogue and endorse the deeds of activist organizations blatantly militating against co-operative ways of settling social disputes.

There are deviations from dialogical ideals inherent in each activist planning mode (Tables 3.1 and 3.2), as in all political practice. These are modes that can potentially be chosen as a process framework by activist communicative planners. The aberrations from dialogical norms are least grave in equity planning and radical planning. Given that the principle of proportional deviations is to be observed, these are the planning modes that can most readily be used in relatively well-functioning liberal societies when a stakeholder in the communicative planning process resorts to coercive, non-deliberative negotiation technique.

Some societies are overall liberal and democratic, while still neglecting or mistreating particular groups of people on criteria of ethnicity, religion, sexual disposition, etc. The discrimination might manifest itself in planning processes and engender severe digression from the norms of dialogue. In such conditions, the planner may be justified in choosing the role of an official partisan or advocacy planner, even when committed to Fung's principles of deliberative activism.

In democratic and liberal societies, the proportionality principle will seldom permit subversive planning, and very few empirical studies deal with this mode. In authoritarian societies, it can be dangerous for the planner to be openly critical. Covert planning may then be warranted even when the proportionality principle is to be respected. However, the more authoritarian and repressive the regime, the less meaningful it is to imagine communicative planning at all.

Claims of justice and fairness are most often linked to the plan and its consequences, implying that activist communicative planning has an obvious substantive aspect. Activists rarely fight only to get the process right. The relationship between process and outcome quality in communicative planning is analyzed in Chapter 7.

Notes

1. This is a parallel to the dilemma that, in situations of lasting disagreement, any democracy needs coercion (Mansbridge 1996).
2. Hillier (2002b) also sees the need to reconcile informal direct action and institutionalized practices. Real possibilities of participation and real possibilities to disagree are welcomed, differing from potentially repressive consensus. She seems to endorse 'the logic of communicative power, based on relations of mutual recognition, respect and reciprocity' (ibid.130). Hillier does not attend to the problem of activists breaking with this framework, however, and it is not on her agenda to discuss how to make the activist/planner relationship work on a CPT value-platform.
3. Castells (1983:305) defined urban social movements as 'a collective conscious action aimed at the transformation of the institutionalized urban meaning against the logic, interest, and values of the dominant class'. Threats to working class people from neo-liberal policies have triggered joint political mobilization between trade unions and community groups (Lier and Stokke 2006, Robinson 2000), seemingly in line with Castells's notion. Others have let go of the anti-capitalist connotations:
    > Many social movements seem not to be easily categorized as progressive. Most cannot even be pigeonholed in any meaningful way as being about identity, justice, gender, ethnicity, class, collective consumption, etc. There is no singular social goal behind the combined (but often fractured) efforts of communities to reshape their urban lives. (Lehrer and Keil 2007:303)
4. See Bang (2005) and Mitlin (2008) for descriptions of a different type of activist. Also, Larner and Craig (2005) describe local activists working through neo-liberal partnerships, new hybrid forms of governance that fuse policy-makers and communities (ibid.19).
5. Chaskin (2005) draws attention to the difficulties of combining two conflicting frameworks for action, which have similarities with the activist/planner co-operation discussed here. 'One is an ideology of associational action and local democracy associated with fluid grassroots movements and voluntary associations; the other is an adherence to rational-planning, essentially bureaucratic approaches common to the world of government, philanthropy, and the professions' (ibid.408–09). The problem is illuminated by analyzing comprehensive community initiatives.

PART II
THE NEO-LIBERAL CHALLENGE

The prevalent economic-political ideology, neo-liberalism, is a challenge to CPT. The values of this ideology, as well as the policies it recommends for urban development, differ considerably from the ideas of governance and dialogue embedded in CPT. The challenge is all the greater, as neo-liberal ideas of how to reform the public sector through new public management (NPM) have permeated and transformed many agencies and administrations where numerous planners are working. Planners who feel attracted to the ideas of CPT face the dilemma of pursuing dialogical values in agencies that are being managed according to economic values and private business ethics. The three chapters in the second part of this book study different aspects of the relationship between CPT and neo-liberalism: the set of planning-related policies for urban development that have strong neo-liberal features, the contrasting values of CPT and neo-liberalism applied to the public sector (NPM), and the possibilities of preventing CPT from unintentionally aiding the implementation of neo-liberal agendas.

Neo-liberal urban policies are engendered by the nexus between mobile investment capital, inter-city competition, and public entrepreneurialism. The academic literature on urban policy and planning which explicitly links to neo-liberalism is huge. Chapter 5 draws on a comprehensive systematization of this literature between 1990 and 2010 which identifies and describes the most important planning-related urban policies of neo-liberalism. The neo-liberal rationales of the policies are explained, and typical planning concerns are outlined for each of them. The challenges that the neo-liberal urban policies pose to public planning are spelled out. The chapter makes it easier to judge whether plans for regeneration and development of a city push the local society in a neo-liberal direction.

The purpose of Chapter 6 is to show that the current planner role in a number of societies where neo-liberal ideas play an important part in shaping economic-political life, contains tensions which negatively affect the everyday working conditions of many planners. In the Western countries for which data is available, planners are inclined to be in favour of citizen involvement and open processes and opposed to manipulation and lenient control of developers. The hypothesis here is that the attitudes of many planners are much closer to the dialogical ideals of CPT than to new public management (which is neo-liberalism applied to management of the public sector). The planner role is currently under pressure from conflicting values and expectations held by educators and part of the professional community influenced by CPT on the one hand, and politicians and administrators promoting neo-liberalism (new public management) on the other. Patches of what might appear to be common ground are also identified and analyzed, in particular the concern for user influence, service quality, and client satisfaction.

CPT has recently been reproached for facilitating neo-liberal market practices to the disadvantage of broader social interests. Chapter 7 comments on this critique and clarifies what neo-liberalism demands from urban planning. Moreover, the chapter surveys planning theorists' attempts to describe the connection between communicative planning theory and neo-liberalism. This connection is conceived in very different ways, but a variety of arguments support the view that the inherent flexibility of local communicative planning is welcomed by neo-liberals. The critique of being at the service of neo-liberalism should be addressed in CPT by bringing procedural and substantive recommendations closer together. Clearer criteria in communicative planning for judging what is a good plan would make it easier to decide whether planning efforts promote urban developments that are in line with dialogical values or serve other interests. It may be difficult to entirely prevent developer-oriented exploitation of local participatory planning efforts, and communicative planning needs to be critical and alert to the potential misuse of flexible negotiated solutions in order to gain credibility as a form of governance successfully combining inclusive processes and fair outcomes.

The tools developed in Chapters 5, 6, and 7 make it much easier to examine whether a particular urban plan moves society in the direction of neo-liberalism. Part II contributes to the revival of critical planning theory because it becomes less likely that critical pragmatists will unwittingly serve neo-liberal interests.

5

Neo-liberal Policies in Urban Planning

Introduction

A comprehensive literature study has been the foundation for identifying and characterizing the main planning-related, neo-liberal urban policies.[1] The policy overview in the present chapter is an important tool to be used in Chapter 7. That chapter proposes a value-based strategy for determining whether or not plans following from communicative planning processes facilitate implementation of neo-liberal urban policies. In order to answer this question we need to know which planning-related policies can reasonably be called neo-liberal. This will become clear in the following, and actions recommended in plans under scrutiny can then be compared with the content of the policies outlined here.

A neo-liberal policy is one that is promoted by neo-liberal regimes and implies a shift from government to (partly) private strategies, or a conversion from publicly planned solutions to market-oriented ones, or at least the serving of private companies and their favoured customers. Neo-liberalism refers to the repudiation of Keynesian welfare state economics and the ascendance of market liberalization taught by the Chicago School of political economy. Neo-liberal economics views most forms of government intervention as an intrusion into the voluntary contractual arrangements between individuals (Saad-Filho and Johnston 2005). Hence, much of urban public planning is seen as distortion of market mechanisms, and thus as a threat to private motivation and efficient allocation of resources. The neo-liberal doctrine is that virtually all economic and social problems have a market solution (Peck and Tickell 2002). A corollary is that state failure is typically worse than market failure. This lies at the bottom of the neo-liberal critique of planning, in the words of Gleeson and Low:

> What is new ... about the contemporary attack on planning is its conceptual and political reach: neo-liberals desire both to contract the domain of planning (deregulation) *and* then to privatise segments of the residual sphere of regulation (out-sourcing). In both instances, the raison d'etre of planning as a tool for correcting and avoiding market failure is brushed

aside in favour of a new minimalist form of spatial regulation whose chief purpose is to facilitate development. (Gleeson and Low 2000:135, italics in original)

The rhetoric of neo-liberalism aims to give administrative efficiency, entrepreneurialism, and economic freedoms more impetus than democratic political steering. The current neo-liberalization of many societies is shaped by economic globalization and international capital mobility, and characterized by fewer restrictions on business operations, extended property rights, privatization, deregulation, erosion of state-supported economic safety nets, devolution of central government, uneven economic development and increasing social polarization (Harvey 2005). More weight is put on economic indicators of the effectiveness of the political-administrative management system compared to indicators measuring the democratic aspects of politics. The idea is that the market should discipline politics, which is contrary to the social-democratic view that politics should discipline the market (Clarke 2004). The prevailing attitude among planners has been to embrace neither politics nor markets, but rather opt for professionally good solutions. In order to implement these solutions, however, planners tend to argue for the transfer of tasks from markets to public bureaucracies, even if this implies the acceptance of political meddling in professional affairs.

Neo-liberalism can be viewed as a restructuring of the relationship between private capital owners and the state. This restructuring rationalizes and promotes a growth-first approach to urban development. Neo-liberalism has acquired a hegemonic position since the communist implosion around 1990, although it is under duress in the aftermath of the US credit crunch of 2007 followed by the global finance crisis of 2008 (Sheppard and Leitner 2010).[2] The consequences for urban planning are as yet unknown, but the serious cutbacks of public budgets in a number of countries in the wake of the crisis will cause an unusually high number of urban development plans to gather dust on the planner's shelf (Lovering 2010).

Political-economic ideas of neo-liberalism have become deeply entrenched in the public sector administration of countries in most parts of the world, affecting planners in a number of ways (see Chapter 6). The concrete design of neo-liberal policies is, wherever they are implemented, influenced by the legacies of locally inherited institutional frameworks, policy regimes, regulatory practices, and political struggles. The neo-liberalist aspirations are often unevenly and only partly enacted through urban planning.

The sections that follow describe the consequences of mobile investment capital for urban policy and planning, and provide an outline of the chief planning-related, neo-liberal urban policies. By way of conclusion, the final section lists planners' main worries with neo-liberal urban policies and abstracts the challenges posed by these policies to urban planning. The ten policies dealt with here have to do with funding, organizing and constructing physical projects in transport, urban housing, and central business districts, as shown in Box 5.1.

Box 5.1: Neo-liberal, planning-related policies for urban development

---

Expanding the use of private solutions to urban problems:
- Public-private partnerships.
- Private sector involvement in financing and operating transport infrastructure.
- Privatization of public space and sales-boosting exclusion.
- Privately governed and secured neighbourhoods.
- Quangos (quasi non-governmental organizations) organizing market-oriented urban development.

More competition and freer use of private property:
- Competitive bidding.
- Property-led urban regeneration.

Serving developers and their favoured customers:
- Flexible zoning and special business-friendly zones.
- Gentrification.
- Urban development by attracting the 'creative class'.

Place promotion (city branding, local boosterism) could have been entered as a competition-oriented neo-liberal policy in the box, but is instead mentioned as a prominent aspect of inter-city competition in the next section. The sections presenting the neo-liberal policies appear in the sequence shown in Box 5.1. Taken together, the ten policies embrace much of the content of neo-liberal urbanization (compare Peck et al. 2009:59–62). Perhaps needless to say, the need for urban redevelopment is not what is under scrutiny here. What calls for further examination is the role of the private sector in regeneration, and the forms of co-operation between public and private actors.

The consequences of mobile capital for urban policy and planning

This section traces some developments in neo-liberal capitalism that form the economic background for the urban policies presented in the next ten sections. The crucial precondition for the neo-liberal policies is that urbanization and modernization create a need for enormous investments in cities worldwide. It is part of the globalization process that investment capital is local to a decreasing extent, as is also the case with business corporations. The main idea is that highly mobile investment capital forces cities to compete. Cities that want to attract infrastructure capital, company headquarters, and factories have to make their bids more attractive than those of other ambitious cities.

To succeed in this contest, cities must convince private business that their public managers can play as members of a public-private team with the common goal of getting the projects implemented, and securing revenue rather than playing the role of regulation-keen and controlling bureaucrats. In short, the public administration has to demonstrate an entrepreneurial spirit.

Investment capital is mobile at the national level and can more easily cross national borders as financial markets are liberalized and integrated in line with neo-liberal tenets. Besides, an increasing number of metropolises aim to become hubs in the global economic network, and an ever growing number of cities are reaching a population size that can sustain mega-projects. This generates the need for investments to provide infrastructure and housing for the city-dwellers, often of a magnitude that far exceeds what can be raised from local profits and tax revenues. The demographic trends and removal of barriers to capital mobility give rise to intense inter-city competition both on the national and international scale (Turok 2004).

Another backdrop of the inter-urban competition is the widespread deindustrialization with concomitant structural unemployment and, in many countries, fiscal austerity at both national and local levels (Harvey 1989:5). The struggle to reinvigorate the urban economy and raise investment capital entails building a reputation for having a good business climate, attracting corporate head offices, and building safe and pleasant environments for corporate employees, for instance, by constructing shopping precincts and developing recreation facilities and entertainment districts for a sophisticated public. Surely, it helps to offer first-rate telecommunication systems, redevelop the waterfront, and supply land and air transport infrastructure for people who place a high value on time. The pressure to improve the physical attributes of the city to accommodate extant and anticipated corporate segments of the population with high ability to pay, shifts the emphasis of city politics from regulation and welfare issues (such as managing routine service provision and administering social benefits and other support to those in need), to re-imaging and marketing the city, creating employment opportunities, and acting as entrepreneur in implementing large-scale urban development plans.

Urban entrepreneurialism aims at creating conditions conducive to capital accumulation within a city's boundaries. This means adoption of pro-growth policies and new institutional structures of urban governance, expecting local officials to be enterprising, risk-taking, inventive, and profit motivated in their entrepreneurial role. The way cities operate is changed towards business-like strategies, alliances to achieve urban competitiveness, and public-private partnerships. Place promotion is crucial in the competitive environment, and cities are marketed as 'cool towns' or creative centres (Zimmerman 2008).

The physical products of urban entrepreneurship change the pattern of urban spatiality, often by constructing flagship projects or by monumentality in urban design. Typical elements are:

- Out-of-town retail parks and high-rise up-market residential blocks.
- Waterfront developments and walkways.
- Designation of an official cultural district with art galleries, heritage centres, etc.
- High-tech transport nodes.
- Downtown pedestrianized shopping malls.
- Exhibition centres.
- Science parks and technopoles.
- Gentrified inner city neighbourhoods, often converting former industrial premises to apartments.
- Large-scale sports stadiums, often combined with conference facilities or office space.

In addition to creating physical structures like the above, urban entrepreneurs boost their cities through hallmark events in sport and culture, some of which are of a magnitude that requires new infrastructure and implies resetting of priorities among already planned municipal projects. The idea that creativity, cosmopolitan diversity and the cultural industries are vital to the economy of large cities is increasingly embraced (Amin and Thrift 2007) and has led to the incorporation of cultural display among the tools of neo-liberal urban development strategies that are deliberately transforming the images and identities of cities.[3]

An entrepreneur starts or organizes a commercial enterprise, especially one involving financial risk. It is associated with a busy person of action, an enterprising and gambling person who does not take lightly to being slowed down by public deliberation and planning ordinances. Entrepreneurialism and neo-liberal governance require flexible planning and the speeding up of public inquiry procedures and development plan preparation (Prior 2005). Planning authorities are compelled to adopt a positive view of market-led development, and simplification of the planning process and relaxation of planning control are key objectives. The planner has become more of an enabler of development and therefore runs the risk of being less preoccupied with community impact or environmental quality.[4]

Naturally, the idea of solving planning problems by privatizing urban planning itself is close at hand. This can be done by hiring private consultants to do planning work (Saint-Martin 1998), by letting private developers take over the plan-making (Shatkin 2008), and by outsourcing planning-related tasks, such as building control (Meijer and Visscher 2006). Based on Australian data, Heijden (2010) found that private certifiers in building control increased technical efficiency and effectiveness of the regulatory enforcement. Outsourcing requires transformation of routine government functions into packageable units which can then be marketed and sold like private goods. Many countries see planning proposals being more frequently made by private developers, and important planning documents, such as environmental impact assessments, are often compiled by private consultants. In the UK, 'most of the contracted-out work has been for specialist aspects of planning', such as topic studies during development plan preparation and specialist advice on appeals (Higgins and Allmendinger 1999:64). Assessment of quality and contract compliance would be difficult for non-professionals, which is an argument against contracting out (ibid.). Fordham (1990:245) warns that the urban planning system is designed to regulate private developers, and so there are difficulties in transferring this function to the private sector. 'To do that would be to give planning to one of the sectional interests involved in the process, and one whose concern is profit'.

The shift from managerialism to public entrepreneurialism has had a tremendous effect on urban planning, for a large part through the policies dealt with in the ensuing sections. Policies that have been discussed repeatedly in planning-related literature over the last two decades are selected to provide an overview of how neo-liberalism manifests itself in urban development. The sections bring out the rationale of the policies as seen from the neo-liberal point of view and put forward some planning concerns with each policy.

Public-private partnerships

There are many forms of public-private partnerships (PPP), and no single definition is likely to both include them all and describe precisely the characteristics of the types that are most commonly used for solving planning-related tasks. A useful working definition is that partnerships are joint working relationships where the parties:

- Are otherwise independent bodies.
- Agree to co-operate to achieve a common goal.
- Create new organizational structures or processes to achieve this goal.
- Plan and implement a joint programme.
- Share relevant information, risk, and rewards. (Lamie and Ball 2010:111)

Partnerships are 'joint ventures different from the conventional subsidy relationship involving a one-way flow of money, tax incentives, and eased or enhanced regulatory entitlements from government to the private entity' (Sagalyn 2007:8). PPPs are voluntary and durable forms of co-operation between public government and private business that enable those actors to develop products or services jointly. There were cases of PPP even before the rise of neo-liberalism. In general, PPPs can be said to be less neo-liberal the larger the part played by the public sector, and the more private profits are curtailed.

PPPs are widely used in a number of countries, and they are given much attention in planning-related literature. Partnerships are active in several sectors of the economy, for example, local economic development, various transport industries, urban waterfront development and other urban regeneration. A wide variety of tasks is taken on by partnerships, such as building new infrastructure, converting ageing school facilities, restoring historically significant buildings, developing brownfields, revitalizing neighbourhood commercial centres, and transforming former military bases.

Public-private partnership has a long history and takes different forms:

> Partnership forms emanate from the ways in which the state is differentiated from and integrated with capital, the resultant and ever-contested division of resources and responsibilities between the two, and the constant rewriting of ideological justifications that buttress the political economy...
> (Beauregard 1997:53)

PPPs are useful from a neo-liberal viewpoint as they imply a certain load shedding and outsourcing from the public sector, and thus some degree of privatization as well as potential efficiency gains in the production process. Besides, PPPs provide profitable investment opportunities and risk sharing for venture capital. As a management reform, partnerships are promoted as an innovative tool that will change the way government functions, largely by tapping into the discipline of the market. PPPs facilitate implementation of mega-projects that help local image building and the competitiveness of the city. There will usually be gains to private business from the infrastructure provided (Hodge et al. 2010); for example, time savings from increased road capacity.

Partnership classifications are proposed by Edelenbos and Teisman (2008) and Ysa (2007), among others. Edelenbos and Teisman distinguish between the alliance model and the concession model. The alliance is a form of co-operation characterized by intense involvement on the part of the government in the different phases of the project. The concession is a work order, and in this kind of co-operation the government sells the long-term exploitation rights for a lump sum. The concession can take different shapes, such as a design-build contract or a build-operate-transfer contract. The public concerns include use of up-front payments, concession length, and non-compete clauses. All concessions are driven by the same rationale: 'to shift the role of government from that of provider to that of purchaser of public services, with efficiencies achieved by transferring responsibilities and risk to the private sector' (Siemiatycki 2007:389).

Lamie and Ball (2010) study city strategic partnerships that are of particular interest to planning. These are called Community Planning Partnerships in Scotland and Local Strategic Partnerships in England. Under neo-liberal regimes, many countries outsourced part of local service production to quangos and private actors. City strategic partnerships try to reintegrate or 'join up' public service delivery in a local authority area by encouraging all organizations involved in service provision to contribute to the planning process. The partnerships institutionalize cross-sector co-operation while recognizing the jurisdictional integrity of constituent bodies. All partners are expected to align their own plans with the community plan and work towards specific targets. These are formalized in local area agreements between central and local government and other local agencies.

Planners have commented favourably that infrastructure delivery partnerships can help to circumvent the narrow frames of annual public budgets and expedite downtown redevelopment and other infrastructure projects that are sorely missed. When private funds are at hand whenever needed, projects can be built in the most efficient manner, and implementation does not have to be stretched out over many years to fit public budgets (Edelenbos and Teisman 2008:615).

On the other hand, planners are anxious that PPPs might entail subsidies to private business and generally shift attention from the goals of elected governments to the interests of private business (Erie et al. 2010). Especially implementing large projects on the terms of the private competitive sector might entail high user fees and play down considerations of equity between groups and between generations (Ghere 1996). Democratic problems might also arise, in that partnerships can restrict inspection rights and transparency, weaken public accountability, and hamper citizen participation (Lowndes and Sullivan 2004).

Davies (2007) suggests that the new public management driven by national governments is eroding the prospects for partnership democratization. Developers have an interest in maintaining confidentiality for a variety of reasons: it keeps potential competitors in the dark and prevents landowners from gaining information that could affect the price of the land. Confidentiality is also often thought to minimize the risk of developing public opposition and causing delay or even abandonment of the project. Siemiatycki (2010) adds a point confirmed by several empirical results, that non-competition clauses in the concession agreements can restrict government flexibility to respond to changing conditions. Planners also warn that public sector partners tend to underestimate the time and resources needed to negotiate and manage the terms and conditions of the partnership contract (Grimshaw et al. 2002).

Private sector involvement in financing and operating transport infrastructure

In recent years, changes in national institutions have followed neo-liberal trends. These trends have facilitated the withdrawal of state funding of infrastructure, partly shifting responsibility to the private sector. Much is written about neo-liberal policies in the transport sector, dealing with organization and administration of the sector, deregulation of the markets for public transport, and provision and operation of infrastructure. Public-private partnerships construct roads, airports, and seaports in many countries and were dealt with in the previous section. The comments here relate to infrastructure only, as this theme is most relevant for neo-liberal urban development policy.

The neo-liberal policy of down-sizing government has forced municipalities to minimize expenditures by establishing public-private partnerships, systems of 'user pay', and programmes requiring developers to provide the infrastructure for new development. The increase of private suburban roads in some countries may be a neo-liberal policy in itself, but it is also a consequence of the growing number of private, secured neighbourhoods (the theme of a section that follows). It is in line with neo-liberal economics that people should pay for services rendered, so user charges, for example road tolls, are gradually being used more frequently by a number of neo-liberal regimes. Tolling is sometimes linked to PPPs for road construction (Lockwood et al. 2000). The contract then specifies that the private business partner gets paid by the tolls; these tolls generate more income the more attractive the road is made through construction and maintenance. An example is the study by Shaoul et al. (2006) of the first eight design, build, finance and operate roads commissioned by the UK Government's Highway Agency and paid for through a system of shadow tolls. There is also a modest literature on privately operated and maintained roads (Price 2001). Siemiatycki (2005) offers an account of rapid transit infrastructure investment in a planning context which crowded out options other than the neo-liberal, market-oriented ones.

Efficient ports and other transport facilities are an important component of urban competitiveness. While many toll roads make intra-city transport more efficient, airports serve inter-city and international markets. With increased air traffic, the trend has been towards airports developing into commercial centres, with more businesses inside, and more hotels, conference facilities, car hire firms, etc. in the vicinity. This trend is encouraged by privatization of airports, which has been a neo-liberal policy in several countries (Yang et al. 2008). The neo-liberal belief is that efficiency gains will accrue from private ownership and operation of the airports. Urban and regional development is affected through the property markets and the freeways and high-speed railways that are often built between airports and adjacent city centres (Freestone et al. 2006).

Planners have been concerned that privatization of airports means emasculation of the government's ability to handle their immense external effects (May and Hill 2006). Private ownership is also assumed to give less control over the way major airports influence the evolution of the city and region. In some countries, airport land is not subject to the jurisdiction of surrounding municipalities. Conflicts are created when the privatized airports try to extract commercial property revenues in order to supplement aeronautical earnings. In the development of 'fly buy' airport cities, 'non-aviation uses are perceived as a commercial challenge to the economic activity in the surrounding area, a source of extra traffic generation to put additional pressure on local road infrastructure, and a destabilizing influence on the employment numbers and floor space embodied in local and regional planning strategies' (Baker and Freestone 2010:16). The development of 'fly buy' cities resulting from privatization of airports thus calls for careful regulation.

Planners have criticized toll roads mainly because of equity issues. Well-off people hardly notice the tolls, while poorer motorists are forced to shift to less satisfying transport options, so that daily mobility becomes dependent on the ability to pay. Moreover, it seems unjust that people in some towns have to supplement government budgets by user charges to get their new highway, while similar towns get the highway fully paid by the government. Shaoul et al. (2006) found that risk transfer to the private sector does not come cheap, and that the shadow toll schemes of highway funding were costly to the taxpayers. Concerning private suburban roads, local residents paying for their operation and maintenance may want to keep non-residents out in order to reduce wear and tear on the streets. From a planning perspective, residential neighbourhoods with private roads therefore affect the connectivity and social integration of the urban landscape. Finally, planners have felt uneasy that the neo-liberal political agenda might cause policy-makers to lose sight of public transport's longstanding social purpose of providing mobility for people who do not drive a car (Grengs 2005).

Privatization of public space and sales-boosting exclusion

Neo-liberalists advocate private market solutions to most problems. The public realm – understood as the public interest, public services, and collective identity – has been subjected to processes of dissolution (Clarke 2004). This also goes for urban public space, which is increasingly privatized in many countries, even if some of its functions might remain public despite private ownership. City managers make compromises; they may be willing to give private business control over formerly public space in exchange for a productive economic return. Las Vegas in Nevada is a case in point. In accordance with the interests of the casinos and the tourist industry, the county has prohibited prostitution, begging, and activities associated with public homelessness. It has also actively encouraged the privatization of sidewalks along the Las Vegas Strip, where the largest hotels are located (Blumenberg and Ehrenfeucht 2008).

The standard example of quasi-public space is the shopping mall. According to Voyce (2006:280), malls are often fortified cells of inducement that filter the middle classes away from unnecessary social influences and interruptions to the intensity of their spending. Private ownership of public space is not necessarily a self-contradiction when it is believed that '(t)he daily activities in public spaces are what make a space public' (Dijkstra 2000:1). However, others use additional criteria to draw the line of demarcation between public and private space, such as the rules of access and the source and nature of control over entry (Smith and Low 2006:3–4). The issue of ownership can then be decisive.

Downtowns of many cities have been re-aestheticized as corporate landscapes of leisure, and they have simultaneously developed into consumerist 'playscapes' catering to the affluent. Neo-liberalism affects urban planning through the variety of ways public space ceases to be a public good. In losing its publicness, urban space presumably starts excluding some people, although this is sometimes contested (Melik et al. 2009). This tendency is contrary to the inclusiveness aimed for in, for example, communicative planning. Many towns in Western countries have more than half of their commercial floor-space in malls and shopping centres. The further this trend develops, the higher will be the density of out-groups and maladjusted individuals in the shrinking but openly accessible part of the town centre, and the clearer will be the sorting of people, with the socially fearful seeking solace in private space. More segregation limits the recognition by those spending in malls of the conditions of poverty which some people have to endure.

Surveillance, monitoring, discrimination, and exclusion can take place in public as well as private space. Most of the discussion and critique of the neo-liberal policy of privatizing public urban space has nevertheless been linked to the fear of less inclusive and more controlled cities (Kirby 2008). Privatization, control, and exclusion are therefore treated here as different aspects of the same neo-liberal policy for managing urban land. Privatization gives more scope for control, and control yields information about who to exclude. The regulation of access and behaviour is directed against those who do not seem to be potential customers and those who are supposed to make the premises less attractive to shoppers. Clearly, procedures and devices for control have a positive security aspect, but the concerns of the private owners are maintenance, liability, and marketability; the main purpose of neo-liberal exclusionary policies is to protect investments.

Some of the scholarly literature on exclusionary policies focuses on the type of place, such as gated communities, malls, playgrounds, urban parks, city centre plazas and pavements. Planners in local government have regularly opposed efforts to create exclusionary design of 'bonus plazas' in the US. 'The term *bonus* derives from incentive zoning regulations that give builders additional floor area ratio ... allowing them to build larger, taller buildings in exchange for providing public plaza space at street level' (Smithsimon 2008:327, italics in original). Research has shown that such plazas are most often intentionally made barren, uninviting, and inaccessible, and that their management has deleterious effects on concepts of citizenship and representation (Németh 2009).

Other contributions study how particular groups are subjected to discrimination in the city. On the producer and supplier side of the economy, examples are owners of 'adult entertainment', sex workers, drug dealers, independent artists, street musicians, sellers of raffle tickets, hawkers, panhandlers, and buskers (Kerkin 2003). Several groups are targeted even among those who are not using the city centre primarily for commerce, such as homeless street people, bag-ladies, junkies, delinquents, political campaigners, skateboarders and other noisy teenage groups (Mitchell 2001).

Planners and urban theorists have pointed to several problems with the neo-liberal privatization and surveillance policies. Privatization undermines citizens' right to assembly and limits the scope for collective action: '(T)he loss of undifferentiated public spaces leads to a diminution of the ability of individuals to meet and interact freely with others' (Kirby 2008:75). Urban public spaces offer opportunities for interaction and engagement and provide location for democratic initiatives. Are the inclusive dialogues of communicative planning theory less likely to occur in cities restricting access to the centre for some people by turning downtown into an environment controlled by business interests? It may be objected that the individuals and groups most often removed from areas where rules are privately constructed and enforced are hardly of the resourceful kind expected to contribute significantly to the public conversation. However, their dismissal may still be considered a breach of the conditions for open public dialogue. The city centre should be a common good which is accessible even for those adjudged to be unsuitable and unpleasant, as long as they act lawfully. This is a question of justice, and some scholars ask whether the politics of downtown development is skewed to reflect the interests of developers (Turner 2002). Planners need to 'question why non-consumption should be a legitimate basis for removing people from public space' (Hubbard 2004:670) and reflect on the legitimacy of regulating the visibility of disorderly bodies for the benefit of commerce.

Privately governed and secured neighbourhoods

Gated communities can be defined as 'closed urban residential schemes voluntarily lived in by a homogeneous social group where public space has been privatized, restricting access through the implementation of security devices' (Roitman et al. 2010:5). Such enclaves have been much discussed in the planning literature lately. 'There is hardly another form of urban development that has received so much public attention since the late 1990s as privately organised, and often secured, housing developments' (Glasze et al. 2006:1). For this reason this separate section is warranted even though gated communities are a case of privatization of public space, which was the theme of the preceding section.

Balancing the right to a secure environment against the public's right to access is felt to be a pressing concern on all continents, and the global trend is that access loses out to various types of enclosed and guarded residential areas, such as common interest developments, gated communities, and masterplanned residential estates. Masterplanned residential estates may involve varying degrees of securitization, enacted through a range of mechanisms from passive design features through to full gating (McGuirk and Dowling 2009).

Gated communities are not peculiar to neo-liberal societies. Religious, ethnic and other vulnerable minorities might need to protect themselves under different ideological regimes. This can also be the case for political and economic elites. A number of authors writing from around the world nevertheless see the recent trend towards segregated urban enclaves as engendered by neo-liberalism or similar market-centred ideas (in China, for example) (Wu 2005).

Walks (2006) holds that neo-liberalization and aestheticization are intertwined to form a strategy for social exclusion and management of class and other social identities masked by aesthetic appeals. Several others suggest that the need for urban enclaves with special protection arises as a result of policies that:

- Stimulate accumulation of wealth so that a significant segment of the urban population can afford high quality living conditions in enclaves offering extra service and security.
- Create economic differences by dissolving welfare systems or failing to build them in the first place. The threat to the affluent is more serious when there are lots of desperate people around and few welfare arrangements to cater for those who lose out in the competitive labour market.

Neo-liberalism has these characteristics and creates a market for gated communities. The ideology entails, moreover, that demand for consumer goods should be satisfied – housing units in secured neighbourhoods in this case. Harvey (2008:32) sees a connection between the 'neoliberal ethic of intense possessive individualism, and its cognate of political withdrawal from collective forms of action' on the one hand, and the increasing fragmentation of the big cities of many countries into fortified enclaves and gated communities on the other hand. Gated communities are cast as vehicles of civic privatism, extending private property rights, and embedding market logics and neo-liberal modes of privatized governance.

The gated communities most closely associated with neo-liberalism are predominantly a product of market mechanisms, representing class-based preferences for segregation and security rather than ideology, ethnic identity, or special services requested by, for example, elderly people. Planners have voiced concern that this type of gated community – exclusionary enclaves or fortified citadels – increases urban inequality and erodes the public sphere by allowing the retreat of middle-class citizens into private enclaves (Caldeira 1999:125). These enclaves make outsiders of fellow citizens and crystallize patterns of segregation and metropolitan fragmentation, giving ungated parts of the city the imprint of residuals (Goix 2005). On the positive side, gated communities give their residents several advantages protecting identity and lifestyle, such as privacy, quiet, and absence of unwanted social contact.[5]

Quangos organizing market-oriented urban development

Implementation of broad urban policies often requires the establishment of new organizations, as is the case with neo-liberal policies for urban renewal. Urban Development Corporations (UDC) in the UK, the only kind of organization to be described here, are among those on which most scholarly comment has been expended (Imrie and Thomas 1999). The British inner cities of the 1980s were a testing-ground for the enterprise culture in the form of UDCs and Enterprise Zones (explained in a later section on flexible zoning). UDCs were quasi non-governmental organizations (quangos) to which national government devolved power. They were among the flagships of the Thatcher Government's emphasis on the private sector. These single function agencies were to replace local authorities as the lead agents in planned urban regeneration, and they were run by boards with a majority of private-sector members. The organizations were set up by central government to coordinate rapid improvements within depressed city areas, facilitating development led by the private sector rather than acting as developers in their own right (Haughton 1999).

The aims of UDCs were typically to make the local environment more attractive to business, give cash grants to firms setting up or expanding within the area, renovate and reuse buildings, and offer advice and practical assistance to firms considering moving to the location. Deas et al. (2000:1) see UDCs as epitomizing 'the subordination of redistributional to economic growth concerns in urban policy; they embodied the preoccupation with responding to ostensible private sector needs, and embracing the outlook of business in public policy'.

UDCs have been critically scrutinized by planning scholars. Critics railed against the failure of the UDCs to engage with local communities, their lack of concern for the social consequences of their activities, and their disdain for local accountability (Deas et al. 2000:1, Haughton 1999). They were seen as indicative of a new closure of urban politics, a politics of exclusion, especially of local community groups. Planners in Bristol feared that 'the UDC would drive up the development value of existing sites, pricing out the large number of small businesses and industrial undertakings in the area and creating further imbalances in the employment market' (Punter 1993:532). The corporations seem to have developed a commercially realistic and flexible mode of planning, which was, however, primarily orientated to the short-term needs of private capital.

New quangos typically replace older ones as weaknesses in their functionality are uncovered, as urban development programmes come and go, or when a new government with a different agenda comes to power. The period of UDCs in the UK has come to an end; their predecessors and successors (English Partnerships, Homes and Communities Agency, Urban Regeneration Companies) are described by Booth (2005). The function of enabling private-sector development is retained in the successors, as is the responsibility for land acquisition, assembly, and project development – often by means of public-private partnerships. Another reason why UDCs are singled out for mention here, is that their main characteristics have been transferred to market-oriented development organizations in several other countries than the UK (Dodman 2008, Johnson 2004).

Competitive bidding

Neo-liberal administrations in many countries have reorganized established bureaucratic hierarchies and procedural systems to create quasi-markets under the banner of new public management (NPM), which is described in Chapter 6. One of the most notable urban policy innovations in the 1990s was competitive bidding regime for the allocation of public resources, especially for regeneration projects (Oatley 1998). The policy is attractive to central government, as competition 'helps to shift the onus for tackling difficult problems of economic decline and social disadvantage to the local level, while retaining control over the broad direction of expenditure' (Taylor P et al. 2001:46).

The idea is that competition for funds is likely to improve the quality of public output and be a viable alternative to resource allocation based on an assessment of need on a national basis. The competitive process ensures that bidders make promises to improve regeneration efforts in order to get ahead of their rivals. The theory is that sponsors maximize social welfare by choosing the highest quality portfolio among the incoming bids.

Competitive bidding resonates with the ethos of neo-liberalism, as the logic of market competition and economic efficiency determine the allocative outcome, and because a culture of enterprise and winning is encouraged at the expense of egalitarianism (Taylor P et al. 2001). In urban regeneration, one or more national agencies are often on the purchasing side, while local partnerships spanning the public-private sector divide are usually actors on the supply side. Neo-liberal regimes, for example in the UK and the US, aimed to 'change the nature of urban governance by encouraging local authorities to change the way they operated, to become more entrepreneurial, more open to partnership and working across department and agency boundaries' (Oatley 1995:8). Even those that place bids in vain are expected to gain from the stimulus to new thinking and forced exposure to interagency co-operation and partnership working (Taylor P et al. 2001:46).

The planning literature reveals scepticism with the assumptions made about the behaviour of both winners and losers. The bidding process stimulates short-term contracting that can destroy established patterns of trust that develop through long-term funding arrangements (John et al. 2004:406). Unsuccessful bids may cause substantial disillusionment resulting in forced closure of projects and programmes in areas of severe social need. Failure will not necessarily make people work harder together in order to overcome adversity. Moreover, the risk is that the bidding process rewards proficient presentation of the bids rather than their content in terms of the government's objectives (ibid.425). However, the gravest concern of the planners has been with the underlying idea of funding urban regeneration on convincing bids containing a mix of development opportunities and social deprivation instead of helping the groups and neighbourhoods that are most needy according to reasonably objective, statistical criteria of economic decline (Oatley 1995).

A number of countries use competitive bidding in sectors other than urban renewal, for example, in planning of transport infrastructure and tendering processes in public transport. However, Warner and Hefetz (2008) have found that, in the US, local governments tend to substitute mixed public-private delivery of services for other forms of market management, such as competitive bidding. The policies mentioned below concern urban regeneration.

Many changes in the management of public services have involved attempts to gain the advantages of market mechanisms, even where no market previously existed. The City Challenge programme in the UK is an example of the introduction of competition without a proper market. Challenge funding required bidders to apply with specific proposals for action in pursuit of an initiative's overall policy aims. Partnership was nearly always a prerequisite for government funding, and co-financing from the private sector was encouraged (Fearnley 2000). The bidding stage of Challenge funding required the contractor to set up the contract and the conditions that are to govern it, thus relieving the client (government) of many of the problems that arise in defining the detailed terms of contracts (Foley 1999:814). Responsibility for success is thus placed with those that make the bid. Planners' expressed concerns with City Challenge mirror their concerns with competitive bidding in general. In addition, Foley worries that 'the new partnerships created are often corporatist alliances which centralize power to existing main players, whilst marginalizing "peripheral" stakeholders, such as local neighbourhood groups and voluntary sector organizations' (ibid.820).

The Single Regeneration Budget (SRB) superseded the City Challenge programme in 1995 and brought together under one budget 20 existing programmes for regeneration and economic development in the UK. Hence, the word 'single' highlights the claimed innovation: a unified programme with extensive co-operation between central and local agencies. The competitive-bidding funding regime was retained, and central government took a hands-off approach in which guidance and periodic performance review nevertheless played a role. An important innovation was the lack of boundaries or restrictions on the spatial areas that could be covered in the SRB bid (Rhodes et al. 2003:1402). This was not a neo-liberal policy change primarily meant to open up for regeneration where there are economic opportunities, at the expense of more dilapidated areas. Brennan et al. (1999:2082) found that 'all bar 1 of the 99 most-deprived districts received SRB funding and, of this group, the most-severely deprived 20 districts ... received more SRB funding per head of population than the group with less-severe deprivation'. This finding attracts extra interest, as most academic accounts of neo-liberal urban policies end with negative conclusions.

Property-led urban regeneration

The trend away from long-term comprehensive plans and towards project-based or property-led planning has been observed in many countries. Renewal locations have been considered by the private sector as areas of risk and uncertainty. To make developers build on the land provided, the market needed prodding into action with government subsidy. The master plan made by the legitimate public authority used to direct urban development to a larger extent, while it is now commonplace that privately initiated building projects have first priority, and that whatever public plans exist are modified accordingly.

The rationale underpinning regeneration of city centres is one of seeking to engage the private sector in the absence of effective demand for new and costly buildings. This necessitates some form of government intervention to stimulate market activity, for example, the special zones and organizations mentioned in other sections. Property development provides the physical platform for regeneration. It is often assumed that there is a one-way process leading from physical to economic and community prosperity. Property development is seen as a prime catalyst of regeneration, fostering confidence through the demonstration effect created by clearly visible physical transformation of an area. The demonstration effect can be enlarged by flagship projects, mega-events, or cultural festivals of the kinds already mentioned (Taşan-Kok 2010, Temelova 2007).

Property-led regeneration makes the real estate and property development industries lead players in urban renewal. The approach is less an alternative to development by the public sector than a call for extended public-private co-operation. Property-led initiatives are forms of supply-side intervention which facilitate economic development, assuming that development of property can trigger demand for inner city sites and enhance economic activity. Urban competitiveness is directly influenced by property development through the latter's provision of suitable accommodation for economic activity, and indirectly through its cumulative contribution to the built environment (D'Arcy and Keogh 1999:917).

The private sector may lack confidence to invest in inner city projects. Property-led policies are means to restore this confidence and attract private capital via financial support, infrastructure, and site preparation, which all overlap with other neo-liberal policies dealt with in this chapter. For example, urban development corporations made property-led strategies a core component of their approach, and public-private partnerships are a characteristic of most property-led regeneration.

Planners have criticized property-led regeneration for focusing on projects, rather than plans and strategies, as this easily results in a failure to address wider issues of equity and distribution of benefits (Healey 1991). Large-scale property development sometimes has an inherent financial and political weight which pushes the implementation process forwards despite incompatibility with the overall function and aesthetical character of the area. Ball (2004) also points to private partners' scepticism to community participation. The practice of property-led development in districts where conflicts between very different uses call for an overall plan makes a mixed-use planning dilemma acute, as noted by Wolf-Powers (2005:379–80): '(H)ow to govern the use of sought-after land in mixed-use areas near central business districts...that not only are logical sites for commercial and luxury residential expansion but because of their proximity to markets and their unique agglomerative character also constitute prime niches for specialty manufacturing, light industry, and arts-related establishments'.

Flexible zoning and special business-friendly zones

Zoning is a set of development controls separating land uses in order to prevent negative external effects associated with the proximity of incompatible activities. This land-use regulation achieves several urban planning goals, such as protection of natural and social environments, controlling urban sprawl, and historical preservation. The zoning ordinances sometimes conflict with investors' interest in obtaining the most profitable location for their new real estate projects. A prominent neo-liberal point of view is that traditional zoning places excessive restrictions on personal liberty and the use of private property, and adherents of this ideology have sought to establish less restrictive systems that allow market forces to play a greater role in determining land uses.[6] This can be achieved by legalizing more broadly defined and mixed-use zoning districts (Hirt 2007) or performance zoning. Regulation based on performance requires that any development meets specified performance standards, rather than complying with the detailed specification of acceptable uses for specific parcels inherent in traditional zoning regimes (Ottensmann 2005).

Neo-liberals cannot turn a blind eye to the fact that zoning by-laws can be designed so as to serve developer interests. One example is special zoning for homeless shelters to keep them at arm's length from city centre malls and 'playscapes' for the affluent (Ranasinghe and Valverde 2006). In other words, zoning can support the controlling and discriminatory policies mentioned in the section on privatization and sales-boosting exclusion (exclusionary zoning). Another example is zones intended to strengthen the competitiveness of the city by preferential treatment of investors. Consequently, the zoning instrument can be good or bad for business depending on its design, and the neo-liberal attitude to zoning can therefore be somewhat ambiguous.

The entrepreneurial wish to relax zoning ordinances is met with scepticism by many planners. They ask how then to establish city growth boundaries, how to contain the urban built-up area? These questions became pressing with the emerging political goals of reducing energy use and creating sustainable cities with regard to climate and pollution – which in the opinion of many planners depends on creating more compact urban forms. Another main concern of planners with reference to zoning is the potentially exclusionary effects already alluded to. This problem predates neo-liberalism, but it is exacerbated by neo-liberal, business-oriented zoning policies in the city centres.[7] More of the planners' attention is probably directed to exclusionary policies nowadays due to the emphasis on inclusion in contemporary theory, for example, communicative planning theory.

Several types of zones fit neo-liberal ideology, and simplified planning zones, urban enterprise zones, and business improvement districts are mentioned here. The streamlining of planning administration is seen as a mechanism for creating greater confidence and certainty for private sector investment in the land development process. The Housing and Planning Act of 1986 imposed upon local planning authorities in the UK a duty to consider simplified planning zones (SPZ) in their area to achieve this goal (Lloyd 1990). The zones were meant to promote investment and improvement in targeted areas and not simply as the lifting of controls. Detailed control could be relaxed in specified zones and substituted by performance parameters agreed with developers. The rationale of SPZ was that 'detailed case-by-case planning control imposed unnecessary costs in some circumstances and that securing permission in larger blocks would save costs without compromising quality of outcome' (Webster 2005:45). SPZs exhibit a clear link between planning policy and Thatcher's political thinking. Nevertheless, the zones do not seem to having achieved their Thatcherite aims, and they might even have increased rather than decreased regulation. Apparently, the benefits of negotiating an SPZ were usually not worth the costs, and few simplified planning zones were created.

Urban enterprise zones (EZ) are a kind of special economic zone that was established in the UK by the Thatcher government in 1979 and implemented in the US a couple of years later (Greenbaum and Engberg 2004). 'Not only were EZs originally seen as a way of turning around run-down urban areas, they were also a test of free-market ideas which, if they proved successful in inner cities, could be generalised throughout the United Kingdom' (Atkinson and Moon 1994:140). Developers were offered regulatory relaxation, tax relief and public-sector subsidy if they invested in an enterprise zone. Such zones encompassed blighted neighbourhoods and were meant to be an important instrument for renewal of urban areas that the private sector would normally ignore. McGreal et al. (2002:1829) associate taxation-based instruments with New Labour's 'third way'-thinking, 'which seeks a synthesis of traditional forms of interventionism and regulation with sympathy for pricing and the nuances of a market-oriented neo-liberal agenda'. Planners have criticized the lack of attention to the planning process as an element in programme implementation, and contended that derelict areas require much more assistance than the incentives that enterprise zones can provide (Wilder and Rubin 1996).

A third type of zone is the business improvement district (BID) or city improvement district. Downtown business owners who must compete with the safe and orchestrated shopping experience of the malls, devised the business improvement district as a way to emulate the controlled conditions and comprehensive management of such mega shopping centres (Hoyt 2004). BIDs aim to make city centres competitive again. They are associated with neo-liberal ideas, as they ensure business-led innovation at the local level and reduce local government involvement in the provision of services. These improvement districts entail private management of public space; they are often managed by non-profit partnerships between local government and business corporations. BIDs are voluntary associations of local businesses which volunteer to levy an extra fee upon themselves (Clough and Vanderbeck 2006:2266). These fees are collected by the city authorities and typically cover additional services for security, cleaning, marketing of unique events, and capital improvements (for example, installing pedestrian-scale lighting and street furniture, planting trees and shrubbery). The general private goal is to ensure maximal capital accumulation for the fee payers of the district. The public goal is urban revitalization, making selected parts of the city more marketable and attractive for lucrative consumption and investment.[8]

Planners have expressed concern that BIDs can limit the democratic nature of public space and suppress the varied unfolding of human interaction. BIDs are seen as a 'threat to local accountability as well as strategic planning institutions, which presently seek to benefit all groups in society, not merely business interests' (Lloyd et al. 2003:305). In a more balanced account, Justice and Skelcher (2009:739) find that, on the one hand, BIDs offer the potential to increase the responsiveness and efficiency of public policy through the direct involvement of relevant stakeholders, while, on the other hand, 'they also challenge traditional models of democratic governance and accountability because of their high degree of internal autonomy relative to general-purpose, public governments'.

Gentrification

Neighbourhood revitalization encompasses a range of policies that differ over time and space and depend on the type of neighbourhood. Some collaborative policies have explicitly been associated with neo-liberalism (Elwood 2002).

Not surprisingly, this is also the case with neighbourhood regeneration under the New Right regimes in the UK (Tiesdell and Allmendinger 2001). There are also links between revitalization and related discourses, such as conservation and historical preservation (Morris 2008), focusing on the neo-liberal influences.[9] The following paragraphs comment only on the gentrification aspect of neighbourhood revitalization.

Gentrification has been discussed in planning and urban geography for several decades. The essence of gentrification is well articulated by Clark:

> Gentrification is a process involving a change in the population of land-users such that the new users are of a higher socio-economic status than the previous users, together with an associated change in the built environment through a reinvestment in fixed capital. The greater the difference in socio-economic status, the more noticeable the process, not least because the more powerful the new users are, the more marked will be the concomitant change in the built environment. It does not matter where, it does not matter when. (Clark 2005:258, cited from Butler 2007b:166)

Hence, the two key processes of gentrification are 'the class-based colonisation of cheaper residential neighbourhoods and...reinvestment in the physical housing stock' (Atkinson 2003:2344). They are often seen as processes reclaiming the city for the middle classes.

Gentrification has been understood as part of neo-liberal urban development (Butler 2007b), aiming to bring investment capital as well as middle class people back to the central parts of the city through 'creative destruction' and city-centre flagship projects. The urban regeneration process has been tremendously stimulated by financial deregulation and increasing diffusion of the risks of real estate transactions, for example, by commodifying debt through mortgage securitization.[10] Gentrification creates good living conditions for corporate employees and helps to make the city centre attractive for visitors and as a place to do business. Also on the positive side, decaying and derelict districts are upgraded, and sometimes the physical fabric of architecturally valuable neighbourhoods is secured (Atkinson 2003).

Gentrification is in part used as a spatial remedy to break up concentrations of poor people. In such cases, it serves the neo-liberal policy of making urban poverty less visible by 'deconcentrating' the poor without addressing the underlying economic-political causes of poverty. Planning-related literature has pointed out that tenured residents, mainly working class people, 'have often been displaced through rent increases and have been unable to secure another local dwelling' (Atkinson 2003:2345). Revanchism and colonization of the city are phrases used by some scholars to characterize the influx of more affluent citizens at the expense of vulnerable populations (Smith 1995). Studies of mortgage lending have found 'evidence of intensified discrimination and exclusion in gentrified neighborhoods' in the US (Wyly and Hammel 2004:1215).

Urban development by attracting the 'creative class'

There is a steady flow of articles in the planning-related literature in the wake of well-known books about how to make cities creative (Landry 2008) and how to attract the so-called 'creative class' (Florida 2002, 2005). Attention is here directed to Richard Florida's work, as his ideas on how cities can attract the creative class and facilitate the entrepreneurial ventures of its members are seen by several authors as interwoven with neo-liberal urban policies (Gibson and Klocker 2005, Peck 2005).

The gist of Florida's argument is that economically advanced societies have entered a phase of capitalism in which creativity is the central motor of economic development. New technologies, new industries, and most other economic benefits flow from it. About 30 per cent of the workforce makes up the creative class, including groups ranging from artists to high-tech workers and managers. The economic and social fortunes of today's cities allegedly rest on their ability to attract and retain members of this highly mobile class of creative people. City leaders must understand how such people prefer to spend their money and their time. Cities should be buzzing with activity and nurturing the kind of open, diverse and tolerant urban culture favoured by the creative class. Local institutions and business climate must encourage the transformation of creativity into commercial opportunities. This calls for an entrepreneurial city administration supporting the would-be entrepreneurs among the creative.

The creative class needs places for consumption, recreation, and living. Cultural events, nightlife, downtown 'playscapes', and artists' districts would be in demand. Furthermore, housing the creative class requires a shift from working class quarters to hip, varied, and good quality residential areas. The influx of the creative class stimulates gentrification. Overall, the creative class theory fits hand in glove with neo-liberalism, as it takes globalized capitalism, inter-city competition, and the need for urban entrepreneurialism for granted. Furthermore, the focus is on economic growth and on succeeding in the market for creative talent. '(C)reativity is a key concept ... because of its ability to act as a catalyst in the cultural transition from "citizens" into "entrepreneurs" and "consumers", the "idealised companions" of the neoliberal state...' (Gibson and Klocker 2005:94). Peck asserts that:

City leaders … are embracing creativity strategies not as *alternatives* to extant market-, consumption- and property-led development strategies, but as low-cost, feel-good *complements* to them. Creativity plans do not disrupt these established approaches to urban entrepreneurialism and consumption-oriented place promotion, they *extend* them. (Peck 2005:761, emphasis in original)

Planning scholars and urban geographers have criticized creative class theory for being highly affirmative to the concept of class and the current mode of capitalist development (Krätke 2010) and for leading to reallocation of public funds from supporting the deprived to pampering the creative elite. Urban policy in line with the theory implies a shift in investment from social projects to strategies for place promotion and competition for talent. Trip and Romein (2009) warn that the desire for attracting the creative class creates an imminent danger that competing cities become copycats and choose very similar physical forms of urban development.

There seems to be a strong positive correlation between income inequality and measures of creative cities, and this has led to critical reflection on the diversity that is supposed to engender creativity. Some commentators request clarification of the association of diversity and tolerance (Thomas and Darnton 2006) and more emphasis on justice relative to diversity (Fainstein 2005). Other planning academics have focused on methodological questions, for example, the indices used by Florida to rank cities with regard to talent, technology, and tolerance. They find the rationale behind the indices rather vague, which makes them potentially confusing and easily misapplied (JAPA Review Editors 2005:204). Moreover, the methods and conceptual problems of creative class theory cast doubt on the causalities linking creative people with economic growth (Markusen 2006). Finally, there is concern that cultural creativity is not valued in itself but treated merely as attractor of the creative class and thus as an agent of economic boosterism. Although several recent papers conclude that creative professionals do not have a significant or positive impact on the success of urban areas in developing sustainable economic structures (Hoyman and Faricy 2009, Krätke 2010), the ongoing discussion is still lively.

Neo-liberal challenges to urban planning

This section derives neo-liberal challenges to public planning both from planners' concerns with the ten policies delineated in foregoing sections and from other sources. Special neo-liberal challenges faced by CPT are spelled out (see also Chapter 6). Some general difficulties with neo-liberalism from the outlook of urban public planning are articulated by way of conclusion.

Planners' worries about neo-liberal ideas of urban planning and policies most often spring from the following characteristics, as suggested by the preceding sections:

- One-dimensional concentration on efficiency and economy in neo-liberal policy recommendations.
- A predilection for private, competitive, and market-oriented solutions to urban problems, that is:
  - search for development strategies that create profitable investment opportunities, and organizational frameworks that mimic markets and force actors to compete;
  - scepticism to year-long participatory processes preparing for political compromises rather than economically sound decisions.
- Lack of a democratic agenda beyond consultation that elicits information from clients and consumers, and widespread privatization that reduces transparency and thus weakens the inhabitants in their capacity as well-informed citizens.
- Indifference to concerns for unequal treatment, exclusion, segregation, and distributional questions: Private goals of profitability are given higher priority than social goals of improving the living conditions of the economically deprived.

Some authors have found, in connection to the last point, that neo-liberal governance may use processes of symbolic inclusion, yet simultaneously rely on processes of material exclusion (Miraftab 2004). Important consequences of the above points are a determined down-sizing of local government, a simplification of public planning processes, and an emphasis on production and economic efficiency rather than redistribution and fairness.

Three challenges follow from the above critique. Private investors are given preferential treatment, and well-off people can afford to pay for the goods brought about by neo-liberal urban policies and thus stand to gain. In contrast, poorer people are not well served when a programme's success is measured by the so-called 'willingness' to pay for its products in a market. Second, neo-liberal policies will support sustainable urban areas only to the extent that people's preferences for stable climate, clean natural environment, and a rich variety of species are revealed in their willingness to pay for policies with such outcomes. Third, more private sector funding and management of urban development means contraction of the political sphere. Private operators and investors are less vulnerable to political criticism, and it is thus harder for the citizens to put pressure on them to take basic needs, external effects and city-wide consequences into consideration.

A purposeful attack on public urban planning followed the spread of neo-liberalism. Healey (2000:518) notes that '(t)he neoliberal strategy ... is to seek to transform planning systems into quasi-market regulatory mechanisms for dealing with conflict mediation over complex spatially manifest environmental disputes'. She worries that this strongly limits the range of problems that will be handled by public planning. The quality of places is defined not only by how environmental externalities are dealt with. Healey holds the spatiality of relations and the meanings of places – 'place identity' – to be important dimensions of city planning.

There is a tension between market solutions and local empowerment, and scholars tend to expect neo-liberal regimes to give priority to the market and downplay the need for democratic planning processes. Commenting on John Major's regime in the United Kingdom, Allmendinger and Tewdwr-Jones (1997:109) find that '(c)onsultation procedures in plan preparation have been reduced to speed up the policy adoption process and have thereby minimized public involvement while creating greater certainty for those who are still involved in the process'. This is a fairly typical statement, and it is also commonplace that scholars criticize neo-liberal authorities for instrumental use of participatory processes. For example, policies are legitimized by 'playing the user card' and referring to user group opinion in order to buttress elites' own preferred course of action (Harrison and Mort 1998). Protesters may be deliberately co-opted by drawing them into the authority's own discourses and institutional practices through repeated cycles of exchange.

The neo-liberal attitude to public planning has been overwhelmingly negative due to planning's intervention in markets: planning is said to be too inflexible, the public's role is too strong, and approvals take too long (Baker et al. 2006). All this leads to delays, extra costs, and reduced employment. On the other hand, investors in markets where demand is highly exposed to business cycles, and where profitability depends on the hardly predictable preferences of other actors, put a value on reduction of uncertainty. Public planning has survived the neo-liberal onslaught much because it delivers on this point, protecting real estate against negative external effects of neighbouring activities through zoning and land-use plans. Even if it is a main aim of neo-liberalists to liberate markets from public intervention, actors in the property markets do not seem to unambiguously embrace the idea of curtailing planning. Empirical research in the UK indicates that 'landowners, developers and householders actually welcomed the certainty provided by the planning system' (Allmendinger and Thomas 1998:250). Planning tells the urban entrepreneur what to expect from the future evolution of the district in which investment is considered.

From the point of view of CPT, privatization is unwanted to the extent that transparency becomes restricted, thereby eroding the basis for informed conversation about future development of the city. Privatization is also unwelcome when it makes important actors in urban development less responsive to criticism. The surveillance and control aspect of private city centre regeneration can delimit access to central public places where people can come together and express their views, and from where they can launch new political initiatives. Furthermore, policies that imply withdrawal of some groups from the rest of the population are a challenge to communicative planning in that segregation hinders mutual understanding and undermines inclusive public exchange of opinions.

The position of CPT is that the future of urban neighbourhoods should be deliberated and debated in public, and decided in democratic and inclusive processes. In contrast, neo-liberal policy plays on market mechanisms and income differentials to achieve political goals for the city, as, for example, when concentrations of poor people are broken up by the gentrification of parts of their neighbourhoods. The troubles of disadvantaged districts and the underlying problem of severely biased income distribution should be handled politically and not be left to market forces. Reliance on markets to solve political problems that require solidarity is a challenge to communicative planning.

Conclusion

The challenge to planners is to convince the public at large that market-oriented systems for solving urban problems serve those with high ability to pay far better than those with low ability, and that even the well off are being served by neo-liberal policies mainly in their capacity as economic actors (producers and consumers). In contrast, the aim of public planning is to treat people as citizens with political roles, rights, and agendas – not only as entrepreneurs and recipients of service. It is the task of planning to provide public goods even when markets are non-existent, and protect against externalities even when payment systems are not in place. Planners should draw continued attention to collective goods that are not marketable at a profit-giving price, and whose production is therefore not attractive to private companies. Some goods benefiting disadvantaged segments of the population belong to this category, as do redistribution policies in general.

Neo-liberalism aims to improve governance systems by new public management (NPM) (characterized and discussed in Chapter 6), while CPT aims to improve the democratic system through inclusion, participation, and public deliberation. Public planning will be in a better position to resist the neo-liberal attack by succeeding in disseminating the message that broadly based and justifiable collective decisions are generally more important than efficient decision-making in the economic sense.

Notes

1. This chapter is distilled from my systematic overview of the planning-related academic literature on neo-liberal urban policies from the period 1990–2010 (Sager 2011). The literature survey comprises around 770 references and delineates 14 neo-liberal policies, as city marketing, economic development incentives, private sector involvement in procuring water, and liberalization of housing markets are added to those dealt with here. Because of the easily available and well-referenced background article, the number of references to each policy is kept at a moderate level in the present chapter.

2. The trend towards increased international capital flows changed with the financial crisis of 2008 and the following recession. The setback is expected to be temporary. There has been a flight to safety and return of home bias when it comes to investment, and financial protectionism is feared by the IMF. Emerging economies have suffered a broad retrenchment of foreign investors and banks (International Monetary Fund 2009).

3. Related to neo-liberalism, however, more has been written on place marketing through urban festivals, parades, carnivals and the like (Gotham 2005). In neo-liberal inter-city competition, culture is exploited for corporate branding and economic gain. Areas can be gentrified because of their cultural reputation, leading to displacement of indigenous residents and businesses.

4. With regard to the UK and the US two decades ago, Fainstein (1991:22) noted that conservative 'national administrations have stressed market-based solutions to allocative questions and have promoted growth over redistribution'. This describes quite accurately the neo-liberal climate under which planners in large parts of the world are working even today.

5. Two arguments why gated communities do not necessarily lead to more social fragmentation are put forward by Roitman et al. (2010:5). When gated communities are located in poor neighbourhoods, which is often the case in developing countries with high income inequalities, the closer territorial proximity reduces the geographical scale of segregation and produces opportunities for functional integration. Moreover, residents of the enclaves belong to homogeneous social groups with already closed social circles before moving within gates, and therefore it is an already existing social and residential segregation that facilitates the move to gated communities.

6. Houston is a special case of a no-zoning, free enterprise regime, but Buitelaar (2009:1056) finds that even this city 'has almost all the other instruments from the development control tool box'. Qian (2010) concludes that civic and private organizations such as super neighbourhoods and homeowner associations fill the gaps left by the lack of land-use zoning.

7. Several articles deal with exclusionary zoning in the suburban context (Ihlanfeldt 2004, Pendall 2000).

8. New York has become the centre of BID activity, even if BIDs are widespread throughout North America (Hoyt 2004). In the UK, BIDs were adopted as part of a package of measures intended to make cities more beautiful, safe, and vital. This form of urban revitalization is also found in other parts of the world, for example, the city improvement districts in Cape Town and Johannesburg (Bénit-Gbaffou et al. 2008).

9. New Urbanism quite often comes up as a keyword in articles on gentrification and neo-liberal urban development (Butler 2007a). Some authors explicitly associate New Urbanism with facets of neo-liberal gentrification, such as the revanchist city and the luring of homeowners and employers back from the suburbs in order to keep taxes low

and cities safe, thus improving the business climate (Kenny and Zimmerman 2003). My view is that the association between the two is more due to concurrence in time and space than to inherent common traits.

10. Weber outlines the neo-liberal financial policy for the US housing market, pinpointing the mechanisms that engendered the American and then global financial crisis of 2008, a consequence of large numbers of households defaulting on their payment contracts:

> By creating a secondary mortgage market through quasipublic institutions (eg Fannie Mae, formed in 1968), the state has increased the total size of capital flows … These institutions buy mortgages, package them, and guarantee their payments with government backing on mortgage-backed securities held by other institutions, such as pension funds. Securitization connects real-estate credit markets to the nation's general capital markets and creates more liquidity in the system … The secondary mortgage market also enables investors in one part of the country to invest in mortgages originated in another region, effectively ending the geographic segmentation of credit. (Weber 2002:182)

6

Conflicting Values of
Communicative Planning Theory
and New Public Management

Introduction: roles and values

The purpose of this chapter is to show that in a number of societies where neo-liberal ideas play an important part in shaping economic-political life, the current role of planners contains tensions which negatively affect their everyday working conditions. In addition, the values of CPT and new public management (NPM) are made explicit in this chapter, in order to facilitate judgement on whether concrete urban plans tend to change the city in a neo-liberal direction or in ways corresponding with the values of communicative planning. The clarification of values is necessary input to the discussion in Chapter 7. Although planners in a variety of administrations and public agencies will presumably recognize the conflicting demands analyzed in this chapter, the planners most likely to feel the cross pressure work on plans and projects developed through processes that include citizen participation. The administrations where planners work have in many cases been reorganized in accordance with neo-liberal management ideals.

The tensions under scrutiny here spring from differences between communicative planning theory (CPT) and new public management (NPM) regarding the kind of behaviour expected from planners working in the public sector. NPM is a set of ideas applying neo-liberalism to public sector management. Neo-liberalism recommends market solutions to most problems, as accounted for in Chapter 5, and markets are a type of institution grounded in openly strategic action and means-end rationality. CPT, on the other hand, is guided by ideals of dialogue and communicative rationality. Sharp contrasts between NPM and CPT are therefore to be expected.

The role of the communicative planner has notable procedural aspects in that she or he facilitates discussion and attempts to involve even marginalized interests. Those emphasizing participation and dialogue tend to see the role of planners more as that of a facilitator and mediator and less as that of a technical-economic expert. Neo-liberals, on the other hand, see the planner role primarily as providing expertise in substantive and legal-procedural matters rather than promoting participation, consensus building, and empowerment of weak groups. According to neo-liberalism, even planned solutions should be in harmony with the market, thus leaving less room for politics.

Tensions in the planner's role are created by external pressure on the planner to act contrary to her values, and by recurring tasks that imply hard choices, that is, the need to trade off different values. Values are abstract principles that individuals have internalized as desirable standards of behaviour for themselves or society (Dryzek and Braithwaite 2000). Values define what is right and what is wrong. They are central concepts or beliefs regarding final states or desirable behaviour that transcend specific situations, guide decisions and their ex post evaluation, and therefore human conduct, becoming an integrated part of an individual's way of being and acting (Schwartz and Bilsky 1987:551).[1] Values are resistant to change, and this continuity separates them from preferences and opinions. 'Values run deeper than interests ... (W)hen we give up something we value, we often feel we give up part of ourselves, and that's very difficult, very threatening, and hardly compensated by some gain somewhere else' (Forester 1999:463). When non-tradeability is prominent, the cherished virtue is a 'protected value' (Baron and Spranca 1997). Attitudes ('valences') are less abstract than values and linked to a specific context. They 'refer to the subjective attractiveness or aversiveness of specific objects and events within the immediate situation' (Feather 1995:1135).

The following few examples are selected from Rokeach's (1973:57–8) lists of 'quality of life' values. Their description is modified to make it more suggestive as to how an individual might act on them in his or her capacity as a planner. Similar principles are listed under the harmony-oriented dimension of the Social Goal Values Inventory applied by Dryzek and Braithwaite (2000:255).

Freedom: independence, free choice, asserting that adult persons are themselves the right judges of what public goods will serve them best.

Helpfulness: showing social solidarity, implying that society should help individuals out of poverty, and that increasing the capabilities of people should be a primary policy concern.

Responsibility: taking care of the social and natural environment required to uphold the quality of life for everyone.

Social recognition: showing respect; protecting human dignity, integrity, and identity; and preventing things held sacred from being traded off for economic gain.

There is a tendency in mainstream economics and neo-liberalism towards attending to preferences rather than values (Orr 2007), and to downplay the need to protect the latter. Baron and Spranca (1997) found that the thought of trading off moral values evokes anger in people, and that they tend to engage in denial of the need for trade-offs through wishful thinking. Overly economistic ideology threatens the values above, in that all relevant consequences of plans are measured in monetary terms, decisions rest on utilitarian considerations, and efficiency-oriented management is given priority over democracy. These are features that can be recognized in the normative claims of neo-liberalism (and thus NPM) as briefly outlined below.

Neo-liberals espouse economic liberalism as a means of promoting economic development and securing freedom. Political liberty is seen as the freedom of the individual from outside compulsion, for example, from intervention by the state or other government hierarchies. In order to promote economic development, political liberty must also provide opportunities to act: the individual has a moral claim to freedom of action. Neo-liberalism advances individualism, stressing human independence and individual self-reliance, primarily achieved by acting in markets. Competitive markets are hailed both as the crucial way to disperse power and to provide an institutional framework for transactions that are economically beneficial to all parties. As a consequence, neo-liberals seek to disseminate the logic of the market to all institutions and all social action dimensions of human life, making the market the organizing and regulative principle of the state and society. It is a corollary that a generalized calculation of cost and benefit is to become the measure of state practices. According to Brown:

> (E)qually important is the production of all human and institutional action as rational entrepreneurial action, conducted according to a calculus of utility, benefit, or satisfaction against a micro-economic grid of scarcity, supply and demand, and moral value-neutrality. Neo-liberalism does not simply assume that all aspects of social, cultural and political life can be reduced to such a calculus, rather it develops institutional practices and rewards for enacting this vision ... Importantly then, neo-liberalism involves a normative rather than ontological claim about the pervasiveness of economic rationality and advocates the institution building, policies, and discourse development appropriate to such a claim. (Brown 2003:4)

The train of reasoning throughout the present chapter goes as follows: the prominent values of CPT are outlined and linked to the role of the communicative planner. Then NPM is presented with special attention given to market orientation and the aim for economic efficiency. Some values are deduced from this and contrasted with CPT values. A separate section explores patches of common ground between CPT and NPM, especially the common concern for service quality and responsiveness to users. This common emphasis makes it more difficult to read, in the empirical studies of planner values and attitudes surveyed in the subsequent section, whether the values reflect support for communicative planning or managerialism. This difficulty can be overcome, however. I therefore hypothesize that the typical attitudes of planners in the Nordic countries are much closer to CPT than to NPM. Many planners are assumed to experience a tension in their perceived role between dialogical ideals and the neo-liberal realities conveyed by NPM. Preceding the conclusion, theoretical developments are mentioned that might change public administration so as to ease this role conflict.

Communicative planning and new public management (NPM) are both modes of governance. The communicative approach makes sense for planning tasks that require citizen deliberation. Other tasks, such as the routine of issuing permits for uncontroversial changes of built structures, will presumably lend themselves to market adaptations involving people in their capacity as consumers. Agencies working according to NPM principles might provide such service in a satisfactory way. Communicative planning and NPM both take an adaptive and pragmatic approach towards the management of complex coordination problems. The two modes of governance are, however, very different with respect to purpose, ideological foundation, area of application, and potential for transforming organizations in line with the needs of the capitalist economic system. A systematic and general comparison of communicative planning and NPM is superfluous in the present context. Instead, the next two sections demonstrate that these modes of governance encourage conflicting types of behaviour on the part of the planner.

Values and communicative planning

This section reiterates the values of CPT in order to facilitate comparison with neo-liberalism and NPM. The section is brief, as the Habermasian ideals and discourse ethics making up the foundation of dialogical values were outlined in the introductory section of Chapter 1. In later sections of the present chapter, the role and values of communicative planners will be juxtaposed with the ideas of new public management and with the attitudes of practising planners.

The role of the communicative planner is to make stakeholders and affected groups collaborate with each other in a creative process, generating opportunities that offer each participating group more than it would have been able to achieve for itself through alternative processes. The planner facilitates the process, mediates conflict, and exposes domination by recognizing and avoiding distortions. Technical-economic expertise features less prominently in communicative planning than in some other modes of planning, but this does not imply the levelling down of the planner's role to that of any other stakeholder, as is sometimes asserted (Allmendinger 2001:134). Nevertheless, as for every other participant in dialogue, planners must act openly and honestly, be prepared to see their values subjected to scrutiny and criticized by stakeholders, and to yield in the face of arguments that others find more convincing. Throgmorton (2000) describes the planner's role as that of being a 'skilled-voice-in-the-flow' of persuasive argumentation. The planner must take on tasks related both to process and substance. It is part of the planner's role to advance plans that are fair and to the advantage of deprived groups, as well as to design a process based on open exchange of sincere and honest arguments.

From the definition of communicative planning and the associated planner role, it is evident that values peculiar to this mode of planning are closely related to dialogue, communicative rationality, and fairness in the social opportunities to express oneself. The values in Box 6.1 are inherent in CPT and provide a basis for comparison with planner attitudes stated later in the chapter.

Box 6.1: Procedural values in communicative planning theory

Empathy, broad-mindedness, being a good listener, aiming to understand others' point of view.

Empowerment, striving for autonomy and independence in the performance of daily tasks.

Equality of moral worth, equal opportunities for communicative action across race, sex, and religion; that is, respect for diversity.

Fairness, serving people according to criteria of need and communicative difficulties rather than power, money, and social status.

Honesty, sincerity and trustworthiness, abstaining from deception and manipulation.

Inclusiveness, hospitality in the sense of welcoming people with differing sets of values and attitudes into planning processes and other arenas of social and political life.

Responsiveness to other parties in the planning process and to the general public, willingness to engage in deliberation and debate, and to give reasons why one holds a view.

Self-government, defending every citizen's right to influence collective decisions in matters that concern them.

Responsiveness is a basic value in communicative planning. The ideal of dialogue cannot be approached unless the involved parties are willing to listen to each other and respond to each other's utterances and arguments. '(P)racticing responsiveness by developing the ability to listen skillfully reduces the tension between administrative effectiveness and democratic accountability' (Stivers 1994:364). It is considered rude in many cultures to ignore what other interlocutors say in ordinary conversation. Unresponsiveness is a way to exclude a person and breaks with the openness required by discourse ethics. Respect for reasoning is fundamental in deliberative democracy and thus in CPT. All participants must be willing to give justifications for their actions and will rightly demand them of others. Reciprocity suggests a manner of argument in which citizens regard each other as autonomous and equal.

All the values listed in Box 6.1 belong to the harmony dimension of social values, according to Braithwaite (2009). She contrasts harmony with the security dimension, which we return to in the next section, and offers the following characterization of the harmony dimension:

> (T)he harmony value system brings together societal and personal values that aim to further peaceful coexistence through a social order that shares resources, communicates mutual respect, and cooperates to allow individuals to develop their potential to the full. Harmony values orient us toward establishing connections to others, transcending our individual grievances and dissatisfactions, and finding peace within ourselves and with our world. (Braithwaite 2009:89)

Critical pragmatists seek an enlargement of egalitarian values, principally through the extension of cultural respect and moral consideration for a wider range of human communities and natural habitats. According to Gleeson and Low (2000:146), '(i)t is precisely this "meta-concern" of progressive planning that is directly imperilled by the neo-liberal project'. The rest of the chapter provides a background for assessing this statement. NPM is outlined in the next section to facilitate consideration of its compatibility with the values of communicative planning.

New Public Management – the efficiency features

This section describes briefly the economizing core features of NPM, demonstrating a striking contrast to the CPT values. CPT is not intrinsically against efficiency, as that would mean being in favour of wasting resources. The aim for efficiency is seen as reasonable to the extent that it is compatible with a democratic and fair process. Collaborative planners and critical pragmatists should consider the risk that without discipline in all activity areas of the budget, resources meant for participation and dialogue might instead be used for covering deficits in budget chapters that the economizing 'new public managers' hold to be more important. The efficiency-oriented view of NPM is supplemented in the next section, dealing with the aim for consumer satisfaction and related properties of NPM that seem to be more in line with communicative planning.

As explained in Chapter 5, the neo-liberal shift in the organization of government is a broad trend including aspects such as entrepreneurialism, depoliticization, and outsourcing of governmental tasks and activities to separate agencies. Entrepreneurialism reflects the widening responsibility of urban politicians from provision of services, facilities and benefits to local development and employment growth. The notion of a public-private partnership is the centre-piece of this development. Depoliticization is the process of placing at one remove the political character of decision-making (see Harmes (2006:732–34) for the separation of economics and politics in neo-liberalism). This is a precondition for the disaggregation of integrated administrative structures into single purpose semi-independent agencies. Large public agencies are split up to create units that are fit for market competition. In the railway industry, for example, construction and maintenance of infrastructure have been separated from operation of the trains. The purpose is to arrange for competition on the railway network in conditions where the owner of the tracks lacks the motive for giving one operator preferential treatment.

New public management (NPM) is a reform movement challenging the traditional political-administrative systems of Western democracies (Hood 2002, Lane 2000). It is part of the broader current of neo-liberal thinking which has strongly affected right-of-centre politics and even made an impact far into the social democratic parties of many countries (for instance, in the UK, New Zealand and Scandinavia). NPM's stress on delegation, devolution and decentralization, as well as the subsequent need for coordination, has profoundly changed the central agencies and departments where many planners are working (Hart 1998). The aim of the brief account given here is to make clear that the core ideas of NPM differ from the values which in the previous section were found to guide communicative planning.

Traditional government systems 'are based on a complex and often ambiguous set of norms and values related to political-administrative control, codes of professional behaviour, due process and government by rules, democratic responsibility, public service ethics, and participation of affected groups' (Christensen and Lægreid 2001a:93). NPM offers an economic model of governance claiming that market and business rationality can be made to operate as effectively in the public interest as it does in securing private interests. Similarities between the public and private sectors are accentuated, and NPM encourages organizational forms that increase the autonomy and freedom of choice of managers in order to enhance agency efficiency, for example through performance contracts. Administrative bodies at all levels should be competitive, should have management orientation and customer-focused quality improvement systems, and should pay attention to results (benchmarking). The public sector is expected to give lower priority to rules, processes, and various internal considerations, such as expert jurisdictions and job security.

Under NPM, less weight is put on political signals, professional interests, rights, equality, and the preferences of affected third parties (Christensen and Lægreid 2001b:67). This means that traditional bureaucratic virtues, such as formally equal treatment and always acting in conformity with specified rules grounded on technical knowledge, are placed more in the background. Devolution and management by contract rather than control via hierarchy are among the core elements in a reform where cost effectiveness takes centre stage. Financial targets, budget discipline, and monitoring of service provision and performance are standard features. Other means to achieve the efficiency goal are internal accounts, tendering, privatization, outsourcing, and separation of political and administrative functions.

In contrast to communicative planning theory, NPM has given much attention to problems of accountability, meaning answerability for performance and being subject to sanctions for failure to meet defined criteria (Thomas 1998:352). With the increased discretion granted to managers under NPM, relatively more emphasis is put on managerial accountability than political responsibility. The conceptual relationship between accountability and responsibility (which is the theme of Part III) is discussed by Bovens (1998) and Gregory (2009). Extending freedom to managers without strengthening their accountability would undermine the power of politicians. By managerial accountability is meant the obligation to provide an account of one's actions to those in superior positions of authority. Accountability under NPM is mainly based on output measurement, competition, transparency, and contractual relations. It is a problem, however, that political-administrative processes often do not generate the kind of precise, clear-cut objectives and criteria that are necessary for managerial accountability to be a relatively neutral and value-free exercise (Sager and Sørensen 2011). The most common techniques for checking given accounts involve monitoring, audits, and investigation of possible wrong-doings (Power 1997). Merciless accountability procedures induce blame-avoiding behaviour and are therefore purchased at the expense of creative innovation and transparency.

Managerial accountability is mainly performance-based as opposed to compliance-based. The latter requires rule-based processes, so it can be checked whether an agency works in conformity with process regulations. 'Performance-based processes are more concerned with establishing measures of desirable outcomes and using these tools to measure performance than they are with monitoring compliance with rules' (Jos and Tompkins 2004:259). Indeed, impatience with restrictions, rules, and procedures is a dominant theme in NPM. Measuring the performance of processes poses particular difficulties, as discussed by Agger and Löfgren (2008) and Carmona and Sieh (2008). This is more of a problem for CPT than for NPM, as the latter has a more pronounced emphasis on specifying the quality of services rendered.

Critics maintain that NPM is 'threatening to eliminate democracy as a guiding principle in public-sector management' (Box et al. 2001:608). This is controversial, however, and the aim towards devolution, decentralization and delegation might be interpreted as signalling democratic concern (Harmes 2006). A case can also be made that NPM approves efforts to strengthen consumers' interests by widespread consultation (as dealt with in the next section). Furthermore, NPM supports consumers' voice and choice, that is 'consumer sovereignty' and 'freedom of choice', but the individualism behind these values might also lead to selfishness. Selfishness stands in contrast to the empathy and mutual understanding encouraged in CPT. Based on the above outline, six social values are deduced for NPM and displayed in Box 6.2.

Box 6.2: Values embedded in new public management

Individualism, promoting self-reliance, independence, and personal responsibility in decision-making.

Entrepreneurialism, meaning ability to take risks, launch initiatives, and seize opportunities in competitive situations.

Accountability as support for the rule of law and accepted standards of conduct, for example, budget discipline.

Prosperity, through private ownership and minimization of waste, that is, efficient use of labour, capital, and natural resources.

Reward for individual effort through impersonal market mechanisms rather than bureaucratic regulations.

Freedom of choice resulting from competitiveness and from institutions, impartial authority, and social recognition allowing market entry and choice.

The first five values in Box 6.2 belong to the security dimension of social values, as defined by Braithwaite:

The security value system brings together guiding principles that ensure that one is well positioned to protect one's interests and further them within the existing social order. Security values guide us in deciding how we divide up limited resources, what kinds of competition between groups and individuals are legitimate, and how we define winners and losers. (Braithwaite 2009:89)

This description of security values is well in line with the ideological orientation of NPM. The sixth value in Box 6.2, freedom of choice, is placed by Braithwaite within the harmony dimension. This aspect of freedom is nevertheless not far from the security dimension, as can be seen from the fact that freedom of choice is one kind of reward for individual effort. Braithwaite (2009) notes the growing support for individualism in many societies, and reports from Australia that '(i)ncreasing in importance are values that are concerned with enabling individuals to make good through their own efforts' (ibid.91) – such as 'reward for individual effort' and 'freedom'.

The present section does not give a full picture of NPM, as will shortly be shown. It is nevertheless clear from the above that planners working in line with the NPM ideology would have to give priority to economic arguments and make the striving for efficiency a prominent part of their professional role. Moreover, dialogical processes are time consuming, and the solutions emerging from deliberation and mediation might challenge expertise and management preferences. Both elements can cause conflict between the values of NPM and communicative planning.[2] The next section will nevertheless examine whether there are similar features of NPM and communicative planning which point to some overlap of interests. The aim is not to show that CPT and NPM are politically compatible, or that these ideologies rest on a common set of moral and social values. They do not.

Only irreconcilable differences, or patches of common ground?

The techno-bureaucratic style of planning and governance, so strongly advocated in the mid twentieth century, is confronted both by CPT and NPM. These sets of ideas challenge the traditional roles of politicians and professionals, although in different ways. This section draws attention to some ostensible correspondences between communicative planning and the NPM. It turns out, however, that even apparent similarities might conceal significant divergences. The basic contrasts are first recapitulated. The interest of both CPT and NPM in involvement and user satisfaction is then discussed. Finally, it is considered whether – intended or unintended – these two modes of governance benefit strong developers by putting more emphasis on local negotiations (a question which is followed up in Chapter 7).

Restating the contrapositions

In the face of competing values and role ambiguities, according to Hendler (1991:156), planners tend to choose one of the following conflicting responses when forming their own professional role:

- Retreating to a more value-neutral role of technical advisor to politicians.
- Pursuing a value-laden, normatively directed course of action. This is often, but not necessarily, aimed at enhancing social equity and conserving the natural environment.

The first is the traditional expert role, which can be adjusted to NPM, provided considerable decision-making power still lies with the manager of the planning agency. The second role allows for taking a side more openly, without perforce throwing overboard the notion of widely shared interests. This position is chosen by many communicative planners, and can be recognized, for example, in John Forester's sympathy for equity planning (Krumholz and Forester 1990).

Most planners are reluctant to give up their expert status, and some might be tempted to bring the first role above into deliberative planning processes. According to Tewdwr-Jones (2002:73), however, they are caught in a trap: 'to be a professional requires possessing a specialised area of knowledge for which they are rewarded and this fact rests heavily on their mind. But the communicative turn argues for a more pluralistic and equal relationship between "the planner" and the planned...'. In a conscious or subconscious attempt to retain prestige and rewards, planners might hesitate to question their supposed professional status even if they share the values that underpin the attempted dialogue (ibid.73).

In communicative planning, the planner 'should continually foster participatory processes to expand democratic rights, and access to those rights, to support citizens' voices, and to redirect resources to the most needy' (ibid.66). Communicative planning fosters deliberative democracy. NPM, on the other hand, conceives the modern state as a market-based delivery system, and its aim is to satisfy customers and free managers from political shackles and unions' idiosyncrasies. The main feature of NPM is its one-dimensional emphasis on economic norms and values.

Some further tensions between NPM and communicative planning can be read from Imrie's (1999) critique of the regime shift from bureau-professionalism to managerialism. This shift paved the way for business or corporate values and technical-economic procedures and discourses. For planning, the efficiency goal of NPM entails speeding up the turnaround of planning applications, faster completion of local plan preparation, facilitation of development objectives, and the streamlining of procedures. Important procedures in the present context are those arranging for public consultation. The risk is that the pressures on local planning authorities to streamline procedures and reduce delays in plan preparation and development control could diminish the time devoted to public involvement in planning processes (Imrie 1999:117). If this takes place, there is the risk of extra costs further down the line, for example, if objectors resort to direct action or the courts.

The splitting up of strong public agencies and the privatization of their entrepreneurial and commercial divisions have made it difficult in many cases to build large-scale infrastructure as a purely public undertaking. Planners are increasingly being encouraged towards management practices premised on the development of associative and collaborative networks to enable the attainment of planning objectives (Imrie 1999:111). Public-private partnerships are therefore more often becoming a necessary solution, and both parties might have a financial stake (see Chapter 5). There are considerable risks in these circumstances that profit maximization will subvert planning considerations. Commitment might shift from widely shared interests to more narrowly defined intra-organizational goals.

The mutual focus on users' needs

The individualism of neo-liberalism and the collective nature of discourse ethics (Habermas 1990) lead to quite different sets of values in NPM and CPT. Nevertheless, should there be some patches of common ground, it might ease the tension felt by planners if they could be identified and provide a basis for (at least some) action that would be seen as meaningful both from the managerial and the dialogical perspective. After all, empirical studies have shown that most individuals do not regard security and harmony values as necessarily incompatible; rather, their expression is often symbiotic (Braithwaite 2009:89). NPM and CPT do in fact appear to have a central theme in common: both theories stress the importance of user involvement and client satisfaction, and they both have an interest in being responsive to the users or consumers of public plans. However, communicative planners have much broader commitments. There is a crucial difference between serving the consumers, for instance the users of a planned new trunk road, and taking into account all the groups and interests affected by the road. Christensen and Lægreid place the critique in a wider democratic setting:

> (W)hile the term "customer" is meant to empower the public, it may actually turn out to be a more limited role than that of citizen. The rights of a customer are really quite minimal compared to those of a citizen and the relationships to public employees/service providers are short-term and

temporal in nature. Reform efforts that focus on the aggregation of individual customer preferences ignore and weaken the fundamental democratic trusteeship required of both public bureaucrats and citizens. (Christensen and Lægreid 2002:283)

Citizens are bearers of rights and duties within the context of a wider community. They exert power by voting, organizing themselves around salient ideas and values, and working politically for their general acceptance in the constituency. Customers and consumers are different in that they do not share common purposes but rather seek to optimize their own individual benefits. Imrie (1999:116) makes the additional point that consumer influence depends on expressing a preference in a market place through willingness to pay. Willingness is highly correlated with ability to pay. Thus, while planners may be attentive to social difference and unequal opportunities, the consumerist conception of the public seems inattentive to issues of inequality of access to the public realm. Therefore, 'public participation in planning, along consumerist lines, has the capacity to reinforce social exclusions by doing little more than maintaining the power of the professionals to design, develop and implement the range of planning services' (ibid.116).

Purely technical or managerial decisions might easily fall foul of complex political reality. A demand for extensive public consultation therefore came hand in hand with NPM in several countries (OECD 2001, Commission of the European Communities 2001).[3] The main idea is that public plans and services should become more in line with citizen preferences, not that those consulted should also be the decision-makers. The coupling of participation with decision-making is more in demand when people are seen as citizens in a democracy (as in CPT), than when they are regarded as clients or consumers (as in NPM). From the NPM perspective, public involvement is closely linked to the aim of driving up public sector performance. To improve accountability, there is increased emphasis on formal control and concomitant transparency, 'because the theory behind the consumer orientation holds strongly that people need access to detailed information in order to make informed decisions about preferred goods and services' (Aberbach and Christensen 2005:240). The consumer orientation of NPM fits the neo-liberal idea of the citizen, as defined by individual preferences and rights. However, it de-emphasizes collective traditions, as embedded, for example, in discourse ethics and CPT, which underline common goods and collective action through political parties, social movements, neighbourhood groups and participation in community activities (ibid.241).

Clarke (2008) finds a perverse confluence between, on the one hand, participation as part of a project constructed around the extension of citizenship and the deepening of democracy (as with CPT) and, on the other hand, participation associated with the project of a minimal state that requires the shrinking of its social responsibilities and its progressive exemption from the role of guarantor of rights (as with neo-liberalism). 'The perversity of this confluence reflects the fact that, although pointing to opposite and even antagonistic directions, *both projects require an active, proactive civil society*' (ibid.140, italics in original).

Preventing the potential abuse of power is the ultimate goal of the numerous accountability arrangements of NPM and other democratic modes of governance. Keeping illegitimate use of power from influencing public plans is also a central concern of critical communicative planning (Forester 1993a and Chapter 2 of this book), and one might thus expect that accountability has been thoroughly discussed in CPT. This is not the case, despite the usefulness of dialogue in improving accountability (Roberts 2002).

The customer service ideal of the NPM and the aim to empower affected lay people in communicative planning both lead to a profound reorientation of accountability relationships compared to the compliance orientation of traditional bureaucracy. The accountability needs of the manager and the planner become more complex. There is still a chain of command, so managers and planners have to justify their actions up the hierarchy. In addition, however, responsiveness to customers, clients, and the general public becomes the central aspect of accountability (Thomas 1998:355–56). Responsiveness is essential in what Romzek (2000) calls political accountability relationships. They afford NPM managers and communicative planners the discretion of being responsive to the concerns of key stakeholders, such as elected officials, clientele groups, and the public at large (ibid.27). In NPM, the responsiveness is often linked to the use of customer satisfaction surveys and other output performance measures. In communicative planning, on the other hand, responsiveness tends to be regarded as a value in itself, independent of the service improvements it might bring about. There is scepticism in CPT towards citizens being seen as consumers. Public life should not be 'reduced to a series of isolated transactions from which individuals come away feeling more or less satisfied that they have received value for money' (Thomas 1998:378).

It can be concluded that even in the main area of common interest to NPM and communicative planning – involvement and user satisfaction – there are profound differences between these modes of governance. Two additional differences which are likely to create tensions when the two modes are combined, warrant emphasis:

• Communicative planning opens up the process and welcomes all sincere arguments from involved parties. NPM narrows the public debate, in the sense that cost-effectiveness is given a hegemonic position among the arguments.

- NPM seems to induce a depoliticization of decision-making in the public sector, placing the political character of decision-making at one remove, while communicative planning engenders a politicization of public planning by bringing a wide range of interests to the table.

In response to the first point above, one might question the idea of opening up the planning process to extensive and effective lay involvement if it is already given that cost-effectiveness arguments are to be decisive. Aware of the NPM ideology and neo-liberal leanings of her agency and its political principals, is the planner really in the position to act sincerely when propagating dialogue and participation? Or does manipulation sneak into her professional role despite the dislike of manipulation expressed by the typical planner (see the empirical material in the next section)? An affirmative answer to the last question would suggest that tensions easily arise between the role expectations faced by communicative planners.

The second point invites the objection that communicative planning cannot stimulate political processes, as it is striving for rational solutions based on intellectually convincing arguments, and not on compromises achieved by political means. Mouffe (1999) surmises that advocates of deliberative democracy conceive political questions as being of a moral nature and therefore susceptible of being decided rationally. 'This means that they identify the democratic public sphere with the discursive redemption of normative validity claims' (ibid.746).[4] While the second point mentions a concrete and practical characteristic of communicative planning, Mouffe's criticism relates to the theoretical model in which dialogue is communicatively rational. There is admittedly a dilemma here: communicative planners have to choose between a political participation process on the one hand, and striving for a communicatively rational process that will by itself ensure the legitimacy of agreements reached on the other hand.

Actually, even if a political process is chosen, that is, a collaborative and stakeholder-based process that might be quite exclusive and far from the Habermasian dialogical ideal, critics hold that depoliticization can take place. Swyngedouw et al. (2002) studied large-scale urban development projects in Europe, which are 'emblematic examples of neoliberal forms of urban governance' (ibid.543). They found that the collaborative partnerships and networks often set up to organize the projects tend to 'compete with and often supplant local and regional authorities as protagonists and managers of urban renewal … a process that can be described as the "privatization of urban governance"' (ibid.573). It can be questioned, though, how much of the depoliticization is due to the general neo-liberal transfer of competencies, decision-making power, and funding from the public to the private sector, and how much follows from the collaborative mode of project planning.

Flexible planning decisions heeding local knowledge and preferences

Recent managerial restructuring of government has aimed at depoliticizing decisions by making them a matter of operational management. The dispersal of state functions to a range of extra-governmental organizations makes this evident (Flinders and Buller 2006). Social and political issues are reformulated so as to fit market solutions, or they are translated into problems to be managed. Imrie (1999) makes use of this to build a case against communicative planning, contending that it 'is a powerful conception in legitimising a managerialist approach to the problems confronting the planner' (ibid.119). Organizing networks, forging partnerships, and developing processes are seen as managerial tasks, but Imrie also views them as core tasks of communicative planning. Although Imrie has a point, he ignores the contrasting reasons for the process-orientation. The proponents of NPM want to make issues less political and opt for a streamlined managerial process. Communicative planning theorists focus on the process because they acknowledge that the issues are political, and that the groups and interests affected should therefore have a say. Moreover, the process should be participatory and fair not only because this is valuable in itself, but because the process will usually affect the final plan. Taking an interest in process does not therefore imply indifference to substance.

We now turn to a critique of communicative planning put forward by Bengs (2005b). He observes that the deregulation of real estate markets and the decentralization of land-use decision-making coincide in many Western countries, although this connection is rarely made by either the proponents of NPM or by communicative planning theorists. Bengs contends that CPT is an instrument to facilitate the building of social institutions consistent with neo-liberal society, which to him means institutions that match and advance development and the free flow of investments. The common interest of CPT and NPM is, allegedly, manifest in their endorsement of '(a) new planning regime with a minimum of predefined restrictions and guidelines and ample possibilities for striking deals on the local level' (ibid.6).

As mentioned, NPM is interested in having satisfied users. This follows from market logic rather than democratic logic, although satisfaction with public service would presumably help politicians get uncomplaining voters. Displeased customers impair the standing of the manager and reduce the agency's or company's opportunities for supplying the same type of projects or plans in the future. Flexible local planning decisions are attractive to NPM – which has a managerial and entrepreneurial focus – as they give managers (developers) more leeway to negotiate locally instead of risking being stopped by general regulations and by-laws. Big land developers, often with several prospective projects in the municipality, might have a strong hand in negotiations with local stakeholders.

CPT definitely recommends that solutions be searched for in dialogue with local interests. Local knowledge should be respected in decisions on local matters. Decisions should be made by political bodies as close as possible to where the development takes place. This is assumed to give more power to people directly affected by the plans. The democratic principles that are involved are a core concern of communicative planning theorists.

Critics contend that communicative planners acting on the democratic principles above unwittingly risk transferring power to developers. The strength of developers can be balanced by the power of national authorities. Therefore, laws, regulations, and political guidelines can be enacted at the national level, which serve widely shared interests. At lower administrative levels, communities often compete for the employment opportunities, activities, and tax revenues resulting from development projects. Developers are hence often in the position to play local politicians against each other. This can bend local power relations to the developers' advantage and hence bias initiatives in collaborative problem-solving, although this effect may be modified by other local actors.

This critique of CPT is not equally convincing in all institutional contexts. The position of developers is stronger when industry is footloose and can thus locate anywhere, and when the market for land is free enough to supply a choice of properties fit for development in several adjacent administrative districts. Developers are also stronger when they operate in a monopolistic market that allows them to accumulate profit; this makes it more difficult for local administrations to start negotiations with competitors. Finally, developers will have an advantage in local negotiations if they are backed by an entrepreneurial urban regime, and if widely shared environmental interests are insufficiently protected by law.

Summing up

Through empirical studies, Braithwaite (2009:89) has found that most people place importance on both security and harmony, and that security values are often justified in terms of harmony values. Developments in the two value dimensions can be mutually related. For example, in Australia she observed a simultaneous increase in individualism and in the importance of economic equality as a value. The reason may be that globalization and increased reliance on market solutions have widened the gap between rich and poor (ibid.91). This section has revealed a different point of contact between the two value dimensions, in that seemingly common features of CPT and NPM are substantiated both by arguments based on harmony values and argument drawing on security values.

The reasons given for the focus on users' needs from the perspective of NPM are based on a market logic associated with the security dimension. The main subject is the customer; consultation is introduced as a tool for eliciting information on service demand, and consumer satisfaction with public service provision is sought. The reasons given from a CPT perspective are based on a democratic logic associated with the harmony dimension. The main subject is the citizen; participation is seen as an element in the striving for rule by the people, and empowerment of disadvantaged groups is seen as an aim.

Likewise, flexible planning decisions and locally negotiated solutions are supported by both security-related and harmony-related arguments. New public managers want flexibility in order to achieve fuller exploitation of the potential of properties through performance planning, that is, development in accordance with quality standards rather than zoning regulations. This points to security values. Communicative planning theorists want flexibility in order to increase compatibility with local values and needs, thus enhancing citizen empowerment. Their argument relates to harmony values.

This section has compared selected aspects of NPM and communicative planning. Even if reasons differ, some forms of participative practices are supported by both modes of governance. However, the patches of common ground should not be allowed to overshadow the value differences pointed out in previous sections. The consequences of these differences will depend on the typical values and attitudes of practising planners. The next section examines whether the average planner is closer to the NPM values or the values of CPT.

Typical planner values and attitudes

What do we know of the values and attitudes of the 'average planner'? This section briefly reviews results from the empirical literature on European planners' values and attitudes to assess how far the problem analyzed in this chapter is a real one. That is, the aim is to show that many planners actually express values that make it reasonable to assume that they experience tension between conflicting sets of demands. The empirical results are considered only in so far as they record such tensions. The national differences in institutions and social conditions that might affect the results are not discussed.

The values and attitudes of planners have been studied empirically in several countries. The research design developed by Howe and Kaufman (1979, 1981) has been replicated to study the attitudes of planners in Israel (Kaufman 1985), the Netherlands, Spain and the United States (Kaufman and Escuin 2000), Sweden (Khakee and Dahlgren 1990), and Norway (Olsen 2000). Most of the results referred to here are from these studies, and the similar questionnaires facilitate comparisons.[5] The samples of planners studied in European countries are small and probably not statistically representative. The smallest is the Spanish sample of 19 planners questioned in 1995, and the largest consists of 77 Norwegian planners questioned in 1998. The Swedish and Dutch studies were carried out in 1988 and 1995, respectively. The typical attitudes of Nordic planners which emerge from these studies correspond to the ideals and values embedded in communicative planning, while private and market-oriented development is regarded with considerable scepticism.

Negative attitudes to the neo-liberal NPM were indicated by planners' scepticism towards private developers, as revealed in the empirical studies above. From the extensive questionnaires of those studies, the following five characteristics were selected:

- Developers have a bad image, not unjustified.
- Developers have a complaint against many communities for imposing unnecessary and cost-increasing requirements on their development; the complaints are not legitimate.
- There should be tighter controls on private development to protect the public interest.
- Private developers have little or no concern for the good of the community as a whole.
- Developers are only concerned with making profits.

Planners were asked to what extent they agreed with these statements. Norwegian planners turned out to be the most sceptical towards private developers. This negative attitude is taken to indicate scepticism towards the neo-liberal (and NPM) ideas of transferring more urban land-use decisions to private markets. Planners from Spain, Sweden and the Netherlands reveal less distrustful attitudes towards private developers. In addition, Olsen (2000) shows that European planners typically hold positive attitudes towards dealing with local public transport, low-income groups and minorities, and the natural environment. These are themes that are not usually thought to be well catered for in market-led processes favoured by neo-liberalism.

Indications of planners' attitudes towards openness and citizen involvement were also deduced from the empirical studies above, by utilizing planners' responses to the following four themes in the questionnaire:

- In a democratic system, opposition to a policy held by one's own agency should be just as normal and appropriate as support for it.
- Planners should be participants in the open planning process, defending their values in discussions, and openly striving to achieve their ends.
- No one can better define the needs of a community than its residents.
- Planners should involve citizens in every phase of the planning process.

The responses to the first two statements indicate that planners from all four European countries are in favour of open planning processes. However, the last two statements, dealing directly with citizen involvement, reveal significant differences. The typical Norwegian planner is clearly in favour of involving the public, and more so than was found in Sweden. The Dutch and Spanish planners were more cautious and ambivalent about the role of citizens in the planning process.[6]

In CPT, much emphasis has been put on counteracting manipulation and other distortions of information. Critical questioning has been a main strategy for fighting power-based argumentation (Forester 1993a, Sager 1994). Howe and Kaufman (1979) drew up 15 planning scenarios that were designed to elicit planners' opinions on what constitutes ethical and unethical professional behaviour. Their study was replicated in Sweden, where 40 planners were questioned in 1988 (Khakee and Dahlgren 1990). Six of the scenarios were also used in the Norwegian study from 1998 (Olsen 2000). The Swedish results show that wilful distortion of information is considered very unethical planner behaviour. Examples are deliberate omission of facts that erode arguments in favour of the planner's preferred solution, and falsely claiming to have support from groups or agencies that in reality have not backed the planner's solution. The Norwegian planners are also strongly opposed to communicative distortions, and more so than what is typical among the 616 US planners questioned by Howe and Kaufman. The strong dislike of distorted information is taken as an indication of sympathy with the values of communicative planning.

Among the countries contributing empirical data, Norwegian planners display the attitudes most closely aligned to CPT and most disassociated from the neo-liberalism of NPM. They are both the most positive to public participation and the most sceptical to private developers. Swedish planners are also favourable to citizen involvement and express some doubt about private development. Lapintie and Puustinen (2002) report from a survey of the values of 233 Finnish planners that their attitudes towards the idea of communicative planning and participation were quite positive. Seventy-eight per cent of the respondents agreed that participation practices increase the meaningfulness of their work, while about one third agreed that participation practices are wearisome and consume too much planning resources. On this basis I put forward the hypothesis that the attitudes of the typical Nordic planner are much closer to communicative planning theory than to NPM (the pro-CPT hypothesis).

Planners from the United States are also typically of the opinion that citizens should be involved in every phase of the planning process, and that this involvement should go beyond merely allowing citizens to be heard (Kaufman and Escuin 2000:41). However, the average US planner is considerably more positive towards private development than Norwegian planners, making it more uncertain where the American planners stand in relation to neo-liberalism and NPM. Empirical results for European planners outside the Nordic countries disclose only lukewarm attitudes towards citizen involvement. There is no strong evidence to suggest that the attitudes of Israeli or non-Nordic European planners are much closer to CPT than to NPM. The differences between countries may be due to a number of factors, for example, the attitudes in the wider society towards the state and towards private land ownership, but explanatory variables for these differences are not studied further here.

The dialogical ethos and the neo-liberal managerial ethos pull the role of the planner in different directions. New public management is likely to be the strongest influence, as it is aligned with predominant trends in contemporary market-oriented politics. However, communicative planning seems to better match the typical values and attitudes of Nordic planners. The result is a value conflict which is likely to be felt by many in the planning community, presumably also by many reformist planners outside the Nordic countries. This statement and possible steps to take if it is correct, are discussed in the next section.

Relevance and possible consequences of the CPT/NPM value conflict

This section discusses the reasonableness of the hypothesis that the attitudes of the typical Nordic planner are much closer to CPT than to NPM. Then follows a brief account of how NPM has affected government structures and how it is likely to change the working conditions of planners in executive agencies. The relative accentuation of efficient and reliable processes is changed. The discussion is a backcloth for considering whether the 'new public service' – a recently presented alternative set of ideas for public management – offers a possibility of bringing the values of public administration into harmony with those of communicative planning. Importantly, this is not an attempt to modify NPM to establish consensual ground with communicative planning. New public service is not a modification of NPM, but a markedly different alternative to that mode of governance.

Is the pro-CPT hypothesis reasonable?

The European studies of planners' values and attitudes are spread over a 10-year period from 1988 to 1998, and hence none of them is quite up to date. The attitudes both towards communicative planning and NPM may have changed as planners acquired more experience with the practices that have developed from these sets of ideas. New data from 2007 was collected for Norway by Falleth et al. (2008). They obtained answers from 249 planners and planning directors. Three quarters of the respondents thought it important to ensure participation from the local community, and two thirds found such participation important for the quality and feasibility of the resulting plan. The empirical data of Falleth and her co-authors gives communicative planners reason to view developers with some scepticism, as less than 30 per cent of the 296 responding developers see local participation as important in the same sense (ibid.74).

However, the most serious challenge to the pro-CPT hypothesis (that the attitudes of the typical Nordic planner are leaning towards CPT rather than NPM) is that CPT and NPM might have sufficiently much in common through their mutual interest in user involvement and 'customer' orientation, that planner attitudes in favour of participation could also be interpreted as support of NPM. The question is whether the statements in the questionnaire designed by Howe and Kaufman (1979, 1981) allow the distinction between support for citizen participation with a democratic purpose and support for customer consultation with the more narrow purpose of a service quality check. If such a distinction is impossible, most of the empirical research on planner values and attitudes cannot be used to make a case for the pro-CPT hypothesis.

Returning to the list of points concerning openness and consultation, it is possible to infer that the planner responses reflect participation from the perspective of improving democracy. The request for general openness in planning processes, which is explicit in the first two statements on the list, points far beyond the need for consultation to improve the quality of publicly supplied service. The last two statements are directly related to citizen participation. One statement focuses on 'the needs of a community' rather than the quality of service experienced by individual customers or clients. The last statement is about involving citizens 'in every phase of the planning process'. This is usually seen as necessary when the aim is democratic decision-making, but it is quite needless when the purpose is to advise on how to improve service quality.

The conclusion is that the statements on openness and consultation deal with broad participation with the aim of democratic decision-making rather than narrow consultation aiming for product development. Hence, planner attitudes manifested through strong agreement with the statements indicate sympathy with the kind of citizen involvement required by communicative planning. Such openness and democratically grounded participation would be incompatible with administrative processes in which it is predetermined what arguments are going to count as important; open processes do not go well with NPM, where market-orientation and economic efficiency are predetermined core considerations.

NPM and trends in the structure of government: consequences for planners

Norway has been described as a reluctant new public management reformer (Christensen and Lægreid 2009). Neo-liberalism is nevertheless a strong ideological influence which advances individualism at the cost of communal values. Based on an empirical study of media language in Norway between 1984 and 2005, Nafstad et al. (2007:324) maintain that the 'powerful public discourse of individualism undermines and potentially destroys the value foundations of the welfare state: the values of collective responsibility and human equality'.

The main conclusion of Norway's second official study of social power relations is that all elements of popular self-government are being weakened (Selle and Østerud 2006). Some of the reasons are peculiar to Norway, but in the present context it is of more concern that some noted changes in the structure of government are due to the dissemination of NPM:

- The distinction between politics and administration has become clearer and more formal. More discretion has been granted to executive directors of public agencies and public enterprises without any formal political responsibility. The state apparatus has been hollowed out and become more fragmented, and politically accountable bodies have lost or delegated power.
- The National Assembly has tighter control over a more restricted domain following on from the implementation of NPM in public administration.
- Through market orientation, privatization, and forms of public enterprise exempt from political dictate, areas of economic life previously controlled by politicians are transferred to the neo-liberal governance mechanisms of competitive markets.
- Democratic self-government at the local level has been tapped of much content by a combination of state directives, laws granting citizens the right to certain types of service, and limited budgets (compared to assigned tasks). The public persona of Norwegians is undergoing a change from citizen to service recipient and customer.
- In the sum of the current processes of change – including the transfer of authority to administration, independent organizations, the judicial system, and markets – a retreat of politics is embedded. The chain of parliamentary steering is growing weak in all links (Østerud et al. 2003:290–95).

Due to the international impetus of NPM ideas, the above points seem to be valid far beyond the Norwegian borders. A reasonable supposition might be that as NPM procedures become firmly established, planners in executive agencies will become less dependent on political principles. If neo-liberal influence remains strong, they will probably be able to plan with less direct intervention from politicians in the future. They might, however, be working under stricter intra-organizational regimes due to NPM.

With regard to democracy, planners can inform and vitalize public debate on the physical development of places, facilitate public involvement, expose and criticize repressive use of power, and check that market forces are played out within the framework of laws and political guidelines. Judging from the official Norwegian study of social power, it seems more important than ever to develop an interface between the prevalent styles of public planning and public administration that strengthens democracy. I will argue below that such compatibility of communicative planning and administration can be achieved by substituting the new public service for NPM as the prominent ideology of public sector organization.

Reliability versus efficiency

Vickers and Kouzmin (2001) describe the human costs in agencies embracing new public management. A substantial number of employees are not equipped with the coping skills and resilience to handle the strains of a fervently efficiency-seeking organization. The alienation and work-related stress reactions suffered stand in contrast to the empowerment sought by CPT.

Not only empowerment, but also reliability is declining in organizational systems that are single-mindedly pursuing efficiency. While it sets the course for restructuring, organizational down-sizing and outsourcing, NPM shies away from complexity. New public managers look down upon redundancy, duplication, slack, and overlap, which are precisely the features that engender reliability in organizational processes (Landau 1969). These are properties of inclusive deliberation processes that make it unlikely that communicative planning will be the mode chosen by NPM-steered agencies. The idea that all organized action should be both indispensable and inevitable does not sit easily with the ideological cannons of liberal, participatory democracy.

Within the organizational design simplicities of 'lean and mean' prescriptions, the advantages of redundancy, deliberation, rich information, and inclusive consensus building are grossly maligned (Vickers and Kouzmin 2001:110). This is to the detriment of reliability. Repetition and parallel problem-solving processes are general remedies to cure an efficient but vulnerable and too error-prone process or plan. When flexibility is aimed for, more elements and more connections should be included than strictly necessary for the functioning of the system under normal conditions.

Communicative planning aims towards flexibility and is likely to provide the redundancy required because of its inclusion of a varied assortment of people. They should all feel that they have been listened to, and that their involvement has been meaningful. The task may be difficult because the participants usually represent competing interests and therefore may disagree among themselves. Hence the plan design will be a compromise judged suboptimal by any partisan criterion. From this perspective, it is an advantage if a design is chosen that is heterogeneous, complex, and composite. The plan should be composed by loosely interconnected parts, so that some of them are adjusted to the wishes of one interest group, and some correspond with the preferences of another. The redundancy needed is arranged for by:

1. making the whole project more multi-faceted and versatile than is functionally required;
2. letting the plan consist of more elements than are technically necessary; and
3. reducing the interdependence among the elements beyond the level suggested by economic risk analysis, to be able to tailor each part to special interests.

Communicative planning surpasses NPM processes in reliability, but comes second in efficiency. In this sense, inclusion and democracy are achieved at a price. Participation and deliberation are not determined by cost-benefit analysis or other efficiency criteria.

New public service

Denhardt and Denhardt (2003a, 2003b) outline a system of ideas for administering the public sector which offers a distinct alternative to NPM. This ideology is coined 'new public service', and it puts collective decisions based on dialogue at centre stage, while displacing individual decisions based on rational choice. Perry (2007) juxtaposes a new public service with related ideas about a public sector ethos. The contrast to NPM is underlined by the maxim that '(g)overnment shouldn't be run like a business; it should be run like a democracy' (Denhardt and Denhardt 2003a:3). The roots of new public service are ideas of citizenship, community, organizational humanism, and civil society (ibid.Ch.2). The Denhardts propose replacing the ethos of NPM, which is based on market and customers, with a public service ethos that re-establishes the centrality of citizens, democracy, and the public interest. This mode of governance 'seeks shared values and common interests through widespread dialogue and citizen engagement' (ibid.170):

> From this perspective, the role of public administrator is to bring people "to the table" and to serve citizens in a manner that recognizes the multiple and

complex layers of responsibility, ethics, and accountability in a democratic system. The responsible administrator should work to engage citizens not only in planning, but also implementing programs to achieve public objectives. This is done not only because it makes government work better, but because it is consistent with our values. The job of the public administrator is not primarily control or the manipulation of incentives; it is service. (Denhardt and Denhardt 2003a:170)

Denhardt and Denhardt (2003b:9) delineate the principles of new public service, summarized below. The primary role of the public servant is to help citizens articulate and meet their shared interests and commit to shared responsibility. This can be most effectively achieved through collective efforts and collaborative processes. Dialogue is the preferred tool for eliciting shared values and building relationships of trust and mutual respect. Public servants must be attentive to more than the market; they must also attend to statutory and constitutional law, community values, political norms, professional standards, and citizen interests.[7]

Perry (2007:7) aims to contrast NPM and new public service, and starts by condensing the many aspects of NPM into the following four points:

- Catalytic government, steering rather than rowing.
- Customer-driven government, meeting the needs of the customer, not the bureaucracy.
- Community-owned government, empowering rather than serving.
- Enterprising government, earning rather than spending.

New public service, on the other hand, is built on seven mutually reinforcing ideas (ibid.8):

- Serve citizens, not customers.
- Seek the public interest.
- Value citizenship over entrepreneurship.
- Think strategically, act democratically.
- Recognize that accountability is not simple.
- Serve rather than steer.
- Value people, not just productivity.

These points are not meant to sideline values such as efficiency and productivity. However, in a democratic society, democratic values should be paramount in the way we think about public administration.

The gist of the principles is that widely shared interests are better advanced by public servants and citizens committed to dialogical ideals than by entrepreneurial managers acting on market incentives. The accentuation of involvement and deliberation, and the attention given to democratic accountability at the expense of efficiency and cost-effectiveness, would bring public administration in line with communicative planning practice. New public service is much closer to the values of CPT than the ideals of NPM. The similarity of the ideas is acknowledged by Hefetz and Warner (2007), who point out that the reform has been coined 'new public service' in public administration and 'communicative planning' in the planning field. Behind both is the idea of deliberative democracy, where 'the cooperative search of deliberating citizens for solutions to political problems takes the place of the preference aggregation of private citizens or the collective self-determination of an ethically integrated nation' (Habermas 2006a:413).

Conclusion

Several studies of the values and attitudes of planners confirm their inclination to be in favour of public involvement and open processes, and opposed to manipulation and lenient control of developers. The evidence is sufficient to put forward the hypothesis that the attitudes of the typical Nordic planner, in particular, are much closer to CPT than to new public management. Discourse ethics and theories of deliberative democracy have provided inspiration and supportive ideas to planners since the early 1980s. It is nevertheless questionable whether these ideas can stand up to the pressure from main trends in politics, economies, and administration – such as the market orientation and rational choice perspective of NPM. This set of neo-liberal ideas has a marked influence on the planning of many types of public infrastructure and service provision both at the national and the local level. The planner role is currently under contradictory pressures from conflicting values and expectations held by educators and part of the professional community influenced by CPT on the one hand, and politicians and administrators promoting NPM on the other. Patches of common ground have also been identified and analyzed – especially the concern for user influence, service quality, and client satisfaction – but these do not resolve the value conflict.

Imrie (1999:111) notes the dilemma of the present situation, in which 'pressures for community involvement in planning policy processes, and the democratisation of policy practices, are heightening in a context whereby planners are increasingly having to justify their actions by recourse to measures of efficiency and value for money'. In the present confrontation between the one-dimensional economic approach of the NPM and the open and multi-dimensional deliberation recommended by CPT, it seems important that planning retains a critical function (Forester 1993a).

Planners can take on many different roles, but in light of the present discussion of CPT and NPM, and putting nuances aside, there are the following two extremes on the continuum of possibilities:

- Role 1: the planner as intermediary between the multiplicity of society and the economism of neo-liberal public administration. The planner interprets reality in managerial NPM terms. The planner makes a note of the retreat of politics and becomes part of the reductionist movement, working in the service of efficiency and cost-effectiveness.
- Role 2: the planner conveys the variety of views in the polity to the public administration at national and local levels. The planner regards it as her task to prevent the many-faceted public discourse from collapsing into one dimension as issues are filtered through the preparatory stages of planning and policy-making on their way to political decision-makers. The planner brings the outcome of deliberative democracy into planning documents and recommendations.

The present challenge is to simultaneously ease planners' tension and stimulate democracy by forging workable compromises from the stylized planner roles above. New public service has a value content closing the present gap between the ideals of prominent theories of public administration and planning. Hence, by struggling to give the dialogical and democratic ideals of new public service a solid foothold in public administration, and breaking the hegemony of NPM, planners would also relax the contradictory claims that CPT and NPM make on their role in society. This would ease the role tension that might currently be felt by collaborative planners and critical pragmatists, as CPT and new public service are related in their aim to strengthen the deliberative qualities of democracy.

Notes

1. Brooks (2002:62-78) and So et al. (1979:8–20) give overviews of planning values. Hillier (1999) identifies values in environmental planning and indicates the current dominance of economy-based values and the relative invisibility of cultural values. Wart (1998) offers a comprehensive discussion of values in public administration, presenting the major schools of thought. Scott (2002) applies content analysis to identify five organizational moral values: honest communication, respect for property, respect for life, respect for religion, and justice. A number of values are also listed by Braithwaite (1998:582).
2. Value differences between NPM and communicative or collaborative processes for planning and decision-making do not prevent governments from embracing both modes of governance. For example, New Labour under Prime Minister Tony Blair was widely held to institutionalize neo-liberal ideas (Bevir 2003), yet it simultaneously initiated a range of participatory policies (Barnes et al. 2004a).

3. OECD (2001:23) defines three levels of involvement. The lowest level is information given in a one-way relationship. The medium level is consultation, which implies a two-way relationship. Governments define the issues for consultation, set the questions and manage the process, while citizens are invited to contribute their views and opinions. The highest level is active participation in a relation based on partnership with government. Citizens actively engage in defining the process and content of policy-making.

4. See also Kapoor's (2002) clear exposition of Mouffe's argument. Dahlberg (2005) defends Habermas's public sphere conception against critique from the 'difference democrats', Mouffe among them.

5. The values of planners can also be elicited indirectly, for example by asking what are considered important competencies by planning professionals (Guzzetta and Bollens 2003). Communicative skills seem to be valued more than technical and quantitative knowledge, although professional communication should build on a base of broad analytic skills. A more reliable and representative source of knowledge about the values of planners is the professional codes of organizations like the American Institute of Certified Planners in the US and the Royal Town Planning Institute (RTPI) in the UK. Their web addresses are, respectively: www.planning.org/ethics/conduct.html and www.rtpi.org.uk/about-the-rtpi/codecond.pdf. The codes are discussed by Hendler (1991) and Lucy (1996). The codes take a stand against discrimination on the grounds of race, sex, religion and sexual orientation, and they promote equality of opportunity. Even the educational guidelines of the professional organizations reveal values. Poxon (2001) comments on the guidelines of the RTPI, which promote an appreciation of and a respect for the role of government and public participation in a democratic society, among other things.

6. Two focus groups studied by Campbell and Marshall (2001) in 1996 confirm that the view on citizen involvement varies among planners. The more senior British planners, in particular, emphasized the importance of consultation in order to 'give people a say'. What came through on a fairly general basis, however, was the importance of not romanticizing public participation (ibid.102).

7. Some traits of new public service are similar to characteristics of the post-bureaucratic organization, as outlined by Alvesson and Thompson (2005) and Iedema (2003). The latter explains that the post-bureaucratic organization dissimulates authority 'by reducing hierarchy, devolving decision-making power, setting up collaborative decision-making forums, emphasizing flexibility, and dissolving inside-outside boundaries and rigidities' (ibid.193). Post-bureaucratic work is not principally about following pre-determined rules, but about enacting some kind of rule-making.

7

A Strategy for Examining whether Communicative Planning is Serving Neo-liberalism

Introduction: critique of communicative planning theory

The purpose of this chapter is to discuss the relationship between neo-liberalism and CPT. In particular, the aim is to arrive at suggestions of how CPT can be developed so as to increase the chances that communicative planning efforts will not unwittingly serve a neo-liberal agenda. Substantive and procedural recommendations in communicative planning are brought closer together in this chapter. Clearer criteria for what a 'good plan' means in the parlance of communicative planning are necessary for deciding whether a specific plan takes society a step in the direction of neo-liberalism or a step towards realization of the ideals of CPT. The main concepts of neo-liberalism and new public management (NPM) were explained in Chapters 5 and 6. The exposition can therefore be taken fairly directly to the relations and, at least on the face of it, mutual scepticism between neo-liberalism and CPT.

Opinions on the influence of neo-liberalism on living conditions are strong and conflicting. When reading Bourdieu (1998) or Saad-Filho and Johnston's (2005) introduction on neo-liberalism's allegedly miserable track record, one gets the impression that it is lethal on a grand scale, especially to the extent that it is allowed to shape the economic processes of globalization. Bourdieu describes the effects of the neo-liberal utopia as:

> the poverty and suffering of a growing proportion of the population of the economically most advanced societies, the extraordinary growth in disparities in incomes, the progressive disappearance of the autonomous worlds of cultural production ... and above all the destruction of all the collective institutions capable of standing up to the effects of the infernal machine. (Bourdieu 1998:102)

Dangerous is also, by implication, any theory or practice that helps to implement neo-liberal policies, such as planning and planners that 'have been complicit with the neoliberal disaster' (Lovering 2009:3) and in particular CPT, according to Bengs (2005a, 2005b) and Purcell (2008, 2009). At the opposite wing regarding neo-liberalism is McCloskey (2006), asserting that neo-liberalism has 'helped hundreds of millions of people attain higher standards of living, beyond what they, or most economists, thought imaginable but a short while ago' (ibid.248–49). Gerring and Thacker (2008) also hail neo-liberalism for promoting human development across the world by lowering the rates of infant mortality.

My own position is that the neo-liberal ideas were originally useful for reorganizing inefficient and cumbersome bureaucracies. However, in many Western countries the economism inherent in neo-liberalism has been taken too far and has policies biased towards efficiency goals at the expense of equally important goals of democratization, environmental protection, and improved living conditions for deprived groups, for example. Nevertheless, the present chapter is not meant as a long lament over neo-liberalism's unfortunate influence on planning. The important task is to find a way for planning theorists to deal with criticism that applications of their theories end up benefiting ideologies and urban policies at odds with the core values inherent in the theory itself.

Well-known accounts of CPT – such as those by Forester (1989), Healey (2006), and Innes (1995) – point to no obvious reason why collaborative planners and critical pragmatists should not go along with neo-liberalism's fight against self-sufficient and closed bureaucracies, economically wasteful customs, and malpractices like favouritism and corruption. Neither does there seem to be any reason, in principle, to oppose the neo-liberal striving for accountability, or its aim to serve the client or the customer rather than the employees of the service provider. This notwithstanding, the other chapters in Part II of the book have shown that there are tensions between neo-liberalism and CPT, and this picture will be painted more clearly in the sections to come.

The critique of CPT which prompted the writing of this chapter claims that CPT belongs to the set of rules, norms, and bureaucratic procedures (that is, institutions) supporting the neo-liberal state. This critique sees communicative planning as advancing developers' interests and the free flow of investment in real estate. The core argument is that a planning regime with a minimum of predefined restrictions and guidelines, and with ample possibilities of striking deals at the local level, is in conformity with neo-liberal ideals (Bengs 2005b:6). Such a regime is, allegedly, introduced by communicative planning, with detrimental effects for urban development in the interest of the great majority. One objection to a more top-down planning strategy is that the top echelons of politics and administration in many countries are already infused by neo-liberal ideas, and would be happy to let their executive agencies disseminate these ideas through state-led policies.

The remainder of the chapter is organized in six sections. It is first argued that developments in planning theory often follow broad political trends, and that critics' attempts to link CPT to neo-liberalism are in line with this. Second, I explain how neo-liberalism is able to change public planning and describe what the changes are. Third, some critical viewpoints on the relationship between neo-liberalism and CPT are briefly surveyed. Fourth, I consider how CPT can deal with the accusation of being a handmaiden of the neo-liberal state. Emphasis is put on developing substantive value principles that are based on the same values as the procedures of communicative planning. A case study illustrates how the values and practices of a particular planning effort can be compared with CPT values and neo-liberal values and policies in order to determine which ideology's interests are being promoted. The last section concludes the discussion of whether CPT necessarily facilitates neo-liberalism.

Planning theories can reflect broad political trends

Planning theorists *should* ponder the association of their theoretical constructs with politics. This is part of planning theorists' reflection on their own academic field and its place in society at large. Such an exercise is also necessary for planning theory to be considered a socially critical area of research. Does it make sense to interpret emerging planning theories in the context of general political developments? This has to be assumed if the idea of CPT being developed in response to the needs of neo-liberalism is to have credibility. It is necessary but not sufficient to make the idea seem plausible. Whatever one thinks about the claim that CPT facilitates neo-liberalism, there is precedence for linking the emergence of planning theories to contemporary hegemonic political discourses and changes in the general political climate. This is not to say that planning theory is necessarily wholly reactive, and that planning theorists are without agency and power to set their own agendas.

Advocacy planning was a response to the degeneration of many US inner cities in the early 1960s, and the transactive planning of John Friedmann (1973) reflected the radical political trends and the quest for more citizen participation of the late 1960s and early 1970s. Links between shifts in planning theory and prominent political-economic currents are also assumed in recent literature. For example, Beauregard (2005) and Healey (2005) agree that the 'turn' to institutionalist analysis in the planning field in the 1990s and 2000s embodies an opposition to globalization and neo-liberalism. McDermott (1998) suggests that planning exists to serve the varying needs of capitalism.[1] When capitalism faces new problems, public planning is likely to change. Today, planning is formed 'less from the need to mediate capital's conflict with labour and more to mediate or manage the conflicts between production and societal and environmental values' (ibid.635).

The various strands of CPT go well with a liberalized land regime, as they stress communication with stakeholders and put less emphasis on politically mandated public control. Stakeholders increase their influence in such planning systems relative to democratically elected representatives. This development may be seen as an adaptation to the less controlled and more efficient real estate market that follows from neo-liberalism and globalization. To some critics, '(p)lanning reduced to communication is a political statement in line with the building of a neo-liberal society' (Bengs 2005a:3).[2] Such a one-dimensional view of planning practice is not defended by CPT, even if much attention has been given to improvements of interpersonal communication. The next two paragraphs exemplify what other links have been theorized between CPT and neo-liberalization since the 1980s.

Allmendinger (2001:134) holds the denial of a central coordinating role for the planner to be a main theme of collaborative planning. He believes that planners in this mode need to engage with local stakeholders in an unbarred search for local consensus. Allmendinger interprets collaborative planning theorists as wanting a levelling down of the planner's role to that of any other stakeholder. As already mentioned, Throgmorton (2000) describes the planner's role as being a skilled-voice-in-the-flow. The limited authority which is a consequence of this role weakens the ability of planners to stand up against powerful stakeholders. Allmendinger (2001:123) sees the function of communicative planning as 'providing planners with the theoretical justification for their continued existence in the shadow of the deregulatory approaches of the 1980s'. This survival strategy might give private developers more room for manoeuvre in urban planning. Perhaps the coordination challenge inherent in shaping land and property development so that public concerns are addressed has to move to a different institutional site and practice?

Taylor (1998:122–25) points out that negotiation and undistorted dialogue are both types of communication, and that the last type has taken centre stage as an ideal in communicative planning. However, he rightly holds that negotiation and the concomitant mediator planner role are also important in participatory and communicative planning processes and help in taking the step from analysis to action. Theorists analyzing the transformative steps from knowledge to collective action have drawn attention to the importance of interpersonal, communicative skills in general. Taylor therefore regards CPT as a strand of thought following the upsurge of implementation analysis in planning and policy-making throughout the 1970s and early 1980s, but is careful to concede that communicative planning theorists were as interested in fairness and vitalization of democracy as in how to get things done. Efficient implementation, in the form of speeding up the handling of development proposals, is a core interest of the neo-liberal and neo-conservative regimes emerging in the late 1970s and the following decade. Taylor maintains that concerns about implementation can therefore provide a potential stepping-stone between communicative planning and neo-liberalism and asserts that the 'developments in planning theory in the 1980s and 1990s cannot be disassociated from the changes to planning practice brought about by this political shift to the right' (ibid.130).

Even if theories of planning are influenced by the political-economic environment, there may be a number of reasons why CPT gained momentum during the last two or three decades. Some of the candidate answers for partial explanation have no clear connection to neo-liberal politics:

- Many Western societies and cities are becoming more multicultural, with more diverse publics and thus increased need for negotiation and communication in the preparation of public plans and projects.
- The citizenry is more educated than ever before and demands to be heard in public matters.
- Civil society is thoroughly organized in many countries, with a large number of interest organizations, NGOs, and social movements that are strong enough to challenge bureaucratic and political decisions.
- The 1970s saw a large extension of the range of effects deemed relevant to the evaluation of public plans and projects. There is a lack of objective standards for assessing many of the environmental and social consequences, in contrast to the traditional technical and economic ones, so the preferences of affected groups are needed alongside expert calculations.
- CPT links much of contemporary planning firmly to theories of deliberative democracy (Bohman and Rehg 1997). This makes communicative planning part of the efforts to enrich democracy beyond periodical election of representatives. Such revitalization is important in order to maintain the legitimacy of democracy in a period when voter turnout to the polls is low in many Western countries.

My own opinion is that important reasons for the emergence of CPT are to be found among the points on this list. If one nevertheless opens for the possibility that neo-liberalism may have influenced the theory of public planning, the next question is how this effect came about, given that neo-liberal tenets and NPM are probably not taught in most planning programmes. As argued in Chapter 5, there are aspects of neo-liberalism that weaken the position of public planning and shift its focus from regulation to facilitation of urban development. Interurban competition curtails the set of regulative policies that can be used by planners in each single city (Albrechts 1991, Healey 1992a). Rolling back the state and transferring more of urban renewal to private initiatives leaves less room for comprehensive and coordinated plans (Bramley and Lambert 1998). Neo-liberalization means more market and less bureaucracy, outsourcing segments of the residual sphere of regulation, and contracts rather than control via hierarchies. All this gives a narrower scope for public planning and lowers its status (Imrie 1999).

Any reorganization is followed by a new agenda, and NPM-steered organizations direct attention to problems considered important from the neo-liberal outlook, and to policies thought to work without threatening neo-liberal values. This line of reasoning is strengthened by Hammond and Thomas's (1989) theoretical result stating that a neutral hierarchy is impossible. Any particular organizational structure will affect what organizational decision-makers are able to learn and will bias policy-making toward some outcomes and away from others. Since the structure influences which options are to be compared, in what sequence, and by whom, a particular organizational structure is, in effect, the organization's agenda (Hammond 1986:382). It is obvious, then, that neo-liberals would want to change public planning and its agencies.

What do neo-liberals demand from public planning?

Neo-liberals have worked to curtail public planning because it intervenes in markets and, in their opinion, is a threat to efficient allocation of resources (Allmendinger and Thomas 1998:242, McDermott 1998:643). They find that local citizen participation can have the same effect, especially when concerned with local action to solve global problems. The ideological position is that the public planning function gives local and national government too much of a say in urban and regional development. The strong government involvement is seen as a source of inefficiency, as approvals take too long because multiple consents have to be obtained from various government departments. Planning authorities are criticized for taking a negative stand towards market-led development (Prior 2005:475–76). Consequences of the complicated planning procedures are delays, extra costs, wasted capital, and reduced employment (ibid.475). Neo-liberals also criticize public planning for being inflexible. This is a problematic point though, as flexibility reduces predictability which is a priority of both developers and the community. 'Regulatory flexibility ... may actually increase both the size of the administrative apparatus of planning and transaction costs' (Gleeson and Grundy 1997:310), as case-by-case assessment of land-use consents takes much administrative time.

The neo-liberal pursuit of efficiency in planning is part of the general striving for making the economy competitive. Many neo-liberal regimes have institutionalized the use of cost-benefit analysis and management by objectives and results to advance this strategy (Bagley and Revesz 2006, Sager and Sørensen 2011). The increased reliance on such formal techniques also reflects a shift from communication to calculation as the primary source of legitimacy. To make this shift successful, emphasis has to be put on driving up public sector production measured through 'best value' performance indicators and comprehensive performance assessment (Carmona and Sieh 2008).

Baker et al. (2006) discuss performance-based planning in the United States, Australia, and New Zealand. Traditional zoning tends to separate land uses, while the performance-based approach allows more integration of land uses as long as performance criteria are met. This kind of planning 'is supposed to be more flexible, require fewer regulations, speed up the approval process, and encourage a greater dialogue amongst stakeholders' (ibid.396). Baker and co-authors maintain that the performance approach tended to reinforce the general climate and consequences of neo-liberal reform in the Australian public sector, and found that it overlapped with reforms emerging from NPM. The calls for change came from the development community, which alleged that local planning schemes were too inflexible, and that 'the public's role in the decision-making process was too strong' (ibid.401).

Deliberative decision-making and participatory practice involve a great deal of time and effort. 'Decisions will be deferred until there is broad agreement and they will not come quickly' (Gleeson and Low 2000:154). The neo-liberal response was to speed up public inquiry procedures and development plan preparation in order to achieve faster turnaround of planning applications (Prior 2005:476). Streamlining of procedures, for example, the routines for public consultation, was also requested. This is contrary to the stated aim of communicative planning theorists and would make it a risky business for them to run the errand of neo-liberals.

In line with the devolution of governance to local scales, neo-liberals could accept a contracted and more focused planning system that is proactive and positive to development initiatives (Allmendinger and Tewdwr-Jones 2000:1396). The system should assist and not hinder the work of market mechanisms, and planners should to a greater degree become deal-makers rather than regulators. Neo-liberalism can be well served by a planning system that is more flexible with regard to the outcome of planning, and thus relatively more concerned with how to plan. Some scholars surmise that collaborative planning is found useful to neo-liberalism because of its dismantling of old divisions between state and market in order to accommodate new synergistic partnerships (Brand and Gaffikin 2007:283).

Neo-liberalism accentuates the logic of the market in an attempt to 'restore social and institutional order by suppressing the chaotic demands of democratising social movements' (Gleeson and Low 2000:143). The neo-liberal attitude to citizen involvement in planning is a compromise between this felt need for discipline and predictability on the one hand, and the need for client and consumer information about public goods and services on the other. The compromise can be pursued by disciplining citizens through ostensibly open and deliberative planning processes that turn out to be excluding and co-opting (Gunson and Collins 1997), participation being based on selective invitation. Involvement procedures might favour the stakeholders regarded as the most important to a particular partnership, leaving out residents, neighbourhood groups, and non-profit organizations (Turner 2002:536). The visioning process seems to be the most open phase of regeneration planning in many cities, but it is an early agenda-setting exercise which does not necessarily give participants much influence on the final plan. McCann (2001:216) found it to be 'the product of attempts by local elites to negotiate the contradiction between privatized and nominally collaborative planning in a way that produced a certain level of consent for their vision of the future'.

Summing up, then, neo-liberals demand public planning with an ambit restricted to land use and efficient spatial allocation, leaving equity concerns to the politicians. Planning authorities should not interfere in markets unless transaction costs are demonstrably higher there than in public bureaucracies. Moreover, neo-liberal planning procedures should be simple and flexible yet efficient, and planning initiatives should promote local competitiveness. The next section is a selective survey of theorists' interpretations of how CPT has responded to these challenges.

Could CPT possibly be an offspring of neo-liberal ideology?

This section provides a systematic overview of notable attempts to understand how CPT relates to the ideas and practices of neo-liberalism. Much of the critique of CPT's ostensible association with neo-liberalism is based on the idea that both bodies of theory have taken an interest in certain aspects of urban planning and therefore must be related and must somehow further the same cause. The common features mentioned in the planning literature are:

- *Process similarities*
    - Masking conflicts about substantive matters by focusing on process.
    - Weakening the role of public planners as professionals and experts.
- *Authority-weakening similarities*
    - Flexibility as opposed to rigid regulations (as in zoning schemes).
    - Solutions generated by civil society, thus reducing the influence of government.

In addition, Miraftab (2004) puts forth an argument which suggests that community participation – here seen as an approximation to communicative planning – is sometimes not practised with sufficient critical skill to reveal misinterpretation of central value concepts and prevent CPT from serving neo-liberal purposes. Miraftab's somewhat implicit critique of communicative planning theorists is that they let neo-liberals hijack their concepts related to fairness, democracy, and inclusion and twist the interpretation of these terms to fit their market-oriented rhetoric that leads to social and economic differences and exclusion. The conclusion I draw from Miraftab's exposition is that planning theorists have not provided the critical analysis of neo-liberalism in urban planning and policy-making that might have disclosed and prevented this misuse of communicative action theory. When anti-hegemonic work is lacking, more participation might effectively mask the power structure of local communities, potentially resulting in more disempowering planning processes (Kothari 2001:146).

Critique based on alleged process similarities of CPT and neo-liberalism

Recently, Mark Purcell advanced a critique of CPT, arguing that Habermasian communicative and collaborative planning modes 'provide an extremely attractive way for neoliberals to maintain hegemony while ensuring political stability' (Purcell 2009:140). He assumes that the consensus-oriented deals made by the parties to communicative planning will always mask conflict and thus always serve those who benefit from the prevailing system of power relations:

> (E)ven if deliberative processes include more marginalized participants than had been included previously, they tend to reinscribe existing social hierarchies, since all groups must gain from each decision. Moreover, they tend to legitimate those existing hierarchies with a stamp of democratic process. Therefore, deliberative democracy, managed thoughtfully, can be a particularly powerful tool for advancing the neoliberal agenda. (Purcell 2007:201)

Purcell (2008) repeats and sharpens this critique, setting out from Innes's (2004:12) statement that '(c)onsensus building is not, in any case, the place for redistributing power'. With regard to Innes's collaborative planning model, Purcell contends that it offers an undisguised preservation and legitimation of the status quo (Purcell 2008:80). In his opinion, what makes communicative planning such a convenient vehicle for neo-liberals, is that it offers decision-making practices that are widely accepted as democratic and are therefore legitimizing, while they cannot fundamentally challenge existing relations of power (Purcell 2009:141). CPT is allegedly helping to capture the banner of democracy for a neo-liberalism that is experiencing a legitimation crisis.

Purcell finds communicative planning guilty of legitimizing development decisions which do not challenge prevailing capitalist urban regimes. The question of whether the parties to the presumably deliberative process are happy with the solution does not affect his critique; what matters is whether or not the system for trading and developing urban land (which urban planners might hope to affect) is left intact. Purcell is sceptical of communicative planning because he thinks that civil society participants can be carefully selected and effectively disciplined by the competitiveness imperative. He worries that the shift from decisions made within government to decisions made in local consensus-building processes will advance the neo-liberal agenda of 'outsourcing' public decisions to the private sector or to quasi-governmental agencies. 'If the state can be successfully tarred as the enemy of democracy, then outsourcing can be sold as democratization' (Purcell 2008:29).[3]

The worries about communicative planning put forward below by Bramley, Lambert, and Mees, are grounded on the weakening role of professionalism. The strengthening of civil society seems to imply that more solutions to collective problems will be offered by the market or by the co-operative efforts of private actors, and fewer solutions will be offered by experts in the public bureaucracies. Bramley and Lambert (1998:89) see the critique of professionalism as a feature common to New Right thinking and participatory planning theory. In communicative planning, the planner seems to downplay her role as technical or economic expert, while showing herself more in the capacity of being facilitator, mediator, and process organizer. To the extent that the planner is reluctant to profess expertise in substantive matters, more latitude is given to other knowledgeable actors who might turn planning outcomes in partisan directions, for example, towards market-oriented solutions that ignore externalities affecting the broader public.

Referring to communicative planning, Mees (2003) is worried about the alleged lack of a planner role that links planners' expertise with the substance of the plan. Based on his negative experience with long-term planning in Melbourne, Mees holds that the participatory and communicative part of the planning process can often be easily manipulated or contracted to a minimum level even if the planners' engagement with the public was originally advertised as a central characteristic of the process. The problem, according to Mees, is that when this happens, there is nothing left in the ruins of the communicative planning effort that can defend broader social interests. In alternative modes of planning – even in the despised rationalistic or synoptic mode – one would at least have professional recommendations about the substance of the plan to fall back on if there was no outcome from a deliberation process to provide legitimacy to action. In a manipulated and curtailed communicative process, Mees fears that there will be nothing to counteract opportunistic political proposals and market-determined solutions.[4] The criticism is against communicative planning for being risky, as it leaves no defence of non-partisan interests if deliberation fails.

It is not clear that more power to planning professionals would effectively protect against neo-liberal transformation of cities by curbing the policies dealt with in Chapter 5. Planners have political sympathies in different directions, and available data does not show that most planners are strongly pro CPT and contra developers throughout the world (see Chapter 6). Both professionals and regulators can be captured by private interests with the resources to stimulate development, market liberalization or other broad formulas conceived as the cure to many ills.

Critique based on alleged common interest in limiting government influence

Miraftab (2009:43) worries that 'inclusive planning, with its emphasis on citizen participation and civil society partnership, has often become the accomplice of neoliberal governance'. As mentioned in the previous chapter, this is also the complaint of Bengs's criticism of CPT: 'A new planning regime with a minimum of predefined restrictions and guidelines and ample possibilities for striking deals on the local level is in conformity with the neo-liberal ideals' (Bengs 2005b:6). The first part of this description fits CPT, which is consequently seen as a tool for building social institutions consistent with the neo-liberal ideology. As Bengs believes that developers and other strong stakeholders will gain the upper hand in local deal-making, relegating other actors to the role of pure 'extras', he regards CPT as establishing institutions that serve the few rather than the many.

A clear case of linking CPT to a policy for diminishing central government influence comes from Elwood's (2002) analysis of neighbourhood revitalization through collaborative planning in Minneapolis, Minnesota. She indicates that the conclusions on the relations between neo-liberal interests and the collaborative efforts might be generalized to other revitalization programmes throughout the US. The collaborative programmes fit the neo-liberal agenda because:

1. Devolution and collaborative public-private partnerships are means for downsizing the state, giving citizens and civic organizations growing responsibility for local urban planning and service delivery.
2. Grassroots organizations may be co-opted into reproducing neo-liberal priorities and policies at a highly localized level, such as entrepreneurialism,

market-driven competition, and diminished state involvement within neighbourhood level revitalization.

This critique of communicative planning assumes that state intervention can serve the weak groups in urban development processes, and that it is therefore unfortunate that the state withdraws and transfers responsibility to local planning initiatives and civil society. Elwood admits a certain ambiguity, however, in that the neo-liberal planning initiatives studied have afforded new opportunities for participation, enabling some community organizations to contest state agendas. The contention of some scholars, 'that collaborative planning and revitalization initiatives are a way of pacifying community action and co-opting resistance' (ibid.128), is thus modified.

Summing up

The authors referred to in this section have at least one thing in common: they all see a connection between CPT and the predominant neo-liberal politics of many societies. However, ideas immediately differ when describing and explaining this connection. The combination of a neo-liberal economy and government programmes for citizen participation might seem like a clash of ideologies, but can make sense in democracies with a need for legitimizing policies. For example, under a neo-liberal regime, no overall plan sanctioned by the city council that can give legitimacy to each site plan may be in existence. This creates a need for more citizen consultation at the local level as an alternative source of legitimacy.

Critics of CPT claim that dialogue at the local level between those initiating and those being affected by urban plans will serve developers and thus neo-liberalism. However, the planning literature is ambiguous on this point. On the one hand, there are reports that neo-liberal reformation of planning systems has been welcomed partly because the public's role in the planning process was conceived as being too strong and contributing to overly lengthy processes (Baker et al. 2006). On the other hand, some regimes with neo-liberal agendas have launched programmes for engaging citizens and communities. Major's Conservative government in the UK issued its Citizen's Charter in 1991, featuring the principle of information for and openness to the service user, and systematic consultation with users (HM Government 1991). Later in the decade, Tony Blair's New Labour government pleaded for democratic renewal in a White Paper where they wanted to get 'In Touch with the People' (Department of the Environment, Transport and the Regions 1998). This dualism nourished the idea that neo-liberalism and CPT might somehow be related, and that the first might find the second useful.

Purcell (2008, 2009) maintains that communicative planning serves as an important legitimizing technology for neo-liberal urban policies. It is not possible for planners to prevent authorities with a neo-liberal agenda from organizing potentially legitimizing processes. However, critical pragmatists could question the design of such processes and exert pressure to make the participation go beyond mere consultation and instead take the form of co-determination. The planners have to find a way between using their professional position as a springboard for making revolution on the one hand, and 'trying to paper [neoliberalization] over with dreams' (Purcell 2009:160) on the other.

This and the preceding sections have presented some adverse reactions to CPT for being in league with neo-liberalism without any intention on my part of refuting the criticism. Instead my approach is to show that, should it turn out to be warranted to reproach CPT for unwittingly serving neo-liberalism, something can in fact be done about the problem. We now turn to this task.

A strategy for developing CPT to withstand the criticism

It should be clear from preceding sections that neo-liberals have demanded changes to urban planning that have been deeply regretted by communicative planning theorists. They are therefore likely to find allegations of any positive relation between CPT and neo-liberalism paradoxical and hard to believe. After all, CPT challenges neo-liberalism because CPT argues for finding solutions through deliberation rather than market transactions, and because it broadens the notion of representation from deal-makers to all affected groups. The idea that CPT may unwittingly benefit neo-liberalism should nevertheless be discussed rather than ignored. After all, it has long been realized that good intentions are no guarantee against paving the road to hell – or to serfdom. The classical discussion dealing with this theme tied central planning to socialism, which was pitted against a liberal society based on markets. Hayek (2008 [1944]) argued forcefully that planners' well-intended striving for equality was leading to a society where freedom would be lost. In this section, I put forward a development of CPT that will hamper applications breaking with the values of discourse ethics, and impede exploitation of this planning theory for neo-liberal purposes. A few preliminaries must first be addressed.

Preliminary ideas

Only a few of the theorists giving attention both to planning and to neo-liberalism have explicitly dealt with CPT. Among those who have, even fewer have provided a critical and thorough analysis of the connection between

CPT and neo-liberal economic and political currents. Nevertheless, as recorded in the previous section, some planning theorists comment on that relationship; the potential advantage communicative planning provides to neo-liberalism is sufficiently indicated to suggest that the conception of CPT as the unsuspecting handmaiden of neo-liberalism warrants further analysis.

Attack is sometimes considered to be the best defence, and it is tempting to look for arguments that neo-liberalism might indirectly help communicative planning catch the wind instead of the other way around. One line of reasoning assumes that neo-liberal policies are hostile to labour unions and other movements for working people that could interfere with market mechanisms, entrepreneurial government, and corporate accumulation of capital. Social unionism has been the response in some places, shifting the emphasis from wages and workplace concerns to activist agendas promoting community development, social justice, and economic equity (Baines 2010, Lier 2006). When the work-based parts of organized civil society are under siege and become less influential, people may be motivated to join other kinds of civic associations and forums of public protest. New outlets have to be found for the frustration and despair engendered by neo-liberal policies that erode welfare. Community organizations and even involvement in communicative planning processes might sometimes be useful substitutes. The state apparatus is fragmented, not least under neo-liberal regimes with their emphasis on decentralization, devolution, and outsourcing of tasks to semi-autonomous agencies. One resistance strategy for civic groups is to build alliances with elements in sympathetic agencies with a hidden agenda to resist neo-liberal policies from the inside.

Thus, when neo-liberalism and communicative planning are observed together, the reason is not necessarily that communicative planning has been called upon to support neo-liberal policies. It might be that (1) neo-liberalism and concomitant entrepreneurialism have created many controversial projects and plans; (2) that neo-liberalism has rolled back the state and its local tentacles, thereby leaving room for new forms of public-private governance; (3) that progressive planners have taken this opportunity to offer relational goods (see Chapter 1) by establishing new social networks, building social capital, engaging civil society in processes of visioning, and assessing and amending development initiatives; and (4) that communicative planning has consequently emerged as a check on developers' efforts to alter places in accordance with their own economic interest. There are virtually no empirical studies to underpin the above sequence of theoretical arguments, though.

It might not be possible to completely eradicate the suspicion that CPT may be a useful pawn on the neo-liberal side of the political game. Capitalist-led market systems provide such an intricate web of incentives at all levels, from individuals to national governments, that it is difficult to entirely escape their subtle persuasion. David Harvey concedes this much when writing that:

> If ... urban entrepreneurialism ... is embedded in a framework of zero-sum inter-urban competition for resources, jobs, and capital, then even the most resolute and avantgarde municipal socialists will find themselves, in the end, playing the capitalist game and performing as agents of discipline for the very processes they are trying to resist. (Harvey 1989:5)

It might be possible to design an empirical and statistical study of a great number of urban planning cases which could provide more convincing results as to whether a participatory and communicative local process tends to produce developer-friendly plans. However, available case studies are by no means in agreement on the potential and the success so far of communicative planning. For example, Barnes et al. (2004b), Brownill and Carpenter (2007), Ferreyra and Beard (2007), and Margerum (2002a, 2002b) conclude in a balanced or largely positive tone, while Bedford et al. (2002), Gunson and Collins (1997), McGuirk (2001), and North (2000) are more sceptical. They conclude that experience with communicative planning has been discouraging or that real gains have still to be proved.

The ideas above do not take us far in devising an approach that can give CPT a fair trial. For lack of conclusive empirical material, a different strategy is needed that can make CPT less vulnerable to accusations of running the errands of ideologies other than deliberative democracy. The suggested approach is outlined in the next sub-section.

The value approach to examining whose interests CPT is serving

CPT is often criticized for single-minded preoccupation with the qualities of the planning process at the expense of the planning outcome. As long as the process is open, striving for dialogue in the Habermasian sense, and aiming for local consensus – so the criticism goes – there is little in CPT to prevent the plan itself from serving neo-liberal purposes.

One can endorse democratic procedures (or the ideal process of CPT) either because they are believed to be intrinsically valuable, or because they are instrumentally valuable and thus tend to produce good outcomes. The prevailing view in CPT is that communicative planning has the potential to deliver on process and outcome qualities alike. It is nevertheless conceded by many communicative planning theorists that there is a need to bring process qualities and outcome qualities closer together (Forester 2009b). This means it must be made evident that what is required from the plan (the outcome) is grounded in substantive principles that are closely associated with the values behind the process design. The value approach sketched in the present section is meant to do just that; and by insisting on consistency between the values of the process and the principles of good outcome, it offers a way to address the charge that CPT facilitates the progress of neo-liberal urban development.

The idea of the value approach is to identify a set of criteria for what constitutes a good plan in the spirit of CPT. This set of substantive criteria or principles should explicitly point back to – and be closely associated with – the procedural values that are the basis of planning process design and desirable planner conduct according to CPT. Process values for CPT were articulated in Chapter 6. The profound differences between these values and the values of new public management (neo-liberalism) were also demonstrated there, in that the values of CPT and NPM were shown to be very different, and belonging to the harmony and the security value dimensions, respectively. Given this contrast, it is unlikely that urban plans complying with a set of substantive criteria that mirror the process values of CPT, will also serve the purposes of neo-liberalism.

The discussion between adherents of procedural and substantive theories is an old one in planning, as is clear from the overview chapter in Faludi (1987:68–87). For most theorists who then dealt with the issue, it was a question of relative emphasis rather than either/or.[5] The dichotomy has later been discussed from a radical perspective by Feldman (1995) and from a post-positivist standpoint by Allmendinger (2002), who suggests doing away with the distinction. Alexander (2002a) nevertheless separates substantive and procedural concepts of the public interest; the first being concerned with the content of actions and their consequences, and the second focusing on the quality of the planning and decision-making process. Planning rights are also divided into substantive and procedural concepts; this division is of interest here because rights are closely related to values. Alexander (2002b:198) sees the values of human dignity, equal treatment, and free enjoyment of property as underlying substantive planning rights. The relationship between participatory process and planning outcome was recently analyzed by MacCallum (2008). She notes that the values and norms guiding the process 'are not the values that shape the structure and content of the conventional "good" plan. ... A participatory process and a conventional product, then, are underwritten by different ideal-type logics' (ibid.326).

A number of empirical studies analyze the effects of participatory processes on the quality of planning outcome. Positive effects on quality are found by Brody (2003), Burby (2003), Innes and Booher (2010:41–88), Loring (2007), and Susskind et al. (1999). Warnings about potentially negative effects of participatory and communicative planning processes are put forward by Abram (2000), Pelletier et al. (1999), and Voogd and Woltjer (1999). The range of differing results is evidence that the debate about procedures' relation to substance is still ongoing.

The main idea in this section is to underline the difference between neo-liberal planning and CPT by requiring that the planning outcomes of the latter mirror its procedural values. CPT must change its balance of process- and product-orientation towards the outcome. The plan should be designed to promote the realization of the intrinsic values of the planning process. As a result, participants will feel they have been listened to, and that their involvement was meaningful. Redundancy techniques (an aspect of flexible planning) can be used in order to design plans that underpin the procedural values (Sager 1994:232). Giving general recommendations about plan design is problematic in CPT, as free dialogue is at the heart of the communicative mode of planning. Pre-given values or criteria pertaining to planning outcomes must therefore be on a form restricting the open discussion as little as possible.

The idea of linking outcome evaluation to process values is developed further here by drawing on Sen's (2009) concept 'comprehensive outcome' and Brettschneider's (2005, 2006) value theory of democracy. Sen argues against a narrow consequentialism where a state of affairs is evaluated by considering 'culmination outcome' only. The culmination outcome includes the ultimate results of an action that are detached from process, agencies and relations. In contrast, comprehensive outcome evaluation takes the dynamic context of the choice of action into account; for example, the properties of the planning process leading up to the recommendation of a certain planning alternative (Sen 2009:215). Sandbu (2007) extends and deepens the analysis of comprehensive outcomes. It is of significance to CPT that he studies the evaluation of voice and participation. Communicative planning processes draw their value partly from their instrumental effect on culmination outcomes; '(y)et in their symbolic and evidential role, they represent something much broader: they represent our autonomy as subjects who can shape our reality, rather than objects whose lives merely happen to them' (ibid.226). Participants in democratic processes value their *causal* role in producing culmination outcomes.

The local public can value the substantive outcome of a planning effort differently depending on whether it was imposed on them by fiat or it emanated from a deliberation process with extensive public participation. Consider an example. The local evaluation of a windfarm on nearby mountain ridges is likely to differ in the following two alternative situations. Situation 1: a business-oriented economic analysis is the basis of the decision. The process is expert-driven, and windmills are the only technology for electricity production taken into account by the planners. Situation 2: in a co-operative process with local politicians, the planners have compared all feasible technologies for producing the electricity required. The impact assessment of the alternative solutions has a local community perspective in addition to displaying financial effects for the energy company. Assessment reports were circulated for public comment and discussed at community meetings.

The windmill plan is likely to be less negatively or more positively received by the affected municipality if local people agree that the alternatives to a windfarm have been properly assessed. A participatory process creating a feeling among local people that their concerns have been clearly conveyed to the decision-makers, is also likely to influence locals' views of the plan, although not necessarily in a positive direction. Disappointment over an undesirable decision, despite having thoroughly explained the disadvantages accruing to the local community, can make the local constituency judge the plan very unfavourably. The different evaluations imply that people's judgement is founded on a comprehensive approach to outcomes and thus affected by the quality of the planning process.

Brettschneider's (2006) value theory of democracy offers an alternative to the traditional divide between procedural theories of democracy and substantive theories of justice. She argues that the democratic ideal is fundamentally about a core set of values with both procedural and substantive implications. I adopt the idea of linking both process and outcome to the same set of core values, and propose a value approach to the problem of bringing process and outcome closer together in CPT. In the present value approach, as in the value theory of democracy, '(i)t is the ambition ... to reconcile the ideal of self-government with the protection of substantive individual rights by appealing to a set of core values' (ibid.261).[6] The CPT values identified in the previous chapter are empathy, equality, fairness, honesty, inclusiveness, responsiveness, and self-government. As seen, some of these values have relevance both for process and outcome, which is required in order to link the substantive value content to the process values. Brettschneider's set of democratic core values – equality of interest, political autonomy, and reciprocity – is included among the values of CPT.

The purpose of the present value approach is to combine the ideal of dialogically agreed plans with the effective safeguarding of quality outcomes by appealing to the set of values that characterizes exemplary processes of communicative planning. The set of core values of CPT has, for instance, implications of fairness for planning outcomes as well as for the deliberative planning process. For example, affected individuals should be given a fair hearing, but also a fair compensation if some of their property is expropriated for the production of public goods. The value approach applied here to communicative planning rests on respect for all citizens as lay planners. Citizens authorize legitimate plans through their participation in communicative and democratic planning processes (see Chapter 1). Respecting a citizen's status as a lay planner requires that planning outcomes resulting from CPT procedures do not undermine this status. Communicative planning must be by and for the people. The criteria that safeguard the virtues of outcomes ensure that plans will not undermine citizens' fundamental interest in being treated as competent lay planners who know what is for their own good and in the best interest of their community (Brettschneider 2006:268–70). Thus, professional communicative planners cannot, for example, first invite local citizens into the planning process in the name of empowerment, self-government, honesty and empathy, and then come up with planning outcomes that disregard their arguments and recommendations. In cases where higher level government chooses a solution different from the one desired by the local community, good reasons must be given, and adjustments must be made to accommodate local interests.

In the planning literature, values expressed through the substantive features of the plan are usually not dealt with directly, but instead transformed into planning goals and displayed as such (Keeney et al. 1996). Some substantive goals are clearly process-dependent, such as Gormley's (1987:156) 'community integration', and are more readily achieved with the support of participatory and communicative planning processes. Planners and politicians usually want a neighbourhood plan with a substance that most residents feel a strong commitment to implement. Such commitment must, however, be built through the planning process, thus making certain demands on the design of this process. The demands on the substantive outcome of the deliberative planning process – the plan – are not in themselves values, but the demands correspond to the procedural values of CPT and are here named substantive value principles or value criteria.

Before listing a set of substantive principles or criteria, I would like to clarify a couple of issues concerning CPT's value-related principles for planning outcomes. One-to-one correspondence between the procedural CPT values and the quality criteria to be satisfied by desirable planning outcomes is not necessary in the value approach. Every procedural value might not have an equivalent in the virtues of a particular planning outcome, but the plan can still be deemed satisfactory from a CPT perspective. There may also be substantive value principles (characterizing a particular planning outcome) that are not process-dependent and thus do not refer back to the set of CPT values identified in the previous chapter. When the primary purpose is to acquire the ability to distinguish the effects of communicative planning from neo-liberalism, as is the case here, the occurrence of process-independent values inherent in the outcome is not a problem as long as they do not advance neo-liberal policies. However, for the value approach to lead to the conclusion that the plan under scrutiny does not primarily serve neo-liberal sectional interests, the overlap between the substantive value principles and the procedural CPT values for this particular planning effort must be broad. The overlap must preclude all reasonable doubt that the plan is in the spirit of deliberative democracy and CPT and does not bolster contrasting ideologies. When the overlap between substantive value principles and CPT process values is quite limited, and several outcome criteria underline the worth of efficiency, optimal resource allocation, employment opportunities, market solutions, and individual choice, the chances are much higher that the planning effort in question serves neo-liberal urban development.

The vision of the good city can be articulated as an ethic of care, 'an expanding habit of solidarity and ... a practical but unsettled achievement, constantly building on experiments through which difference and multiplicity can be mobilised for common gain and against harm and want' (Amin 2006:1020–21). This needs to be fleshed out, but how concretely should the substantive value principles be articulated in CPT? If evaluation criteria and value principles for the planning outcome are made overly concrete and without explicit reference to the CPT set of process values, they will have to be reformulated for each new planning task. The chief purpose of the substantive value criteria is to advance consistency between process and planning outcome, and the level of concreteness should be adapted to this need. Some quite general substantive value principles are listed in Box 7.1. The list makes no claim to be exhaustive, but taken together, the principles on the list are associated with all the procedural CPT values identified in the previous chapter. The substantive principles in Box 7.1 are process-dependent in that the likelihood of their fulfilment depends on the design of the planning process.

Communicative planning is an integral part of deliberative democracy, and this could be reflected in a substantive value principle saying that public space should be created 'where the values of democracy are enacted, by providing a social scene for spontaneous encounters, discussions and expressions of values' (Jacob and Hellström 2010:662). The city, as well as city planning, should be inclusive. In many planning cases this would lead to substantive value criteria such as keeping urban space public and open to a wide range of activities.

Inclusiveness is also about promoting urban housing in all price classes. This is an inclusion policy which CPT shares with some other prescriptions for city improvement, such as the vision of the eco-city or sustainable city. One principle is to 'create decent, affordable, safe, convenient, and racially and economically mixed housing' (Roseland 1997:198). Modernization of central areas should not force low-income groups out of inner-city neighbourhoods. There should be restrictions on the size of enclaves allowed to be gated or to interfere with the right of free passage by other means.

Box 7.1: Suggestions for substantive value principles in communicative planning theory

---

A selection of substantive value principles for CPT:

- The plan should accommodate diverse lifestyles and not hinder legitimate groups from living in accordance with their self-chosen identity. For example, cultural minorities should find places in the city which are fit for their rituals and ways of socializing (empathy).
- The plan should respect what is culturally essential to affected groups, such as their heritage and their conception of that which is sacred (equality of moral worth).
- The plan should hold something for each affected group, if not in the main physical manifestation of its purpose, then in the form of compensation. Especially, the situation of underprivileged groups should not be aggravated (fairness).
- The plan should correspond to the information and the planner intentions conveyed to the participating parties throughout the planning process. The plan should not give reason to suspect previously hidden agendas (honesty).
- The plan should not make it difficult for certain groups to take part in public life, to work, or to access basic public and private services (inclusiveness).
- The plan, even when designed contrary to the wishes of a particular group, should include elements signalling to this group that it has been listened to. At least some details of the plan should be fashioned to accommodate the needs of protesting groups (responsiveness).
- Widely accepted solutions negotiated in the communication process (especially consensus proposals) should be incorporated in the final plan, possibly with modifications catering for the interests of people who may not be part of a local consensus; for example, tax payers in general and future generations (self-government).

It is important that some of the CPT substantive value principles point directly at social justice, as:

> there has been something of an acrimonious debate in urban planning theory between those who have advanced a communicative action or argumentative approach and those who have sought to reaffirm a more traditional political-economic orientation which has, among other things, emphasized social justice. (Fischer 2009:52)

Critical writing on *social justice and the city* was much stimulated by Harvey's (1973) book with the same title. Ideas on social justice are wide-ranging, and I have no intention of listing them all. Planning-related claims are, for example, equal maintenance levels for roads, parks, etc. in all parts of the city, and satisfactory provision of public services in all districts (water, electricity, waste collection, security). Demand for universal design is entering the political agenda in a growing number of countries, making buildings and public transport – and thus the city centre – accessible for people with various handicaps. Marcuse (2009) lists many other demands from right-to-the-city activists.

Some issues of the 'just city' have to do with power and security. If it is not okay that systematic power differentials bias city planning, why should it be acceptable that exertion of power biases the use of the city itself? A substantive value criterion could call for a safe urban environment for all groups, day and night. Fear of terrorism can easily lead to restrictions on access and prohibition of certain activities. The public sphere is contracting in such cases, and more so for groups regarded as suspicious. This is taking us farther away from the ideal of the just city. Finally, the homeless have lost the right to many cities, as it is made more difficult for them to find places to rest, spend the night, and go about their daily routines (Mitchell 2003). Working on the issues above to make cities more just corresponds well with the agenda of critical pragmatists focusing on respect, inclusion, and an open and vigorous public sphere.

Many values are of the kind that can be advanced both through the design of processes of interaction and through the design of physical realities. The purpose of the substantive value principles is to make sure that the planning process and the plan itself serve the same values. When the physical manifestation of the plan is designed in accordance with a CPT substantive value principle, this will further one or more of the CPT procedural values. However, the value approach is based on the realization that good process does not by itself guarantee an outcome that is good, as judged from the same set of values as the process; extra criteria are needed in order to ensure value consistency between process and outcome. In principle, the possible inconsistency between the value contents of the process and the plan is analogous to the tensions between popular sovereignty and liberal rights. In the literature on legislation and political science, this dilemma between democratic proceduralism and substantivism is sometimes characterized as the core of the legitimacy problem of collective decisions (Mármol 2005:262).

The substantive value principles listed in Box 7.1 are quite abstract, and they need to be supplemented by more concrete criteria in order to assess whether a particular plan serves neo-liberal interests or the development of an inclusive, egalitarian, and caring society.[7] An example will clarify what kind of value formulations is required, and how the concrete substantive principles and goals can be juxtaposed with CPT values and neo-liberal policies.

On the wrong side of the tracks: the case of Svartlamon

The purpose of this section is to illustrate the 'value approach' of the previous section by a real life example. The case comprises the planning going on in Svartlamon, an area situated about 1.5 km north-east of the central business district of Trondheim, Norway. I give an account of the urban regeneration in this small, run-down neighbourhood, where a long-standing conflict over demolition versus restoration was transformed into a communicative development planning process. Figures 7.1 to 7.4 give an impression of the area. The analysis identifies the procedural values implicit in the planning process and demonstrates that the design of the development plan is in line with the substantive value principles of CPT. These sets of normative statements are compared to the values identified in previous sections as being typical of CPT and neo-liberalism, respectively. In addition, the practical policies implemented in Svartlamon are juxtaposed with the neo-liberal, planning-related urban policies surveyed in Chapter 5. The comparisons show how to examine whether or not the process and outcome of a particular planning effort serve neo-liberal development of the city.

Many cities have districts where anti-authoritarian and ecologically conscious people fight to realize more communal alternatives to the mainstream lifestyle and way of organizing local society. One pedagogical advantage of selecting such an area for illustration purposes is that the value contents of both process and plan are often relatively easy to extract.

Description of the case area

The quarter of Svartlamon developed during the years 1860–1890 and was inhabited by workers from the nearby factories.[8] In 1889 the railway was constructed, and Svartlamon became disconnected from the city district of Lademoen. From this period onwards, the area was known as one of the poorest neighbourhoods of the city and got its nickname Svartlamon (dirty Lademoen). New building restrictions were enacted in 1905 to prevent timber houses from being built within the city limits. Some of the buildings along the access street to the area (Strandveien) were replaced by three to four storey brick houses, but most houses in Svartlamon are still made of timber. Almost half of the Svartlamon neighbourhood was torn down after the Second World War, and the area was regulated for the purposes of port, industry, and transport infrastructure. By the early 1980s, Svartlamon was a squatter area threatened by total demolition.

Even today, in 2012, the railway is a border preventing Svartlamon from being fully integrated with the surrounding city. All access routes are underneath the railway track. The old houses in the area are now considered worthy of preservation (about 5000m²). There is a potential for increasing the building density by adding about 5000m² in two and three storey buildings. Among the activities on the 32000m² of land making up Svartlamon are an art-and-culture kindergarten, café, project- and performance hall, artist residence building, office for a work training centre, centre for creative recycling, a free shop, book café, clothes shops, scenic dance studio, shop for redesigned clothes, and a restoration workshop. A co-operative ecological food shop opened in 2009 and a vegan People's Kitchen in 2010, both manned by local volunteers. Outdoors there are the Freedom Park, a playground, open courtyards, and small common gardens. A mobile artist's home (Husly), made as an ecological, prefabricated house based on recirculated European pallets, was moved to Svartlamon in 2008. The rock festival Eat the Rich is arranged annually and is a non-profit grass-roots event. Some 200 people are living in about 30 buildings in Svartlamon in 2011, and no flats are uninhabited except a few that are being restored.

The use of the area is mixed, but many of the cultural and business activities are concentrated in the buildings formerly owned by the car dealer Strandveien Auto. This company was a main party to the local land-use conflict throughout the 1990s. The firm wanted to expand its property at the expense of old, dilapidated working class houses, and for several years, up to 1998, the expansion plan of the car dealer was actively supported by the municipality of Trondheim.

Figure 7.1 Overview of Svartlamon, also showing part of the concrete submarine shelter Dora 1 from the Second World War to the right of the little-used industrial railway track

Figure 7.2 Wooden block of flats from about the turn of the nineteenth century

Figure 7.3 Workman's house that is now inhabited by young people with an unconventional lifestyle

Figure 7.4 Decorated block of flats adjacent to a showroom formerly owned by the car dealer Strandveien Auto

The activists' relationship with the municipality of Trondheim: from strife to talks

The Svartlamon case demonstrates that very different strategies can be used by a protest group – conflict-oriented action and co-operative discussion – and that both can serve the group's purpose well, contingent on the situation. Svartlamon residents achieved the decisive breakthrough for their preservation cause in 1998 following a conflict strategy, while Svartlamon's status as a (partly) self-governed, alternative, and experimental area for sustainable, cheap, and participatory urban regeneration in 2001 was achieved through a communicative and co-operative strategy.

In 1991, the Svartlamon Residents Association ('Svartlamon beboerforening') was established to prevent municipal authorities from ruining the housing quarters and turning them into an industrial zone. People from certain political movements, musicians and artists wanted to use the area as a base for activity. Some flats were inhabited by occupants from the late 1980s onwards, but most of the tenants had legal contracts. Housing occupants justified their actions by referring to the cynicism of the neo-liberalizing housing market. The national government and the municipalities were eager to privatize and sell off subsidized public housing units, leaving the poorer segments of the population to a speculative market with rising prices. A broad movement consisting of local inhabitants, artists, media, 'green' and left-wing politicians and others gradually took form and protested effectively. Demonstrations, music festivals, media stunts, and clever lobbying created lots of political noise which never let city council members have a moment of peace.

Svartlamon residents and municipal authorities were in continuing conflict for almost a decade. Even though some decisions that were threatening to Svartlamon were made, and housing contracts were eliminated, the preservationists prevailed. In 1998, the Trondheim City Council voted to keep Svartlamon as a housing area, and the industrial interests had to move out and were given compensation and business property elsewhere. After that, the communication between the Residents Association and the municipality gradually improved, despite challenges to co-operation between a flat and egalitarian activist culture and a hierarchical and technocratic administrative culture. Bureaucrats found it problematic that the Residents Association very often changed their representatives from meeting to meeting. As far as the residents were concerned, they were frustrated that they were not initially allowed to participate in all working groups planning for Svartlamon. The disagreements were resolved, and the residents were involved in all working groups and also got to keep their somewhat untraditional practice of rotating representatives (Thorkildsen 2006:24). Later, disagreement sometimes still flared up, for example, over the choice and quality of ecological solutions for rehabilitating buildings.

After years of struggling to survive as a residential area, the neighbourhood of Svartlamon eventually became a pilot project for sustainable social housing, direct democracy and ecological city planning. In an early phase of the project, the municipality and the Residents Association organized a joint study trip to Copenhagen. This helped to build mutual trust regarding the parties' intentions and plans. Following two years of planning and co-operation between Svartlamon inhabitants and the politicians and bureaucrats of the municipality, Svartlamon Housing Foundation was formally established, along with a foundation given the responsibility for running 3500 square metres of industrial locations left vacant by Strandveien Auto. These foundations, as well as other conditions and goals guiding the interactions between local residents and the municipality, receive their authority from the legally binding development plan for Svartlamon that was approved by Trondheim City Council in 2001.

Svartlamon Residents Association appoints one representative to the five-member board of Svartlamon Culture and Business Foundation, which is now managing the former car dealer site. One other member is appointed by the renters of office and business space, and three members represent the municipality. The purpose of the Culture and Business Foundation is to establish and rent out space for culture, small business, restoration activities, and other services. The superior goal of the foundation is to help Svartlamon become an alternative urban district with extensive possibilities of experimenting with sustainable restoration and resident participation (compare with Shaw 2005).

Resident participation

In a comment to the city council decision of October 2001 on the legally binding development plan for Svartlamon, the majority of representatives announced that:

> The principles of Local Agenda 21 have been central in the entire process leading to the development plan. Participation from the inhabitants, private businesses, and the research community has brought important competence and resources to the project. It is essential that this principle also be the foundation of future work. (Trondheim City Council 2001)[9]

Chapter 28 of Agenda 21, dealing with local authorities' initiatives in support of Agenda 21, lists objectives urging municipalities to start consultative processes with the population, and commends implementation and monitoring of 'programmes which aim at ensuring that women and youth are represented in decision-making, planning and implementation processes' (UN 1993). Dialogue, consultation, and consensus building are among the recommended activities.

The goals of Local Agenda 21 are meant to guide the processes in Svartlamon, and the development plan announces the aim to test new models of resident involvement and active participation at all levels (Trondheim Municipality 2006:1–2). Participation is a right and a duty for every resident in Svartlamon. About 40 per cent of the adults participated on a regular basis in activities of the Residents Association in 2002. A large part of the work of restoring and maintaining Svartlamon is done by the residents. These efforts are made as voluntary communal work and in working groups open to all who want to take part. In 2010 there were working groups for caretaker services, allotment of housing units, recycling and other environmentally friendly solutions, activities for children, and information and media. Members of the latter group have produced the monthly bulletin "Blant blomster og vrak" (Among Flowers and Wrecks) since 1995. The working group for culture and business activities co-operated with the municipality and the architects concerning the reconstruction and alteration of the Svartlamon Auto site. Several open dialogues and workshops were organized.

According to the residents (Svartlamon Housing Foundation 2002), the key to their involvement has been the sense of belonging and a strong sense of regarding the Svartlamon quarters as their own. The opportunity for participating in the development of a central area of Trondheim, and the right to take part in decisions on matters that directly affect their daily life, have been very motivating. Many residents take some interest in the local economy, as their rent payments go to the implementation of environmentally sustainable solutions, regeneration projects in the area, and administering the Housing Foundation in co-operation with the municipality – all of which closely affects them. Because of relatively low housing standards and obligatory own maintenance efforts, rents in Svartlamon are about half of the level in similar places elsewhere in the city.

The monthly residents meeting is the highest institution governing daily operations in the Svartlamon quarters. In the year 2000, the average number of persons attending the meetings was 16, rising to 20 in 2001 and to 36 in 2002. The attendance varied greatly in 2010, with an average of about 20. These numbers are still higher than when the area was threatened by demolition. As the level of activity grew, the length and frequency of residents meetings increased. In order to reduce the burden of meetings on each resident, Svartlamon was divided into five small neighbourhoods, which could separately handle some issues of consequence primarily to the few houses in a single neighbourhood block. The residents meetings are gatherings of peers, and consensus decisions are highly valued. In Svartlamon, as everywhere else, new ideas will meet some resistance, and the aim for consensus can lead to delays and quite 'conservative' decisions. This is somewhat paradoxical in a community meant to be experimental.

The Residents Association established in 1991 was originally the task force of Svartlamon against demolition. Since the formal victory in 1998, it has served to coordinate the activities of the inhabitants, and one of the most important tasks has been to work out plans for the future of Svartlamon. The association has a completely flat structure: everyone in the area has an equal right to meet, speak, and decide at the meetings. The association does not have a leader or an executive committee; limited practical tasks (but no political decisions) can be delegated to working groups or single persons. A chairperson and reporter are chosen for each meeting. All posts and tasks are mandated by the residents meetings.

Svartlamon Housing Foundation was established by Trondheim City Council in 2001 to manage the area. The board has five members, of which two represent Svartlamon Residents Association according to the statutes, and the other three are appointed by the executive committee of the City Council. In practice, however, a third member of the Residents Association has been appointed, giving residents de facto decision power. The Housing Foundation is the formal landlord of all housing units in Svartlamon, except for three private houses, and it has the economic and legal responsibility for managing and maintaining the buildings. The board of the foundation deals with economic issues such as budget, accounts, lending applications, engagements, and larger planning assignments. Meetings of the Residents Association deal with planning within the given economic frames, environmental tasks, organization of work, information exchange, political matters, and anything that the inhabitants might want to discuss with each other. The development plan and the ordinances of the Housing Foundation give the residents direct influence on the management and development of Svartlamon.

An important discussion in 2011 concerns the type of contract that should be offered to future inhabitants of a planned new house that won the Europan competition of 2010. Compared to rented apartments, a housing co-operative would bring in more money. It would be owned by the part-holders living in the co-operative who would be free to sell their parts. Thus the Residents Association is afraid of losing control of who is coming to live in Svartlamon.

Goals and values guiding the operation and development of Svartlamon compared to CPT

In order to identify goals and values, I sometimes refer to municipal practice as contained in public documents, and at other times to the goals, plans, and concrete practices of the residents as articulated in their Environmental Plan, for example (Svartlamon Residents Association 2005). The public documents referred to are in line with prevailing Svartlamon resident ideology. Both sources of information are therefore relevant for deciding whether or not the communicative planning for Svartlamon has been in the service of neo-liberal urban regeneration.

The points below list some values that are easily recognized in the planning and operations of Svartlamon. For each value, its relevance to the work going on in the case area is explained.

- Self-government: residents of the area struggled nearly a decade for self-government in local matters. They succeeded, and write on their web pages that 'the area is managed jointly by us who live and work here' (www.svartlamon.org/portal/index.php?section=2). It is clear from the 2002 annual report of the Housing Foundation that self-government has been a leading motivation for residents' activism (Svartlamon Housing Foundation 2002:4).
- Responsibility for the environment: the 2001 decision of the Trondheim City Council declares as a superior goal that Svartlamon should become an alternative urban district with plenty of room for experimentation regarding ecological solutions and energy conservation. 'Development of the area should be based on sustainability and ecological principles. The area is to be regulated as an urban ecological experimental district' (Trondheim City Council 2001:5). The restoration activities of the residents, for instance their emphasis on use of recycled materials, are in line with this goal, and so is the intention of keeping Svartlamon free from cars (Trondheim Municipality 2006:9) and the voluntary work in the shop selling ecological food. The residents worked out environmental guidelines for the area after three years of co-operation with the Trondheim-based SINTEF research foundation (Svartlamon Residents Association 2005). Private car ownership is limited to less than one fourth of the households.
- Identity and protection of cultural heritage: according to the development plan, it is a primary goal 'to preserve the existing cultural environment and develop it further, putting special emphasis on safeguarding the area's diversity and its character as a district of wooden houses' (Trondheim Municipality 2006:1). The timber houses are to be carefully rehabilitated, keeping the focus on modest use of resources at all levels of the process.
- Equality: all tenants in Svartlamon have equal rights and duties, and, as mentioned, the Residents Association has a completely flat structure. The plan is to achieve equal opportunities for living in the area by aiming for Universal Design of the ground floor in every new or renovated building.

- Inclusiveness: the low-cost restoration entails a deliberatively chosen lower housing standard in Svartlamon than in other parts of the city. This makes Svartlamon a possible address for people who cannot or will not pay high rents. However, new tenants must be accepted by the working group that decides on allotment of housing units. The working group selects according to criteria of age, need for a dwelling, economic and social difficulties, immigration status, artisan skills, artistic skills, and activist potential. The discretion of the working group must allow for the fact that Trondheim municipality has the right to reserve 20 per cent of the housing units for people with social and economic problems. Hence, Svartlamon is not inclusive toward everyone from the outside world. It is different for those inside, though. The accentuation of social interchange, indoor and outdoor meeting places, consensus decisions, and collective services (laundry and bathroom) promote inclusion.
- Social belonging: residents in Svartlamon see the strong sense of belonging to the area as important for enduring the long struggle of the 1990s, and as a motivation for adapting to the voluntary communal work regime. The high level of self-government and the strong focus on environmental action, which is of common interest to most residents, are assumed to foster the sense of belonging.

Accessibility is a goal in Svartlamon, as in other parts of the city, as witnessed by the wish to have more walkways and bicycle lanes connecting the area with adjacent districts. It is clear from the opposition to private car use in the area, however, that speed is not a priority. Accordingly, it is a policy to minimize the space dedicated to car traffic and parking, and transform the main access road (Strandveien) to an urban street with aesthetic qualities and facilities for bicyclists and pedestrians. A further objective is to improve the internal lanes and paths of Svartlamon.

The question is now whether the activities in Svartlamon and the values embedded in Svartlamon policies point back to the values of CPT. Self-government and equality are found on both lists of values. This is also the case with inclusiveness. Low rent for small businesses in Svartlamon helps some people enter the labour market, and low housing rent makes it easier for some people to have a decent life and feel included in society. Moreover, the Svartlamon value of social belonging is related to the experience of being part of a community, thus of being included.

The CPT values of empathy, responsiveness, fairness, and honesty do not have direct parallels on the above value list for Svartlamon. Some Svartlamon practices nevertheless point in the direction of these values. First, empathy is indicated by Svartlamon Solidarity Fund, which supports political, social, and environmental work. The fund receives about $5 monthly from each tenant household, and the money can be used to assist people who are in economic difficulties. In the important trust-building period leading up to the development plan of 2001, empathy was also expressed on the part of the municipality. One of the representatives said that the process had become an important part of her life, and that Svartlamon residents – through 'their unselfish attitudes and conduct' – had made her understand 'that it is possible to think differently from the way she had been thinking in her stable and somewhat rigid and conventional way of living' (Thorkildsen 2006:15). Second, the CPT value of responsiveness is built into the organizational forms of development planning in Svartlamon. Unresponsiveness on the part of municipal planners toward initiatives from the Residents Association would break with one of the superior goals of the development plan, which is 'to base the development on Local Agenda 21-principles and a high level of resident participation, so that competence and resources in the area can be exploited and the sense of belonging to the area will be reinforced' (Trondheim Municipality 2006:1). Third, the fairness value shines through as much in the overall ideology as in concrete Svartlamon policies. The Environmental Plan of the residents requires that fair trade products and environmentally certificated goods be chosen, if available. The central conviction is that opportunities should be provided for leading a decent life in the city even for people at the margins of the highly individualistic consumer society and the commercialized culture. The fairness value is implicit in the striving for an *alternative* urban district. Finally, I rely on a citation from Thorkildsen to shed light on the relation between the Residents Association's process policy and the CPT value of honesty:

> There are indications that both parties ... managed to be open with regard to their goals and intentions, and thus were able to marginalize actions that were purely strategic. The residents have by and large opted for an open, honest, and matter-of-fact communication practice. They have chosen to show their cards, telling the other party about their intentions and how they plan to proceed. This impression is to a great extent supported by the politicians and the municipal bureaucrats who have met with the residents throughout the planning process. They use words such as 'frank', 'businesslike', and 'well organized' when describing the practice of the residents. (Thorkildsen 2006:26–27)

A list of process-dependent substantive value principles for CPT was presented at the end of the previous section. The development plan for Svartlamon and the planning practice in the area correspond to most of the values on that list.[10] It can be concluded that several values and goals of Svartlamon planning are closely associated with central values of CPT. Self-government, equality, and inclusiveness are important common priorities.

220   *Is Communicative Planning Serving Neo-liberalism?*

Comparison of Svartlamon practices and neo-liberal urban policies

Overall, the planning ideas implemented in Svartlamon are a reaction to galloping housing prices, exaggerated and privatized consumption, the throw-away society, wasteful use of the earth's resources, the automobile society, conformist and commercialized city culture, municipal power politics at the neighbourhood level, and urban development on the terms of people with high willingness and ability to pay. Even the moderately conservative local newspaper Adresseavisen became gradually more positive to the regeneration of Svartlamon:

> The fight for Svartlamon is not only about the preservation of a few houses. The struggle is about lifestyles and the possibility of choosing a low-cost way of living, without carport and fully tiled bathroom with floor heating. It is about the possibility of opting for city life without being swallowed up by the material rat race. (Adresseavisen 24 January 1998, cited from Thorkildsen 2006:14)

The flat internal governance structure, the broad participation, and the power-sharing with the municipality are not in line with the neo-liberal NPM slogan 'let the managers manage'. The development of Svartlamon, through ecological and social experimentation, is different from neo-liberal development on the terms of private business. The municipal commitment to the subsidized low-rent policy deviates from the neo-liberal belief in allocating resources through market prices. The biggest private business in Svartlamon – a car dealer – was eventually forced to leave the place instead of expanding through demolition of old working class houses. Already from the outset, then, one would expect to find disharmony between Svartlamon practices and neo-liberal policies. In order to make the differences clearer, the points below nevertheless juxtapose each of the planning-related, neo-liberal urban regeneration policies with Svartlamon practice.

- Public-private partnerships: there is a partnership between the municipality of Trondheim and Svartlamon Residents Association. The co-operation involves private business only to a small extent, which does not suffice to see this PPP as a neo-liberal policy.
- Private sector involvement in financing and operating transport infra-structure: not used in Svartlamon.
- Privatization of public space and sales-boosting exclusion: the tendency in Svartlamon seems to lead in the opposite direction. For example, part of the open area bordering the World War II submarine bunker Dora 1 is proposed as public space that should be seen as an attraction not only for people in the area, but for the whole city and visitors from other places

(Europan Norge 2009). However, a change in the use of the existing rail tracks has been vetoed by the Norwegian National Rail Administration. The Environmental Plan calls for as many attractive common meeting places as possible both indoors and outdoors (Svartlamon Residents Association 2005).

- Privately governed and secured neighbourhoods: even if Svartlamon is partly governed by the Residents Association, it is very different from a gated community. Svartlamon wants to open up to its surroundings, not to be secluded. A new pathway has been built under the railway. Moreover, security against crime is not a big issue, and the policy is to keep lots open rather than to close them off.
- Gentrification: not going on in Svartlamon. The decision of the City Council before restoration started was that: 'Present inhabitants can continue to stay in the area. Svartlamon is meant to be for people who are in need of cheap housing. Subletting is not permitted' (Trondheim City Council 2001:5). The biggest new house in Svartlamon is a five storey construction in solid wood. Far from being a gentrification object, this building, financed by the municipality of Trondheim, contains cheap flats for youth and small collectives. Gentrification is made virtually impossible by the Residents Association's control of who is moving into the area.
- Flexible zoning and special business-friendly zones: zoning in Svartlamon is flexible in that a mixture of functions – for example, housing, culture-based activities, and small businesses – is allowed. The low rents are helpful when setting up a small shop, but there is no room for big business, tax exemptions, or high-standard municipal service provision as in the Business Improvement Districts mentioned in Chapter 5.
- Quangos organizing market-oriented urban development: quangos are not involved, and the urban development in Svartlamon is not market-oriented.
- Property-led urban regeneration: development in Svartlamon is not property-led, but instead sticks to a plan for the entire area.
- Competitive bidding: some contracts with carpenters, plumbers, and other firms have been entered into after a tendering process. Restoration based on competitive bidding has not made much of an imprint on the area, as the inhabitants of Svartlamon have an obligation to do most of the rehabilitation themselves.
- Urban development by attracting the 'creative class': one aim in the plan for Svartlamon is to attract people creative in music, theatre and other cultural branches through well-suited locales and low rents. The segment of the creative class seeking out Svartlamon for a living area does not have much purchasing power, however. The plan for the area does not lead to reallocation of public funds from supporting the needy to

pampering the creative elite. The development plan for Svartlamon is in itself a social project. Internationally, planners have feared that attempts to attract the creative class would imply a shift in investment from social projects to strategies for place promotion and competition for talent. There is an element of place promotion in the municipal dealings with Svartlamon. At the time of rezoning the area to housing, the protests against demolition had grown to a mass movement and got publicity on a national scale; it was a question of avoiding giving Trondheim a bad reputation. Later, a number of delegations from other cities visited Svartlamon to learn about ways of realizing Local Agenda 21 in practice, and to see the massive new wooden house which has received an architectural prize.

The above list of comparisons shows little overlap between the planning policies implemented in Svartlamon and the 10 neo-liberal policies for urban regeneration listed in Chapter 5. It can therefore be concluded that communicative planning in Svartlamon has not enhanced neo-liberal urban development in Trondheim.

It may be objected that the chosen example, Svartlamon, is not typical, and that its history and eventual support from the municipality of Trondheim allow practices and policies that make it seductively easy to see its anti-neo-liberal profile. In most other cases of urban development guided by communicative planning, the extent of correspondence with neo-liberal policies and business interests would presumably be more difficult to judge. However, the Svartlamon case is offered in order to illustrate how one can reason when the task is to determine whether or not one particular communicative planning effort enhances the continued spread of neo-liberal urban development. This case is not presented to indicate or suggest that most communicative planning processes result in plans that are in opposition to neo-liberal urban policies, but to suggest a method for studying the subject. Whether processes inspired by CPT commonly result in such plans is an empirical question that I do not have the knowledge to answer.

Conclusion

It is easier to assess the effects of communicative planning on the neo-liberalization of cities when some other aspects of the relationship between planning and neo-liberalism have been clarified. The neo-liberal view on public planning was therefore outlined, and planning scholars' critique of CPT's alleged links to neo-liberalism was surveyed, before a strategy was proposed for enquiring into the charges against CPT for running the errands of neo-liberals. It is the main purpose of this chapter to develop such a strategy for dealing with accusations that CPT is unwittingly supporting ideologies and policies whose values are quite different from CPT's own.

The critique of being at the service of neo-liberalism should be addressed in CPT by bringing procedural and substantive recommendations closer together. It must be made evident that what is required from the plan (the outcome) is grounded in substantive value principles that are closely associated with the values behind the process design.

The proposed strategy does not aim to show that communicative planning is unlikely to bolster ideologies deviating from its own theoretical core. Instead it employs a value approach to investigate whether this might be the case for particular planning efforts and, if so, it proposes a solution to the problem. Whether the critique of CPT turns out to be valid or misconceived, planners should be warned not to approve of solutions without first taking a critical look at the role played by developers and other powerful actors in the communicative process. In his early books, Forester (1989, 1993a) tried to make it clear that a capitalist economy always provides a structurally unequal context for planning. The critique of CPT for serving neo-liberalism is a reminder that appeals to dialogue which ignore structural inequality are disingenuous and cannot be expected to be part of a democratic bulwark against the hegemony of particular interests. If this attention to structured inequality gets lost, then indeed appeals to dialogue facilitate neo-liberal market-oriented problem-solving. In other words, there needs to be a critical side to communicative planning. Accepting a toothless kind of CPT which lets conformity to market regulation assume the mantle of flexibility and furthermore fails 'to engage in the critical analysis necessary to inform planners of the possible range of responses would be to confirm the claim of planning's redundancy by detractors of the right' (McDermott 1998:633).

Planners can have some responsibility both for the plan and for the process leading up to it. Critical pragmatists must be prepared to question outcomes that break with the substantive value principles of CPT even if no party complains about communicative distortions in the process.

In rounding off this chapter, it should be conceded that even in seemingly straightforward cases like Svartlamon, some doubt about the anti-neo-liberal effects of communicative planning may linger, as can be seen when the assessment is widened from the small planning area to the entire city. The possibility is that neo-liberals and the business community may see their interests well served by concentrating counter-cultural elements, rebellious youth, and low-paying tenants to a particular district, especially one which has not got much attraction for most of the urban population anyway. Even if neo-liberals occasionally lose a battle, they may regard this as a necessary cost helping them to win the war. This suspicion cannot effectively be removed by studying single processes and plans for small districts, such as the case analyzed in this chapter.

It is difficult for planning theorists to find protection against the suggestion that CPT *unintentionally* enhances neo-liberalism. Proponents of neo-liberal ideology might exploit the ideas of CPT in ways that the theorists did not anticipate. This points to the subject matter of Chapter 8, dealing with the responsibility of planning theorists for the end use of their theories.

Notes

1.   Another relationship between neo-liberalism and communicative planning consists of neo-liberal (Hayekian) critique of citizen participation, deliberative democracy and, by implication, communicative planning, as put forward by Pennington (2003, 2004), for example. Such a critique is not dealt with in this chapter, although it is interesting in the present context that deliberative democracy based on Habermas's ideas has been seen as a challenge to neo-liberal ideology and subjected to criticism from that perspective.

2.   On the other hand, there are scholars who see a purely antagonistic relationship between neo-liberalism and communicative planning. Miller contends that:

    (U)nder neoliberalism we are seeing a fundamental shift away from communicatively rational, democratic forms of social action coordination based on the model of the (urban) public citizen, toward more instrumentally and strategically rational forms of social action coordination based on the model of the (suburban) private consumer. (Miller 2006:210)

3.   Similar points about outsourcing and legitimacy were made by McCann some years earlier, but then in the context of a critique of collaborative visioning in planning processes. McCann (2001) saw such visioning as an attempt by local elites to negotiate the contradiction between privatization and the rhetoric of consensus-based decision-making (ibid.208).

4.   Swain and Tait (2007) contend that trust in the planning system and in the planners' ability to provide expert knowledge about land-use planning issues has been denigrated (ibid.242). However, somewhat more optimistically than Mees, they regard communicative planning as valuable for rebuilding trust that has been eroded in a pluralist society permeated by neo-liberal ideology.

5.   Critique of overly proceduralist reasoning is also brought against approaches to deliberative democracy, which has inspired CPT (Cohen 1997). O'Neill (2000) maintains that normative frameworks that bring certain substantive features of democratic life into focus, should supplement Habermas's procedural approach. Estlund (2005) contends that influential strands in democratic theory – Habermas's approach among them – claim to rely only on the values of democracy itself, and to eschew independent standards for deciding which political decisions are good. He finds that the normative plausibility of these theories depends on their acceptance of a role for procedure-independent standards of good outcomes. Gilabert (2005) defends deliberative democracy and aims to show that its proceduralism is not an empty formalism by spelling out the substantive dimension of deliberation. Some contributions on democracy focus on deliberative outcomes – such as agreement, meta-consensus, and inter-subjective rationality (Niemeyer and Dryzek 2007). Meta-consensus means agreement about the nature of the issue at hand, and inter-subjective rationality means

that individuals have taken into account all the relevant considerations determined by meta-consensus. These process outcomes are different from the substantive planning outcomes dealt with here.

6. The identification of a core set of values to guide both process and outcome is the main idea adopted from Brettschneider (2005, 2006). In other respects the present approach differs from hers. Brettschneider argues that a set of procedure-independent core values constitute the democratic ideal; for her, the foundation is the substantive values.

7. The Universal Declaration of Human Rights (www.un.org/en/documents/udhr/) contains many paragraphs that promote values corresponding to the list of process-dependent substantive CPT value principles. There are clauses about democracy, liberty, freedom of movement, recognition, and equality – for example, equal right to public service – and furthermore, the Human Rights call for protection against arbitrary interference, for instance, against being arbitrarily deprived of one's property. Individuals should also have protection of social and cultural rights indispensable for personal dignity.

8. The following description draws heavily on the information material from Europan Norge (2009), compiled for an architectural competition.

9. Agenda 21 is an action plan of the United Nations related to sustainable development; it was an outcome of the UN Conference on Environment and Development held in Rio de Janeiro, Brazil, in 1992. Some national and state governments have legislated or advised that local authorities take steps to implement the plan locally. Such programmes are known as Local Agenda 21.

10. The comments in this note concern a few points where there might be some doubt about the correspondence between the substantive CPT value principles and Svartlamon planning: First, the plan should respect what is culturally essential to affected groups. It is neither sacred things nor the cultural heritage of the young activists themselves that are at stake in this planning process, rather it is the heritage of a group they identify with: the poor working class people once living in this former industrial part of town. Second, the plan should accommodate diverse lifestyles. The point is not that a wide range of lifestyles should be present in Svartlamon, but that the governance of this area helps to increase the presence of varied lifestyles in the city, which it does. Third, the plan should contain something for each affected group. Svartlamon became a show-case for the municipality of Trondheim with regard to its work on Local Agenda 21. Svartlamon residents got non-profit housing, environmentally sustainable regeneration, and participatory power. The car dealer Strandveien Auto received about $4 million in compensation.

PART III
RESPONSIBILITIES

As a consequence of the criticism raised against CPT in the first two parts of the book, planning theorists might come to wonder what can reasonably be expected of them. What does it mean to act and to make a decision in a fully responsible manner? In what conditions can individuals be said to have responsibility for the final consequences of their actions? Are these conditions likely to be fulfilled in the case of end-uses of planning theories? The purpose of Part III is to help planning theorists reflect on responsibilities associated with their daily work and its consequences.

Part III looks at very different ways in which questions of responsibility come up in the professional workings of communicative planning theorists. These questions spring from the theorists' delivery of ideas shaping planning practice, their promotion of inclusion and hospitality which can create democratic risks when pursued into the extreme, and their obligations as teachers, colleagues and social critics in academia. I argue that the way planning scholars deal with responsibilities in these areas affects the status and social acceptance of critical planning theory. Were planning theory inconsequential, there would be no point in making it critical or feeling responsible for its effects. Significance breeds responsibility, and responsibility is a motivation for being critical.

The views among scientists and other theorists have differed a great deal concerning their responsibility for the final practical consequences of their work. Neffe writes about Albert Einstein in the latter's very productive years during the First World War:

> Although he adamantly opposed war and all things military, he fell silent on the subject of military weapons and what they owed to science. 'As long as I am interested in working along lines of research ... the practical aspect, that is, every practical result that is found simultaneously or arises out of it later, is a matter of complete indifference to me', he once said. He drew no distinction between basic theoretical research of the type he conducted and applied science, which uses 'pure' knowledge to produce objects and systems – including gas grenades and atomic bombs. (Neffe 2007:253)

The focus of Chapter 8 is on planning theorists' responsibility for the end-uses of the theories they produce. Recent criticism of CPT alleges that it may sometimes serve authorities in repressive ways (as can other planning theories), and thus not always fulfil the communicative planning theorists' aim of empowering the citizenry. This is the background for introducing the concept of 'dual planning theory', which is compared to the dichotomy of light/dark sides of planning. What should planning theorists do to protect against misuse of their ideas? Responsibility for consequences depends on theorists' possibilities of predicting and affecting end-uses, prompting discussion of unintended effects and the problem of many hands.

Chapter 9 deals with communicative planning theorists' responsibility for laying the groundwork for inclusive planning processes. They should develop frameworks for public planning that invigorate democracy by rendering the public realm more conducive to lay involvement and deliberation. I explore the potential of Emmanuel Levinas's ethical theory for being a lodestar for communicative planning theorists. The comparison with Habermasian discourse ethics reveals profound differences concerning their views on reciprocity, dialogue, and responsibility for the Other. The uncompromising inclusion and hospitality advocated by Levinas is a challenge to liberal democracy. An opening for reconciling Levinas's belief in responsibility for the Other with practical applications of CPT is created by his admission of the need for making compromises in the political realm. There, the planner has responsibilities toward several people and therefore cannot give unlimited attention to a single Other. Hospitality and thus inclusion cannot be unconditional in practice. The problem of setting the terms is clarified by examining the concept of toleration.

Chapter 10 concentrates on decisions, and Jacques Derrida's ideas on responsible decisions provide the basis for the analysis. Planning theorists have responsibilities as educators, and issues of improvisation and creativity, critical theory, and reflection on professional practice are discussed. Teaching should not deal only with the need to plan but also accentuate the need for changing plans. The responsibilities of planning theorists as university faculty are multi-faceted, as they are directed towards colleagues, students, administrative leaders, and the general public. The chapter must thus be selective, and the issues dealt with relate to truth-searching and independence from strong outside interests, such as the armed forces and corporate industry. It is argued that the independent role of university scholars as social interpreters and critics comes under pressure with the entry of neo-liberal ideas into academia. The commercialization of universities gives less favourable conditions for critical theory.

8

Responsibility for the End-use of Theory

How can a discussion of the responsibility for end-uses of theories contribute to the revival of critical planning theory? Planning theories will to some extent be used in the shaping of practice, whether in planning or in other kinds of political-administrative practice. These practices will be less than ideal. Some will have obvious weaknesses and therefore be met with deserved criticism. The repercussions on CPT (and thus critical planning theory) will presumably be more balanced if it is made clear that planning theorists have, in general, limited information about and limited power to influence the end-uses of their theories.

I argue in this chapter that communicative planning theorists most often cannot take full responsibility for use of their ideas in processes that might possibly lead to co-optation, implementation of neo-liberal policies, and agreements that are unfair. This contributes to the revival of CPT as a critical theory.

Introduction on the responsibility of planning theorists

This chapter discusses in what sense planning theorists are responsible for end-uses of their theories, and the circumstances in which they are responsible for the consequences of proposing design of planning processes in accordance with theories they have constructed and offered to the public. Questions of responsibility usually arise when certain actions cause problems for another party, especially when the problems were foreseeable to some extent, and the actor may have had the power to prevent them. Can planning theorists be morally blamed for the critiques they make, the theories they produce, or for the socially undesirable consequences of the use of these theories? The purpose of the chapter is to stimulate a debate on ethics in the field of planning theory by encouraging planning theorists to reflect on the social impact of their research and on the proper response to various kinds of applications.[1]

Any researcher putting forward new ideas should be subject to the critique of peers. This also goes for planning scholars presenting their thoughts in the form of critique of others' theories. Does the critic have a responsibility for coming up with an alternative theory that is better than the one being criticized? I do not think so. Very worthwhile critique would in many cases be delayed if a presentation of that critique had to wait until a better solution was found. Besides, striking and appropriate critique is likely to stimulate the creativity of other researchers so that an improved theory will appear more quickly. This is what counts, not that the improvement is hit upon by the critic. The research process moves forward in a spiral of critique, counter-critique, and new hypotheses and suggestions. But I see no reason to demand that any particular scholar should be equally heavily involved in each phase of the process.

The situation of planners may be very different from that of planning theorists. Consider a planner working in a textbook-like rationalistic (synoptic) planning process: The goals of both the plan and the planning process are externally given, and the task assigned to the planner is to examine different strategies and tell the politicians how available means can best be combined and used in order to reach the goals set by them. The planner provides recommendations but does not decide on the plan. Juridically, although perhaps not morally, the planner avoids responsibility because goals are formally set by others, and the important decisions are formally made by others. The planners cannot be entirely exempt from moral responsibility, however, as their expertise and agenda-setting power are likely to influence decision-makers. Moreover, if the planners mindlessly let the goals of others determine their work, they are acting irresponsibly. The situation of the planning theorist is different from the one just sketched for the planner. The purpose of theory building is often determined by the theorists themselves. Furthermore, the theorist can also be considered the decision-maker in the sense that she decides whether the theory she has in mind should be developed and made known to others. Hence, the theorist cannot entirely deny responsibility.[2]

Planning theorists might be seen as responsible for informing practising planners and other parties to planning processes about how their theories can be transformed into actions for designing and guiding planning processes and for making plans. This task seems to be particularly hard to evade for communicative planning theorists. It is an aspect of 'relational responsibility' (McNamee and Gergen 1999), a concept that is of particular interest to communicative planners because so much of their work is about tending relationships. In relational responsibility, the relational process replaces the individual as the central unit of concern. This invites practices that put meaning-building conversation in the place of isolation and alienation. Participants in deliberation have relational responsibility for the 'means of valuing, sustaining, and creating forms of relationship out of which common meanings – and thus moralities – can take wing' (ibid.xi).

It is instructive to outline the conditions for ascribing moral responsibility, as a point of reference for ensuing examples and analysis. Forester (1989:xi) linked responsibility to power when telling the reader what his book is about, namely 'the vulnerabilities of democracy, about power and professional responsibility...', and responsibility can indeed be seen as the ethical side of power. Planning theorists are here considered responsible for particular consequences in so far as:

1. their theoretical work is a cause of these consequences; and
2. their theoretical work is not carried out in ignorance of these consequences or under compulsion.

Very similar claims are put forward by Jonas (1984:90) and Thompson (2005:18). Jonas sums up the two points by stating that responsibility is a function of power and knowledge (op.cit.123). There are strong and weak causal links, and there are degrees of knowledge of these links and degrees of power to affect consequences. The degree of moral responsibility varies, but in principle, 'responsibility extends as far as our powers do in space and time' (Ricoeur 2000:29).

Condition (1) above can be met even if several other causal factors would also have to be present for the particular consequences to follow. Requiring that the consequences in question would not have been realized but for the work of the planning theorist, might be too strong. Responsibility can follow from facilitating a certain consequence even if not being decisive in bringing it about. The degree of compulsion in condition (2) is usually linked to the theorist's role in a research project or an educational programme, and the pressure to participate would rarely be strong enough to exempt theorists from moral responsibility. The point is that construction of the theory in question must be under the planning theorist's control for questions of responsibility to arise. The problem of ignorance in condition (2) is linked to the problem of unintended consequences. Ignorance counts as an excuse only when the ignorance is not negligent.

Many aspects of planning theory have been criticized; for example, the weak link between planning theory and planning practice, and the undue preoccupation with process at the expense of substance. Accusations of universalism are also put forward: There is an alleged tendency among planning theorists to write as if the analysis and procedural recommendations are equally relevant everywhere, both in the North-Atlantic countries and the global South (Watson 2002, 2006, Yiftachel 2006). Claims regarding the theorists' responsibility can be derived from much of this critique (Jazeel and McFarlane 2010, Raghuram et al. 2009) and indeed from many other sources: Are planning theorists who argue for restrictive development practices to protect environmental amenities responsible for the increased housing prices resulting from constrained supply (Adams and Tiesdell 2010:197)?

The considerations mentioned above relate to all procedural planning theory and indicate that the need for thinking through responsibilities applies to planning theorists in general. This chapter nevertheless focuses on theorists writing about communicative (collaborative) planning, which is the mode of planning that has been most discussed over the last couple of decades. Although CPT has been subjected to some criticism for inviting misuse (see the next section), there is no reason to assume that CPT has led to more undesirable social effects than other approaches to planning. Rationalistic (synoptic) planning, for example, is blamed for repressive practices in many places (Kamete 2007, Misselwitz and Weizman 2003, Yiftachel 1995a).

The train of thought throughout the chapter goes as follows. The next section discusses features of CPT which critics think have detrimental effects. Since such effects are in stark contrast to the good intentions of planning theorists, they raise issues of responsibility. Thereafter, we turn to the conditions limiting theorists' information about end-use. The concept of 'dual planning theory' is introduced to complement the light-side/dark-side dichotomy and help analyze the equivocality that affects responsibility by making prediction of end-use more difficult. Unintended consequences make prediction a very blunt tool with regard to the application of theories. Moreover, planning theories are read, re-read, circulated, picked up in new settings, criticized, and re-written. Reading and re-writing are creative actions in the sense that new meanings are created. Simultaneously, new possibilities for applications emerge, which may have been wholly unexpected by the authors when they published the theory in its original form. This affects their responsibility. A separate section analyzes conditions that limit the theorists' power to affect end-use. The section brings up the issue of how the involvement of many hands and intermediary actors complicates the question of responsibility. So do the lack of patent or monitoring and the loose theory-practice relationship.

Critique of communicative planning theory: three examples

The purpose of this section is to show examples of criticism levelled against CPT as a backcloth for analyzing the responsibilities of planning theorists. I make no attempt to counter the objections. The three critiques suggest that CPT can serve masters with contrasting goals, and the examples will be used in the next section to explain the concept of 'dual planning theory'. The examples criticize CPT for co-optation of activists, for facilitating the development of neo-liberal economic governance, and for illusory search for consensus across incompatible value positions, respectively.

The co-optation example

This subordinate section considers the criticism raised against both CPT and the earlier advocacy planning theory for leading spokespersons of protesting groups into long-lasting and pacifying processes of deliberation and negotiation. Involvement in such processes tends to co-opt group leaders and take the sting out of local direct action. This criticism against CPT is chosen because it is a well-known point of departure, and because it sheds light both upon responsibility and upon ambiguous effects of theory, and because it is the only example in this chapter where it is quite obvious that the communicative planning theorists knew about the problems at the root of the criticism.

Advocacy planning has been criticized for diverting the poor from their most effective forms of action. After having presented several discouraging cases, Piven (1970) goes on to say that:

> What all of this suggests is that involving local groups in elaborate planning procedures is to guide them into a narrowly circumscribed form of political action, and precisely that form for which they are least equipped. What is laid out for the poor when their advocate arrives is a strategy of political participation which, to be effective, requires powerful group support, stable organization, professional staff, and money – precisely those resources which the poor do not have...
>
> (T)he planning advocates ... have not added to the political force of the ghetto. Quite the contrary, for the advocates are coaxing ghetto leaders off the streets, where they might make trouble. The absorbing and elaborate planning procedures which follow are ineffective in compelling concessions, but may be very effective indeed in dampening any impulse toward disruptive action which has always been the main political recourse of the very poor. (Piven 1970:35)

According to Piven, the effect of advocacy planning may well be to absorb slum leadership and render it ineffective. Conflict is deflected by preoccupying protesters with procedures that pose little threat to entrenched interests and instead promote the political stability that serves the city elites.

It is important in the present context that communicative planning pulls protesting local people into the same sort of long-lasting deliberation and negotiation as does advocacy planning. In fact, this critique can be strengthened in the case of communicative planning and especially collaborative planning: the more emphasis that is put on communicative rationality and consensus building, the less room is left for partisan protests and the fight of the under-privileged for their own interests without modifying their grievances into politically correct public interest terms.

If the above critique is valid, communicative planning – like Davidoff's (1965) theory of advocacy planning – can be used to weaken spontaneous protest and direct action as weapons of deprived groups, and thus make it harder for them to enhance their living conditions (see Gunson and Collins 1997 for an example). CPT might then support city authorities through top-down initiatives, as well as backing bottom-up efforts initiated by citizens. This is referred to as the co-optation example later in the chapter. It indicates that the typical CPT paternalism mentioned in Chapter 1, asserting that everyone should participate in dialogical planning processes for their own good, is not innocent.

Even if co-optation is a risk that communicative planning theorists should be aware of, the fuzziness of the causalities makes it unclear whether they can be held morally responsible. Piven-inspired criticism and the experience from advocacy planning had, however, been available to the planning community for a decade or more when CPT began to spread through planning journals. Communicative planning theorists can hardly claim ignorance of the possibility that similar criticism might apply to communicative planning. However, since the co-optation issue is still contested, this diminishes any responsibility of communicative planning theorists, should spokespersons for under-privileged groups be co-opted through the communicative processes prescribed.

The neo-liberalism example

The general problem exemplified in this subordinate section is that well-meant contributions to deliberative democracy at the local level might have adverse effects on democracy at higher administrative levels and in the long run. A theory that can simultaneously serve incompatible interests is more likely to be in demand in such situations.

A standard Marxist critique of public land-use planning argued that the social function of planning is to make the capitalist markets run smoothly in order to enhance the perpetual accumulation of capital (Scott and Roweis 1977). Bengs (2005a, 2005b) and Purcell (2008) restate this critique, specifically targeting communicative planning. They contend that CPT flourishes due to the prevalence of neo-liberal ideology, and in particular neo-liberalism's need for legitimacy and for establishing social institutions that match and advance urban land markets and the free flow of investment. The critique raised by Bengs and Purcell was presented in Chapter 7, noting the core point that a planning regime with a minimum of predefined restrictions and guidelines and ample possibilities to strike deals at the local level might be in conformity with the neo-liberal ideals.

The critique of CPT for serving neo-liberalism gains credibility if communicative planners invite local people affected by proposed land developments to join in consensus-building deliberation without having an effective strategy for how to help them stand up to real estate interests and resourceful developers. This is exactly the objection most often voiced against CPT (Flyvbjerg and Richardson 2002, Huxley and Yiftachel 2000). The problem is how to hold back those trying to influence the planned solution by leaning on their power base instead of on arguments that sound reasonable to the wider public. For all its good intentions of counteracting such behaviour by fighting communicative distortions through critical questioning (Forester 1993a) and by decreasing the political transaction costs of fair-playing actors and groups that stand to lose from the project (see Chapter 2), critics are not convinced that such measures can be used by communicative planners in ways that are effective.

The critical points above, to the extent that they are valid, readily identify CPT as a theory that diametrically opposite interests might try to exploit to their advantage. CPT is meant to back bottom-up planning, but it might also, according to the critics, support top-down planning that serves the entrepreneurial interests of private business and public authorities. This is referred to as the neo-liberalism example later in the chapter. The neo-liberalism example suggests that CPT may serve authorities as well as grass root organizations. Several examples from recent planning-related literature confirm that theories and concepts sometimes cross borders and are introduced in contexts that are very different from those in which they originated. The travelling concepts may also support purposes and interests they were not meant to serve. For example, Whitzman and Perkovic (2010) recount the changing use of 'women's safety audits', which were intended to support local activists in identifying safe and unsafe places, and to suggest how places that are unsafe for women can be improved. Women's safety audits are a participatory planning tool that enjoyed rapid international diffusion. However, in new settings, the tool soon lost its focus on gender and activism. The emphasis on empowering and listening to the voices of the people most affected by violence and insecurity faded. In some cases the once active women's safety audits were turned into a means for furthering traditional conservative policy: 'in communities without strong women's groups it became easy for police or gender-neutral crime prevention organizations to "act in a traditional 'protector' paternalistic pattern", wherein safety audits became "opportunities for the police to show women dangerous places to avoid"' (ibid.227).[3]

Returning to the accusations for serving neo-liberalism, some questions can be posed: what if the planning theorist warns the local people about the potential advantages that developers with access to money and expertise can have from deliberative, consensus-building processes instead of strict laws, rules, and politically binding plans? What if the theorists try to devise ways of counteracting developer power in planning processes? Critics might say that this is all very well but it is not a solution to the problem. It does not change the logic of the game between developers, planners, politicians and local people. Warnings and theoretical analysis of interactions do not necessarily change anything in practice, as inadequate information may not be the reason why outcomes tend to be biased in favour of developers. Even with clearer warning and more critical analysis, it might well be rational for the players of the planning game to continue acting as they do, instead of changing their behaviour. Critics contend that in order to produce outcomes that are contrary to neo-liberal interests, one might have to change institutions (the rules of the game), for example, by introducing a less flexible planning regime. However, this is not the intention of communicative planning theorists.

So, is it at all possible for communicative planning theorists to avoid moral responsibility for promoting neo-liberalism in their writings if the critics have a valid point? The position taken here is that theorists writing as protagonists of communicative planning have some moral responsibility to the extent that there is a causal relationship between the implementation of CPT and a stakeholder-led regime for land development and thus facilitation of neo-liberalism, and also to the extent that such a relationship could be foreseen by the theorists. However, it is controversial both whether there is such a causal relationship between CPT, investor interests and neo-liberalism and, if there is, whether communicative planning theorists could reasonably be expected to foresee it and act upon it.

One element in both the co-optation example and the neo-liberalism example is that local people who feel threatened by a plan are somehow led to sit peacefully at the table and let themselves be outmanoeuvred by their stronger counterparts. Some scholars blame the putative emphasis on consensus building in CPT, and the criticism of this practice is delineated in the next subordinate section.

The consensus example

This sub-section considers the critique raised against CPT for stimulating planners to aim for unrealistic and harmful consensus, thereby downplaying inherent problems of exclusion (Connelly and Richardson 2004, Dahlberg 2005). Except for the bracketing-of-power critique, this is the objection most often launched against CPT. The important critical points are listed in the section on strife, consensus, and the public interest in Chapter 1. The critique is only briefly revisited here to clarify what communicative planning theorists might be held responsible for.

Critics see consensus as utopian, excluding, necessarily shallow, and as a threat to freedom.[4] As a whole, the criticism implies that consensus can only be illusory, which is just as well, because actually achieved consensus would be increasingly repressive the more significant the differences eradicated in the process. In any case, consensus formation as an emancipating and empowering project cannot succeed, according to the critics. Communicative planning theorists would be responsible for leading practitioners astray if the critics are right, and if the theorists should have foreseen the difficulties of obtaining meaningful consensus.[5]

Moreover, if assimilation of identities and harmonization of interests are furthered by planning processes to the extent that consensus is occasionally achieved, these processes of deliberative democracy would challenge other aspects of democratic systems – for example, the authority of representatives elected by majority vote. As several critics see it, communicative planning theorists would be responsible for eroding the foundation of freedom more than they consolidate it.

Should the criticism in this consensus example be considered valid, it still does not show CPT to be indiscriminately on the side of both top-down state initiatives and bottom-up planning processes initiated by local civil society. It is not obvious that political and economic authorities stand to gain if representative government is devitalized. Besides, it might be easier for elites to govern by central directives than having to trust the outcome of myriads of local consensus processes. Furthermore, in consensus building modelled on communicative rationality, the authorities' superior availability of legal and economic expertise would mean less, since local conceptions of fairness might easily deviate from legal reasoning. It would vary with the situation at hand whether it is the authorities or the grass roots who would reap the benefits from reconciling differences in a consensus-building process instead of treating them as 'agonist strife' (Pløger 2004).

Conditions limiting theorists' information about end-use

Planning theorists' information about end-use is limited for several reasons, three of which are discussed in this section:

- It is unknown who will use the theory. More specifically, this is the problem of 'dual planning theory': a planning theory is here defined as dual when it can be used for organizing both bottom-up and top-down processes. Such theories are likely to serve very different masters, purposes, and ideologies. This makes it difficult to predict applications.
- The effects of applying the theory are not known. More specifically, this is the problem of unintended consequences: theory travels, and with modern media, search motors, and publication channels, a particular planning theory can be picked up on the other side of the world, possibly by interests

outside urban planning. Its application can have unexpected consequences in foreign cultures, political systems, and professional traditions.

• The directions in which the theory will be developed are not known. More specifically, this is the problem of creative reading and re-writing: every reader has his or her own reference points and interprets a theoretical exposition slightly differently from the original author. The theory can be developed by cross-fertilization with other theories and be re-written as a hybrid with effects that could not be foreseen by the original theorist.

Dual communicative planning theory

Dark-side studies have often focused more on planning practice (Graham 2005, Yiftachel 1995b) than on planning theory. Nevertheless, it is Allmendinger and Gunder's (2005) critical study of planning theory that is most useful here, as it contains a conceptual discussion of what 'the dark side of planning' might mean. Referring to Yiftachel (1995a, 1995b), the starting point is the widely shared interest in individual liberties and social equity, environmental sustainability, and improved quality of places, including residential amenity. The term 'dark-side planning' denotes practices that are contrary to these causes of action and instead involve social repression, exclusion, economic retardation or environmental degradation (Allmendinger and Gunder 2005:97). The distinction of light and dark planning reflects opinions of what enhances or degrades people's living conditions, hence 'our ideological illusions and fetishes as to what constitutes good or bad' (ibid.108). While, for example, civil/military is a bisection of categories that can be distinguished by using criteria approaching objectivity, the dichotomy of light/ dark planning is based on a normative and subjective categorization.

Allmendinger and Gunder (2005:105) seem inclined to delimit use of the term 'dark side' to planning with a *systematic* orientation towards repression and exclusion. It is this kind of planning they find it particularly appropriate for academics and others to explore and expose. Plans that degrade living conditions can also follow from the hijacking of planning by powerful stakeholders. This, however, seems to Allmendinger and Gunder 'a price we sometimes pay for having an "open" process focused, initially at least, at the local level' (ibid.). The labelling of this more haphazard phenomenon as 'dark-side' planning is to them like paying too little respect to the cases revealing systematic and procedural prejudice. Although Allmendinger and Gunder's distinction is useful, the line between systematic orientation and hijacking by powerful stakeholders in special situations is not always easily drawn. Somehow the situation at hand often tends to seem special. The 'haphazard' hijacking of urban plans by strong developers in 'special' situations might turn out to be typical.

The term 'dual-use planning theory' – or 'dual planning theory' for short – is adapted from 'dual-use technology', which refers to tools and techniques that have both military purposes and civil commercial applications (Alic 1994). Considerations of dual use play an important role in technology transfer policy. For example, the International Atomic Energy Agency attempts to monitor Iran's nuclear programme, which is allegedly based on dual-use technology. And the technology used for synthesizing poliovirus in the laboratory and producing weakened vaccine strains fast, can also help terrorists manufacture viruses such as smallpox (New Scientist 2006).

'Military' is too narrow a category for characterizing the authorities whose interests are served by various planning theories. When importing the term 'dual-use' to planning theory, it is therefore proposed here to substitute the duality civil/military by bottom-up/top-down; that is, civil society at the grass roots as opposed to civil and military authorities defined as the upper echelons of formal hierarchies. Planning theory underpinning bottom-up initiatives organizes the strategic efforts of a variety of civil society actors, such as local protest groups, national environmental associations, residents' associations, NGOs, and social movements. Their purposes are sometimes insurgent or counter-hegemonic, thereby challenging established systems or protecting life-worlds. Planning theory espousing top-down initiatives organizes the strategic efforts of public or private authorities in politics and the economy. Policies managed from the top might favour the elites, paternalistically aim to benefit ordinary people, or actually reflect the stated needs of the populace.

'Dual planning theory' is defined as planning theory with both top-down and bottom-up applications; it offers insightful descriptions and recommendations for organizing important aspects of both kinds of processes. Authorities and grass-roots organizations can both see their interests well served by processes moulded from dual planning theory. Because of this, it is hard to foresee who will apply a dual theory, what purpose it will serve, and which interests will reap the biggest advantage from it. This uncertainty is what makes dual planning theory a potentially interesting concept in the context of responsibility.

The above definition of dual theory does not deny that planning from the top can provide benefits to the public at large, or that authorities can give street level planning initiatives sympathetic consideration. There is no basis for associating top-down with 'bad' and bottom-up with 'good'. The purpose of introducing 'dual planning theory' is to offer a conceptual tool that is less value-laden and normative than the light/dark distinction but still draws attention to the unpredictable outcomes of actions derived from planning theory. The concept of dual planning theory would not deserve much attention if the interests of government and governed were always in harmony; in such a perfectly functioning democracy there would be no real duality. As it is, however, it is worth pondering how one and the same planning theory can be found suitable for organizing processes initiated and managed from the grassroots as well as from head offices in 'agonistic' societies characterized by conflicting interests (Hillier 2003).[6]

Since the duality of some theories adds to the difficulty of predicting applications, researchers working on dual theories can to a lesser degree be held responsible for practical impacts. Awareness of possible dualities should nevertheless alert planning theorists to what Alpern (1983:41) calls the Principle of Care: 'Other things being equal, one should exercise due care to avoid contributing to significantly harming others'. Not only should one try to foresee the harm that may result from one's theoretical work; one should also take precautions to avoid such harm, and be ready and willing to make sacrifices in order to minimize it. As a corollary to the Principle of Care, Alpern states that: 'When one is in position to contribute to greater harm or when one is in a position to play a more critical part in producing harm, one must exercise greater care to avoid so doing' (ibid.42). This corollary warns influential planning theorists to take extra care when potentially harmful dual use is suspected. But how far should planning theorists go to protect against misuse of their ideas? They must situate themselves on the spectrum of responsibility between the legally narrow and the impossibly demanding. The aim should not be to become 'moral saints' (Wolf 1982).

It is time to look back and sum up what the three examples in the previous section say about CPT as a dual theory. The criticism in the co-optation example suggests that CPT is not unambiguously to the advantage of street level activists but can also work as a co-optation tactic that authorities may use for pacifying unruly protesters. The criticism in the neo-liberalism example indicates that the flexibility and locally adapted solutions that follow from communicative planning, while intended by theorists to give ordinary citizens more influence, can also serve the interests of developers and growth-oriented, neo-liberal local regimes. The criticism in both examples provides arguments for regarding CPT as dual theory. In comparison, what is new in the consensus example is that the criticism does not lead one to expect that CPT is a dual theory. A local consensus on a planning issue, which is established outside the representative democratic system, is usually a challenge to elected politicians and top-down policy implementation. Should the authorities happen to endorse the locally mediated agreement, the criticism still makes the consensus a less forceful legitimation tool. Taken together, the examples make it reasonable to classify CPT as dual theory.

Unintended consequences

This sub-section on unintended effects links the problem of the manifold end-uses that can be spawned by dual planning theory and the question of planning theorists' responsibility for the use made of their ideas. Theorists can hardly be held morally responsible for consequences that could not be anticipated at the time the theory was first published.

'Thanks to the connection of willed effects with external necessity, action has consequences that we can say escape the circumspection of the intention' (Ricoeur 2000:33). Such unintended consequences are a recurrent topic in the planning literature (Burby 1999, Sager 1994:187–89), and a recent contribution ventures to say that 'there is hardly a corner of program or policy planning that has not seen analyses of unintended consequences' (Morell 2005:444). The general significance of such consequences is illustrated by the unending stream of noteworthy examples reported in the scholarly literature, such as development aid promoting arms races (Collier and Hoeffler 2007) and raised legal minimum drinking age increasing the prevalence of marijuana consumption (DiNardo and Lemieux 2001). A third example concerns military planning. During the military campaign against the PLO in Lebanon in 1982, captured Palestinian fighters were sent to the Ansar Prison Camp, where the internal inter-human dynamics engendered profound social integration and subsequently a solid social, political, and military coherence. The unintended effect was, as retired IDF Brigadier General Dov Tamari complained, that '(a)t Ansar, we established the military of the future Palestinian state' (Tamari 2001:45). The classical planning-related example is Hayek's (2008) accusation that planners' good intentions of pursuing equality and the public interest lead to serfdom.

Morell (2005:456) maintains that 'circumstances force continual revision in any plan that was fixed at any point in time'. The phenomenon of unintended consequences is not made interesting by the obvious fact that pundits occasionally fail to foresee even first and second-order impacts of planned actions. What makes the theme an essential one to planning and social theory is the far stronger claim made by Sartre (1982:38-9): in the dialectic inherent in the interrelations between individuals, the consequences of our actions always finally escape us. The core message is aptly restated by Jonas:

The consequences of the single action enmesh with the immensity of strands in the causal fabric of the whole, which defies analysis even for the now, and exponentially so into the future … (A)lmost every purpose is destined to become estranged from itself in the long run. (Jonas 1984:117)

Vernon (1979:57) imparts that for Sartre as well as for Popper, '(u)nintended consequences figure as an explanatory bridge between the "human" character of action and the "alien" character of history'. Prominent scholars have singled out unintended consequences as the main target for social research. Merton (1957:66) suggests that 'the *distinctive* intellectual contributions of the sociologist are found primarily in the study of unintended consequences ... of social practices, as well as in the study of anticipated consequences...' (emphasis in original). He points to evidence that the major contributions of sociologists were made when they shifted their attention to consequences which were neither intended nor recognized. Popper has put the matter more squarely:

> (I)t is one of the striking things about social life that *nothing ever comes off exactly as intended*. Things always turn out a little bit differently. We hardly ever produce in social life precisely the effect that we wish to produce, and we usually get things that we do not want into the bargain. ... To explain why they cannot be eliminated is the major task of social theory. ... The characteristic problems of the social sciences arise only out of our wish to know the *unintended consequences*, and more especially the *unwanted consequences* which may arise if we do certain things. (Popper 1972:124, emphasis in original)

There are connections between unintended consequences on the one hand, and dark-side planning and dual planning theory on the other hand, although the linkages are not unambiguous or obvious. CPT's potential facilitation of neo-liberalism is an example of dark-side effects of planning theory to those who believe that neo-liberal policies degrade living conditions. Dark-side planning effects would habitually be seen as unintended only by a profession used to seeing itself in a heroic light. Should this happen to be the situation in planning, the profession would do well to heed Reade's (1991:186) warning, that prominent planning theorists are 'very much in a tradition absolutely central to planning, the tradition in which planners search endlessly for a more glamorous way of presenting themselves'.

The way dual planning theory was defined in the previous sub-section makes unintended consequences a potentially important notion. Dual planning theory is found useful both in organizing top-down planning processes and in bottom-up planning initiated by ordinary citizens. One might assume that those starting up a planning effort have the knowledge and power to implement a plan limited to serving their own interests. However, it is often not the party launching the plan whose interests are being served by the unintended consequences; these can strike in all directions. A planning theory may be intended to have favourable effects on the emancipation and empowerment of a particular group. It might nevertheless be known to the planning theorists working on this theory that its implementation is likely to have the side effect of underpinning a market-based political-economic system that undermines public planning in the long run (compare the neo-liberalism example). When the theorists continue working on such a dual theory and encourage its practical use, they allow the detrimental side effects to happen, and thus have some responsibility for them. This is all the more so if the theorists do not warn the practitioners about the predictable long-term side effects and take no measures to prevent them. Intending the good does not necessarily exonerate from responsibility for the bad (Thompson 2005:37–41). Researchers might be morally responsible for consequences of their theory if these consequences were foreseen, even if they were not intended. The word 'might' in the previous sentence indicates that the consequences in question must be sufficiently likely to occur for the theorists to be held responsible (Baldwin 1979:354). It cannot be foreseen in the abstract what a particular idea may look like when concretely materialized.

Creative reading and re-writing

The writing of theory is both reality construction and a way to model and paint a simplified picture of an already existent reality (Mallon 2007). Therefore, theoretical development is not only an attempt at more advanced reflection or explanation. It also changes people's view of the physical and social materiality, processes and events that plans aim to alter, and thus implants new ideas in change agents of what might be possible and desirable. Tsivacou (1996) explicitly notes that ideas and meanings do not precede the very act of writing plans, 'the written form of planning generates a new kind of logic which guides the behaviour and worldviews of the actors today' (ibid.72). This means that writing planning theory, as well as writing plans, is a creative act that has consequences and thus potentially evokes questions of responsibility.

The creative aspect of writing, 'writing as a method of nomadic inquiry', is emphasized by Richardson and Adams St.Pierre (2005). They commend the inquiry of flux, becoming, and heterogeneity, as opposed to the stable, eternal, and constant. Writing is not only representation; it can also be used to disrupt the known and the real. In so doing, they say (with reference to Foucault), that we might loosen the hold of received meaning limiting our work and our lives and investigate to what extent the exercise of thinking our own histories can free thought from what it thinks silently and to allow it to think otherwise (ibid.969). This emancipative aspect of writing reinforces the idea that the resulting theory is the writer's own product and hence – in some sense – her responsibility. In fact, were planning theorists unwilling to accept and recognize their role in the construction of reality, merely purporting to represent a reality existing 'out there' as a fact, they would be irresponsible. It would amount to insisting on equivalence between an externally located reality and planning theories as representations, thereby rejecting the main mechanism by which theorists influence the lives of others, namely by constructing reality by generating and disseminating ideas and concepts by which the world is conceived and manifested in language.[7]

Thus from a constructivist outlook, planning theorists have a measure of power in their capacity as writers. Of course, this also goes for authors developing, criticizing, re-writing, and applying planning theories, and this is the important thing in the present context. When other authors use the work of planning theorists, they always introduce a twist based on their own experiences and idiosyncrasies. That is, they continue the construction of reality in slightly different directions than those taken by the planning theorists from whom they borrow. These twists and deviations cannot be foreseen by the planning theorists.

Creativity can be found in theory consumption as well as in theory production. This is emphasized by Certeau (1984) who questions the association of reading and passivity, asserting that every reading modifies its object. The reader – the theory user in the present context – invents in texts something different from what the theory builder originally had in mind. The reader combines the fragments and aspects of the text with personal intuitions and creates something new and unknown in the space organized by the text's capacity for allowing an indefinite plurality of meanings (ibid.169). As Adams St.Pierre (1996:537) professes, '(b)eing a responsible reader becomes crucial in that relation where theories ricochet and have the power to inscribe and reinscribe lives'.[8]

Theories may be transformed into actionable knowledge due to the conditions of their dissemination and the needs of the users, not necessarily because of any intrinsic properties or claims to truth. Compare this to the 'garbage can' model of organizational decision-making (March and Olsen 1986) according to which events are determined by the arrival and departure times of problems, resources, decision-makers' attention, and choice opportunities. In the context-dependent flows of these ingredients for choice, intention is lost, and a temporal order is substituted for an order based on cause and effect which is probably taken for granted by most planners. In the present context, ideas can be reinterpreted and customized by the theory consumers (readers) and incorporated in their repertoire of actions. This kind of 'creative bricolage' implies that the researcher originally constructing the theory loses control of its application. Moreover, it opens for dark-side use, as it is '(a) fundamental feature of bricolage ... that it does not worry about "proper" and "improper" uses of objects' (Gabriel 2002:139).

In concluding this section, consider the situation in which a particular theory of planning has not been misunderstood, the theory is applied by the appropriate persons (planners), and it is applied for the purpose it was meant to serve. The consequences of the theory's end-use may still not measure up to the theorist's expectations. If they do not, one reason can be that the theory does not provide a helpful interpretation of the segment of the real world that it is intended to cover. It is the responsibility of the planning theorist to see to it that the theory is not inadequate in this sense.

Conditions limiting the power of theorists to affect end-use

Restrictions on theorists' ability to predict end-uses, and restrictions on their power to affect end-uses are not easily separated. Each phenomenon that limits the theorists' ability to predict end-use also diminishes their power to influence end-use – and vice versa. As used here, the distinction is mainly a device for structuring the exposition. The mechanisms mentioned in the present section (related to power) nevertheless rely more on institutional context and organization of the activities related to public planning. Planning theorists' power to affect end-use is limited by several factors, of which the problems of many hands, no patent protection, and a loose theory-practice relationship are dealt with.

Many hands and intermediary actors

Theorists are continually interacting in their minds with what others have written and discussed. In this sense, theory production is not the lone endeavour of a single scholar. Moreover, clients and principals influence commissioned research, power may be shared with team members, and intermediaries (planners) strongly affect applications. Similar situations are those in which the theorist is aware that the theory in question is developed further or applied by others whom he or she does not trust to use it correctly, but can do little to prevent this 'unauthorized' use from taking place.[9]

The problem of many hands must be taken into account when ascribing responsibility to theorists (Thompson 2005:11–32). A theory often results from the work of many researchers. Even if there is a leading figure – an initiator digging out the diamond – many others may have helped to cut and polish it. It may not be possible to identify one single theorist, or even one particular team, who was in control of the construction of a theory. The process of refining and perfecting the theory can take years, and researchers influence each other in the mutual learning process. Each person must still answer for his or her own written work, but when CPT is used or misused, it is nevertheless hard to know how much responsibility should be ascribed to single theorists. How much weight could be put on causal effectiveness as a criterion? An academic who does mediocre research and has the capacity to improve CPT only insignificantly may be less responsible for its use in planning practice and other applications, and thus be less morally responsible for its consequences.

Imagine that a university planning department has completed a large commissioned research project on the increasing private initiatives in city planning throughout Europe; the project has involved most of the department's professors. The project is criticized, and the department is held responsible for left-leaning conclusions and a theoretical approach which the client finds incomprehensible. Can this collective responsibility be apportioned to individual professors who contributed to the allegedly unsatisfactory collective effort? The standard argument against is that employees in organizations act not as individuals but within the confines of roles which they do not themselves define, and so they do not fulfil the necessary conditions for bearing moral responsibility. The general view of Flores and Johnson (2005) is that 'the role constraints on the individual's behavior are not in themselves sufficient to undermine the autonomy of the individual nor the responsibility one bears as an individual for the consequences of one's behavior' (ibid.345). This conclusion seems particularly apt in the case of university professors who have some influence on how to form their professional role and are enjoying a fair amount of academic freedom.

There is usually the presence of an intermediary actor in the causal chain from the researchers' publication of their theory to the end-use. The practising planner is often in that position. When intermediaries are identifiable, the quality of applications can be safeguarded by disseminating information on reasonable and effective use of the theory in question among them. The researcher producing procedural planning theory can be seen as an adviser to the planner, and the latter often has significant power in designing the planning process, even when the broad outline is laid out in guidelines or laws. The question is what significance should be attributed to the argument that advisers are not responsible for the results of policies since the person whom they advise is free to accept or reject their counsel (Thompson 2005:33–49).

No patent or monitoring

Planning theories are not patented; Lindblom's (1959) 'science of muddling through' can serve as an example. Based on this seminal article, disjointed incrementalism was developed in various directions: mixed scanning (Etzioni 1967), logical incrementalism (Quinn 1980), dialogical incrementalism (Sager 1994), and many more. The original researcher can revisit his or her theory

(Lindblom 1979), and in so doing choose to criticize the twists and turns grafted on the theory since its inception, but can do little else to prevent strange progeny from spreading throughout academia and beyond. There is copyright on published work but not on the ideas expressed therein, and there is (fortunately) no monitoring of theory development. As soon as the work is published, the planning theorist loses control of others' further development of the theory.

This is so even if theorists often watch and check on each others' work. Academic debate and critique have been lively in the case of CPT. Types of critique affect end-use in different ways. When the theory is simply dismissed, the criticism probably leads to a narrower set of end-uses. But when the critics revise the original theory, end-uses can diversify and be less predictable.

Loose theory-practice relationship

It is often questioned whether practitioners make much use of planning theory. When they occasionally do, it is mostly in a pragmatic way and quite independent of the theorists. Planners are free to apply bits and pieces of theory as they see fit. The uncertainties of the process of implementing plans further diminish the theorist's ability to control effects on physical and economic reality. Theorists might not ever imagine exercising such control, which may have contributed to the loose theory-practice relationship in the first place.

If plans sometimes do not change the world but remain forever on the office book-shelf, it seems even less likely that the theory behind the plans will have practical significance. Real-world impact of theory would at least be modest to the extent that effects come via implemented plans, as planners seem to make little explicit use of planning theory (a statement supported by Sanyal (2002) but disputed by Friedmann (2008)). Social effects of planning theory do not always rely on plans as an intermediate link, though. For example, those familiar with communicative planning theory are exposed to arguments for participation and dialogue likely to influence the practices they will advocate both inside and outside planning processes. Moreover, theories travel and might be put to use in disciplines and problem areas thematically far from their origin (Healey and Upton 2010, Perry 1995, Tait and Jensen 2007).

Assuming that planning theory is without effect, which would leave the theorists impotent in their roles as teachers and researchers, it would not be of much interest to raise questions of responsibility for its applications. 'The first and most general condition of responsibility is causal power, that is, that acting makes an impact on the world' (Jonas 1984:90). Responsibility is a correlate of power and should be commensurate with the latter's scope and that of its exercise (ibid.x). The position taken here, in light of the examples of CPT critique given in this chapter, is that planning theory does indeed affect the real world. As Friedmann (2003:9) answers the question of why do planning theory: 'because … it does matter, because it is essential to the vitality and continued relevance of planning as a profession'.

Numerous studies in administrative and political science have shown that plans, programmes, and policies are frequently imperfectly implemented, if at all. DeLeon and deLeon (2002:469) warn of 'the immense vale of troubles that [lie] between the definition of a policy and its execution'. This means that the theorist will in many cases not be responsible for physical and economic consequences even if his or her theory was used as a 'template' for designing real world planning processes. DeLeon and deLeon argue that the probability of seeing physical-economic effects is highest when the planning theory is mainly deployed as inspiration for bottom-up processes (ibid.477–78). Implementation of plans can be hampered because 'the planning staff … is often composed of different individuals than the implementing staff. In the transition between these two groups responsibility is often lost' (Gottschalk 2001:208).

The loose theory-practice relationship in the field of planning contributes to the powerlessness of the planning theorists in several situations: when the theorist knows what unintended effects can occur, but cannot prevent them; when the theorist is aware that the theory is used for purposes other than those which it was constructed for, but has no say in deciding the area of use; and when the planning theorist knows that the theory in question is applied in contexts and under conditions that are not in line with its assumptions, but is unable to prevent improper use.

Conclusion

Responsibility requires a demonstrable chain of cause and effect. Furthermore, the scholar held responsible for adverse consequences of a planning theory must have knowledge about this chain and her ability to affect it. Theorists cannot entirely prevent misuse of their theories. They can, however, significantly reduce the chances that perversion of theory is predicated on misunderstandings. Communication, debate and dissemination of knowledge are the best measures for guiding well-intended use of planning theory. This notwithstanding, a dilemma cannot be completely avoided: The more widespread the information about a theory, the higher the likelihood that someone picks it up for dark-side purposes. The more efficiently published in far-reaching media, the more likely it is that planning theory travels to foreign fields and cross-fertilizes into hybrids with unpredictable and uncontrollable end-uses. Hence, when communicative planning theorists are conscious of their responsibility to communicate, their theories become more exposed to people and causes their work was not meant to serve.[10]

Habermas (1984:14) holds that, '(i)n the context of communicative action, only those persons count as responsible who, as members of a communication-community, can orient their actions to intersubjectively recognized validity claims'. Building on this idea, planning theorists can be seen as acting responsibly when:

- Discussing their theories with peers and potential users.
- Listening to criticism and making corrections as appropriate.
- Trying to avoid misunderstandings in application of their theories.
- Making clear when they use assumptions or other theoretical elements that are known to be notable simplifications or stylizations of reality.
- Answering the important questions in their field, but also ensuring that they are asked.

Theorists are responsible to the research community for making their reasoning comprehensible and for putting forward only theories that can be defended (that are reasonable in this sense). The argument is not always fully developed when the theory is first presented. In the early stages of evolution it is hard to imagine what criticism will be raised against the theory. When this becomes clear, however, the theorist has a moral responsibility to respond to criticism, as this exchange of views and mutual examination of pros and cons constitute the logic by which the research community expands its knowledge. At the political level, being a responsible communicative planning theorist means anticipating how existing social relations of power are likely to support or constrain a deliberative democratic planning process and then acting in ways to nurture such a process.

To say that theorists may be morally responsible for the consequences of their work is not necessarily to claim that they should stop working on the theory in question when they become aware of applications that offend their conscience. Other applications of the same theory might serve society well and override the misuse, to the best of the theorists' judgement. In any case, the existence of detrimental effects implies that the theorists' choice of whether to develop the theory further is a moral one, and that they have a continuing obligation to consider and question the uses to which their contributions are put.

Finally, planning theorists are responsible to practising planners for providing theories that produce helpful consequences when applied in planning processes. Judging from the allegedly modest use of planning theory among planners, this is an area where many members of the planning community think that planning theorists still face a great challenge.

Notes

1. Gunder and Hillier (2007, 2009:157–79) are mainly preoccupied with the responsibilities of planners, which was a contributory factor when choosing to concentrate on the responsibility of planning theorists in this chapter. I avoid the philosophical discussion of what comes first, ideas or actions. Why should a cause-effect chain arbitrarily start with the planning theorists? Surely they too must be influenced from somewhere, and perhaps by someone's actions. In this endless regress, the likely outcome is that the person linked up with the original idea or action will not be identified, and responsibility would in any case be dissolved along the limitless causal chain. Search for the ultimate source of an idea is probably the surest way of making the question of planning theorists' responsibilities uninteresting.

2. Most planning theorists work in colleges or universities which are committed to the protection of academic freedom. Academics in these organizations enjoy the privilege of defining and pursuing their own research agenda (Brinkman 2009:107). This autonomy is codified in the American Association of University Professors' 'Statement of Professional Ethics' (www.aaup.org/AAUP/pubsres/policydocs/contents/statementonprofessionalethics.htm) and in the American Council of Education's 'Statement on Academic Rights and Responsibilities Offered by Higher Education Communities (www.acenet.edu/AM/PrinterTemplate.cfm?Section=Search&template =/CM/HTMLDisplay.cfm&ContentID=21564) (accessed 10 November 2010).

3. Two other examples shed considerable light on the difficulties of predicting future use of concepts and theories. Vidyarthi (2010) gives an account of the changing political use of the concept 'neighbourhood unit' when it 'migrated' from the US to India. Clarence Perry, who conceptualized the neighbourhood unit as a physical planning tool, imagined that the spatiality of the neighbourhood unit would help to repair deteriorating links between the individual, the family, and the community. In India, Otto Koenigsberger and Albert Mayer substituted this by the imagination that the disciplined spatiality of neighbourhood units would 'civilize' their residents. Pioneering planners inverted the conundrum that had prompted the invention of the neighbourhood unit concept in the first place:

    > Perry's aim in conceiving the neighborhood unit was to inculcate 'neighborliness' by creating a village-like state in American cities. Mayer and Koenigsberger, on the other hand, faced a more complicated situation because they wanted to create 'neighborliness' by preserving the best elements of existing village life while modernizing Indian cities. However, in doing so, they were ironically aiding the very processes of urbanization that, to Perry, were the root of the problem. (Vidyarthi 2010:90)

    Massey (2008) tells how she was confronted with a different political use of her concept 'power geometry' when invited to Venezuela. The concept originated as a tool for analyzing UK economic-political conditions, but was applied in the South American context for arguing the case for President Hugo Chávez's Bolivarian revolution. Massey writes that 'This concept (of "mine") has travelled, been adopted by Chávez. It's being used in a particular way. What responsibilities does one have in a situation like this? Whose concept is it now?' (ibid.496).

4. A few critical remarks can be mentioned to supplement those listed in Chapter 1. Flyvbjerg (1998a:229) writes that: 'If societies that suppress conflict are oppressive, perhaps social and political theories that ignore or marginalize conflict are potentially oppressive, too.' Fischler (2000:364) holds consensus building in accordance with communicative rationality to imply public exposure of the inner self: '(O)ne may

wonder whether the transformation of personal and cultural issues into public ones will not lead to the further "colonization of the lifeworld"…'. He also finds that consensus building comes with political costs. Local consensus can undermine representative democracy and state intervention. 'Without state intervention, civil society would soon be reduced to a marketplace (or a jungle), in which the vulnerable would fair (sic) extremely poorly' (Fischler 2000:365).

5. Some critics seem to believe that CPT assumes the existence of a 'consensus society' binding people into a cohesive polity and civil society. But many communicative planning theorists see the opposite: a society with many tensions and a multitude of conflicts between social groups and interests. Communicative planning is often proposed as a way to enable at least sufficient agreement to be reached, so some plan to deal with pressing problems can be identified and acted upon.

6. Criteria for deciding whether one and the same theory guides the design of both top-down and bottom-up processes can presumably be made less arbitrary and subjective than criteria to distinguish the politically good and bad. This is one difference between deciding if a planning theory has a dual character and deciding if a theory promotes dark-side planning. There is also another difference: Demonstration of the dark side of a planning theory requires that the theory, when informing planning practice as intended, systematically leads to deteriorating living conditions. Demonstrating that a planning theory is dual requires showing that it inspires both bottom-up and top-down practices which are not inherently good and bad, respectively, and which are not necessarily planning practices.

7. It follows from this constructivist standpoint that the work of planning theorists is partly fictional. Truth telling cannot be the only or even the predominant goal for planning theorists. Paradoxically, for planning theorists to be responsible they must not claim to convey truth in any objective sense (Rhodes and Brown 2005:480). If the planning theorists' situation were such that they had to adapt to a predetermined programme for representing 'the true reality', little room would be left for responsibility. (See the Derridean responsibilities of planning theorists in Chapter 10.) But if planning theorists cannot demonstrate responsibility primarily by telling the truth, it needs to be clarified what they are responsible for (ibid.478).

8. The interpretation theory of Paul Ricoeur is highly relevant to the theme of creative reading and re-writing. His view on interpretation was linked to flexibility in planning and integrated with CPT in Sager (1994:230, 254–5).

9. The average number of authors to peer reviewed journal articles is steadily increasing in many academic fields, for example ecology, bioethics, physics, and medicine (Bennett and Taylor 2003, Tarnow 2002). The life sciences are experiencing a rapid increase in the number of articles with more than 100 authors. Articles published in, for example, *The Lancet*, have more than six authors on average. The risk is that the high number of authors pulverizes responsibility for the published text. If there is a trend towards multi-author articles in planning, it has not yet been regarded as a problem.

10. The organizations of planning academics and planning theorists (AESOP, ACSP, APSA, etc.) can try to guard against misuse of planning theory, for example, through initiatives administered by thematic groups on ethics. AESOP has formed a thematic group on Research Ethics and Planning with the purpose of exploring ways of thinking about planning research which consider the social context of moral perception and behaviour. Concerning the topics to be discussed, the chairs of the group write that: 'Planning research, like any other kind of social science research, is an intervention in people's lives. … (R)esearchers in public policy disciplines like planning must face the possibility that their findings will be used by others in ways of which they disapprove' (AESOP 2007).

9

Responsibility for Inclusive Deliberation in Planning: Struggling with Deep Difference

Critical CPT argues for open processes, inclusive participation, and broad deliberation. But in some contexts limits must be set, because potential participants do not respect the basic rules of decision-making in liberal societies and loath the superior idea of democracy itself. Even critical pragmatism – a watchdog for openness and inclusion – can in exceptional cases limit hospitality for the sake of protecting democracy. CPT is more credible as a critical theory defending democracy if it also reflects critically on its own inclusive tenets and recommendations and dares take the unpleasant discussion of how to exclude in order to protect primary values.

Inclusion is at the core of democratic theory (Young 2000). Democratic political movements and designers of democratic processes and institutions can promote greater inclusion in public planning and decision-making as a means of advancing more just outcomes. The joint consideration of responsibility and inclusion is topical in societies where neo-liberal ideology fosters new relations of individual obligations and responsible citizenship. For example, the unemployed are being encouraged to act responsibly by re-educating themselves in order to acquire salaried employment (Ilcan 2009). They are seen as responsible for including themselves in the labour market system and in mainstream society in general.

Inclusion is a central theme for Jürgen Habermas, as for Emmanuel Levinas and Jacques Derrida. The topic is often treated under headings of welcoming, hospitality, toleration, recognition, or multiculturalism (Chan 2010). This chapter explains the implications of Levinas's ethical relationship between the subject (self) and the Other for face-to-face conversation, and then compares such Levinasian conversation with the Habermasian dialogue often aimed at by communicative planning theorists. The differences between the ethical and the political realms are highlighted, and special attention is given to hospitality and toleration. The purpose is to analyze the implications of Levinasian ethics for the responsibility of planning theorists to prepare for the inclusion of very different Others in public deliberation. With this limited intention, there is no need here to attempt a broad introduction to Levinas's ideas.

Levinas's consideration for the Other is extreme and cannot be sustained when third parties are transforming the dyad into a web of relationships. The following section establishes a principled ethical position that has to be modified when dealing with multiple Others, as in planning processes. It starts with the concept of 'the Other' and only brings in additional notions that shed light on the links between otherness, inclusion and dialogue.

Dialogue with the different Other

Dialogue is an ideal in CPT, and the principles of discourse ethics state that the communicative process should be open, undistorted, truth-seeking, and empathic, as explained in Chapter 1. Openness implies that communicative planning must be inclusive and admit radical otherness (alterity) into deliberation. The guiding intuition in Habermas's work is that the legitimacy of democratic political authority has to be secured by broad popular involvement in public deliberation and decision-making (Habermas 2003). Dialogue between the parties participating in planning or affected by public plans is the ideal of such deliberation. The World Planners Congress Vancouver Declaration 2006 states that: 'We stand for planning as an inclusive process' (Harper et al. 2008:4). Even so, Allmendinger and Tewdwr-Jones (2002:19) question whether public-sector urban planners actually have a moral obligation to enhance community participation. Building on the arguments in this book, I see it as the responsibility of theorists working on participatory and communicative planning to develop and analyze models inspiring and preparing for inclusive planning processes. The purpose of the chapter is to discuss problems related to this obligation.

The relationship to the Other is the main theme of Emmanuel Levinas, considered by many to be among the leading ethicists of the twentieth century (Arnett 2003, Critchley 2004). It is appropriate to draw on Levinas here, as his ideas about responsibility for the Other have implications for inclusive deliberation in planning, and because he was an important influence on Jacques Derrida, to whom we return for a discussion of the concept of hospitality later in this chapter, and for the discussion of responsible decisions in Chapter 10. The Other is what the subject is not, '(a)nd the Other cannot be wholly interpreted or translated into the language, experience, or perspective of the self since it would, at that point, no longer be other' (Critchley 2004:139). Moreover, as argued by Hendley (2000), Levinas's preoccupation with language as exposure to the Other provides a corrective to Habermas's focus on the procedural aspects of communication.[1] It is the future of the Other, not the past of what the subject has already done, that is the focus of Levinasian responsibility, which is well in line with the future orientation of planning.

The ethical relationship between the subject and the Other differs much in the writings of Levinas and Habermas, and Levinas's position (and his hyperbole) helps to set the dialogical foundation of CPT in sharp relief. The subject in Levinasian ethics is subordinated to the Other through an ethical injunction to respect him or her as an absolute alterity. The idea of subordination to others is foreign to Habermasian discourse ethics, which instead aims for equal status and reciprocity. Power relations are ideally levelled out in Habermasian dialogue, while they are constituted by moral obligations in Levinasian face-to-face conversation:

> Indeed, whoever advocates a Levinasian ethics will be confronted with a merciless irony as soon as he or she comes up to someone else and face-to-face declares, 'You should subject yourself to the Other', which then literally means, 'You should subject yourself to Me, you should obey My law'. (Hägglund 2004:53)

Levinas's ethical relation is one in which the Other is passively granted his or her alterity. Taking responsibility for the Other is part of the human condition and is not a commitment freely chosen by the subject. The challenge for the self is to come into dialogue with, and unmask the 'face' of, an individual who cannot be fully conceptualized in its otherness. There is always the need for disclosing more of the 'face' of the Other in dialogue in order to clarify and deepen the responsibilities of the subject. The face, as the concept is used in this chapter, is a metaphor for the other person in all his or her vulnerability, which presents itself to the subject as a moral summons to be acknowledged.

To use language in order '(t)o intervene or establish common territory would be to conceptualize alterity, which is tantamount to enacting its violation' (Trey 1992:417). This is far from Habermas's aim of using dialogue for establishing intersubjectivity and mutual understanding. Trey explains how respect for the absolute alterity of the Other makes the consensus-building efforts of communicative planning suspect, as interpreted from a Levinasian perspective. This line of reasoning underscores the critique of consensus building for unduly repressing difference, which was put forward in Chapter 8. Trey fears, in line with Levinas, that 'Habermas's normative accord involves a political subsumption of alterity into rational agreement' (ibid.421). Rationally deliberated consensus would then seem to close off dissent, resistance, and alterity – establishing the absolute authority of reason. In my view, it is rather a question of establishing a situated authority of reasoning among parties who are affected in different ways by a certain policy or project and disagree on how to react to it.

But here, Levinas would claim, a power strategy is enacted. By introducing content into the discursive relationship between I and the other, and by formulating that content in such a way that it can be shared, the alterity which originally situated the relationship is excluded. By appealing to the authority of 'we', the other to whom I am responsible becomes mine. (Trey 1992:421)

However, such an adoption of the Other by the subject betrays the ethical relationship, which is utterly independent of any active force and 'situated in terms of domination free speech' (ibid.417).

Critics of Habermas's handling of otherness in the theory of communicative action object that full acceptance of otherness in dialogue would make rational consensus all but impossible. Consensus would require exclusion or modification of alterity, thus necessitating an exertion of power from which communicative action theory dissociates itself. For example, Coole (1996:221) concludes that Habermas 'is unable to attribute any emancipatory potential to alterity, or otherness … because his basic ideas concerning communicative reason and an emancipatory project of modernity are predicated on its exclusion'. The response in CPT to this critique is that repeated deliberation in long-lasting collaborative processes can impact on people's subjectivities in ways that are likely to modify alterity without use of force (Innes and Booher 2010). Scepticism to alterity based on non-rational, mystical or unverifiable beliefs is at the heart of Habermas's opposition to post-modernism.

An immediate problem when assuming responsibility for others is whether the geographical distance to the others should be allowed to influence the responsibility relationship. There is the question of whether concerns for people in the neighbourhood can be transformed into active concern for distant strangers. This question is of the utmost importance to planning. If nearness in time and space is seen as decisive, responsibility to future generations is discounted to insignificance, and much of the sustainability literature would be a waste of time. Exclusion from processes of planning and policy-making upholds distance and might be disastrous for the group denied admission, and face-to-face conversation would be privileged and count for even more than it does in communicative and collaborative planning practice. If distance leads to indifference, most long-range and macro level planning should be looked at with suspicion.

To some extent, felt responsibility for those in the circles nearest to us may spring from gratitude for the relational goods created in interaction with people who are culturally, temporally, and spatially close to us (friendship, self-esteem, belonging; see Chapter 1 and Brock 2005:5–6). Besides, conditions for deliberative democracy are greatly enhanced when participants share a sense of solidarity with co-members of the community. 'There needs to be such a special bonding if compatriots are to govern in a way that responsibly promotes the common good and sometimes requires sacrifices on the part of the members' (ibid.6). Citizens of democratic countries have benefited from participation in a mutually advantageous co-operative scheme, and they have obligations to other members of the same scheme, such as indigenous minorities (Sandercock 2000). The question is whether they have the same obligations to more distant strangers; Levinas insists that they do.

Inclusion ideally means engaging with the Other in dialogue. As there cannot be any instrumental thinking in the ethical relationship, the subject is not to expect reciprocity in the dialogue; to recognize the Other is to give and not at all to consider what is in it for oneself. As soon as calculation enters the scene or reciprocity is sought, the pure alterity of the Other disappears and the interlocutors exit the ethical plane. The Other may be responsible for me, but that is his or her own affair and of no consequence in defining my moral obligations. It is my opinion that the insistence on *absolute* alterity can be overdone, if not in philosophical and ethical academic discussion, then at least in practical policy-making and planning, where a more pragmatic balancing of differences and similarities between people is required.

Ethical principles notwithstanding, the need for technological mastery and political self-preservation cannot be ignored: 'Indeed, without these political and technological structures of organization we would not be able to feed mankind. This is the great paradox of human existence ... to ensure the survival of the other we must resort to the technico-political systems of means and ends' (Levinas and Kearney 1986:28). Note, however, that this admission is about instrumentality in the political sphere, not the ethical – a distinction to which we will now turn. The following sections deal with Levinas's ideas of the Third and the political in order to examine if these ideas point to a strategy for narrowing the gap between Levinasian responsibility and Habermasian dialogue (Levinas 1969, 1981).

Politics and planning: ethical consequences of multiple Others

Focus on the relationship of responsibility between the subject and a singular Other has triggered the question whether Levinas's philosophy is not a 'solipsism for two' and therefore incapable of properly understanding responsibility in social settings (Zaborowski 2000:56). This is a salient question when using Levinas's ideas to illuminate the responsibilities of planning theorists, as planning is always a collective affair. Part of the rationale for public planning is precisely its identification and management of consequences to third parties. Hence, if Levinas is to have anything to offer planning theorists, his theory building must show a way out of the infinite responsibility for a singular Other. The introduction of the Third – that is, multiple Others – and the distinction between the realms of ethics and politics, opens up such an escape route. It was nevertheless necessary to start this chapter with Levinas's ideas about a responsible relationship between the subject and a singular Other, both in order to introduce his concepts and because political interactions cannot do without corrective from this fundamental dyadic relationship.

There are often several people in proximity of the self, so the attention of the subject cannot be undividedly directed to a single Other. Since the Third exists in a condition of parity with respect to the Other, the subject is no less responsible for the welfare of the third party than it is for the other person. The Third is not necessarily a singular person; it might in principle represent the rest of humanity (Gauthier 2007:165). In reality there is always a Third, although not necessarily in proximity. Hence, in the meeting with another person's naked 'face', the subject is confronted with other people as well, who may be just as much in need of consideration and help as the one who is in proximity. The planning theorist is responsible not only to the PhD student she happens to know well, but also to her other students; she is responsible not only to the good colleague who poses a question after her conference presentation, but also to everyone else in the audience. The Third introduces the realm of politics, in which responsibility extends beyond the dyad. This has consequences for the theory and practice of inclusion, to which we return later in this chapter.

A wholly new communicative situation arises with the recognized presence of the Third. Intimate one-on-one discourse is no longer sufficient. 'Faced with two parties who simultaneously vie for its attention and concern, the self is compelled to weigh competing ethical obligations' (Gauthier 2007:166). The sphere of moral concern is thus enlarged, and 'the Third serves as a corrective to the danger of ethical myopia' (ibid.167).

As the Third inspires the creation of institutions, laws, and the state, the presence of the Third projects the subject into the realm of politics. While ethics concerns the unique imperative arising from a unique Other, politics concerns the negotiation of multiple and competing imperatives. Politics is understood as the (epistemological) realm of decision-making, in contrast to ethics which belongs to the (phenomenological) realm of the encounter with the Other (Murray 2003b:41). By virtue of their general quality, laws make no allowance for human alterity and uniqueness. Even in the most enlightened and liberal societies, laws oppress the individual as seen from a Levinasian perspective. Laws belong to the political, and as Levinas writes, 'politics left to itself bears a tyranny within itself; it deforms the I and Other who have given rise to it, for it judges them according to universal rules' (Levinas 1969:300).

Hence, there is a lacuna between ethics and politics, and politics cannot be derived from ethics in Levinas's conceptual universe. In everyday interaction with others, moral responsibility is mediated by 'the political world of the impersonal "third" – the world of government, institutions, tribunals, prisons, schools, committees, and so on' (Levinas and Kearney 1986:30). In daily life, we have to compare the needs and wishes of different individuals, set priorities and make decisions that will inevitably reflect the fact that we are unable to fulfil everybody's needs. Planning theorists must acknowledge this situation, as they write for planning which is embedded in the realm of the political.

Communicative planning processes always involve more than two individuals and are preoccupied with justice, fairness, and equity. However, '(t)here is a certain measure of violence necessary in terms of justice … if one speaks of justice, it is necessary to allow judges, it is necessary to allow institutions and the state; to live in a world of citizens, and not only in the order of the Face to Face' (Levinas 1998:105). Even if inevitable, justice and politics in all its forms must always be held in check by the responsibility inherent in the initial dyadic relation. There is a never-ending oscillation between ethics and politics in the practice of planning which must be reflected in planning theory. The norm that must continue to inspire and direct the moral order of the political realm is the ethical norm of the inter-human (Levinas and Kearney 1986:30).

In politics, the Other, whoever he or she may be, is bound by the same institutions, laws and norms as the self. Politics forms a sphere in which the subject can reasonably expect to be treated with reciprocity from the others (Simmons 1999:94). The self is restored to a position where it may demand suspension of unidirectional responsibility. 'Reciprocity emerges here as impartiality demands that I take the interests of every other into account, including myself, as an other to the others' (Hendley 2000:48).

In order to encompass those Others who cannot be reached in face-to-face encounters, ethics must be transfixed into language, justice, and politics; hence ethics needs politics. Politics also needs ethics, and it is useful to note one similarity between Levinas's and Habermas's views on language in the realms of political/strategic action and ethical/communicative action. Habermas holds that there can be no completely strategic application of language that could be abstracted from its communicative use. Levinas contends that inter-human relations cannot be purely political; they have to retain elements of the ethical and must be formed on the basis of the subject's responsibility for the Other. Even as we use language strategically, we must also use it communicatively. Even as we use language politically, we must also use it to reveal the face of the Other (Hendley 2000:18–19).

Universalization of responsible actions into common norms and rules of conduct distances self from Other, but is nevertheless required to reach the multiple Others not in proximity (Simmons 1999:97). In the state's web of generalizations, classifications and power relations, the subject is unable to respond directly to the face of the unique Other. Response is institutionalized and formed by the rights and duties of broader categories of people. 'Even when the state functions perfectly it is, by its very nature, opposed to ethics' (ibid.98). Public planners thus have a role that is partly at odds with Levinasian ethics, and so have planning theorists as teachers and researchers for the state. This is not the full picture, however, as theorists of communicative planning may help to answer the question of how to set priorities between competing obligations and duties in order to act in line with principles of ethics in the public arena. According to Levinas (1969:298): 'Justice consists in … making possible expression … Justice is a right to speak.' This does not answer the question, but hints at the inclusion of Others in dialogue-like conversation as part of the solution.

Murray (2003a) suggests that the competing calls of multiple Others can be prioritized not by invoking an external hierarchy of principles, but through dialogue (in theory) and deliberation (in practice). This attributes an important role to dialogue in the realm of politics, in addition to its role of unmasking the face of the Other in the ethical sphere. Something like Habermas's 'ideal speech situation' would be required for dialogue to fulfil its political role, and besides, a model of justice that seeks a dialogical prioritization of calls is needed but not yet developed (ibid.4). Murray tries to explain why dialogical engagement with Others can reveal the relative moral force of an ethical summons. '(T)he stronger voice, understood as a reflection of ethical priority, will prevail precisely through its greater capacity to unsettle the self's own preconceptions, justifications, arguments, and rebuttals' (ibid.19). The face of the Other is experienced as a calling into question of the self, 'an uprooting of the I' (Levinas 1969:83). Murray proposes that the degree to which the Other's testimony disables and disrupts the rhetoric of the subject is a reliable, though by no means assured, measure of the relative ethical priority of that demand.

Emotional and rational appeal both count when reducing to order the competing claims from multiple Others. This use of dialogue differs from Habermas's (1990:198) claim that '(a)rgumentation insures that … nothing coerces anyone except the force of the better argument'. It is also worth noting that the use of dialogue for calling into question the argumentation and rhetoric of the subject is an inversion of John Forester's strategy for counteracting misuse of power in planning processes. Forester (1989:109–11) suggests that critical pragmatists should foster open and authentic political debate by questioning infeasibilities and shaping responses of hope in the face of societal values and norms restricting openness, power relations maintaining domination, and conflict repressing legitimate interests. In this power-levelling strategy, the planning theorist (the self) recommends questioning the arguments and rhetoric of supposedly strong actors in the process, while in Murray's revelation of the urgency of calls, the arguments and motives bringing the planning subject into the conversational relationship are themselves questioned. In any case, the Third is 'the birth of the question' (Derrida and Dufourmantelle 2000:5), opening for divided attention in deliberation and for reciprocity requiring that questions be answered. The practice of questioning comes up again in the next section because of its problematic relationship with Derrida's concept of hospitality.[2]

Responsibility and inclusion: hospitality

The contradiction that links Levinas's theory to the responsibility theme is this: To act morally according to Levinas is to give total attention to the Other. When there is a Third, as is always the case in planning, acting morally implies exclusion in the sense of not responding to the Third. The Third is ignored, and this is irresponsible action. The introduction of politics and justice in Levinas's system of ethics is essential in order to navigate out of this dilemma. It is the responsibility of planning theorists to develop models for including the Third in public deliberation and dialogue and to analyze how this can be done with the least relaxation of ethical principles. This section leans on Derrida's analysis of the Levinasian obligation to welcome the Other. The open dialogue is the paradigmatic form of interpersonal action in CPT, but there are dangers hidden in indiscriminate entry to planning deliberation.

In a few places, for example, in *Totality and Infinity* (1969:254), Levinas applies the terms 'hospitality' and 'welcome' of the Other, but this is not typical. These terms will nevertheless be used in the remainder of this chapter, as they are convenient for analyzing inclusion of the Other and the Third in planning communication. Use of the terms does not mean that I stray far from Levinas's ideas, rather it means reading Levinas through the glasses of Jacques Derrida (1999, 2000 (with Dufourmantelle), 2006). Derrida writes that: 'Although the word is neither frequently used nor emphasized within it, *Totality and Infinity* bequeaths to us an immense treatise of hospitality' (1999:21, italics in original). Derrida understands Levinas as attempting to elaborate an interpretation of welcoming and hospitality, offering a genuine ethics of hospitality, even ethics *as* hospitality.

Against the concept of hospitality as a capability or power of the subject based on control of a self-assured proper place, Derrida (1999) emphasizes the originality and radicality of Levinas's concept of hospitality which result from the subject's infinite responsibility for the Other. In the realm of ethics, the self welcomes the Other beyond its own capacities of welcoming. The subject receives beyond its capability. When hospitality, like responsibility, is infinite, the subject opens to an Other which is greater than itself. In planning dialogue this would be tantamount to inviting anyone in unconditionally, installing the new entry in the position of a master. Are people received in planning processes as Others – as inherently different – or as objects of assimilation that can legitimately be co-opted into identity?

The Other is for Levinas and Derrida unidentifiable and unforeseeable. The alterity brought into the planning process by the Other may not further or even go in for rational analysis (of any familiar sort). Therefore, the otherness to be dealt with because of unconditional hospitality undermines the predictive aspect of planning, whether statements about the future consequences of the plan are made on the basis of communication or calculation. When trying to accommodate pure otherness in their writings, communicative planning theorists may run into conflicting responsibilities. For example, the responsibility for fully open planning dialogues can make it more difficult to fulfil responsibilities for preparing planning input for political decision-making.[3]

The idea of unconditional hospitality can be criticized for its 'ethical overload' (Critchley 2006:103), and the absolute of responsibility and hospitality must be modified in the political realm. Invitation into deliberation on planning matters is not necessarily unconditional. In setting conditions, however, the planning theorist should be very alert to respecting alterity. All limitations of hospitality are exposed to what they seek to exclude, haunted by those who question the legitimacy of the restrictions.[4] CPT and Habermasian dialogue aim to be inclusive, while Derrida holds that 'the ethical question concerns the relationship to an other who ultimately escapes inclusion because she cannot be included and remain other at the same time' (Thomassen 2006a:115). This is the same warning against levelling difference as was sounded against consensus in Chapter 8.

Derrida (2006:225) admits that hospitality has a paradoxical trait, and the essay *Hostipitality* plays on this by combining the extremes of hostility and hospitality. Hospitality should be unconditional from the ethical point of view, but Derrida concedes that he would nevertheless be unable to open up or offer hospitality without reaffirming that he must be the master of his house, without being 'assured of his sovereignty over the space and goods he offers or opens to the other as stranger' (ibid.225). He sees self-limitation or self-contradiction in the demand for hospitality. In the political realm where there should be reciprocity, and one expects 'being oneself in one's own home' even when hosting a stranger, hospitality 'remains forever on the threshold of itself' (ibid.225). Differentiation is necessary, as Hägglund writes:

> (I)f I did not discriminate ... between what I welcome and do not welcome, what I find acceptable and unacceptable, it would mean that I had renounced

all claims to be responsible, make judgments, or pursue any critical reflections at all. Moreover, it would mean that I had opened myself without reservations to whatever is violently opposed to me and can extinguish everything that is mine, including my principles of hospitality. (Hägglund 2004:66)

Hägglund criticizes Levinas for having nothing to say regarding all the situations where the subject is confronted with an other who assaults her, turns down the offered hospitality, and in turn denies help when the subject needs it (ibid.52). The same contrariety is inherent in planning dialogue. Fundamentalists regard their own beliefs, lifestyles and values as dictated by an absolute authority and therefore beyond discussion. Is it still the responsibility of communicative planning theorists to argue for a deliberation in planning that should be open also for fundamentalist groups? In difficult cases, a line has to be drawn between groups that find it hard to contribute meaningfully in deliberation because all their traditional standpoints and practices are taken for granted, and groups that see deliberation as a serious attack on their beliefs and ideology and therefore aim to destroy deliberation itself.

From the principles of discourse ethics in Chapter 1, it is seen that Habermasian dialogue aims to be open and inclusive, qualities which are also recommended in CPT. Everyone is welcome to participate, but those entering the dialogue must follow the rules of discourse ethics. Communicative planning faces the democratic dilemma at the micro level: Deliberation should not include individuals whose aim is to destroy deliberation. Participation in planning discussions is not unconditional; the insiders remain masters. The ideal of inclusion must be balanced with political rationality which protects the capacity to make collective decisions by means of a desired type of political institution (Diesing 1962). Inclusion can take place on the condition that procedures are in place for protecting the deliberative institutions. The responsibility of communicative planning theorists is not only to the singular Other – to build theory that supports her welcome into dialogue. The theorists are also responsible for keeping up deliberative democracy by fortifying the institution of deliberation in planning. This implies some gate-keeping, maintaining the threshold of compliance with the tenets of discourse ethics.

There must be an extended welcome into planning deliberation, however. For it is in the welcoming of the face of the Other that equality is founded (Levinas 1969:214) – and thus justice. The credibility of the claim made by CPT that it seeks fairness in public planning – both in procedure and substance – depends on our willingness to let the Other reveal herself to us and, according to Levinas, let the Other command the relationship; otherwise equality 'is but an abstract idea and a word' (ibid.214). The line between inclusion and exclusion should not be drawn once and for all. The need for inclusion, on the one hand, and the need for protecting democratic processes, on the other hand, has to be balanced anew with every effort to plan communicatively.

In analyzing hospitality, Derrida negotiates between two imperatives: the obligation to unconditionally welcome the Other in advance of any knowledge, recognition or identity, and the moral command of welcoming and effectively interacting with someone in particular, someone with a name, an identity and a social origin. Hospitality requires compliance with both imperatives (Derrida and Dufourmantelle 2000). Surely though, the hospitable question for a name, for information opening the subject up to difference and surprise, can turn into an interrogation bent on closing doors and raising the threshold for entry into deliberation. This may be the effect of asking about the Other's interests in the planning process at hand, her partiality, objectivity and willingness to contribute to mutual understanding. As Derrida stresses: 'The question of hospitality is thus also the question of the question' (ibid.29).

The disputed issue of whether participants in deliberation should be questioned and possibly contradicted, or whether they should be offered unquestioning welcome, seems analogous to the difference between politics and ethics. In the realm of ethics, the responsibility of the subject to the Other 'is prior to dialogue, to the exchange of questions and answers' (Levinas 1981:111). In the realm of politics, on the other hand, if someone disagrees with me, I should not automatically accept this criticism as a law that is not to be questioned or countered – as such an indulgent stance could harm both myself and the Third. The strategy of 'questioning and shaping attention', recommended by Forester (1989:109–11) to counteract misuse of power in critical communicative planning, belongs to the realm of politics, for example, deliberation and debate in the public sphere.

The strategy of questioning assumptions in forecasts, criteria for judgement and assessment, and the impartiality of arguments is valuable to critical pragmatists. So is the strategy of directing attention to contradictions, unfairness, and new possibilities. These are their primary tools for reducing the political transaction costs of deprived groups and augmenting the political transaction costs of groups misusing their sources of power to shift planning towards recommendation of an alternative that further builds their power base (see Chapter 2). Nevertheless, this flexible course of action is compatible with the entire gamut of welcomings, from real inclusion to formal invitation followed by disregard. This last type of reception, inclusion as pure formality, would result from a questioning process leaving the arguments of the 'welcomed' group with zero weight, and from an attention-shaping process that allows the interests of the group to be completely ignored in the plan-making. In practice, the 'exigencies of political community require some form of closure, exclusion, and calculation. But these nonetheless offend against a norm of unconditional welcome that continues to serve as a principle of immanent critique of existing practices' (Barnett 2005:14). Questioning and shaping attention necessarily introduces a degree of calculation into the practice of care.

This section includes some paragraphs that put the Other in a superior position, and some paragraphs assuming reciprocity. This reflects dilemmas created by the planner's need to have one foot in the ethical realm and the other in the political realm. Inclusive planning deliberation implies welcoming others into both ethical and political relationships. The planner (the host) has a complicated role. She cannot escape from the responsibility of the face-to-face relationship, although her attention has to be shared between the Other and the Third. Her behaviour must be formed by her participation in asymmetric ethical relations. It is nevertheless also her task to ensure that the deliberation fulfils its political purpose, enhancing mutual understanding and exploring the possibilities for agreement on matters related to the plan. In her capacity as facilitator and mediator, the planner must arrange for symmetrical, reciprocal relations between the parties. She must work politically while attending to her moral obligations. Contradictions between the responsibilities of the ethical and the political realm force the planner to live with double binds. This predicament must be grasped by the scholar developing normative theories that are to be helpful in the planners' daily struggle.

Responsibility and inclusion: toleration

This section on toleration presents a mostly Habermasian analysis of Levinas's welcoming theme.[5] As shown in the preceding sections, Levinas makes a distinction between the ethical and the political realm, and is thus able to circumvent the ethical injunction of infinite responsibility for the Other. Habermas also needs to delimit the ethical, and does so by contrasting it with the moral. The ethical point of view concerns what is good for a person in the long run; that is, goals relative to a particular subjective history, tradition, or way of life. The moral point of view, on the other hand, concerns what is equally good for all, and as such, not relative to a particular subject (Thomassen 2006b:442). By moral reasoning one can promote political integration; for example, inclusive deliberation in planning processes.

Habermas seeks 'a *nonlevelling* and *nonappropriating* inclusion of the other *in his otherness*' (ibid.442, emphasis in original). Inclusive deliberation in politics and planning allows for difference and otherness in the ethical realm, but the inclusion of the other in her ethical difference is conditional on her acceptance of the ethical-moral (political) distinction and on her acceptance of the common political culture, for example, the principles of the constitution. A political community along these lines will not exclude a priori persons with different values or ethical backgrounds. 'Inclusion', Habermas writes, 'means that the political community stays open to include citizens of any background without confining those *Others* within the uniformity of a homogeneous national community' (Habermas, *The Postnational Constellation*, page 73, cited from Thomassen 2006b:443, italics in original).

Successful inclusion in planning is essential to comply with the tenets of discourse ethics. Each group partaking in deliberation must be willing to listen and respond to viewpoints from every other group even if the listener finds the arguments ill-conceived or of little merit.

It is worth examining whether toleration is the right criterion for deciding who should participate in the planning process. Jones identifies two standard conceptual features of toleration:

> First, toleration in its orthodox sense entails disapproval or dislike. We tolerate only that to which we object; if we find something unobjectionable, we have no occasion to tolerate it. Thus, when people conform to the model case of toleration, they are usually thought to possess two sorts of reason: (a) a reason for objecting to and so for preventing x and (b) a reason for not preventing x. Their reason not to prevent x overrides their reason to prevent it; hence they tolerate x.
>
> Secondly, we can tolerate only what we are able to prevent. If we object to x, but are powerless to prevent it, we cannot tolerate x. (Jones 2007:384)

This is in accordance with Cohen's (2004:69) definition, that 'an act of toleration is an agent's intentional and principled refraining from interfering with an opposed other (or their behaviour, etc.) in situations of diversity, where the agent believes she has the power to interfere'.

Borradori (2003) points to the religious origin of the notion of toleration. She holds that this origin makes toleration 'the remnant of a paternalistic gesture in which the other is not accepted as an equal partner but subordinated, perhaps assimilated, and certainly misinterpreted in its difference' (ibid.16). Derrida and Habermas both acknowledge that toleration is traditionally conceived as an asymmetrical and one-sided relationship where the tolerated depends on the tolerating bestowing toleration upon her as an act of grace. This view of toleration as paternalism makes Derrida reluctant to accept toleration as much better than a form of charity (ibid.127), while Habermas seeks to develop the concept and provides an inter-subjectivist interpretation grounded in dialogue.

Derrida sees toleration as inextricably linked with biased power relations:

> Tolerance is always on the side of the 'reason of the strongest', where 'might is right'; it is a supplementary mark of sovereignty, the good face of sovereignty, which says to the other from its elevated position, I am letting

you be, you are not insufferable, I am leaving you a place in my home, but do not forget that this is my home… (Derrida in Borradori 2003:127)

As the visitor metaphor in the above citation shows, Derrida finds it reasonable to juxtapose toleration and hospitality. He regards toleration as the opposite of hospitality, or at best its lower limit: 'Tolerance is a conditional, circumspect, careful hospitality' (Derrida in Borradori 2003:128). Derrida describes toleration as a scrutinized hospitality that is always under surveillance; it is parsimonious and protective of its sovereignty. Toleration as conceived by Derrida is sufficient neither for inclusive dialogue as prescribed by discourse ethics nor for the reciprocity between interlocutors of equal standing aimed for in Habermasian planning dialogue. This points to a dilemma, as conditional hospitality is all one can hope for in practice: 'An unconditional hospitality is, to be sure, practically impossible to live; one cannot in any case, and by definition, organize it' (ibid.129). Levinasian hospitality would, moreover, eliminate the predict-ability required for planning; whoever comes, comes, and then whatever happens, happens.

Conceptual development of toleration is required because deliberative democracy demands the critical engagement of citizens with each other; 'toleration in the sense of non-interference is too minimal for cooperative and yet engaged deliberation' (Bohman 2003:758). Arguments must be taken seriously and not be disqualified ex ante, but this does not entail that we refrain from criticizing them. Indeed, the opposite is true, according to Bohman, since without criticism 'others will not form the expectation that *their* reasons as publicly expressed shaped the course of the debate' (ibid.764, italics in original). Habermas develops the non-interference conception of toleration by analyzing how this process of mutual criticism should be designed. One weakness of the standard formulation is that the threshold of toleration, which separates what is acceptable from what is not, is arbitrarily established by the existing authority. In contrast, Habermas argues for a deliberative democracy where 'tolerance emerges from the parties' mutual recognition as equal partners in a dialogue over the norms that should govern society' (Thomassen 2006a:195). Habermas maintains that: 'Within a democratic community whose citizens reciprocally grant one another equal rights, no room is left for an authority allowed to *one-sidedly* determine the boundaries of what is to be tolerated' (Borradori 2003:41, italics in original). For Habermas, toleration is defensible if practised in the context of a democratic community where the limits of toleration are dialogically determined through rational exchange of arguments among citizens.

When toleration is embraced as an integral part of CPT, it is at the same time conceded that deliberation in planning cannot be fully inclusive (Neill

2008). Gunder (2005:85) examines the concept of diversity as represented in multiculturalism and finds it to signify a desire for toleration of the Other 'that may run counter to society's most fundamental desire for security, inclusiveness, and completeness'. Habermas (2006b:197) articulates the paradox: '(E)ach act of toleration must circumscribe the range of behaviour everybody must accept, thereby drawing a line for what can *not* be tolerated. There can be no inclusion without exclusion' (italics in original). If the democratic state is to prevail, it must resort to intolerance towards enemies of the constitution (ibid.198), and if inclusive deliberation is to be feasible in planning, all parties must reciprocally take the perspectives of the others.

Indifference to the Other is contrary to Levinas's demand for responsibility and welcoming. It is also contrary to Derrida's idea of hospitality, even conditional hospitality. Moreover, indifference to the Other's opinions and attitudes exempts the subject of the obligation from being tolerant. We can only exercise toleration towards other people's beliefs if we reject them for subjectively good reasons.

Two kinds of reason have to be involved to make toleration a suitable political option: 'reasons to reject the convictions of others and reasons to accept nevertheless common membership of essentially disagreeing people within the same political community' (Habermas 2006b:199). However, civic inclusion is not only about overcoming controversy caused by different convictions and opinions. Equally important and problematic are different identities, and inclusion of different identities in planning deliberation entails recognition rather than toleration. In fact, the norm of mutual recognition of all as members of the political community – with equal rights – must be accepted before all of us can mutually expect one another to be tolerant. 'Thus, tolerance only begins where discrimination ends' (ibid.200).

The toleration of identities is not primarily about extending the range of liberties available to certain groups, according to Jones (2006:125). Rather it is about granting recognition to those groups. The primary concern when aiming to make deliberation in planning inclusive is, most often, 'not to allow people to do something to which others might object but to accord respect and standing to their identities so that there is no bar to their full inclusion in society' (ibid.125). The toleration of others' perspectives is part of recognizing them as equal members of a political community. Recognition should be granted despite the potential for persistent disagreement and deep conflict. What toleration expresses is recognition of others as entitled to contribute to the definition of our common society (Bohman 2003:765).

In the context of cultural difference, Taylor (1994:64) insists that the politics of recognition demands 'that we all *recognize* the equal value of different cultures; that we not only let them survive, but acknowledge their *worth*' (italics in original). However, the combination of toleration and recognition creates a puzzle which Jones (2006:128) brings to our attention: 'According recognition to a group entails ascribing it some sort of positive value. Yet we can tolerate only that to which we object'. This puzzle is not troublesome when recognition is only associated with, and given to, identities, while toleration is associated with opinions, beliefs, and behaviour – but not identities.[6]

Conclusion

Even if face-to-face interaction is important, dialogue does not have the privileged status in Levinas's ethical theory of responsibility and Derrida's theory of hospitality as it has in Habermas's (1990, 1999) discourse ethics. Dialogue is an exchange relation, in that the interlocutor expects something in return for an uttering, an argument, or a question. Levinas and Derrida are instead looking for ethical content in the generous act of gift-giving, which anticipates no response:

> (E)stablished ways of thinking about the relational encounter between Self and Other – in terms of dialogical, reciprocal, dialectical or symmetrical relations of co-implication – might actually obstruct rather than advance the cultivation of ethical responses to otherness. (Barnett 2005:13)

If the gift relationship is to be seen as the ethical ideal consistent with Derridean hospitality, then the Habermasian communicatively rational dialogue is imperfect in the sense that it inscribes the 'gift' of a presented argument within an anticipated circuit of mutual questions and counter-arguments. Generosity departs as expectations are allowed in. The principle of hospitality can be contravened by introducing a degree of anticipation and reciprocity into the practice of care, and this is what the mutuality expected in dialogue does. The demand for reciprocity is defended by arguing that inclusion is the primary goal, and that moral harm is primarily rendered by excluding or disavowing otherness, not by appealing to reciprocity and mutual empathy.

Important values such as responsibility for the Other, hospitality, and inclusion must be modified in order to be part of politics and planning practice. Not to go morally astray in this modification process, the planner and the planning theorist need an ethic, a system of moral principles or rules of behaviour. The Levinasian ethic outlined in this chapter is one of several options. International controversies over the role of human rights in politics show that the balancing of the ethical and the political realms is of great consequence to contemporary government.

Some conclusions on communicative planning theorists' responsibility for inclusion are listed below:

- Indifference cannot be an attitude commended by communicative planning theorists. It would drain motivation from participants in the planning process for responding to Others, as it would not matter who Others are or what they say. Mutual understanding is not based on indifference.
- Levinas's absolute ethical regard for the Other, and the concomitant claim for non-instrumentality in all self-Other relationships, must be relaxed in planning processes. Planning theory is about collective decision processes and has to give priority to reciprocity and mutuality rather than infinite responsibility and hospitality to the Other.
- Lack of recognition, that is, discrimination against cultural or ethnical identities, excludes people from deliberation even before their arguments are heard. Fighting discrimination should be part of the responsibility of planning theorists, as such struggle is crucial for making planning processes inclusive.
- Intolerance 'is evidenced in the inability of citizens to raise vital and significant concerns in deliberation, in the exclusion of relevant reasons, and in the illicit and unspoken generalization of the dominant or majority perspective' (Bohman 2003:775). These features of intolerance break with the tenets of discourse ethics and represent distortions of deliberation which communicative planning theorists have the responsibility to counteract.
- Communicative planning theorists are responsible for promoting toleration in the Habermasian sense. This means arguing for institutions to work in line with discourse ethics in order to let the various parties to a planning endeavour reciprocally determine whether certain opinions, beliefs, and behaviours should be tolerated.

When working on normative planning theories, scholars have a responsibility to encourage practices for decent and respectful treatment of people who are involved in planning processes or affected by plans. Planners should be led to take others into account in an ethically responsible manner even if the unspecified other person is distant in space, time, culture or social identity. The overall conclusion of this chapter is that even in light of Levinas's ideas of responsibility, the CPT ideal of approaching Habermasian dialogue turns out not to be unreasonable as a lodestar in the political realm of urban planning.

Notes

1. Levinas (1969) analyzes 'the Other' in *Totality and Infinity*, and brief accounts of his ideas on this topic are offered by Arnett (2003), Barnett (2005) and Gunder and Hillier (2007:21–22).

2. Forester's strategic use of questioning is foreign to Levinas's ethical relationship. Sometimes, however, there is a fine line between questioning for strategic reasons and for reaching mutual understanding, and it is hard to see how Levinas can wholly dispense with the subject's questioning of the Other. Through this aspect of conversation and by taking the Other's response into consideration, the subject can develop with the Other a shared sense of context. Then a more or less univocal meaning of what is said can emerge for the two interlocutors (Hendley 2000:7).

3. Spivak (1994:43–64) writes about a planning case, the Flood Action Plan in Bangladesh. He studies how responsibility is associated with a consultation process (dialogue) in this case. It is described how dialogue collapsed when otherness posed a challenge. This happened when an 'authentic' representative of the Bengali peasants got the floor (ibid.60–2). See Thomassen (2006b) for a discussion of dilemmas concerning unlimited inclusion.

4. Brettschneider illustrates by comparing with a restriction on participation in democratic election:

    Consider a case in which a majority disenfranchised one quarter of the population. Here the justification of democracy, that it includes as many citizens as possible in an act of self-rule, conflicts with the results of majoritarian procedure. The result is a tension between the procedure and the reasons that underlie it. Accordingly, if it is not to be self-defeating, majoritarianism should recognize some limits on policy outcomes to ensure that its fundamental justification is not undermined. (Brettschneider 2007:13)

5. Some scholars distinguish 'toleration' as behaviour, from 'tolerance' as attitude. Toleration would then characterize the action or practice of tolerating something, while tolerance would be the willingness or ability to tolerate something. Most authors referred to in this section do not adhere to this distinction. I therefore choose to use the term toleration about the attitude as well as the behaviour.

6. This delimitation of toleration is defended by Churchill (1997:201) who claims that the 'objects of toleration ... are not persons per se, but beliefs, attitudes, behavior (including verbal), and practices subject to change or alteration by the persons who hold these beliefs and attitudes or exhibit or participate in the behaviors in question'. This also seems to be Habermas's solution:

    Tolerance can only come to bear if there are legitimate justifications for the rejection of competing validity claims: 'If someone rejects people whose skin is black we should not call on him to be "tolerant toward people who look different" ... For then we would accept his prejudice as an ethical judgment similar to the rejection of a different religion. A racist should not be tolerant, he should quite simply overcome his racism.' In this and similar cases, we consider a critique of the *prejudices* and the struggle against *discrimination* to be the appropriate response – and not 'more tolerance'. (Habermas 2006b:200, quoting R. Forst, italics in original)

10

Responsible Decisions in Teaching and Academic Life

Reviving critical planning theory is easier when the theorists are not looked down on for failing to practise what they preach. CPT is about dialogue, inclusion, and democratizing decision-processes. There is no good reason why these properties should be desirable in planning processes only. On the contrary, one would expect the properties to be reflected even in the planning theorist's dealings with administrators, colleagues, and students. Demonstrated consistency between words and deeds is likely to result in both the academic and his or her theoretical work being held in higher esteem.

Most planning theorists in academia divide their working hours between research, teaching, and administration. Their responsibilities as researchers were analyzed in the two previous chapters. Many decisions with immediate consequences for students and colleagues are made by planning theorists in their capacity as teachers and administrators at course level and department level in universities. It is to decision-making and to these roles that attention is now directed.

Derrida on responsible decisions

Jacques Derrida's ideas on responsible decisions are taken as the point of departure (see also Gunder and Hillier 2007). This is potentially rewarding, as he wrote repeatedly about the responsibility of the university, the theorists (philosophers), and the teachers. I set out from some publications in which Derrida directly addresses responsibility in the university and the research community (Derrida 1983, 1986, 2002, 2004a, 2004b). Connections are drawn back to the notions of dual theory, unintended effects, neo-liberalism, inclusion of the Other dealt with in the previous chapter, and importantly, the possibilities for doing critical planning theory addressed in the whole book.

Responsible action requires that a decision has to be made; it occurs at junctions where someone faces a choice. In the conceptual system of Derrida responsible action can only take place when the actor faces an aporia, that is, an impasse or a contradiction.[1] This refers to situations in which no rule or similar guideline applies, and established knowledge does not point out the obvious way to proceed. Neither does any authority tell the actor how to choose. The situation is marked by undecidability, meaning that the decision-maker has to invent the reason for choice. If I choose on the basis of a rule and employ the rule as a reason for my 'decision', then I let the rule and the authority that supports it take some moral responsibility for the choice. When the choice is taken on the basis of doctrine, tradition, rule or other authority, it is not entirely *my* choice, and then I cannot be fully responsible. I can be responsible only if not offered a handhold by any institution (set of rules); that is, when I find my own way out of a situation of double-binds and undecidability (Gunder and Hillier 2007:78–81).

Were planning to consist only of applying rules, it would create nothing that is new. It would merely impose 'a stale past onto the future that annihilates the possibility that is promised by it' (Sokoloff 2005:345). If rules are imposed without acknowledging their contingent origin, they may become repressive and reactionary. Derridean 'decision', on the other hand, is an act of invention that cannot be fully grounded on anything that precedes it. As opposed to maintaining the political order, decisions have the potential to transform it (ibid.). Derrida's concept of decision can therefore prove helpful in critical planning theory. This chapter reflects the belief that if the problems of ethics, justice, and responsibility could be solved by the mere use of rules and algorithms that produce certain results with certain kinds of data, there would be little reason why learned persons should bother to make so much fuss about these notions in politics and planning research.

To explore the role of planning theory in relation to Derridean responsibility, a dictum of John Forester's can be used as a springboard: 'good theory is what we need when we get stuck' (Forester 1989:12). Planning theory is assumed to be helpful in situations where no rule applies and no practical knowledge tells the planner how to proceed. Yet, in order to preserve the possibility of responsibility, planning theory cannot remove the planner from a tight spot by completely filling the gap between practical knowledge and action. Rather, planning theory must facilitate reformulation of the problem or devise frameworks for seeing practical problems from new perspectives (Rein and Schön 1993). The responsible planner cannot let decision follow directly from planning theoretical precepts without further reflection. However, with a theoretical foundation to draw on, the final judgement that the planner has to make may look less frightening, less impossible, closer to problems the planner has dealt with before, and therefore less paralyzing.

Dividing the responsibilities of theorists into obligations they have as writers, teachers, and university academics, respectively, makes it easier to see who planning theorists are responsible to. The accountability aspect of moral responsibility suggests that scholars may be requested to explain (to account for) their actions 'by an audience presumed to have some capability or moral authority to pass judgment' (Deetz and White 1999:113). Several types of audience can call on planning theorists to explain and defend their theoretical contributions to research and education. Academics must try to make their theories stand up to scrutiny by their colleagues at internal seminars, answer students at lectures, and counter the critique of the research community at conferences. As writers, theorists must account for their reasoning to referees, editors, and the research community in the capacity of readers. Finally, as every other employee, scholars in tertiary education must answer to superiors, who in many universities and colleges are influenced by neo-liberal management ideology that is at odds with the respect many academics have for the critical and Enlightenment-oriented ethos.

Responsibility of planning theorists as educators

Teaching is necessary for research, and this goes for planning theory as for every other academic field. The teachers are the reproductive organs of the research community. Knowledge in the field will stagnate, dry up and be forgotten unless passed on to new generations of prospective researchers. Post-graduate education is about creating and forming an offspring (Habermas 1987:11). For planning theory to be sustainable, theorists' responsibility for research must extend to include the responsibility for teaching. Writing about the responsibility of philosophers, Derrida (2004b:170) insists that 'we have the right to demand that philosophical research and questioning never be dissociated from teaching'. Generalized to other fields, this means that researchers in academic disciplines should have the right to shape their own reproduction.

Having established that planning theorists hold a responsibility for teaching, there is the question of *what* they should be responsible for conveying to their successors. The ensuing account does not by any means aim to be complete. Just a few central points are elaborated, beginning with the linking of Derridean undecidability and responsibility to Jonas's (1984) ideas on unintended effects, and continuing with improvisation and creativity, critical theory, postcolonial responsibility, and reflection on professional practice.

Jonas is right that 'the excessively intricate web of events will, in principle, never conform to plan' (ibid.118), making it necessary to preserve the capacity for spontaneity at all times. In the future-oriented field of planning, there is an ultimate unpredictability. Without the ability to improvise, plans would soon be useless and forgotten – or simply harmful when used as guidelines for collective action, if the plans are out of touch with reality. Dvir and Lechler

(2004) state the quandary in its extreme form: plans are nothing, changing plans is everything.

Accentuation of the fundamental need for improvisation depicts a situation from where knowledge does not point in any particular direction. This is where Jonas can be linked up with Derrida. The concept of undecidability defines such situations from where processed knowledge manifested in rules and the like – in Jonas's case the plans – are unhelpful in guiding the next steps. Impromptu action and ad hoc measures could lead anywhere, however, and are likely to bring about effects that are unintended and not dealt with in the plan. Thus, when planners and decision-makers act responsibly and improvise in order to protect what still makes sense in the plan, they produce consequences unintended at the time of releasing the original plan. This risk is unavoidable, as unrevised plans lead to aporia – nonpassage. (See Chapter 8 on unintended consequences.)

Jonas (1984:118) stresses 'that any total responsibility ... is always responsible also for preserving ... the *possibility* of responsible action in the future' (italics in original). It is thus the responsibility of planning theorists 'not to plug up the indispensable, though not calculable, wellspring of spontaneity' (ibid.) from which creative and improvised planning revisions can erupt in future unanticipated conditions. Neither in the goal nor on the road to its fulfilment must the planning theorist 'create a condition in which the potential candidates for a repetition of his own role have become lackeys or robots' (ibid.). Protecting creativity means that planning theory should not be a doctrine but have an open structure allowing for ideas to develop in many directions. This comes with the risk that planning theory which can be used responsibly by planners in escaping from impasse, might also facilitate measures that many find repulsive, such as the neo-liberal policies dealt with in Chapter 5. The same can be said of planning as Jonas says of political action: it 'has always been beset by the excess of causal reach over that of prediction and so was never free of an element of gambling' (ibid.118).

Favourable conditions for creativity imply acceptance of uncertainty (Kunzmann 2005). Encouraging creativity in theoretical and practical work means welcoming solutions that were previously unheard of and could not be foreseen. Creative planning emphasizes the will-formation side of planning at the expense of the forecasting side (Albrechts 2005, Healey 2004). Communicative planning is creative only in so far as discussions and compromises – the mutual adjustment of competing ideas – can lead to something significantly different from what exists already. The creative potential of communicative planning is ambiguous: the conflicting interests and preferences of the involved parties delimit the scope for acceptable innovative solutions, while the participants' increasing mutual understanding throughout the dialogical process enhances their capacity for creatively combining ideas into novel packages that offer something to every stakeholder. Responsible planning decisions must be creative to offer escape from the undecidable situations caused by the double binds of inclusion/exclusion, deliberation/implementation, and acceptance/critique.

Teachers should beware of imposing a paralyzing weight of critique and conceptual conundrums on students, so they can see no possibility of meaningful action. Nevertheless, attention to undecidability and the consequences dealt with above is essential in the teaching of planning theory, as the general attitude towards revision of plans shapes the relationship between planners and elected politicians. Planning students must be taught to acknowledge the likely presence of unintended consequences and the absolute necessity that responsible decision-makers ask for revisions that inevitably will sometimes produce effects that conflict with the planners' intentions in the original plan. Contempt for politicians and democratic politics will easily breed in planning circles if the above mechanisms are misconstrued, and it is not realized that necessarily risky spontaneity and improvisation can save plans even when altering them.

For Derrida, responsibility begins by questioning the origin of universal rules and confronting established concepts and practices. 'There is no responsibility without a dissident and inventive rupture with respect to tradition, authority, orthodoxy, rule, or doctrine' (Derrida, cited from Wang 2005:49). Derrida calls for questioning of academic texts – be it a reading, an interpretation, the construction of a theoretical model or the rhetoric of an argument. Teaching responsibility to planners entails developing the habit of open-minded critique and the positioning of planning theory as a critical theory, such as critical pragmatism (Forester 1993a), for example. Derrida writes about the responsibility of philosophers, but the analogy with planning theorists is pertinent, as philosophy stands in a theory-practice relationship with empirical sciences that has similarities to the relationship between planning theory and planning.

The questioning of philosophy by philosophers is perceived by Derrida as a most compelling duty. The responsibility of a philosopher arises from the request that '(a) philosopher is always someone for whom philosophy is not a given, someone who, in essence, must question the essence and the purpose of philosophy. And re-invent it' (Derrida, cited from Egéa-Kuehne 2003:276–7). Analogically, planning theorists should question the essence and the purpose of planning and planning theory. The theorist has an obligation which involves the risk of asking questions that are unsettling because they challenge established traditions, beliefs and certitudes (ibid.277). The questioning of planning tools and procedures prepares students for making decisions without trying to draw final answers solely from the tenets of their professional training; that is, it prepares them for acting responsibly. Planning theorists must teach students that even if the planning toolkit offers decision support, this apparatus draws on the kind of fuzzy criteria that allows for the possibility of things being different.

Universities are criticized for allowing too much 'preprofessionalism or "vocationalism", in the narrow sense of adaptation of one's college education to the putative demands of a future job in the so-called outside world' (LaCapra 1998:44). Planning education has this decried characteristic. The purpose of teaching planning theory is to make vocationally trained planners reflect on their vocation and to show how their techniques, procedures, rules and professional practices are grounded in theoretical foundations put down by non-vocational disciplines taught at the university, such as philosophy, ethics, and social theory. Hence, the task and the responsibility of the teachers of planning theory are to bridge the gap between vocational training and 'the humanistic goals of increasing self-understanding and furthering critical inquiry into culture and society' (ibid.44). This is what Derrida calls his 'double responsibility':

> I think I have to make two gestures simultaneously: to train people, to teach them, to give them a content, to be a good pedagogue, to train teachers, to give them a profession; and at the same time to make them as conscious as possible of the problems of professionalisation. (Derrida 1986:7)

Planning theorists' responsibility as educators is a perilous engagement, a commitment to staying over the abyss and at the same time overcoming it (Derrida 1983). This involves efforts to bestride the opposition between practice and theory, technology and metaphysics, and vocational guidelines and the principle of reason. It is clear from the above passages that planning academics should not teach as if planners are to be critics only. Planners should also be able to point towards possible solutions. Commenting from a critical and left-of-centre position, Massey thinks that:

> It is salutary, and politically important ... not always to be in a position of critic (I think of all the easy, anti-State stuff, and sniping from 'the margins' – which academics rarely inhabit – that litters much theoretical and 'critical' writing); to be forced to be constructive and to take a different kind of responsibility (including responsibility for compromises). (Massey 2008:495)

In his reassessment of the critical planning education he received at the Graduate School of Architecture and Urban Planning at the University of California, Los Angeles, Sanyal (2008) stresses that critical thinking, if it is to become central to planning education, must appreciate the need for problem-solving. 'Planners are expected to assist with problem solving, and to do so they have to go one step beyond social criticism and commit themselves ... to propose policies that would address issues of general public interest' (ibid.153).

The breakthrough for neo-liberal ideology has not made it easier for university academics to combine conveyance of vocational knowledge with the critical knowledge necessary for the enlightenment of the political public sphere. It used to be the responsibility of university teachers to induct students into the culture of ideas and arguments so that they can partake in intellectual conversations which endow them with the capacity to become public actors and be part of a productive democratic citizenry (McLean 2006). In many countries with neo-liberal regimes, universities are required to compete with each other for students and research funding. This encourages giving priority to what students perceive as immediately useful to their future work, career skills, and credentials. The trend is towards privatizing higher education or putting a price on it, so that citizens will have to buy university studies at market value rather than have them provided by the state. Students and parents demand value for money, meaning knowledge that will ensure work after completed studies.

Finally, responsibility for opening up to the Other is highly apposite to teaching, in the encounter with students. Considering the increasing number of foreign students in many countries, effects of the multiple dimensions of distance on the student–teacher relationship become an issue of both pedagogical and moral interest (see Chapter 9). The destinations of the migrating student population are overwhelmingly the western-style liberal democracies (Madge et al. 2009). Most familiar modes of planning are designed to improve democracy in one way or another. Western teachers of planning theory must try to make sense of such modes to international students, many of them without experience of democracy at the national or regional level. When international students have personal experience with democratic forms of local government, the cultural context and social structure that makes these models work well (or sometimes badly) are most often little known to the teacher. Following Spivak (1988), it can be argued that in the wake of colonialism the views of many students are not 'heard' as a consequence of the privileged position that, for example, Euro-American academics occupy. A postcolonial responsibility of planning teachers is to gain knowledge of others who occupy those spaces most closed to the western privileged view, and attempting to speak to those others in such a way that they might take their teachers seriously and be able to answer back (Jazeel and McFarlane 2007). Critical pedagogy points to the connections between conception and practice, and it honours students' experiences by connecting what goes on in classrooms to their everyday lives (Giroux 2003:11).

Learning from one another is an ethical imperative in communicative planning, and cultural diversity should inform learning in the universities. Dialogue joins hands with a critical teaching of planning to 'contest the hegemonic discourse of western "best practice"... and to imagine everyday academic practices from a multitude of different perspectives and centres' (Madge et al. 2009:43). It is the responsibility of teachers in universities with an international student population to make visible the multiple global voices and respond to the claims made by these voices. Grappling with this 'hospitality' problem and the other teaching problems above prepares the theorist for the wider range of tasks set for university academics.

Responsibility of planning theorists as university academics

Most planning theorists have responsibilities as members of a university staff. These academics popularize and impart research results and do outreach work as part of their responsibility to society, but this is not further discussed here. Both for Habermas and Derrida, social responsibility centres on keeping the scientific and philosophical discourse alive and vigorous. They are both quite concrete on this particular point. Habermas (1987:21) emphasizes stimulation of the specialized public spheres of the university which retain their vitality through associations, annual conferences, journals, etc.[2] Derrida holds that:

> The unacceptability of a discourse, the noncertification of a research project, the illegitimacy of a course offering are declared by evaluative actions: studying such evaluations is, it seems to me, one of the tasks most indispensable to the exercise of academic responsibility, most urgent for the maintenance of its dignity. (Derrida 1983:13)

More abstractly, Derrida asks members of the academic community to 'respond to the call of the principle of reason' (ibid.8). This means 'to explain effects through their causes, rationally; it is also to ground, to justify, to account for on the basis of principles or roots' (ibid.). The imperative for responding is the initial form and minimal requirement of responsibility.

The university is also there to tell the truth: 'It declares and promises an unlimited commitment to the truth' (Derrida 2002:202). University academics need to position themselves as participants in the battle over the status and functioning of truth. Even apart from the prominent view that truth is as much constructed as disclosed in the research process, this unqualified priority of truth-telling is problematic. Does it mean only that university scholars should 'discern and decide between the true and the false' (Derrida 2004a:97), or is it a new call for the Galilean Imperative: 'explore every domain, unravel every mystery, penetrate every unknown, explain every process. Consider not the cost, abide no interference, in the holy pursuit of truth' (Lakoff 1980:111–12). Is there, moreover, any real difference between the two interpretations? New situations will always unfold, in which true and false can be distinguished only by exploring new domains and penetrating further into the unknown. Derrida prescribes a rule by which responsible academics cannot abide: For planning theorists who are in doubt whether to continue working on a new theory with anticipated sinister side-effects, the imperative of truth would always give a green light. Suspicions of dark-side effects will never stop a theory project when commitment to truth is unlimited. But then again, Derrida asks who is more faithful to reason's call than the one who offers questions in return, even about the unfailing superiority of truth and reason (Trifonas 2000:110).

Truth-searching affects reading, and planning theorists have responsibilities as readers of plans, for instance. Mandelbaum (1990:353) conveys the distinct impression that it is the responsibility of theorists to read plans critically and 'free ... [themselves] from the control of the text'. This should be the theorists' chief concern when 'reading against the grain of the textual style – treating an urban design plan as a policy analytic argument, reading a budget as a theatrical narrative, transforming a policy argument into a design opportunity' (ibid.353), even if it implies a serious danger of misreading the text. The critical reading takes precedence in order to penetrate the plan's structure and thus enable the theorist to grasp what is important or central to a plan. The overall intention is to do this reading in public and 'extend and enrich the domain of public discourse' (ibid.356).

One consequence of the imperative of truth-searching is the ideal of the commitment of university scholars to tireless questioning in order to establish truth, and tireless argumentation in order to disseminate verity. The critical strategy of questioning is familiar to communicative planning theorists (Forester 1989). It comes as no surprise that in its critical capacity, the university is not only a community of thought but a community of the question. It might be an impossible community, though, as it is one of dissension and not consensus. 'The university should ... be the place in which nothing is beyond question' (Derrida 2002:205), not even the idea of critique or the idea of thinking as questioning. Derrida's conceptualization of 'the university without condition' implies the right to say everything and to publish it (ibid). It is the responsibility of scholars to resist attempts to restrict free and fair argument. Universities are to be spaces for the 'lovely competition' of ideas (Derrida, in Myerson 1995:127) and sites of unconditional resistance to every other sovereignty but that of the principle of truth. Scholars should defend the importance of ideas: show why they must be investigated and explored, discussed and debated, taught, published, and put into practice if surviving scrutiny.

Discreet coordination and collaboration between the university and other functionally autonomous subsystems, such as the economic-military-administrative complex, worries both Habermas (1987:7) and Derrida:

> The problem of the relationship between the research – fundamental or end-oriented research – and the state, the military and industrial structure of the state, is one of our main concerns, I would say. I think that this is the responsibility of the teacher or scholar today. (Derrida 1986:6)

Derrida notes that one can no longer separate some scientists, some politicians, and some military decision-makers. He maintains that '(o)ne of the responsibilities of the university today is not to let those people do everything by themselves' (ibid.10). On the other hand, neither Habermas nor Derrida would advocate a university cut off from society. Hence, scrutiny of the complex and dangerous liaisons just mentioned must comprise critique of the university itself. It is noteworthy in the present context that the connected university, with its diffuse borders between inside and outside, facilitates development of dual theory (see Chapter 8) that catches the interest of both authorities and civil society organizations.

Derrida is alert to the dangers of dual use of theory in the original meaning of serving both civil and military purposes. Mentioning a long list of academic fields both in the social sciences and the humanities, Derrida concedes that theory within these disciplines may be just as useful in ideological warfare as it is in peaceful accumulation of knowledge:

> Such a theory may always be put to work in communications strategy, the theory of commands, the most refined military pragmatics of jussive utterances ... One can just as easily seek to use the theoretical formulations of sociology, psychology, even psychoanalysis in order to refine what was called in France during the Indochinese or Algerian wars the powers of 'psychological action' – alternating with torture. From now on, so long as it has the means, a military budget can invest in anything at all, in view of deferred profits: 'basic' scientific theory, the humanities, literary theory and philosophy. (Derrida 1983:13)

Collaboration with the military sector is a business strategy also for some publishers of academic journals and books. Chatterton (2008) tells the story of Reed Elsevier's involvement in organizing the biannual Defence Systems Exhibition International arms fair at London's ExCel centre. The around 1000 exhibitors sell everything from battleships and attack helicopters to cluster bombs and machine guns. Reed Elsevier publishes key journals in geography and several branches of planning. Some academics noted that the engagement in the arms fair 'would seem to be divorced from the journals where critical geographers seek to publish their work and to debate issues such as human rights, corporate social responsibility and the politics of violence' (Chatterton and Featherstone 2007:3). The critical geographers could not accept a situation whereby their work was published by a company with links to the aggressive promotion of the arms trade, and they felt the responsibility to start a campaign. As the pressure grew, Reed Elsevier decided to pull out of the arms fair business in 2007.

The Elsevier case shows that some academics regard being critical as insufficient. They feel the responsibility to follow up their critique by taking on an activist role. This felt obligation to span two disparate worlds – studying society from a detached position simultaneously with changing society while living in it – easily brings them into difficulties. Pickerill (2008) offers a telling example of the squeeze experienced by activist academics because their activist compatriots voice expectations that are incompatible with ordinary university research. In 2004 Pickerill started a research project called 'Autonomous Geographies', which explored the everyday lives of anti-capitalist activists. Activist friends thought it smacked of an attempt to find a niche in academic circles with activist kudos. In their view, political transformation would now be a by-product of her career, not the other way around, and one of them wrote to her:

> Getting involved in a project like Autonomous Geographies looks like it's uncomfortably straddling the two worlds ... Simply working within an institution frames your work. The political line will have to go somewhere down the middle because of this ... it is actually totally disgusting for me to see (you) ... becoming an 'expert on the subject' in the eyes of the academy, and taking a salary for it, yet operating in a parasitical relationship to those who are doing the real work and have made financial/lifestyle sacrifices. (Pickerill 2008:482)

The possible leap from being a critical academic to being an activist academic places some planning scholars in an aporia, in a situation characterized by Derrida's undecidability. An impossible choice between deeds and words is called for. Activist academics conceive this choice as having to choose between identities, experiencing the academic alternative as selling out their activist principles and lifestyle for a paid and relatively safe career. The choice is between being a person who uncompromisingly tries to improve man-made reality through direct action, or being one who aims to achieve progressive social change only indirectly by studying and explaining societal phenomena.

It should be evident from Chapter 4 that activist scholars work in dialogue, collaboration and alliance with people who are struggling to better their lives. 'Activist scholarship embodies a responsibility for results that these "allies" can recognize as their own, value in their own terms, and use as they see fit' (Hale 2008:4). For the activist scholar, the people who are subjects of research play a central role, not as informants or data sources, but as knowledgeable, empowered participants in the entire research process. Most activist scholars assert that a good part of their insight and analysis – not just their data – comes from the communities, organizations, and movements with which they are aligned (ibid.15). This is a main source of the difficulties many activist scholars experience in universities. Their challenge is to credibly claim methodological rigour while rejecting the positivist notion of objectivity that has been the lynchpin of such claims for a century.

Because no theory seems any longer to be shielded from goal-oriented use in various directions, it has to be the task of the university to unmask 'all the ruses of end-orienting reason, the paths by which apparently disinterested research can find itself indirectly reappropriated, reinvested by programs of all sorts' (ibid.16). Trifonas (2003:291) declares that '(e)ven the most underground thinking … can be rehabilitated or reappropriated to serve a "highly traditional politics of knowledge" … if the conditions of exposition…are not analysed with a vigilant wariness, a radical suspicion'. Derrida subscribes to this strategy for warding off misuse of dual theory but does not assert its success. On the contrary, he believes there is an unavoidable risk that socio-political forces in certain situations find it in their own interest to exploit university research, even theories not intended to have end-orientation; 'it is the risk of the future itself' (Derrida 1983:17). In these circumstances, ascribing moral responsibility to planning theorists for the consequences of their research is often unwarranted.

Academic responsibilities versus neo-liberal demands

Higher education can be seen as a public good that constitutes a semi-autonomous sphere for the development of a critical and productive democratic citizenry (Aronowitz and Giroux 2000). It is a system that, in many countries, enables scholars to evade the control of powerful vested interest groups. Universities have traded on their Enlightenment inheritance that they are the guardians and creators of knowledge produced for the greater good of humanity:

> They are seen and claim to be seen as the watchdogs for the free interchange of ideas in a democratic society; they claim to work to protect freedom of thought, including the freedom to dissent from prevailing orthodoxies. They are quintessentially defined as public interest institutions and their research is granted status and credibility on the basis of its disinterestedness. (Lynch 2006:1)

It is suggested in this section that neo-liberal influence on the university must be limited if the university degree is not to develop into simply another commodity delivered on the market to those who can afford to buy it.

Several roles and responsibilities have been set up for university academics within the Enlightenment-inspired system. For example, McLean (2006:17) recommends that they should address the inequities of the connections between origins and destinies in terms of class, ethnicity, religion, gender and disability; rebalance the emphasis on economic wealth and individual prosperity against more weight on individual fulfilment and transformation as well as citizenship in a democracy; and deal with complex and serious global problems – in particular, poverty, the natural environment and social conflict.

I concentrate here on the scholar as social interpreter and critic, and thus as a source of inspiration for reform. Doring (2002:143) expects university teachers to devote time and attention to participating in conversations crucial to the transformation of both students and community. Questions should be kept open; the less dialogue is distorted by power and interests, the more transforming the effects of learning. Critical theorists should practise a pedagogy which is attentive to how their students might, as citizens of the future, influence politics, culture and society in the direction of justice and reason (McLean 2006:1). It is the social responsibility of university academics to question current orthodoxy, one-dimensional thinking, and religious, ethnic and economic fundamentalism. University staff with academic freedom should seek the truth behind the veil of misrepresentation, ideology and interests of class and nation through which the events of current history are presented. Blomley (1994:384) contends that to neglect that responsibility is, at the very best, to acquiesce to oppression.

Calavita and Krumholz (2003) address planning academics directly and want them to become more engaged in the public debate about the role of government and public planning in today's society:

> Planning academics also carry the responsibility for publicly challenging the downtown-based model of economic development that, in both decaying rust belt and expanding sun belt cities, starves urban neighborhoods of basic public infrastructure while lavishing public resources on proposals for downtown stadiums, convention centers, and festival market places. (Calavita and Krumholz 2003:403)

Finally, the university must prove to society the quality of its teaching and academic production, and be attentive to the social and cultural demands of its environment. As will be clear, this responsibility forms a link to the description below of neo-liberalism's effects on the university. New public management (NPM), transposing the neo-liberal ideology to the public sector, relies on performance indicators, audits, monitoring, and management by objectives and results. This leads to a predilection for measurable outcome, such as the number of peer reviewed articles in high-standard journals. In numerous universities, the budgetary gains from engaging in conversations that are crucial in the transformation of both students and community are far less than for research articles. What is more, the journals defined as being of high standard are most often international and written in the English language. For planning academics in many non-English speaking countries, the reward system of academic life means that 'good' academics are encouraged to become silent scholars in their own society, inaudible in the public sphere and muted locally by virtue of engaging in discussions mostly with academic peers outside their own country (Lynch 2006:9).

The competition so central to neo-liberalism is not conducive to a critical academic community; emphasis is put on marketable rather than critical skills. Research assessment exercises and periodic teaching quality reviews encourage 'individual academics to "look after themselves", to make sure that whatever else is the case, *their* performance does not fall below expectations' (Thomas 2005:242, emphasis in original). The resulting time squeeze leads to less interest in the substance of the work of colleagues and to an inflated interest in external markers of achievement (ibid.243). Besides, some people feel a deep alienation in the experience of constantly living to perform. It evokes feelings of personal inauthenticity and a culture of compliance, as externally controlled performance indicators become the constant point of reference for one's work, regardless of how meaningless they might be (Lynch 2006:7). In stagnant environments, the extra incentives for research can nevertheless do some good even in the traditional model of university pedagogy. The belief in research-led teaching is widespread, and positive budgetary effects can spur departments with a weak research record to make an extra effort.

Is the successful educated person of today seen as one who is autonomous, rational, market-oriented, consuming and self-interested? The currently hegemonic ideology seems to push in this direction; neo-liberal institutions seek to shape the individual as a competitive entrepreneur. Neo-liberalism is concerned with contributions to society's economic progress through performance measurement, whereas the Enlightenment-inspired education project is concerned mainly with disinterested knowledge, critical reason, and the formation of responsible, democratic citizens. 'Neo-liberalism shifts academic life towards the authority of the market and is less concerned about freedom of thought and action' (Harland et al. 2010:86).

One risk aggravated by competition and commercialization is the subordination and trivialization of educational programmes that have low market value. This is a threat to critical and transformative perspectives that might well strike planning theory. University scholarship serving these perspectives is by its nature oppositional and reflexive. It is founded on the assumptions of independence and autonomy. 'If universities become too reliant on industry-funded research, or too beholden to the business-driven agenda of the government of today (even if it comes coded in the guise of advancing science), there is a danger that the interests of the university become synonymous with powerful vested interests' (Lynch 2006:7).

When universities openly pursue commercialization, it powerfully legitimizes and reinforces the pursuit of economic self-interest by students and contributes to the widespread sense among them that they are at the university solely to gain labour market advantages (Lynch 2006:7). The development of curious inquirers with their own inner dedication is not facilitated. What professors do and what the university does are likely to affect the attitudes of the students and their understanding of why they are studying.

The role of university academics as the critic and conscience of society must include the right to perform this role even in relation to their own university. This is complicated by increasing expectations in several countries that universities will supplement their income from private sources, even when they are within the state sector. Universities are seen as key drivers in the knowledge economy, and they are expected to develop links with industry and business in a series of new venture partnerships (Olssen and Peters 2005:313). However, criticism of one's own university is sometimes hard to keep up when lucrative research contracts are at stake. Neo-liberal organizing of universities generates a concern with market reputation, corporate loyalty and the use of discipline against employees who criticize their university (ibid.327).

The preceding brief account of neo-liberal influences on the institutions of tertiary education suffices to show that the more the economistic lopsidedness of neo-liberalism becomes ingrained in the management of academia, the more difficult it is to live up to the traditional responsibilities of the Enlightenment-oriented university. Critical thinking is not a primary asset in commercialization, social conscience is not indispensable in marketization processes, and the creation of competitive entrepreneurs is unlikely to develop social interpreters and critics.

Some responsibilities can be more easily fulfilled in the entrepreneurial, neo-liberal university, such as the responsibility for keeping up productivity and disseminating research results, and showing to society that quality research has been done. University teachers will experience incentives for efficiently providing vocational training to the many technical, economic and other professions crucial to the smooth working of modern society. Furthermore, there will be remuneration for establishing the academy-industry relations that facilitate the refinement and development of scholars' ideas and patents into marketable products to the benefit of society at large. In short, some features of the neo-liberal university are valuable to society, and university academics could do some good by contributing to the development of these aspects.

The two ends of realizing Enlightenment values and meeting neo-liberal demands cannot both be fully achieved by a university academic, so the need arises for deciding where to put the emphasis. This is similar to the 'double responsibility' that Derrida was faced with himself: to train university teachers for their profession and at the same time raise their consciousness of the problems of professionalism. There are conflicting norms and incentives pulling academics partly towards the traditional critical university and partly towards the neo-liberal commercialized university, trapping scholars in an undecidable situation. The choice between the conflicting roles in the contemporary university must be taken responsibly by each academic. In the Derridean sense this means not letting rules and the authority of others substitute for personal judgement.

Conclusion

Most theories of planning are normative. Procedural theories may describe and analyze, but they also say how some theorists think that processes of public urban planning should be structured and organized. There is always guidance for planner action embedded in planning theories. It stands to reason that the planner should seek support in general frameworks for organization of collective action. However, to act with Derridean responsibility, she must put the general guidelines aside before making up her mind. For theorists and practitioners alike, the final steps on the way to conclusions must go through fairness-seeking introspection, detached reflection on the validity of supporting rules, and inventive intuition. Only then will the individual's own judgement play a decisive role in shaping her standpoint, making her fully responsible, according to Derrida.

Ideally, the university teacher should not only convey knowledge of a subject to the student, but also help him or her develop as a responsible person. The student should grow into someone who not only can think critically and deliberate in a tolerant manner, but who also connects or embeds reason and judgement into actual conduct (Hansen 2001). Making a character-forming impact on students requires close and time-consuming relationships, however. Teachers in research universities would soon be squeezed between student contact and need for reading and writing, challenging the scholar's own ability to balance different responsibilities.

Moreover, universities can make misguided decisions in their dealings with the surrounding society, which backfire on teaching that aims at developing responsible students:

Universities are concerned with education, and their response to social issues will affect the education of their students just as surely as the lectures and the readings that go on in their libraries and classrooms. If we would teach our students to care about important social problems and think about them rigorously, then clearly our institutions of learning must set a high example in the conduct of their own affairs. (Bok 1982:10)

The moral responsibility of university academics should thus extend to critique of their own institutions. Finally, the protection enjoyed by tenured staff in their efforts to teach and write comes with social responsibilities. Advances in knowledge are sometimes unsettling and distasteful to the existing order, so academic freedom needs to be defended. This right of professors to speak their minds freely as teachers and scholars is associated with the general right to freedom of speech.

Despite difficulties and reservations, the conclusion is that the main responsibility of planning theorists is to keep deliberation open and expand it on matters of joint concern within the community of planning research, in academic teaching relations, in planning processes, and in arenas of policy-making and collective choice throughout society at large. Enrichment of the public conversation is a worthy goal.

Notes

1. An aporia is an impasse that cannot be dissolved by a rational principle or ground. It is the condition causing undecidability. As an example, Thomassen (2006b:447) mentions that 'defense of democracy, and by extension, inclusion and tolerance, is only possible in ways that simultaneously limit democracy, inclusion, and tolerance'. Thomassen, referring to Habermas, makes reference to the self-destructive inclusion of the Nazis in Germany in the late 1920s and early 1930s.
2. One undecidable situation regarding publishing is quite topical and illustrates well the call for responsibility in academia. Scholars are asked by their universities both to publish in established elite journals in order to obtain status and increase department budgets by earning publishing points, and to publish in new open access journals in order to undermine the hegemony of elite journals and bring their prices down to the advantage of university libraries.

References

Aberbach, J.D. and T. Christensen (2005): 'Citizens and consumers. An NPM dilemma', *Public Management Review* 7(2)225–45.

Abram, S.A. (2000): 'Planning the public: some comments on empirical problems for planning theory', *Journal of Planning Education and Research* 19(4)351–57.

Adams, D. and S. Tiesdell (2010): 'Planners as market actors: rethinking state-market relations in land and property', *Planning Theory and Practice* 11(2)187–207.

Adams St.Pierre, E. (1996): 'The responsibilities of readers: toward an ethics of responses', *Qualitative Sociology* 19(4)533–38.

Adler, P.S. and S.-W. Kwon (2002): 'Social capital: prospects for a new concept', *Academy of Management Review* 27(1)17–40.

AESOP (2007): 'Research ethics in planning: proposal for an AESOP thematic group'. www.aesop-planning.com/Groups_webpages/Ethics/index_ethics.htm (accessed 26.11.10).

Agger, A. and K. Löfgren (2008): 'Democratic assessment of collaborative planning processes', *Planning Theory* 7(2)145–64.

Alanen, A.R. and T.J. Peltin (1978): 'Kohler, Wisconsin: planning and paternalism in a model industrial village', *Journal of the American Planning Association* 44(2)145–59.

Albrechts, L. (1991): 'Changing roles and positions of planners', *Urban Studies* 28(1)123–37.

——(1999): 'Planners as catalysts and initiators of change: the new Structure Plan for Flanders', *International Planning Studies* 7(5)587–603.

——(2005): 'Creativity as a drive for change', *Planning Theory* 4(3)247–69.

Albrechts, L. and S.J. Mandelbaum (Eds) (2005): *The Network Society. A New Context for Planning.* London: Routledge.

Alcoff, L.M. (1995): 'The problem of speaking for others', pp 229–53 in L.A. Bell and D. Blumenfeld (Eds): *Overcoming Racism and Sexism.* Lanham, Maryland: Rowman and Littlefield.

Alexander, E.R. (2001a): 'A transaction-cost theory of land use planning and development control', *Town Planning Review* 72(1)45–75.

——(2001b): 'Governance and transaction costs in planning systems: a conceptual framework for institutional analysis of land-use planning and development control – the case of Israel', *Environment and Planning B: Planning and Design* 28(5)755–76.

——(2001c): 'The planner-Prince: interdependence, rationalities and post-communicative practice', *Planning Theory and Practice* 2(3)311–24.

——(2002a): 'The public interest in planning: from legitimation to substantive plan evaluation', *Planning Theory* 1(3)226–49.

——(2002b): 'Planning rights: toward normative criteria for evaluating plans', *International Planning Studies* 7(3)191–212.

Alexander, E.R. and A. Faludi (1996): 'Planning doctrine: its uses and implications', *Planning Theory* 16, 11–61.

Alic, J.A. (1994): 'The dual use of technology: concepts and policies', *Technology in Society* 16(2)155–72.

Alinsky, S. (1965): 'The professional radical: conversations with Saul Alinsky', *Harper's Magazine* 230(June)37–47.

——(1971): *Rules for Radicals. A Pragmatic Primer for Realistic Radicals*. New York: Vintage Books.

Allen, A. (2002): 'Power, subjectivity, and agency: between Arendt and Foucault', *International Journal of Philosophical Studies* 10(2)131–49.

Allmendinger, P. (2001): *Planning in Postmodern Times*. London: Routledge.

——(2002): 'Towards a post-positivist typology of planning theory', *Planning Theory* 1(1)77–99.

——(2009): *Planning Theory* (Second Edition). Basingstoke, Hampshire: Palgrave.

Allmendinger, P. and M. Gunder (2005): 'Applying Lacanian insight and a dash of Derridean deconstruction to planning's "dark side"', *Planning Theory* 4(1)87–112.

Allmendinger, P. and M. Tewdwr-Jones (1997): 'Post-Thatcherite urban planning and politics: a Major change?', *International Journal of Urban and Regional Research* 21(1)100–16.

——(2000): 'New Labour, new planning? The trajectory of planning in Blair's Britain', *Urban Studies* 37(8)1379–1402.

——(2002): 'The communicative turn in urban planning: unravelling paradigmatic, imperialistic and moralistic dimensions', *Space and Polity* 6(1)5–24.

Allmendinger, P. and H. Thomas (1998): 'Conclusions', pp 236–53 in P. Allmendinger and H. Thomas (Eds): *Urban Planning and the British New Right*. London: Routledge.

Alpern, K.D. (1983): 'Engineers as moral heroes', pp 40–51 in V. Weil (Ed.): *Beyond Whistleblowing: Defining Engineers' Responsibilities* (Proceedings of the Second National Conference on Ethics in Engineering). Chicago: Center for the Study of Ethics in the Professions, Illinois Institute of Technology.

Alvesson, M. and P. Thompson (2005): 'Post-bureaucracy?', pp 485–507 in S. Ackroyd, R. Batt, P. Thompson and P. Tolbert (Eds): *The Oxford Handbook of Work and Organization*. Oxford: Oxford University Press.

Amin, A. (2006): 'The good city', *Urban Studies* 43(5–6)1009–23.

Amin, A. and N. Thrift (2007): 'Cultural-economy and cities', *Progress in Human Geography* 31(2)143–61.

Ansell, C.K. (2004): 'Legitimacy: political', pp 8704–06 in N.J. Smelser and P.B. Baltes (Eds): *International Encyclopedia of the Social and Behavioral Sciences*. Amsterdam: Elsevier.

APA (2005): *AICP Code of Ethics and Professional Conduct*. www.planning.org/ethics/ethicscode.htm (accessed 25.11.08).

Apte, T. (2007): 'Future in their hands! Strategies for making a people's plan', *Futures* 39(5)597–613.

Arendt, H. (1958): *The Human Condition*. Chicago: University of Chicago Press.

——(1970): *On Violence*. London: Penguin Press.

Arnett, R.C. (2003): 'The responsive "I": Levinas's derivative argument', *Argument and Advocacy* 40(1)39–50.

Arnstein, S.R. (1969): 'A ladder of citizen participation', *Journal of the American Institute of Planners* 35(4)216–24.

Aronowitz, S. and H.A. Giroux (2000): 'The corporate university and the politics of education', *Educational Forum* 64(4)332–39.

Atkinson, R. (2003): 'Introduction: misunderstood saviour or vengeful wrecker? The many meanings and problems of gentrification', *Urban Studies* 40(12)2343–50.

Atkinson, R. and G. Moon (1994): *Urban Policy in Britain: The City, the State and the Market*. London: Macmillan.

Augoustinos, M. (1999): 'Ideology, false consciousness and psychology', *Theory and Psychology* 9(3)295–312.

Austen-Smith, D. and T.J. Feddersen (2009): 'Information aggregation and communication in committees', *Philosophical Transactions of the Royal Society B* 364(1518)763–69.

Bagley, N. and R.L. Revesz (2006): 'Centralized oversight of the regulatory state', *Columbia Law Review* 106(6)1260–1329.

Baines, D. (2010): 'Neoliberal restructuring, activism/participation, and social unionism in the nonprofit social services', *Nonprofit and Voluntary Sector Quarterly* 39(1)10–28.

Baiocchi, G. (2001): 'Participation, activism, and politics: the Porto Alegre experiment and deliberative democratic theory', *Politics and Society* 29(1)43–72.

Baker, D. and R. Freestone (2010): 'From public icon to private corporation: planning for airports in Australia', Paper for the 51st Annual Meeting of the Association of Collegiate Schools of Planning (ACSP), Minneapolis, 7–10 October 2010.

Baker, D.C., N.G. Sipe and B.J. Gleeson (2006): 'Performance-based planning: perspectives from the United States, Australia, and New Zealand', *Journal of Planning Education and Research* 25(4)396–409.

Baldwin, T. (1979): 'Foresight and responsibility', *Philosophy* 54(209)347–60.

Ball, M. (2004): 'Co-operation with the community in property-led urban regeneration', *Journal of Property Research* 21(2)119–42.

Bang, H.P. (2005): 'Among everyday makers and expert citizens', pp 159–78 in J. Newman (Ed.): *Remaking Governance: Peoples, Politics and the Public Sphere*. Bristol: Policy Press.

Barnes, M., J. Newman and H. Sullivan (2004a): 'Power, participation, and political renewal: theoretical perspectives on public participation under New Labour in Britain', *Social Politics* 11(2)267–79.

Barnes, M., A. Knops, J. Newman and H. Sullivan (2004b): 'The micro-politics of deliberation: case studies in public management', *Contemporary Politics* 10(2)93–110.

Barnett, C. (2005): 'Ways of relating: hospitality and the acknowledgement of otherness', *Progress in Human Geography* 29(1)5–21.

Baron, J. and M. Spranca (1997): 'Protected values', *Organizational Behavior and Human Decision Processes* 70(1)1–16.

Beard, V.A. (2002): 'Covert planning for social transformation in Indonesia', *Journal of Planning Education and Research* 22(1)15–25.

——(2003): 'Learning radical planning: the power of collective action', *Planning Theory* 2(1)13–35.

Beauregard, R.A. (1997): 'Public-private partnerships as historical chameleons: the case of the United States', pp 52–70 in J. Pierre (Ed.): *Partnerships in Urban Governance. European and American Experiences*. London: Macmillan.

——(2005): 'Introduction: institutional transformations', *Planning Theory* 4(3)203–07.

Becchetti, L., A. Pelloni and F. Rossetti (2008): 'Relational goods, sociability, and happiness', *Kyklos* 61(3)343–63.

Bedford, T., J. Clark and H. Harrison (2002): 'Limits to new public participation practices in local land use planning', *Town Planning Review* 73(3)311–31.

Beetham, D. (1991): *The Legitimation of Power*. London: Macmillan.

Benditt, T.M. (1973): 'The public interest', *Philosophy and Public Affairs* 2(3)291–311.

Bengs, C. (2005a): 'Time for a critique of planning theory', *European Journal of Spatial Development*, Editorial No. 3, June 2005. www.nordregio.se/EJSD/editorials.html (accessed 29.04.09).

——(2005b): 'Planning theory for the naïve?', *European Journal of Spatial Development*, Comment July 2005. www.nordregio.se/EJSD/debate050718.pdf (accessed 29.04.09).

Benhabib, S. (1996): 'Toward a deliberative model of democratic legitimacy', pp 67–94 in S. Benhabib (Ed.): *Democracy and Difference*. Princeton: Princeton University Press.

Bénit-Gbaffou, C., S. Didier and M. Morange (2008): 'Communities, the private sector, and the state. Contested forms of security governance in Cape Town and Johannesburg', *Urban Affairs Review* 43(5)691–717.

Bennett, D.M. and D. McD. Taylor (2003): 'Unethical practices in authorship of scientific papers', *Emergency Medicine* 15(3)263–70.

Bevir, M. (2003): 'Narrating the British state: an interpretive critique of New Labour's institutionalism', *Review of International Political Economy* 10(3)455–80.

Black, L.W. (2008): 'Deliberation, storytelling, and dialogical moments', *Communication Theory* 18(1)93–116.

Blomley, N.K. (1994): 'Activism and the academy', *Environment and Planning D: Society and Space* 12(4)383–85.

Blumenberg, E. and R. Ehrenfeucht (2008): 'Civil liberties and the regulation of public space: the case of sidewalks in Las Vegas', *Environment and Planning A* 40(2)303–22.

Bohman, J. (1998): 'The coming of age of deliberative democracy', *Journal of Political Philosophy* 6(4)400–25.

——(2003): 'Deliberative toleration', *Political Theory* 31(6)757–79.

Bohman, J. and W. Rehg (Eds) (1997): *Deliberative Democracy*. Cambridge, Mass.: MIT Press.

Bok, D. (1982): *Beyond the Ivory Tower. Social Responsibilities of the Modern University*. Cambridge, Mass.: Harvard University Press.

Bollens, S.A. (1998): 'Urban planning amidst ethnic conflict: Jerusalem and Johannesburg', *Urban Studies* 35(4)729–50.

Booher, D.E. and J.E. Innes (2002): 'Network power in collaborative planning', *Journal of Planning Education and Research* 21(3)221–36.

Booth, P. (2005): 'Partnerships and networks: the governance of urban regeneration in Britain', *Journal of Housing and the Built Environment* 20(3)257–69.

Borradori, G. (2003): *Philosophy in a Time of Terror. Dialogues with Jürgen Habermas and Jacques Derrida*. Chicago: University of Chicago Press.

Bourdieu, P. (1998): *Acts of Resistance: Against the New Myths of Our Time*. Cambridge: Polity Press.

Bovens, M. (1998): *The Quest for Responsibility: Accountability and Citizenship in Complex Organisations*. Cambridge: Cambridge University Press.

Box, R.C. (2007): 'Redescribing the public interest', *Social Science Journal* 44(4)585–98.

Box, R.C., G.S. Marshall, B.J. Reed and C.M. Reed (2001): 'New Public Management and substantive democracy', *Public Administration Review* 61(5)608–19.

Bozeman, B. (2007): *Public Values and Public Interest: Counterbalancing Economic Individualism*. Washington, D.C.: Georgetown University Press.

Brabham, D.C. (2009): 'Crowdsourcing the public participation process for planning projects', *Planning Theory* 8(3)242–62.

Braithwaite, V. (1998): 'The value orientations underlying liberalism-conservatism', *Personality and Individual Differences* 25(3)575–89.

——(2009): 'The value balance model and democratic governance', *Psychological Inquiry* 20(2–3)87–97.

Bramley, G. and C. Lambert (1998): 'Planning for housing: regulation entrenched?', pp 87–113 in P. Allmendinger and H. Thomas (Eds): *Urban Planning and the British New Right*. London: Routledge.

Brand, R. and F. Gaffikin (2007): 'Collaborative planning in an uncollaborative world', *Planning Theory* 6(3)282–313.

Braybrooke, D. and C.E. Lindblom (1963): *A Strategy of Decision*. New York: Free Press.

Brennan, A., J. Rhodes and P. Tyler (1999): 'The distribution of SRB challenge fund expenditure in relation to local-area need in England', *Urban Studies* 36(12)2069–84.

Brenner, N. (2009): 'What is critical urban theory?', *City* 13(2–3)198–207.

Brettschneider, C.L. (2005): 'Balancing procedures and outcomes within democratic theory: core values and judicial review', *Political Studies* 53(2)423–41.

——(2006): 'The value theory of democracy', *Politics, Philosophy and Economics* 5(3)259–78.

——(2007): *Democratic Rights: The Substance of Self-government*. Princeton: Princeton University Press.

Briassoulis, H. (1997): 'How the others plan: exploring the shape and forms of informal planning', *Journal of Planning Education and Research* 17(2)105–17.

Brinkman, P.A. (2009): 'The responsibility to ask questions: the case of bias in travel demand forecasting', pp 107–18 in F.L. Piccolo and H. Thomas (Eds): *Ethics and Planning Research*. Farnham, Surrey: Ashgate.

Brock, G. (2005): 'Does obligation diminish with distance?', *Ethics, Place and Environment* 8(1)3–20.

Brody, S.D. (2003): 'Measuring the effects of stakeholder participation on the quality of local plans based on the principles of collaborative ecosystem management', *Journal of Planning Education and Research* 22(4)407–19.

Brookfield, S.D. (2005): *The Power of Critical Theory for Adult Learning and Teaching*. Maidenhead, Berkshire: Open University Press.

Brooks, M.P. (2002): *Planning Theory for Practitioners*. Chicago: Planners Press.

Brown, W. (2003): 'Neo-liberalism and the end of liberal democracy', *Theory and Event* 7(1). http://muse.jhu.edu/journals/theory_and_event/v007/7.1brown.html (accessed 26.02.11).

Brownill, S. and J. Carpenter (2007): 'Participation and planning: dichotomies, rationalities and strategies for power', *Town Planning Review* 78(4)401–28.

Bruni, L. (2010): 'The happiness of sociality. Economics and eudaimonia: a necessary encounter', *Rationality and Society* 22(4)383–406.

Buitelaar, E. (2007): *The Cost of Land Use Decisions. Applying Transaction Cost Economics to Planning and Development*. Oxford: Blackwell.

——(2009): 'Zoning, more than just a tool: explaining Houston's regulatory practice', *European Planning Studies* 17(7)1049–65.

Burby, R.J. (1999): 'Unleashing the power of planning to create disaster-resistant communities', *Journal of the American Planning Association* 65(3)247–58.

——(2003): 'Making plans that matter. Citizen involvement and government action', *Journal of the American Planning Association* 69(1)33–49.

Burkhalter, S., J. Gastil and T. Kelshaw (2002): 'A conceptual definition and theoretical model of public deliberation in small face-to-face groups', *Communication Theory* 12(4)398–422.

Butler, T. (2007a): 'Re-urbanizing London Docklands: gentrification, suburbanization or New Urbanism?', *International Journal of Urban and Regional Research* 31(4)759–81.

——(2007b): 'For gentrification?', *Environment and Planning A* 39(1)162–81.

Calavita, N. and N. Krumholz (2003): 'Capturing the public interest: using newspaper op-eds to promote planning in conservative times', *Journal of Planning Education and Research* 22(4)400–06.

Caldeira, T.P.R. (1999): 'Fortified enclaves: the new urban segregation', pp 114–38 in J. Holston (Ed.): *Cities and Citizenship*. Durham: Duke University Press.

Cameron, J.D. (2009): '"Development is a bag of cement": the infrapolitics of participatory budgeting in the Andes', *Development in Practice* 19(6)692–701.

Campbell, H. and R. Marshall (2000): 'Moral obligations, planning, and the public interest: a commentary on current British practice', *Environment and Planning B: Planning and Design* 27(2)297–312.

——(2001): 'Values and professional identities in planning practice', pp 93–109 in P. Allmendinger and M. Tewdwr-Jones (Eds): *Planning Futures. New Directions for Planning Theory*. London: Routledge.

——(2002): 'Utilitarianism's bad breath? A re-evaluation of the public interest justification for planning', *Planning Theory* 1(2)163–87.

Canovan, M. (1983): 'A case of distorted communication: a note on Habermas and Arendt', *Political Theory* 11(1)105–16.

Carmona, M. and L. Sieh (2008): 'Performance measurement in planning – toward a holistic view', *Environment and Planning C: Government and Policy* 26(2)428–54.

Castells, M. (1983): *The City and the Grassroots*. London: Edward Arnold.

Certeau, M. de (1984): *The Practice of Everyday Life*. Berkeley: University of California Press.

Chan, W.F. (2010): 'A shared or multicultural future? Community cohesion and the (im) possibilities of hospitable social capital', *Space and Polity* 14(1)33–46.

Chaskin, R.J. (2005): 'Democracy and bureaucracy in a community planning process', *Journal of Planning Education and Research* 24(4)408–19.

Chatterton, P. (2008): 'Demand the possible: journeys in changing our world as a public activist-scholar', *Antipode* 40(3)421–27.

Chatterton, P. and D. Featherstone (2007): 'Intervention: Elsevier, critical geography and the arms trade', *Political Geography* 26(1)3–7.

Cheung, S.N.S. (2002): *Economic Explanation Book III: The Choice of Institutional Arrangements*. Hong Kong: Arcadia Press.

Choi, Y.-C. (1999): 'The politics of transaction costs', *Public Money and Management* 19(4)51–56.

Christensen, T. and P. Lægreid (2001a): 'New Public Management – undermining political control?', pp 93–119 in T. Christensen and P. Lægreid (Eds): *New Public Management. The Transformation of Ideas and Practice*. Aldershot: Ashgate.

——(2001b): 'New Public Management i norsk statsforvaltning' (New Public Management in the Norwegian public administration), pp 67–95 in B.S. Tranøy and Ø. Østerud (Eds): *Den fragmenterte staten. Reformer, makt og styring* (The Fragmented State. Reforms, Power and Steering). Oslo: Gyldendal.

——(2002): 'New Public Management: puzzles of democracy and the influence of citizens', *Journal of Political Philosophy* 10(3)267–95.

——(2009): 'Public management reform in Norway: reluctance and tensions', pp 300–16 in S.F. Goldfinch and J.L. Wallis (Eds): *International Handbook of Public Management Reform*. Cheltenham: Edward Elgar.

Churchill, R.P. (1997): 'On the difference between non-moral and moral conceptions of toleration: the case for toleration as an individual virtue', pp 189–211 in M.E. Razavi and D. Ambuel (Eds): *Philosophy, Religion, and the Question of Intolerance*. Albany: State University of New York Press.

Clark, E. (2005): 'The order and simplicity of gentrification – a political challenge' pp 256–64 in R. Atkinson and G. Bridge (Eds): *Gentrification in a Global Context: The New Urban Colonialism*. London: Routledge.

Clarke, J. (2004): 'Dissolving the public realm? The logics and limits of neo-liberalism', *Journal of Social Policy* 33(1)27–48.

——(2008): 'Living with/in and without neo-liberalism', *Focaal – European Journal of Anthropology* Issue 51, 135–47.

Clavel, P. (1980): 'Opposition planning', pp 206–18 in P. Clavel, J. Forester and W.W. Goldsmith (Eds): *Urban and Regional Planning in an Age of Austerity*. New York: Pergamon Press.

——(1983): *Opposition Planning in Wales and Appalachia*. Philadelphia: Temple University Press.

Clough, N.L. and R.M. Vanderbeck (2006): 'Managing politics and consumption in business improvement districts: the geographies of political activism on Burlington, Vermont's Church Street Marketplace', *Urban Studies* 43(12)2261–84.

Cohen, A.J. (2004): 'What toleration is', *Ethics* 115(1)68–95.

Cohen, J. (1989): 'Deliberation and democratic legitimacy', pp 17–34 in A. Hamlin and P. Pettit (Eds): *The Good Polity*. Oxford: Basil Blackwell.

——(1997): 'Procedure and substance in deliberative democracy', pp 407–37 in J. Bohman and W. Rehg (Eds): *Deliberative Democracy*. Cambridge, Mass.: MIT Press.

Collier, P. and A. Hoeffler (2007): 'Unintended consequences: does aid promote arms races?', *Oxford Bulletin of Economics and Statistics* 69(1)1–27.

Commission of the European Communities (2001): *European Governance: A White Paper*. Brussels: European Commission.

Congleton, R.D. (2007): 'Informational limits to public policy: ignorance and the jury theorem', pp 206–19 in J.C. Pardo and P. Schwartz (Eds): *Public Choice and the Challenges of Democracy*. Cheltenham: Edward Elgar.

Connelly, S. (2010): 'Participation in a hostile state: how do planners act to shape public engagement in politically difficult environments?', *Planning Practice and Research* 25(3)333–51.

Connelly, S. and T. Richardson (2004): 'Exclusion: the necessary difference between ideal and practical consensus', *Journal of Environmental Planning and Management* 47(1)3–17.

Coole, D. (1996): 'Habermas and the question of alterity', pp 221–44 in M. Passerin d'Entrèves and S. Benhabib (Eds): *Habermas and the Unfinished Project of Modernity*. Cambridge: Polity Press.

Cooper, T.L. (1998): *The Responsible Administrator* (Fourth Edition). San Francisco: Jossey-Bass.

Corey, K.E. (1972): 'Advocacy planning: a reflective analysis', *Antipode* 4(2)46–63.

Coughlan, P.J. (2000): 'In defense of unanimous jury verdicts: mistrials, communication, and strategic voting', *American Political Science Review* 94(2)375–93.

Critchley, S. (2004): 'Five problems in Levinas's view of politics and the sketch of a solution to them', *Political Theory* 32(2)172–85.

——(2006): 'Frankfurt impromptu – remarks on Derrida and Habermas', pp 98–110 in L. Thomassen (Ed.): *The Derrida-Habermas Reader*. Edinburgh: Edinburgh University Press.

Crocker, A. (2006): *Identity and Environmentalism in Zapatista Public Discourse on the Montes Azules Biosphere Reserve*. Master thesis in history. Saskatoon: Faculty of Graduate Studies and Research, University of Saskatchewan.

D'Arcy, É. and G. Keogh (1999): 'The property market and urban competitiveness: a review', *Urban Studies* 36(5–6)917–28.

Dahlberg, L. (2005): 'The Habermasian public sphere: taking difference seriously?', *Theory and Society* 34(2)111–36.

Davidoff, L., P. Davidoff and N.N. Gold (1971): 'The suburbs have to open their gates', *New York Times Magazine* 12 November, 40–44, 46, 48, 55, 58, 60.

Davidoff, P. (1965): 'Advocacy and pluralism in planning', *Journal of the American Institute of Planners* 31(4)331–338.

——(1978): 'The redistributive function in planning: creating greater equity among citizens of communities', pp 69–72 in R.W. Burchell and G. Sternlieb (Eds): *Planning Theory in the 1980s*. New Brunswick: Center for Urban Policy Research, Rutgers University.

——(1982): 'Comment', *Journal of the American Planning Association* 48(2)179–80.

Davidoff, P., L. Davidoff and N.N. Gold (1970): 'Suburban Action: advocate planning for an open society', *Journal of the American Institute of Planners* 36(1)12–21.

Davies, J.S. (2007): 'The limits of partnership: an exit-action strategy for local democratic inclusion', *Political Studies* 55(4)779–800.

Dawkins, C.J. (2000): 'Transaction costs and the land use planning process', *Journal of Planning Literature* 14(4)507–18.

Deas, I., B. Robson and M. Bradford (2000): 'Re-thinking the urban development corporation "experiment": the case of Central Manchester, Leeds and Bristol', *Progress in Planning* 54(1)1–72.

Deetz, S. and W.J. White (1999): 'Relational responsibility or dialogic ethics?', pp 111–20 in S. McNamee and J. Gergen (Eds): *Relational Responsibility*. Thousand Oaks: Sage.

deLeon, P. and L. deLeon (2002): 'What ever happened to policy implementation? An alternative approach', *Journal of Public Administration Research and Theory* 12(4)467–92.

Denhardt, J.V. and R.B. Denhardt (2003a): *The New Public Service. Serving, not Steering*. Armonk, New York: M.E. Sharpe.

Denhardt, R.B. and J.V. Denhardt (2003b): 'The New Public Service: an approach to reform', *International Review of Public Administration* 8(1)3–10.

Department of the Environment, Transport and the Regions (1998): *Modern Local Government – In Touch with the People*. White Paper. London: DETR.

Derrida, J. (1983): 'The principle of reason: the university in the eyes of its pupils', *Diacritics: A Review of Contemporary Criticism* 13(3)2–20.

——(1986): 'Jacques Derrida on the university. An interview' (with I. Salusinszky), *Southern Review* 19(1)3–12.

——(1999): *Adieu to Emmanuel Levinas*. Stanford: Stanford University Press.

——(2002): 'The university without condition', pp 202–37 in J. Derrida: *Without Alibi*. Stanford: Stanford University Press.

——(2004a): 'Mochlos, or the conflict of the faculties', pp 83–112 in J. Derrida: *Eyes of the University. Right to Philosophy 2*. Stanford: Stanford University Press.

——(2004b): 'The antinomies of the philosophical discipline: letter preface', pp 165–74 in J. Derrida: *Eyes of the University. Right to Philosophy 2*. Stanford: Stanford University Press.

——(2006): 'Hostipitality', pp 208–30 in L. Thomassen (Ed.): *The Derrida-Habermas Reader*. Edinburgh: Edinburgh University Press.

Derrida, J. and A. Dufourmantelle (2000): *Of Hospitality*. Stanford: Stanford University Press.

Devas, N. (2001): 'Does city governance matter for the urban poor?', *International Planning Studies* 6(4)393–408.

Diani, M. and D. McAdam (Eds) (2003): *Social Movements and Networks: Relational Approaches to Collective Action*. New York: Oxford University Press.

Diesing, P. (1962): *Reason in Society: Five Types of Decisions and Their Social Conditions*. Urbana: University of Illinois Press.

Dijkstra, L.W. (2000): 'Public spaces: a comparative discussion of the criteria for public space', *Research in Urban Sociology* 5(1)1–22.

DiNardo, J. and T. Lemieux (2001): 'Alcohol, marijuana, and American youth: the unintended consequences of government regulation', *Journal of Health Economics* 20(6)991–1010.

Dinerstein, A.C. (2009): 'The Snail and the Good Government: a critique of "civil society" (the Zapatistas in Mexico)'. Paper read at the conference *Beyond NGOs: Civil and Uncivil Society in the 21ˢᵗ Century*, 26–27 February 2009. London: Goodenough College.

Dixit, A.K. (1996): *The Making of Economic Policy: A Transaction-cost Politics Perspective*. Cambridge, Mass.: MIT Press.

Dodge, J. (2009): 'Environmental justice and deliberative democracy: how social change organizations respond to power in the deliberative system', *Policy and Society* 28(3)225–39.

Dodman, D. (2008): 'Developers in the public interest? The role of urban development corporations in the anglophone Caribbean', *Geographical Journal* 174(1)30–44.

Dogan, M. (2004): 'Conceptions of legitimacy', pp 110–19 in M. Hawkesworth and M. Kogan (Eds): *Encyclopedia of Government and Politics. Volume 2* (Second Edition). London: Routledge.

Doring, A. (2002): 'Challenges to the academic role of change agent', *Journal of Further and Higher Education* 26(2)139–48.

Dryzek, J.S. (2001): 'Legitimacy and economy in deliberative democracy', *Political Theory* 29(5)651–69.

Dryzek, J.S. and V. Braithwaite (2000): 'On the prospects for democratic deliberation: values analysis applied to Australian politics', *Political Psychology* 21(2)241–66.

Dryzek, J.S. and C. List (2003): 'Social choice theory and deliberative democracy: a reconciliation', *British Journal of Political Science* 33(1)1–28.

Dryzek, J.S. and S. Niemeyer (2006): 'Reconciling pluralism and consensus as political ideals', *American Journal of Political Science* 50(3)634–49.

Dvir, D. and T. Lechler (2004): 'Plans are nothing, changing plans is everything: the impact of changes on project success', *Research Policy* 33(1)1–15.

Dworkin, G. (1983): 'Paternalism: some second thoughts', pp 105–111 in R. Sartorius (Ed.): *Paternalism*. Minneapolis: University of Minnesota Press.

——(2005): 'Paternalism', 8 pages in *Stanford Encyclopedia of Philosophy*. http://plato.stanford.edu/entries/paternalism/ (accessed 12.01.09).

Edelenbos, J. and G.R. Teisman (2008): 'Public-private partnership: on the edge of project and process management. Insights from Dutch practice: the Sijtwende spatial development project', *Environment and Planning C: Government and Policy* 26(3) 614–26.

Egéa-Kuehne, D. (2003): 'The teaching of philosophy: renewed rights and responsibilities', *Educational Philosophy and Theory* 35(3)271–84.

Elliott, S.J. and J. McClure (2009): 'There's just hope that no one's health is at risk: residents' reappraisal of a landfill siting', *Journal of Environmental Planning and Management* 52(2)237–55.

Elwood, S. (2002): 'Neighborhood revitalization through "collaboration": assessing the implications of neoliberal urban policy at the grassroots', *GeoJournal* 58(2–3)121–30.

Epstein, D. and S. O'Halloran (1999): *Delegating Powers. A Transaction Cost Politics Approach to Policy Making under Separate Powers*. Cambridge: Cambridge University Press.

Erie, S.P., V. Kogan and S.A. MacKenzie (2010): 'Redevelopment, San Diego style: the limits of public-private partnerships', *Urban Affairs Review* 45(5)644–78.

Eriksen, E.O. and J. Weigård (2003): *Understanding Habermas. Communicative Action and Deliberative Democracy*. London: Continuum.

Eriksson Baaz, M. (2005): *The Paternalism of Partnership: A Postcolonial Reading of Identity in Development Aid*. New York: Zed Books.

Estlund, D. (1994): 'Opinion leaders, independence, and Condorcet's Jury Theorem', *Theory and Decision* 36(2)131–62.

——(2005): 'Democratic theory', pp 208–30 in F. Jackson and M. Smith (Eds): *The Oxford Handbook of Contemporary Philosophy*. Oxford: Oxford University Press.

——(2006): 'Democracy and the real speech situation', pp 75–92 in S. Besson and J.L. Martí (Eds): *Deliberative Democracy and Its Discontents*. Aldershot: Ashgate.

Etzioni, A. (1967): 'Mixed-scanning: a "third" approach to decision-making', *Public Administration Review* 27(5)385–92.

Europan Norge (2009): *E10 Trondheim_Norway*. Oslo: Europan Norge.

Evans-Cowley, J.S. (2010): 'Planning in the age of Facebook: the role of social networking in planning processes', *GeoJournal* 75(5)407–20.

Eversley, D. (1973): *The Planner in Society. The Changing Role of a Profession*. London: Faber and Faber.

EZLN (2005): *6th Declaration of the Selva Lacandona*. Chiapas: Zapatista Army of National Liberation. www.anarkismo.net/newswire.php?story_id=805 (accessed 26.02.10).

Fainstein, S.S. (1991): 'Promoting economic development. Urban planning in the United States and Britain', *Journal of the American Planning Association* 57(1)22–33.

——(2000): 'New directions in planning theory', *Urban Affairs Review* 35(4)451–78.

——(2005): 'Cities and diversity: should we want it? Can we plan for it?', *Urban Affairs Review* 41(1)3–19.

Falleth, E.I., G.S. Hanssen and I.-L. Saglie (2008): *Medvirkning i byplanlegging i Norge* (Participation in Urban Planning in Norway). NIBR-report 2008:37. Oslo: Norwegian Institute for Urban and Regional Research.

——(2010): 'Challenges to democracy in market-oriented urban planning in Norway', *European Planning Studies* 18(5)737–53.

Faludi, A. (1987): *A Decision-centred View of Environmental Planning*. Oxford: Pergamon.

Fearnley, R. (2000): 'Regenerating the inner city: lessons from the UK's City Challenge experience', *Social Policy and Administration* 34(5)567–83.

Feather, N.T. (1995): 'Values, valences, and choice: the influence of values on the perceived attractiveness and choice of alternatives', *Journal of Personality and Social Psychology* 68(6)1135–51.

Feldman, M.M.A. (1995): 'Regime and regulation in substantive planning theory', *Planning Theory* (Franco Angeli Series) No. 14, 65–95.

Ferreyra, C. and P. Beard (2007): 'Participatory evaluation of collaborative and integrated water management: insights from the field', *Environmental Planning and Management* 50(2)271–96.

Finlayson, J.G. (2000): 'What are "universalizable interests"?', *Journal of Political Philosophy* 8(4)456–69.

Fischer, F. (2009): 'Discursive planning: social justice as discourse', pp 52–71 in P. Marcuse, J. Connolly, J. Novy, I. Olivo, C. Potter and J. Steil (Eds): *Searching for the Just City. Debates in Urban Theory and Practice*. London: Routledge.

Fischler, R. (2000): 'Communicative planning theory: a Foucauldian assessment', *Journal of Planning Education and Research* 19(4)358–68.

Fishkin, J.S. (2006): 'Beyond polling alone: the quest for an informed public', *Critical Review* 18(1–3)157–65.

Flinders, M. and J. Buller (2006): 'Depoliticization, democracy and arena shifting', pp 53–80 in T. Christensen and P. Lægreid (Eds): *Autonomy and Regulation. Coping with Agencies in the Modern State*. Cheltenham: Edward Elgar.

Flores, A. and D.G. Johnson (2005) [1983]: 'Collective responsibility and professional roles', pp 339–47 in M. Davis (Ed.): *Engineering Ethics*. Aldershot: Ashgate.

Florida, R. (2002): *The Rise of the Creative Class*. New York: Basic Books.

——(2005): *Cities and the Creative Class*. New York: Routledge.

Flyvbjerg, B. (1998a): 'Habermas and Foucault: thinkers for civil society?', *British Journal of Sociology* 49(2)210–33.

——(1998b): *Rationality and Power: Democracy in Practice*. Chicago. University of Chicago Press.

——(2002): 'Bringing power to planning research. One researcher's praxis story', *Journal of Planning Education and Research* 21(4)353–66.

Flyvbjerg, B. and T. Richardson (2002): 'Planning and Foucault. In search of the dark side of planning theory', pp 44–62 in P. Allmendinger and M. Tewdwr-Jones (Eds): *Planning Futures: New Directions for Planning Theory*. London: Routledge.

Flyvbjerg, B., M.S. Holm and S. Buhl (2002): 'Understanding costs in public works projects. Error or lie?', *American Planning Association Journal* 68(3)279–95.

Foley, P. (1999): 'Competition as public policy: a review of Challenge funding', *Public Administration* 77(4)809–36.

Fordham, R. (1990): 'Planning consultancy: can it serve the public interest?', *Public Administration* 68(2)243–48.

Forester, J. (1977): *Questioning and Shaping Attention as Planning Strategy: Toward a Critical Theory of Analysis and Design*. Ph.D. dissertation in city planning. University of California: Berkeley.

——(1980): 'Critical theory and planning practice', *Journal of the American Planning Association* 46(3)275–86.

——(1981): 'Hannah Arendt and critical theory: a critical response', *Journal of Politics* 43(1)196–202.

——(1985): 'Lest planning be seen as a tool…', *Built Environment* 10(2)124–31.

——(1989): *Planning in the Face of Power*. Berkeley: University of California Press.

——(1990): 'Reply to my critics…', *Planning Theory* (Franco Angeli Series) No. 4, 43–60.

——(1993a): *Critical Theory, Public Policy, and Planning Practice. Toward a Critical Pragmatism*. Albany: State University of New York Press.

——(1993b): 'Learning from practice stories: the priority of practical judgment', pp 186–209 in F. Fischer and J. Forester (Eds): *The Argumentative Turn in Policy Analysis and Planning*. London: UCL Press.

——(1994a): 'Lawrence Susskind: activist mediation and public disputes', pp 309–54 in D.M. Kolb (Ed.): *When Talk Works: Profiles of Mediators*. San Francisco: Jossey-Bass.

——(1994b): 'Bridging interests and community: advocacy planning and the challenges of deliberative democracy', *Journal of the American Planning Association* 60(2)153–58.

——(1999): 'Dealing with deep value differences', pp 463–93 in L. Susskind, S. McKearnan and J. Thomas-Larmer (Eds): *The Consensus Building Handbook*. Thousand Oaks: Sage.

——(2000): 'Conservative epistemology, reductive ethics, far too narrow politics: some clarifications in response to Yiftachel and Huxley', *International Journal on Urban and Regional Research* 24(4)914–16.

——(2001): 'An instructive case study hampered by theoretical puzzles: critical comments on Bent Flyvbjerg's *Rationality and Power*', *International Planning Studies* 6(3)263–70.

——(2009a): *Dealing with Differences. Dramas of Mediating Public Disputes.* Oxford: Oxford University Press.

——(2009b): 'Learning from the process versus outcomes debates' (Editorial), *Planning Theory and Practice* 10(4)429–33.

Forester, J. and D. Stitzel (1989): 'Beyond neutrality: the possibilities of activist mediation in public sector conflicts', *Negotiation Journal* 5(3)251–64.

Foucault, M. (1980): *Power/Knowledge.* Brighton: Harvester Press.

Freestone, R., P. Williams and A. Bowden (2006): 'Fly buy cities: some planning aspects of airport privatisation in Australia', *Urban Policy and Research* 24(4)491–508.

Friedman, J., J. Kossy and M. Regan (1980): 'Working within the state: the role of the progressive planner', pp 251–78 in P. Clavel, J. Forester and W.W. Goldsmith (Eds): *Urban and Regional Planning in an Age of Austerity.* New York: Pergamon Press.

Friedmann, J. (1969): 'Notes on societal action', *Journal of the American Institute of Planners* 35(5)311–18.

——(1973): *Retracking America. A Theory of Transactive Planning.* Garden City, New York: Anchor Press/Doubleday.

——(1979): *The Good Society.* Cambridge, Mass.: MIT Press.

——(1987): *Planning in the Public Domain: From Knowledge to Action.* Princeton: Princeton University Press.

——(2003): 'Why do planning theory?', *Planning Theory* 2(1)7–10.

——(2008): 'The uses of planning theory. A bibliographic essay', *Journal of Planning Education and Research* 28(2)247–57.

——(2011): *Insurgencies: Essays in Planning Theory.* London: Routledge.

Fung, A. (2003): 'Survey article: recipes for public spheres: eight institutional design choices and their consequences', *Journal of Political Philosophy* 11(3)338–67.

——(2005): 'Deliberation before the revolution: toward an ethics of deliberative democracy in an unjust world', *Political Theory* 33(3)397–419.

Gabel, M.J. and C.R. Shipan (2004): 'A social choice approach to expert consensus panels', *Journal of Health Economics* 22(3)543–64.

Gabriel, Y. (2002): 'On paragrammatic uses of organizational theory – a provocation', *Organization Studies* 23(1)133–51.

Gächter, S. and E. Fehr (1999): 'Collective action as a social exchange', *Journal of Economic Behavior and Organization* 39(4)341–69.

Gastil, J. and J.P. Dillard (1999): 'Increasing political sophistication through public deliberation', *Political Communication* 16(1)3–23.

Gauthier, D.J. (2007): 'Levinas and the politics of hospitality', *History of Political Thought* 28(1)158–80.

Gerring, J. and S.C. Thacker (2008): 'Do neoliberal economic policies kill or save lives?', *Business and Politics* 10(3) Article 3. www.bepress.com/bap/vol10/iss3/art3 (accessed 29.04.09).

Ghere, R.K. (1996): 'Aligning the ethics of public-private partnership: the issue of local economic development', *Journal of Public Administration Research and Theory* 6(4)599–621.

Gibson, C. and N. Klocker (2005): 'The "cultural turn" in Australian regional economic development discourse: neoliberalising creativity?', *Geographical Research* 43(1)93–102.

Gibson-Graham, J.K. and J. Cameron (2010): 'Community enterprises: imagining and enacting alternatives to capitalism', pp 291–98 in J. Hillier and P. Healey (Eds): *The Ashgate Research Companion to Planning Theory. Conceptual Challenges for Spatial Planning*. Farnham, Surrey: Ashgate.

Gilabert, P. (2005): 'The substantive dimension of deliberative practical rationality', *Philosophy and Social Criticism* 31(2)185–210.

Gill, S. (1995): 'Globalisation, market civilisation and disciplinary neoliberalism', *Millennium: Journal of International Studies* 24(3)399–423.

Giroux, H.A. (2003): 'Public pedagogy and the politics of resistance: notes on a critical theory of educational struggle', *Educational Philosophy and Theory* 35(1)5–16.

Glasze, G., C. Webster and K. Frantz (Eds) (2006): *Private Cities. Global and Local Perspectives*. London: Routledge.

Gleeson, B.J. and K.J. Grundy (1997): 'New Zealand's planning revolution five years on: a preliminary assessment', *Journal of Environmental Planning and Management* 40(3)293–313.

Gleeson, B.J. and N. Low (2000): 'Revaluing planning: rolling back neo-liberalism in Australia', *Progress in Planning* 53(2)83–164.

Goix, R. le (2005): 'Gated communities: sprawl and social segregation in Southern California', *Housing Studies* 20(2)323–43.

Goldie, R.L.S., D.J. de Matteo, L.M. Wells, G.R. Ackroyd and S.M. King (2000): 'Social planning in Canada for families with HIV infection', *Canadian Journal of Public Health* 91(5)353–56.

Goodin, R.E. and J.S. Dryzek (2006): 'Deliberative impacts: the macro-political uptake of mini-publics', *Politics and Society* 34(2)219–44.

Gordon, N. (2001): 'Arendt and social change in democracies', *Critical Review in International Social and Political Philosophy* 4(2)85–111.

——(2002): 'On visibility and power: an Arendtian corrective of Foucault', *Human Studies* 25(2)125–45.

Gormley, W.T. Jr. (1987): 'Institutional policy analysis: a critical review', *Journal of Policy Analysis and Management* 6(2)153–69.

Gotham, K.F. (2005): 'Theorizing urban spectacles. Festivals, tourism and the transformation of urban space', *City* 9(2)225–46.

Gottschalk, P. (2001): 'Descriptions of responsibility for implementation: a content analysis of strategic information systems/technology planning documents', *Technological Forecasting and Social Change* 68(2)207–21.

Goudsmit, I.A. and J. Blackburn (2001): 'Participatory municipal planning in Bolivia: an ambiguous experience', *Development in Practice* 11(5)587–96.

Graham, S. (2005): 'Remember Fallujah: demonising place, constructing atrocity', *Environment and Planning D: Society and Space* 23(1)1–10.

Greenbaum, R.T. and J.B. Engberg (2004): 'The impact of state enterprise zones on urban manufacturing establishments', *Journal of Policy Analysis and Management* 23(2)315–39.

Gregory, R. (2009): 'New public management and the politics of accountability', pp 66–87 in S.F. Goldfinch and J.L. Wallis (Eds): *International Handbook of Public Management Reform*. Cheltenham: Edward Elgar.

Grengs, J. (2002): 'Community-based planning as a source of political change: the Transit Equity Movement of Los Angeles' Bus Riders Union', *Journal of the American Planning Association* 68(2)165–78.

——(2005): 'The abandoned social goals of public transit in the neoliberal city of the USA', *City* 9(1)51–66.

Griffiths, R. (1986): 'Planning in retreat? Town planning and the market in the eighties', *Planning Practice and Research* 1(1)3–7.

Grimes, M. (2006): 'Organizing consent: the role of procedural fairness in political trust and compliance', *European Journal of Political Research* 45(2)285–315.

Grimshaw, D., S. Vincent and H. Willmmott (2002): 'Going privately: partnership and outsourcing in UK public services', *Public Administration* 80(3)475–502.

Gui, B. (1996): 'On "relational goods": strategic implications of investment in relationships', *International Journal of Social Economics* 23(10–11)260–78.

——(2000): 'Beyond transactions: on the interpersonal dimension of economic reality', *Annals of Public and Cooperative Economics* 71(2)139–69.

Gunder, M. (2005): 'Obscuring difference through shaping debate: a Lacanian view of planning for diversity', *International Planning Studies* 10(2)83–103.

Gunder, M. and J. Hillier (2007): 'Problematising responsibility in planning theory and practice: on seeing the middle of the string?', *Progress in Planning* 68(2)57–96.

——(2009): *Planning in Ten Words or Less. A Lacanian Entanglement with Spatial Planning.* Aldershot, Hampshire: Ashgate.

Gunder, M. and C. Mouat (2002): 'Symbolic violence and victimization in planning processes: a reconnoitre of the New Zealand Resource Management Act', *Planning Theory* 1(2)124–45.

Gunson, D. and C. Collins (1997): 'From the *I* to the *We*: discourse ethics, identity, and the pragmatics of partnership in the West of Scotland', *Communication Theory* 7(4)278–300.

Guzzetta, J.D. and S.A. Bollens (2003): 'Urban planners' skills and competencies', *Journal of Planning Education and Research* 23(1)96–106.

Habermas, J. (1977): 'Hannah Arendt's communications concept of power', *Social Research* 44(1)3–24.

——(1983): *Philosophical-Political Profiles.* Cambridge, Mass.: MIT Press.

——(1984): *The Theory of Communicative Action. Volume One: Reason and the Rationalization of Society.* London: Heinemann.

——(1987): 'The idea of the university: learning processes', *New German Critique* 41, 3–22.

——(1990): *Moral Consciousness and Communicative Action.* Cambridge, Mass.: MIT Press.

——(1999): *On the Pragmatics of Communication.* (Edited by M. Cooke). Cambridge: Polity Press.

——(2003): 'Toward a cosmopolitan Europe', *Journal of Democracy* 14(4)86–100.

——(2006a): 'Political communication in media society: does democracy still enjoy an epistemic dimension? The impact of normative theory on empirical research', *Communication Theory* 16(4)411–26.

——(2006b): 'Religious tolerance – the pacemaker for cultural rights', pp 195–207 in L. Thomassen (Ed.): *The Derrida-Habermas Reader.* Edinburgh: Edinburgh University Press.

Hager, C. (2007): 'Three decades of protest in Berlin land-use planning, 1975–2005', *German Studies Review* 30(1)55–74.

Hägglund, M. (2004): 'The necessity of discrimination: disjoining Derrida and Levinas', *Diacritics: A Review of Contemporary Criticism* 34(1)40–71.

Hale, C.R. (Ed.) (2008): *Engaging Contradictions. Theory, Politics, and Methods of Activist Scholarship.* Berkeley: University of California Press.

Hall, C. (2007): 'Recognizing the passion in deliberation: toward a more democratic theory of deliberative democracy', *Hypatia* 22(4)81–95.

Hammond, T.H. (1986): 'Agenda control, organizational structure, and bureaucratic politics', *American Journal of Political Science* 30(2)379–420.

Hammond, T.H. and P.A. Thomas (1989): 'The impossibility of a neutral hierarchy', *Journal of Law, Economics, and Organization* 5(1)155–84.

Hansen, D. (2001): *Exploring the Moral Heart of Teaching*. New York: Teachers College Press.

Harb, M. (2008): 'Faith-based organizations as effective development partners? Hezbollah and post-war reconstruction in Lebanon', pp 214–39 in G. Clarke and M. Jennings (Eds): *Development, Civil Society and Faith-based Organizations. Bridging the Sacred and the Secular*. Basingstoke, Hampshire: Palgrave Macmillan.

Harland, T., T. Tidswell, D. Everett, L. Hale and N. Pickering (2010): 'Neoliberalism and the academic as critic and conscience of society', *Teaching in Higher Education* 15(1)85–96.

Harmes, A. (2006): 'Neoliberalism and multilevel governance', *Review of International Political Economy* 13(5)725–49.

Harper, T.L. and S.M. Stein (2006): *Dialogical Planning in a Fragmented Society*. New Brunswick: CUPR Press, Rutgers.

Harper, T.L., A. Gar-On Yeh and H. Costa (Eds) (2008): *Dialogues in Urban and Regional Planning. Volume 3*. New York: Routledge.

Harrison, S. and M. Mort (1998): 'Which champions, which people? Public and user involvement in health care as a technology of legitimation', *Social Policy and Administration* 32(1)60–70.

Hart, J. (1998): 'Central agencies and departments: empowerment and coordination', pp 285–309 in B.G. Peters and D.J. Savoie (Eds): *Taking Stock. Assessing Public Sector Reforms*. Canadian Centre for Management Development, Montreal: McGill-Queen's University Press.

Hartman, C.W. (2002): *Between Eminence and Notoriety: Four Decades of Radical Urban Planning*. New Brunswick: CUPR Press.

Harvey, D. (1973): *Social Justice and the City*. Oxford: Basil Blackwell.

——(1989): 'From managerialism to entrepreneurialism: the transformation in urban governance in late capitalism', *Geografiska Annaler Series B: Human Geography* 71(1)3–17.

——(1999): 'Frontiers of insurgent planning', *Plurimondi* 1(2)269–86.

——(2005): *A Brief History of Neoliberalism*. Oxford: Oxford University Press.

——(2008): 'The right to the city', *New Left Review* 53, 23–40.

——(2010): 'An interview with David Harvey' (conducted by Michael J. Thompson), pp 99–105 in A.L. Buzby (Ed.): *Communicative Action. The Logos Interviews*. New York: Lexington Books.

Harvey, N. (2001): 'Globalisation and resistance in post-cold war Mexico: difference, citizenship and biodiversity conflicts in Chiapas', *Third World Quarterly* 22(6)1045–61.

Harwood, S.A. (2003): 'Environmental justice on the streets. Advocacy planning as a tool to contest environmental racism', *Journal of Planning Education and Research* 23(1)24–38.

Hasan, A. (2006): 'Orangi Pilot Project: the expansion of work beyond Orangi and the mapping of informal settlements and infrastructure', *Environment and Urbanization* 18(2)451–80.

Haughton, G. (1999): 'Trojan horse or white elephant? The contested biography of the life and times of the Leeds Development Corporation', *Town Planning Review* 70(2)173–90.

Hayek, F.A. (2008 [1944]): *The Road to Serfdom*. (The Collected Works of F.A. Hayek, Volume II: The Road to Serfdom. Texts and Documents. The Definitive Edition, edited by B. Caldwell). New York: Routledge.

Healey, P. (1991): 'Urban regeneration and the development industry', *Regional Studies* 25(2)97–110.

——(1992a): 'The reorganisation of state and market in planning', *Urban Studies* 29(3–4)411–34.

——(1992b): 'Planning through debate: the communicative turn in planning theory', *Town Planning Review* 63(2)143–62.

——(2000): 'Planning in relational space and time: responding to new urban realities', pp 517–30 in G. Bridge and S. Watson (Eds): *A Companion to the City*. Oxford: Blackwell.

——(2003): 'Collaborative planning in perspective', *Planning Theory* 2(2)101–23.

——(2004): 'Creativity and urban governance', *Policy Studies* 25(2)87–102.

——(2005): 'On the project of "institutional transformation" in the planning field: commentary on the contributions', *Planning Theory* 4(3)301–310.

——(2006): *Collaborative Planning. Shaping Places in Fragmented Societies*. Basingstoke, Hampshire: Palgrave Macmillan.

——(2009): 'The pragmatic tradition in planning thought', *Journal of Planning Education and Research* 28(3)277–92.

——(2011): 'The idea of "communicative" planning: practices, concepts and rhetorics', in L. Vale and B. Sanyal (Eds): *History of Planning Ideas*. Cambridge, Mass.: MIT Press.

Healey, P. and R. Upton (Eds) (2010): *Crossing Borders. International Exchange and Planning Practices*. London: Routledge.

Hefetz, A. and M. Warner (2007): 'Beyond the market versus planning dichotomy: understanding privatisation and its reverse in US cities', *Local Government Studies* 33(4)555–72.

Heijden, J. van der (2010): 'On peanuts and monkeys: private sector involvement in Australian building control', *Urban Policy and Research* 28(2)195–210.

Heller, P. (2001): 'Moving the state: the politics of democratic decentralization in Kerala, South Africa, and Porto Alegre', *Politics and Society* 29(1)131–63.

Hendler, S. (1991): 'Do professional codes legitimate planners' values?', pp 156–67 in H. Thomas and P. Healey (Eds): *Dilemmas of Planning Practice*. Aldershot: Avebury.

Hendley, S. (2000): *From Communicative Action to the Face of the Other. Levinas and Habermas on Language, Obligation, and Community*. Lanham, Maryland: Lexington Books.

Hendriks, C.M. (2005): 'Consensus conferences and planning cells: lay citizen deliberations', pp 80–110 in J. Gaskil and P. Levine (Eds): *The Deliberative Democracy Handbook. Strategies for Effective Civic Engagement in the Twenty-first Century*. New York: Jossey-Bass.

——(2006): 'When the forum meets interest politics: strategic uses of public deliberation', *Politics and Society* 34(4)571–602.

Hendriks, C.M., J.S. Dryzek and C. Hunold (2007): 'Turning up the heat: partisanship in deliberative innovation', *Political Studies* 55(2)362–83.

Heskin, A.D. (1980): 'Crisis and response. A historical perspective on advocacy planning', *Journal of the American Planning Association* 46(1)50–63.

Hibbard, M. and M.B. Lane (2004): 'By the seat of your pants: indigenous action and state response', *Planning Theory and Practice* 5(1)95–102.

Hiemstra, N. (2010): 'Immigrant "illegality" as neoliberal governmentality in Leadville, Colorado', *Antipode* 42(1)74–102.

Higgins, M. and P. Allmendinger (1999): 'The changing nature of public planning practice under the New Right: the legacies and implications of privatisation', *Planning Practice and Research* 14(1)39–67.

Hillier, J. (1995): 'SDC or how to manipulate the public into a false consensus without really trying', pp 111–26 in G. Dixon and D. Aitken (Eds): *Institute of Australian Geographers: Conference Proceedings, 1993*. Monash Publications in Geography Number 45. Melbourne: Department of Geography and Environmental Science, Monash University.

——(1999): 'What values? Whose values?', *Ethics, Place and Environment* 2(2)179–99.

——(2000): 'Going around the back? Complex networks and informal action in local planning processes', *Environment and Planning A* 32(1)33–54.

——(2002a): *Shadows of Power. An Allegory of Prudence in Land-use Planning*. London: Routledge.

——(2002b): 'Direct action and agonism in democratic planning practice', pp 110–35 in P. Allmendinger and M. Tewdwr-Jones (Eds): *Planning Futures: New Directions for Planning Theory*. London: Routledge.

——(2003): 'Agonizing over consensus: why Habermasian ideals cannot be "real"', *Planning Theory* 2(1)37–59.

——(2007): *Stretching beyond the Horizon*. Aldershot, Hampshire: Ashgate.

Hirschman, A.O. and C.E. Lindblom (1962): 'Economic development, research and development, policy making: some converging views', *Behavioral Sciences* 7(2)211–22.

Hirt, S. (2007): 'The devil is in the definitions – contrasting American and German approaches to zoning', *Journal of the American Planning Association* 73(4)436–50.

HM Government (1991): *The Citizen's Charter – Raising the Standard*. London: HMSO.

Hoch, C.J. (2007): 'Pragmatic communicative action theory', *Journal of Planning Education and Research* 26(3)272–83.

Hodge, G.A., C. Greve and A. Boardman (2010): *International Handbook on Public Private Partnerships*. Cheltenham: Edward Elgar.

Holgersen, S. and H. Haarstad (2009): 'Class, community and communicative planning: urban redevelopment at King's Cross, London', *Antipode* 41(2)348–70.

Holston, J. (2009): 'Insurgent citizenship in an era of global urban peripheries', *City and Society* 21(2)245–67.

Hood, C. (2002): 'New Public Management', pp 12553–56 in N.J. Smelser and P.B. Bates (Eds): *International Encyclopaedia of the Social and Behavioral Sciences. Volume 8*. Oxford: Elsevier.

Horen, B. van (2002): 'Planning for institutional capacity building in war-torn areas: the case of Jaffna, Sri Lanka', *Habitat International* 26(1)113–28.

Howe, E. (1992): 'Professional roles and the public interest in planning', *Journal of Planning Literature* 6(3)230–48.

Howe, E. and J. Kaufman (1979): 'The ethics of contemporary American planners', *Journal of the American Planning Association* 45(3)243–55.

——(1981): 'The values of contemporary American planners', *Journal of the American Planning Association* 47(3)266–78.

Hoyman, M. and C. Faricy (2009): 'It takes a village. A test of the creative class, social capital, and human capital theories', *Urban Affairs Review* 44(3)311–33.

Hoyt, L.M. (2004): 'Collecting private funds for safer public spaces: an empirical examination of the business improvement district concept', *Environment and Planning B: Planning and Design* 31(3)367–80.

Hubbard, P. (2004): 'Revenge and injustice in the neoliberal city: uncovering masculinist agendas', *Antipode* 36(4)665–86.

Humphrey, M. (2006): 'Democratic legitimacy, public justification and environmental direct action', *Political Studies* 54(2)310–27.

Hutchinson, J. and A. Loukaitou-Sideris (2001): 'Choosing confrontation or consensus in the inner city: lessons from a community-university partnership', *Planning Theory and Practice* 2(3)293–310.

Huxley, M. and O. Yiftachel (2000): 'New paradigm or old myopia? Unsettling the communicative turn in planning theory', *Journal of Planning Education and Research* 19(4)333–42.

Iedema, R. (2003): *Discourses of Post-bureaucratic Organisation*. Amsterdam: John Benjamins.

Ihlanfeldt, K.R. (2004): 'Exclusionary land-use regulations within suburban communities: a review of the evidence and policy prescriptions', *Urban Studies* 41(2)261–83.

Ilcan, S. (2009): 'Privatizing responsibility: public sector reform under neoliberal government', *Canadian Review of Sociology* 46(3)207–34.

Imrie, R. (1999): 'The implications of the "New Managerialism" for planning in the millennium', pp 107–20 in P. Allmendinger and M. Chapman (Eds): *Planning Beyond 2000*. New York: John Wiley.

Imrie, R. and H. Thomas (1999): *British Urban Policy: An Evaluation of the Urban Development Corporations* (Second Edition). London: Sage.

Innes, J.E. (1995): 'Planning theory's emerging paradigm: communicative action and interactive practice', *Journal of Planning Education and Research* 14(3)183–89.

——(2004): 'Consensus building: clarifications for the critics', *Planning Theory* 3(1)5–20.

Innes, J.E. and D.E. Booher (1999a): 'Consensus building and complex adaptive systems: a framework for evaluating collaborative planning', *Journal of the American Planning Association* 65(4)412–23.

——(1999b): 'Consensus building as role playing and bricolage: toward a theory of collaborative planning', *Journal of the American Planning Association* 65(1)9–26.

——(2010): *Planning with Complexity. An Introduction to Collaborative Rationality for Public Policy*. London: Routledge.

International Monetary Fund (2009): *World Economic Outlook April 2009. Crisis and Recovery*. Washington, DC: IMF.

Isaac, T.M.T. and R.W. Franke (2002): *Local Democracy and Development: The Kerala People's Campaign for Decentralized Planning*. New York: Rowman and Littlefield.

Isaac, T.M.T. and P. Heller (2003): 'Democracy and development: decentralized planning in Kerala', pp 77–110 in A. Fung and E.O. Wright (Eds): *Deepening Democracy. Institutional Innovations in Empowered Participatory Governance*. London: Verso.

Jacob, M. and T. Hellström (2010): 'Public-space planning in four Nordic cities: symbolic values in tension', *Geoforum* 41(4)657–65.

JAPA Review Editors (2005): 'Review roundtable: cities and the creative class – discussion and response', *Journal of the American Planning Association* 71(2)203–20.

Jazeel, T. and C. McFarlane (2007): 'Responsible learning: cultures of knowledge production and the North-South divide', *Antipode* 39(5)781–89.

——(2010): 'The limits of responsibility: a postcolonial politics of academic knowledge production', *Transactions of the Institute of British Geographers* NS 35(1)109–24.

Jennings, B. (2008): 'Disaster planning and public health', pp 41–44 in Hastings Center: *From Birth to Death and Bench to Clinic: The Hastings Center Bioethics Briefing Book for Campaigns, Journalists and Policymakers*. Garrison, New York: Hastings Center.

Jennings, E.T. Jr. (2000): 'Welfare reform at the millennium: personal responsibility, race, paternalism, and the quest for solutions' (Book review), *American Review of Public Administration* 30(3)334–60.

John, P., H. Ward and K. Dowding (2004): 'The bidding game: competitive funding regimes and the political targeting of urban programme schemes', *British Journal of Political Science* 34(3)405–28.

Johnson, K. (2004): 'Community development corporations, participation, and accountability: the Harlem Urban Development Corporation and the Bedford-Stuyvesant Restoration Corporation', *Annals of the American Academy of Political and Social Science* 594(1)109–24.

Jonas, H. (1984): *The Imperative of Responsibility*. Chicago: University of Chicago Press.

Jones, P. (2006): 'Toleration, recognition and identity', *Journal of Political Philosophy* 14(2)123–43.

——(2007): 'Making sense of political toleration', *British Journal of Political Science* 37(3)383–402.

Jos, P.H. and M.E. Tompkins (2004): 'The accountability paradox in an age of reinvention. The perennial problem of preserving character and judgment', *Administration and Society* 36(3)255–81.

Justice, J.B. and C. Skelcher (2009): 'Analysing democracy in third-party government: business improvement districts in the US and UK', *International Journal of Urban and Regional Research* 33(3)738–53.

Kahneman, D. (1994): 'New challenges to the rationality assumption', *Journal of Institutional and Theoretical Economics* 150(1)18–36.

Kamat, S. (2004): 'The privatization of public interest: theorizing NGO discourse in a neoliberal era', *Review of International Political Economy* 11(1)155–76.

Kamete, A.Y. (2007): 'Cold-hearted, negligent and spineless? Planning, planners and the (r)ejection of "filth" in urban Zimbabwe', *International Planning Studies* 12(2)153–71.

Kaplan, M. (1969a): 'Advocacy and the urban poor', *Journal of the American Institute of Planners* 35(2)96–101.

——(1969b): 'The role of the planner in urban areas', pp 255–73 in H.B.C. Spiegel (Ed.): *Citizen Participation in Urban Development. Volume II: Cases and Programs*. Washington, D.C.: NTL Institute for Applied Behavioral Science.

Kapoor, I. (2002): 'Deliberative democracy or agonistic pluralism? The relevance of the Habermas–Mouffe debate for Third World politics', *Alternatives: Global, Local, Political* 27(4)459–87.

Karpowitz, C.F., C. Raphael and A.S. Hammond (2009): 'Deliberative democracy and inequality: two cheers for enclave deliberation among the disempowered', *Politics and Society* 37(4)576–615.

Kasachkoff, T. (1994): 'Paternalism: does gratitude make it okay?', *Social Theory and Practice* 20(1)1–23.

Kaufman, J.L. (1985): 'American and Israeli planners – a cross-cultural comparison', *Journal of the American Planning Association* 51(3)352–64.

Kaufman, J.L. and M. Escuin (2000): 'Thinking alike. Similarities in attitudes of Dutch, Spanish, and American planners', *Journal of the American Planning Association* 66(1)34–45.

Keeney, R.L., T.L. McDaniels and V.L. Ridge-Cooney (1996): 'Using values in planning wastewater facilities for metropolitan Seattle', *Water Resources Bulletin* 32(2)293–303.

Keevers, L., L. Treleaven and C. Sykes (2008): 'Partnership and participation: contradictions and tensions in the social policy space', *Australian Journal of Social Issues* 43(3)459–77.

Kenny, J.T. and J. Zimmerman (2003): 'Constructing the "genuine American city": neo-traditionalism, New Urbanism and neo-liberalism in the remaking of downtown Milwaukee', *Cultural Geographies* 11(1)74–98.

Kerkin, K. (2003): 'Re-placing difference: planning and street sex work in a gentrifying area', *Urban Policy and Research* 21(2)137–49.

Khakee, A. and L. Dahlgreen (1990): 'Ethics and values of Swedish planners: a replication and comparison with an American study', *Scandinavian Housing and Planning Research* 7(2)65–81.

King, L.A. (2003): 'Deliberation, legitimacy, and multilateral democracy', *Governance* 16(1)23–50.

Kirby, A. (2008): 'The production of private space and its implications for urban social relations', *Political Geography* 27(1)74–95.

Klemek, C. (2008): 'From political outsider to power broker in two "great American cities": Jane Jacobs and the fall of the urban renewal order in New York and Toronto', *Journal of Urban History* 34(2)309–32.

Klosterman, R.E. (1980): 'A public interest criterion', *Journal of the American Planning Association* 46(3)323–33.

——(2011): 'Planning theory education: a thirty-year review', *Journal of Planning Education and Research* 31(3)319–31.

Kohl, B. and L. Farthing (2008): 'New spaces, new contests: appropriating decentralization for political change in Bolivia', pp 69–85 in V.A. Beard, F. Miraftab and C. Silver (Eds): *Planning and Decentralization: Contested Spaces for Public Action in the Global South*. New York: Routledge.

Kothari, U. (2001): 'Power, knowledge and social control in participatory development', pp 139–52 in B. Cooke and U. Kothari (Eds): *Participation: The New Tyranny?* New York: Zed Books.

Krätke, S. (2010): '"Creative cities" and the rise of the dealer class: a critique of Richard Florida's approach to urban theory', *International Journal of Urban and Regional Research* 34(4)835–53.

Kraushaar, R. (1988): 'Outside the whale: progressive planning and the dilemmas of radical reform', *Journal of the American Planning Association* 54(1)91–100.

Krumholz, N. (1994): 'Dilemmas in equity planning: a personal memoir', *Planning Theory* (Franco Angeli Series) No. 10–11, 45–56.

Krumholz, N. and P. Clavel (1994): *Reinventing Cities. Equity Planners Tell Their Stories*. Philadelphia: Temple University Press.

Krumholz, N. and J. Forester (1990): *Making Equity Planning Work: Leadership in the Public Sector*. Philadelphia: Temple University Press.

Kunzmann, K.R. (2005): 'Creativity in planning: a fuzzy concept?', *disP* 162(3)5–13.

Laburn-Peart, C. (1997): 'Holding the knife on the sharp side: rural women and planning in Mogopa, South Africa', *Third World Planning Review* 19(1)71–90.

LaCapra, D. (1998): 'The university in ruins?', *Critical Inquiry* 25(1)32–55.

Laffont, J.-J. (2003): *The Principal Agent Model. The Economic Theory of Incentives*. Cheltenham: Edward Elgar.

Lakoff, S.A. (1980): 'Moral responsibility and the "Galilean Imperative"', *Ethics* 91(1)100–16.

Lamie, J. and R. Ball (2010): 'Evaluation of partnership working within a community planning context', *Local Government Studies* 36(1)109–27.

Landau, M. (1969): 'Redundancy, rationality, and the problem of duplication and overlap', *Public Administration Review* 29(4)346–58.

Landry, C. (2008): *The Creative City: A Toolkit for Urban Innovators* (Second Edition). London: Earthscan.

Lane, J.-E. (2000): *New Public Management*. London: Routledge.

Lane, M.B. and M. Hibbard (2005): 'Doing it for themselves. Transformative planning by indigenous peoples', *Journal of Planning Education and Research* 25(2)172–84.

Lapintie, K. and S. Puustinen (2002): 'Towards a reflexive planner: the planning profession and the communicative challenge', Unpublished manuscript available from the authors, Helsinki University of Technology.

Larner, W. and D. Craig (2005): 'After neoliberalism? Community activism and local partnerships in Aotearoa, New Zealand', pp 9–31 in N. Laurie and L. Bondi (Eds): *Working the Spaces of Neoliberalism. Activism, Professionalisation and Incorporation*. Oxford: Blackwell.

Leavitt, J. (1982): 'A progressive planning identity: the import of the founding of the planners' network, 10 May 1981', *International Journal of Urban and Regional Research* 6(2)268–75.

——(1986): 'Feminist advocacy planning in the 1980s', pp 181–94 in B. Checkoway (Ed.): *Strategic Perspectives on Planning Practice*. Lexington, Mass.: Lexington Books.

——(1994): 'Planning in an age of rebellion: guidelines to activist research and applied planning', *Planning Theory* (Franco Angeli Series) No. 10–11, 111–29.

Lehrer, U. and R. Keil (2007): 'From possible urban worlds to the contested metropolis: research and action in the age of urban neoliberalism', pp 291–310 in H. Leitner, J. Peck and E.S. Sheppard (Eds): *Contesting Neoliberalism: Urban Frontiers*. London: Guilford Press.

Levinas, E. (1969): *Totality and Infinity. An Essay on Exteriority*. Pittsburgh: Duquesne University Press.

——(1981): *Otherwise than Being or beyond Essence*. The Hague: Martinus Nijhoff.

——(1998): *Entre Nous: On Thinking-of-the-Other*. New York: Columbia University Press.

Levinas, E. and R. Kearney (1986): 'Dialogue with Emmanuel Levinas', pp 13–33 in R.A. Cohen (Ed.): *Face to Face with Levinas*. Albany: SUNY Press.

Lewis, C.W. (2006): 'In pursuit of the public interest', *Public Administration Review* 66(5)694–701.

Lier, D.C. (2006): 'Maximum working class unity? Challenges to local social movement unionism in Cape Town', *Antipode* 38(4)802–24.

Lier, D.C. and K. Stokke (2006): 'Maximum working class unity? Challenges to local social movement unionism in Cape Town', *Antipode* 38(4)802–24.

Lindblom, C.E. (1959): 'The science of "muddling through"', *Public Administration Review* 19(2)79–88.

——(1979): 'Still muddling, not yet through', *Public Administration Review* 39(6)517–26.

Lipsey, R.G. and K. Lancaster (1956–57): 'The general theory of second best', *Review of Economic Studies* 24(1)11–32.

List, C. (2006): 'The discursive dilemma and public reason', *Ethics* 116(2)362–402.

List, C. and R.E. Goodin (2001): 'Epistemic democracy: generalizing the Condorcet jury theorem', *Journal of Political Philosophy* 9(3)277–306.

Lloyd, M.G. (1990): 'Simplified planning zones in Scotland: government failure or the failure of government?', *Planning Outlook* 33(2)128–32.

Lloyd, M.G., J. McCarthy, S. McGreal and J. Berry (2003): 'Business improvement districts, planning and urban regeneration', *International Planning Studies* 8(4)295–321.

Lockwood, S.C., R. Verma and M. Schneider (2000): 'Public-private partnership in toll road development: an overview of global practices', *Transportation Quarterly* 54(2)77–91.

Loring, J.M. (2007): 'Wind energy planning in England, Wales and Denmark: factors influencing project success', *Energy Policy* 35(4)2648–60.

Lovering, J. (2009): 'The recession and the end of planning as we have known it', *International Planning Studies* 14(1)1–6.

——(2010): 'Will the recession prove to be a turning point in planning and urban development thinking?', *International Planning Studies* 15(3)227–43.

Low, N.P. (1991): *Planning, Politics and the State. Political Foundations of Planning Thought.* London: Unwin Hyman.

Lowndes, V. and H. Sullivan (2004): 'Like a horse and carriage or a fish on a bicycle: how well do local partnerships and public participation go together?', *Local Government Studies* 30(1)51–73.

Lowry, K. (1994): 'The legitimation of planning', *Planning Theory* (Franco Angeli Series) No. 10–11, 99–109.

Luban, D. (1979): 'Habermas on Arendt on power', *Philosophy and Social Criticism* 6(1)79–95.

Lucy, W.H. (1996): 'APA's ethical principles include simplistic planning theories', pp 479–84 in S. Campbell and S. Fainstein (Eds): *Readings in Planning Theory.* Cambridge, Mass.: Blackwell.

Lynch, K. (2006): 'Neo-liberalism and marketisation: the implications for higher education', *European Educational Research Journal* 5(1)1–17.

MacCallum, D. (2008): 'Participatory planning and means-ends rationality: a translation problem', *Planning Theory and Practice* 9(3)325–43.

Madge, C., P. Raghuram and P. Noxolo (2009): 'Engaged pedagogy and responsibility: a postcolonial analysis of international students', *Geoforum* 40(1)34–45.

Majone, G. (2001): 'Nonmajoritarian institutions and the limits of democratic governance: a political transaction-cost approach', *Journal of Institutional and Theoretical Economics* 157(1)57–78.

Mallon, R. (2007): 'A field guide to social construction', *Philosophy Compass* 2(1)93–108.

Mandelbaum, S. (1990): 'Reading plans', *Journal of the American Planning Association* 56(3)350–56.

Manin, B. (1987): 'On legitimacy and political deliberation', *Political Theory* 15(3)338–68.

Mansbridge, J. (1996): 'Using power/fighting power: the polity', pp 46–66 in S. Benhabib (Ed.): *Democracy and Difference. Contesting the Boundaries of the Political.* Princeton: Princeton University Press.

Mansbridge, J., J. Bohman, S. Chambers, D. Estlund, A. Føllesdal, A. Fung, C. Lafont, B. Manin and J.L. Martí (2010): 'The place of self-interest and the role of power in deliberative democracy', *Journal of Political Philosophy* 18(1)64–100.

Mäntysalo, R. (2002): 'Dilemmas in critical planning theory', *Town Planning Review* 73(4)417–36.

——(2008): 'Dialectics of power: the case of Tulihta land-use agreement', *Planning Theory and Practice* 9(1)81–96.

March, J.G. and J.P. Olsen (1986): 'Garbage can models of decision making in organizations', pp 11–35 in J.G. March and R. Weissinger-Baylon (Eds): *Ambiguity and Command. Organizational Perspectives on Military Decision Making.* Marshfield: Pitman Publishing.

Marcuse, P. (2009): 'Postscript. Beyond the Just City to the Right to the City', pp 240–54 in P. Marcuse, J. Connolly, J. Novy, I. Olivo, C. Potter and J. Steil (Eds): *Searching for the Just City. Debates in Urban Theory and Practice*. London: Routledge.

Margerum, R.D. (2002a): 'Evaluating collaborative planning. Implications from an empirical analysis of growth management', *Journal of the American Planning Association* 68(2)179–93.

——(2002b): 'Collaborative planning: building consensus and building a distinct model for practice', *Journal of Planning Education and Research* 21(3)237–53.

Markusen, A. (2006): 'Urban development and the politics of a creative class: evidence from a study of artists', *Environment and Planning A* 38(10)1921–40.

Mármol, J.L.M. (2005): 'The sources of legitimacy of political decisions: between procedure and substance', pp 259–81 in L.J. Wintgens (Ed.): *The Theory and Practice of Legislation*. Aldershot: Ashgate.

Marris, P. (1994): 'Advocacy planning as a bridge between the professional and the political', *Journal of the American Planning Association* 60(2)143–46.

Martí, J.L. (2006): 'The epistemic conception of deliberative democracy defended. Reasons, rightness and equal political autonomy', pp 27–56 in S. Besson and J.L. Martí (Eds): *Deliberative Democracy and Its Discontents*. Aldershot: Ashgate.

Massey, D. (2008): 'When theory meets politics', *Antipode* 40(3)492–97.

May, M. and S.B. Hill (2006): 'Questioning airport expansion – a case study of Canberra International Airport', *Journal of Transport Geography* 14(6)437–50.

McCann, E.J. (2001): 'Collaborative visioning or urban planning as therapy? The politics of public-private policy making', *Professional Geographer* 53(2)207–18.

McCloskey, D.N. (2006): *The Bourgeois Virtues: Ethics for an Age of Commerce*. Chicago: University of Chicago Press.

McCloskey, M.C. (1971): 'Planning and regional planning – what are they? An annotated bibliography of definitions', *Exchange Bibliography No. 174*. Monticello, Illinois: Council of Planning Librarians.

McDermott, P. (1998): 'Positioning planning in a market economy', *Environment and Planning A* 30(4)631–46.

McGreal, S., J. Berry, G. Lloyd and J. McCarthy (2002): 'Tax-based mechanisms in urban regeneration: Dublin and Chicago models', *Urban Studies* 39(10)1819–31.

McGuirk, P.M. (2001): 'Situating communicative planning theory: context, power, and knowledge', *Environment and Planning A* 33(2)195–217.

McGuirk, P.M. and R. Dowling (2009): 'Neoliberal privatisation? Remapping the public and the private in Sydney's masterplanned residential estates', *Political Geography* 28(3)174–85.

McLean, I. and F. Hewitt (1994): *Condorcet: Foundations of Social Choice and Political Theory*. Brookfield, VT: Elgar.

McLean, M. (2006): *Pedagogy and the University. Critical Theory and Practice*. London: Continuum.

McLeod, J.M., D.A. Scheufele, P. May, E.M. Horowitz, R.L. Holbert, W. Zhang, S. Zubric and J. Zubric (1999): 'Understanding deliberation: the effects of discussion networks on participation in a public forum', *Communication Research* 26(6)743–74.

McNamee, S. and K.J. Gergen (Eds) (1999): *Relational Responsibility: Resources for Sustainable Dialogue*. Thousand Oaks: Sage.

Medearis, J. (2005): 'Social movements and deliberative democratic theory', *British Journal of Political Science* 35(1)53–75.

Mees, P. (2003): 'Paterson's curse: the attempt to revive metropolitan planning in Melbourne', *Urban Policy and Research* 21(3)287–99.

Meijer, F. and H. Visscher (2006): 'Deregulation and privatisation of European building-control systems?', *Environment and Planning B: Planning and Design* 33(4)491–501.

Meir, A. (2005): 'Bedouin, the Israeli state and insurgent planning: globalization, localization or glocalization?', *Cities* 22(3)201–15.

——(2009): 'Socially sustainable development: planning empowerment among the Bedouin in Israel', Paper for *REAL CORP 2009*, 14th International Conference on Urban Planning and Regional Development in the Information Society, 22–25 April 2009, Design Centre Sitges, Catalonia, Spain. http://programm.corp.at/cdrom2009/papers2009/CORP2009_25.pdf (accessed 27.02.11).

Melik, R. van, I. van Aalst and J. van Weesep (2009): 'The private sector and public space in Dutch city centres', *Cities* 26(4)202–09.

Merton, R.K. (1957): *Social Theory and Social Structure*. London: Free Press.

Meth, P. (2010): 'Unsettling insurgency: reflections on women's insurgent practices in South Africa', *Planning Theory and Practice* 11(2)241–63.

Metzger, J.T. (1996): 'The theory and practice of equity planning: an annotated bibliography', *Journal of Planning Literature* 11(1)112–26.

Meyer, J.M. (2008): 'Populism, paternalism and the state of environmentalism in the US', *Environmental Politics* 17(2)219–36.

Miller, B. (2006): 'Castells' *The City and the Grassroots*: 1983 and today', *International Journal of Urban and Regional Research* 30(1)207–11.

Miller, N.R. (1986): 'Information, electorates, and democracy: some extensions and interpretations of the Condorcet jury theorem', pp 173–92 in B. Grofman and G. Owen (Eds): *Information Pooling and Group Decision Making*. Greenwich, Connecticut: JAI Press.

Miraftab, F. (2004): 'Making neo-liberal governance: the disempowering work of empowerment', *International Planning Studies* 9(4)239–59.

——(2009): 'Insurgent planning: situating radical planning in the Global South', *Planning Theory* 8(1)32–50.

Miraftab, F. and S. Wills (2005): 'Insurgency and spaces of active citizenship: the story of Western Cape Anti-eviction Campaign in South Africa', *Journal of Planning Education and Research* 25(2)200–17.

Misselwitz, P. and E. Weizman (2003): 'Military operations as urban planning', *Mute Magazine – Culture and Politics after the Net*. www.metamute.org/en/node/6317/print (accessed 01.11.06). (Also in A. Franke (Ed.): *Territories*. Berlin: KW Institute for Contemporary Art).

Mitchell, D. (2001): 'Postmodern geographical praxis? The postmodern impulse and the war against homeless people in the "post-justice" city', pp 57–92 in C. Minca (Ed.): *Postmodern Geography. Theory and Praxis*. Oxford: Blackwell.

——(2003): *The Right to the City: Social Justice and the Fight for Public Space*. New York: Guilford.

Mitlin, D. (2008): 'With and beyond the state – co-production as a route to political influence, power and transformation for grassroots organizations', *Environment and Urbanization* 20(2)339–60.

Moe, T.M. (1990): 'Political institutions: the neglected side of the story', *Journal of Law, Economics, and Organization* 6(Special Issue)213–53.

Monahan, T. (2006): 'Electronic fortification in Phoenix. Surveillance technologies and social regulation in residential communities', *Urban Affairs Review* 42(2)169–92.

Montada, L. (1998): 'Justice: just a rational choice?', *Social Justice Research* 11(2)81–101.

Morell, J.A. (2005): 'Why are there unintended consequences of program action, and what are the implications for doing evaluation?', *American Journal of Evaluation* 26(4)444–63.

Morris, A.W. (2008): 'Easing conservation? Conservation easements, public accountability and neoliberalism', *Geoforum* 39(3)1215–27.

Moser, C.O.N. (1989): 'Gender planning in the third world: meeting practical and strategic gender needs', *World Development* 17(11)1799–1825.

Mouffe, C. (1999): 'Deliberative democracy or agonistic pluralism', *Social Research* 66(3)745–58.

——(2000): *The Democratic Paradox*. London: Verso.

Müller, M.M., E. Kals and J. Maes (2008): 'Fairness, self-interest, and cooperation in a real-life conflict', *Journal of Applied Social Psychology* 38(3)684–704.

Murphy, J.T. (2006): 'Building trust in economic space', *Progress in Human Geography* 30(4)427–50.

Murray, J.W. (2003a): 'The dialogical prioritization of calls: toward a communicative model of justice', *New Jersey Journal of Communication* 11(1)2–23.

——(2003b): *Face to Face in Dialogue. Emmanuel Levinas and (the) Communication (of) Ethics*. New York: University Press of America.

Musole, M. (2009): 'Property rights, transaction costs and institutional change: conceptual framework and literature review', *Progress in Planning* 71(2)43–85.

Myerson, G. (1995): 'Democracy, argument and the university', *Studies in Higher Education* 20(2)125–33.

Nafstad, H.E., R.M. Blakar, E. Carlquist, J.M. Phelps and K. Rand-Hendriksen (2007): 'Ideology and power: the influence of current neo-liberalism in society', *Journal of Community and Applied Social Psychology* 17(4)313–27.

Nash, J. (1997): 'The fiesta of the word: the Zapatista uprising and radical democracy in Mexico', *American Anthropologist* 99(2)261–74.

Needleman, M.L. and C.E. Needleman (1974): *Guerillas in the Bureaucracy*. New York: Wiley.

Neffe, J. (2007): *Einstein. A Biography*. Cambridge: Polity Press.

Neill, W.J.V. (2008): 'Within the city limits: tolerance and the negotiation of difference' (Viewpoint), *Town Planning Review* 79(6)i–viii.

Németh, J. (2009): 'Defining a public: the management of privately owned public space', *Urban Studies* 46(11)2463–90.

New, B. (1999): 'Paternalism and public policy', *Economics and Philosophy* 15(1)63–83.

New Scientist (2006): 'Editorial: Dual-use biotech – proceed with caution', *New Scientist* (14 October) 192(2573)5.

Nicholls, W.J. (2008): 'The urban question revisited: the importance of cities for social movements', *International Journal of Urban and Regional Research* 32(4)841–59.

Niemeyer, S. and J.S. Dryzek (2007): 'The ends of deliberation: meta-consensus and inter-subjective rationality as ideal outcomes', *Swiss Political Science Review* 13(4)497–526.

North, D.C. (1990a): *Institutions, Institutional Change and Economic Performance*. Cambridge: Cambridge University Press.

——(1990b): 'A transaction cost theory of politics', *Journal of Theoretical Politics* 2(4)355–67.

North, P. (2000): 'Is there space for organisation from below within the UK government's action zones? A test of "collaborative planning"', *Urban Studies* 37(8)1261–78.

——(2001): '"It's a problem, is it?" Planning and protest', *Planning Theory and Practice* 2(3)356–61.

Oatley, N. (1995): 'Competitive urban policy and the regeneration game', *Town Planning Review* 66(1)1–14.

——(1998): *Cities, Economic Competition and Urban Policy*. London: Paul Chapman.

Oberdeck, K.J. (2000): 'From model town to edge city: piety, paternalism, and the politics of urban planning in the United States' (Review essay), *Journal of Urban History* 26(4)508–18.

OECD (2001): *Citizens as Partners: Information, Consultation and Public Participation in Policy Making*. Paris: Organization for Economic Co-operation and Development.

Olsen, K.H. (2000): *Ethics, Attitudes and Values of Norwegian Planners*. Working Papers from Stavanger University College 81/2000. Stavanger: Stavanger University College.

Olssen, M. and M.A. Peters (2005): 'Neoliberalism, higher education and the knowledge economy: from the free market to knowledge capitalism', *Journal of Education Policy* 20(3)313–45.

Olsson, G. (1984): 'Toward a sermon of modernity', pp 73–85 in M. Billinge, D. Gregory and R. Martin (Eds): *Recollections of a Revolution. Geography as Spatial Science*. London: Macmillan.

Olsson, J. (2009): 'The power of the inside activist: understanding policy change by empowering the advocacy coalition framework (ACF)', *Planning Theory and Practice* 10(2)167–87.

O'Neill, S. (2000): 'The politics of inclusive agreements: towards a critical discourse theory of democracy', *Political Studies* 48(3)503–21.

Oommen, M.A. (2005): 'Deepening decentralised governance in rural India: lessons from the People's Plan Initiative of Kerala', *Social Change and Development* 3(July)103–18.

Orr, S.W. (2007): 'Values, preferences, and the citizen-consumer distinction in cost-benefit analysis', *Politics, Philosophy and Economics* 6(1)107–30.

Østerud, Ø., F. Engelstad and P. Selle (2003): *Makten og demokratiet* (Power and Democracy). Oslo: Gyldendal.

Ostrom, E. and T.K. Ahn (2009): 'The meaning of social capital and its link to collective action', pp 17–35 in G. Tinggaard Svendsen and G.L.H. Svendsen (Eds): *Handbook of Social Capital. The Troika of Sociology, Political Science and Economics*. Cheltenham: Edward Elgar.

Ostrom, E., R. Gardner and J. Walker (1994): *Rules, Games and Common-pool Resources*. Ann Arbor: University of Michigan Press.

Ottensmann, J.R. (2005): 'Planning through the exchange of rights under performance zoning', *Economic Affairs* 25(4)40–43.

Parkinson, J. (2003): 'Legitimacy problems in deliberative democracy', *Political Studies* 51(1)180–96.

Parviainen, J. (2010): 'Choreographing resistances: spatial-kinaesthetic intelligence and bodily knowledge as political tools in activist work', *Mobilities* 5(3)311–29.

Patashnik, E.M. (1996): 'The contractual nature of budgeting: a transaction cost perspective on the design of budgeting institutions', *Policy Sciences* 29(3)189–212.

Peck, J. (2005): 'Struggling with the creative class', *International Journal of Urban and Regional Research* 29(4)740–70.

Peck, J. and A. Tickell (2002): 'Neoliberalizing space', pp 33–57 in N. Brenner and N. Theodore (Eds): *Spaces of Neoliberalism. Urban Restructuring in North America and Western Europe*. Malden, Mass.: Blackwell.

Peck, J., N. Theodore and N. Brenner (2009): 'Neoliberal urbanism: models, moments, mutations', *SAIS Review* 29(1)49–66.

Pelletier, D., V. Kraak, C. McCullum, U. Uusitalo and R. Rich (1999): 'The shaping of collective values through deliberative democracy: an empirical study from New York's North Country', *Policy Sciences* 32(2)103–31.

Pellizzoni, L. (2001): 'The myth of the best argument: power, deliberation and reason', *British Journal of Sociology* 52(1)59–86.

Pellow, D.N. (1999): 'Negotiation and confrontation: environmental policymaking through consensus', *Society and Natural Resources* 12(3)189–203.

Pendall, R. (2000): 'Local land use regulation and the chain of exclusion', *Journal of the American Planning Association* 66(2)125–42.

Pennington, M. (2003): 'Hayekian political economy and the limits of deliberative democracy', *Political Studies* 51(4)722–39.

——(2004): 'Citizen participation, the "knowledge problem" and urban land use planning: an Austrian perspective on institutional choice', *Review of Austrian Economics* 17(2–3)213–31.

Perry, J.L. (2007): 'Democracy and the New Public Service', *American Review of Public Administration* 37(1)3–16.

Perry, N. (1995): 'Travelling theory/nomadic theorizing', *Organization* 2(1)35–54.

Phadke, R. (2005): 'People's science in action: the politics of protest and knowledge brokering in India', *Society and Natural Resources* 18(4)363–75.

Pickerill, J. (2008): 'The surprising sense of hope', *Antipode* 40(3)482–87.

Piven, F.F. (1970): 'Whom does the advocacy planner serve?', *Social Policy* 1(1)32–37.

Pløger, J. (2004): 'Strife: urban planning and agonism', *Planning Theory* 3(1)71–92.

Polletta, F. (2006): *It Was Like a Fever. Storytelling in Protest and Politics*. Chicago: University of Chicago Press.

Polletta, F. and J. Lee (2006): 'Is telling stories good for democracy? Rhetoric in public deliberation after 9/11', *American Sociological Review* 71(5)699–721.

Popper, K. (1972): *Conjectures and Refutations* (Fourth Edition). London: Routledge and Kegan Paul.

Power, M. (1997): *The Audit Society. Rituals of Verification*. Oxford: Oxford University Press.

Poxon, J. (2001): 'Shaping the planning profession of the future: the role of planning education', *Environment and Planning B: Planning and Design* 28(4)563–80.

Price, W.T. (2001): 'An odyssey of privatizing highways. The evolving case of SR 91', *Public Works Management and Policy* 5(4)259–69.

Prior, A. (2005): 'UK planning reform: a regulationist interpretation', *Planning Theory and Practice* 6(4)465–84.

Prouteau, L. and F.-C. Wolff (2004): 'Relational goods and associational participation', *Annals of Public and Cooperative Economics* 75(3)431–63.

——(2008): 'On the relational motive for volunteer work', *Journal of Economic Psychology* 29(3)314–35.

Punter, J.V. (1993): 'Development interests and the attack on planning controls: "planning difficulties" in Bristol 1985-1990', *Environment and Planning A* 25(4)521–38.

Purcell, M. (2007): 'City-regions, neoliberal globalization and democracy: a research agenda', *International Journal of Urban and Regional Research* 31(1)197–206.

——(2008): *Recapturing Democracy. Neoliberalization and the Struggle for Alternative Urban Futures*. New York: Routledge.

——(2009): 'Resisting neoliberalization: communicative planning or counter-hegemonic movements?', *Planning Theory* 8(2)140–65.

Qian, Z. (2010): 'Without zoning: urban development and land use controls in Houston', *Cities* 27(1)31–41.

Quinn, J.B. (1980): *Strategies for Change: Logical Incrementalism*. Homewood: Irwin.

Rader Olsson, A. (2009): 'Relational rewards and communicative planning: understanding actor motivation', *Planning Theory* 8(3)263–81.

Raghuram, P., C. Madge and P. Noxolo (2009): 'Rethinking responsibility and care for a postcolonial world', *Geoforum* 40(1)5–13.

Ranasinghe, P. and M. Valverde (2006): 'Governing homelessness through land-use: a sociolegal study of the Toronto shelter zoning by-law', *Canadian Journal of Sociology* 31(3)325–49.

Rangan, H. (1999): 'Bitter-sweet liaisons in a contentious democracy: radical planning through state agency in postcolonial India', *Plurimondi* 1(2)47–66.

Rawls, J. (1972): *A Theory of Justice*. Oxford: Oxford University Press.

Reade, E. (1991): 'Review article: the barefoot technocrat', *Scandinavian Housing and Planning Research* 8(3)185–92.

Reardon, K.M. (1998): 'Enhancing the capacity of community-based organizations in East St. Louis', *Journal of Planning Education and Research* 17(4)323–33.

——(2008): 'Planning, hope, and struggle in the wake of Katrina: Ken Reardon on the New Orleans Planning Initiative' (Ken Reardon in conversation with John Forester, in Interfaces), *Planning Theory and Practice* 9(4)518–40.

Rein, M. and D. Schön (1993): 'Reframing policy discourse', pp 145–66 in F. Fischer and J. Forester (Eds): *The Argumentative Turn in Policy Analysis and Planning*. London: UCL Press.

Rhodes, C. and A.D. Brown (2005): 'Writing responsively: narrative fiction and organization studies', *Organization* 12(4)467–91.

Rhodes, J., P. Tyler and A. Brennan (2003): 'New developments in area-based initiatives in England: the experience of the Single Regeneration Budget', *Urban Studies* 40(8)1399–1426.

Richardson, L. and E. Adams St.Pierre (2005): 'Writing: a method of inquiry', pp 959–78 in N.K. Denzin and Y.S. Lincoln (Eds): *The Sage Handbook of Qualitative Research* (Third Edition). Thousand Oaks: Sage.

Ricoeur, P. (2000): 'The concept of responsibility. An essay in semantic analysis', pp 11–35 in P. Ricoeur: *The Just*. Chicago: University of Chicago Press.

Rienstra, B. and D. Hook (2006): 'Weakening Habermas: the undoing of communicative rationality', *Politikon* 33(3)313–39.

Roberts, N.C. (2002): 'Keeping public officials accountable through dialogue: resolving the accountability paradox', *Public Administration Review* 62(6)658–69.

Robinson, I. (2000): 'Neoliberal restructuring and U.S. unions: toward social movement unionism?', *Critical Sociology* 26(1–2)109–38.

Roe, K.M., K. Roe, C.G. Carpenter and C.B. Sibley (2005): 'Community building through empowering evaluation: a case study of community planning for HIV prevention', pp 386–402 in M. Minkler (Ed.): *Community Organizing and Community Building for Health* (Second Edition). New Brunswick: Rutgers University Press.

Roitman, S., C. Webster and K. Landman (2010): 'Methodological frameworks and interdisciplinary research on gated communities', *International Planning Studies* 15(1)3–23.

Rokeach, M. (1973): *The Nature of Human Values*. New York: Free Press.

Romzek, B.S. (2000): 'Dynamics of public sector accountability in an era of reform', *International Review of Administrative Sciences* 66(1)21–44.

Roseland, M. (1997): 'Dimensions of the eco-city', *Cities* 14(4)197–202.

Ross, M. (2006): 'Is democracy good for the poor?', *American Journal of Political Science* 50(4)860–74.

Rostbøll, C.F. (2005): 'Preferences and paternalism: on freedom and deliberative democracy', *Political Theory* 33(3)370–96.

Routledge, P. (1997): 'The imagineering of resistance: Pollok Free State and the practice of postmodern politics', *Transactions of the Institute of British Geographers* NS22(3)359–76.

Roy, A. (2009a): 'Why India cannot plan its cities: informality, insurgence and the idiom of urbanization', *Planning Theory* 8(1)76–87.

——(2009b): 'Civic governmentality: the politics of inclusion in Beirut and Mumbai', *Antipode* 41(1)159–79.

——(2010): 'Informality and the politics of planning', pp 87–107 in J. Hillier and P. Healey (Eds): *The Ashgate Research Companion to Planning Theory. Conceptual Challenges for Spatial Planning*. Farnham, Surrey: Ashgate.

Rugendyke, B. (Ed.) (2007): *NGOs as Advocates for Development in a Globalising World*. London: Routledge.

Ryan, V.D., K.A. Agnitsch, L. Zhao and R. Mullick (2005): 'Making sense of voluntary participation: a theoretical synthesis', *Rural Sociology* 70(3)287–313.

Rydin, Y. (2003): *Conflict, Consensus, and Rationality in Environmental Planning. An Institutional Discourse Approach*. Oxford: Oxford University Press.

Rydin, Y. and M. Pennington (2000): 'Public participation and local environmental planning: the collective action problem and the potential of social capital', *Local Environment* 5(2)153–69.

Saad-Filho, A. and D. Johnston (Eds) (2005): *Neoliberalism: A Critical Reader*. London: Pluto Press.

Sagalyn, L.B. (2007): 'Public/private development. Lessons from history, research, and practice', *Journal of the American Planning Association* 73(1)7–22.

Sager, T. (1994): *Communicative Planning Theory*. Aldershot: Avebury.

——(1995): 'Teaching planning theory as order or fragments?', *Journal of Planning Education and Research* 14(3)166–73.

——(2002): *Democratic Planning and Social Choice Dilemmas. Prelude to Institutional Planning Theory*. Aldershot: Ashgate.

——(2005): 'Planning through inclusive dialogue: no escape from social choice dilemmas', *Economic Affairs* 25(4)32–35.

——(2007): 'Dialogical values in public goods provision', *Journal of Planning Education and Research* 26(4)497–512.

——(2011): 'Neo-liberal urban planning policies: a literature survey 1990–2010', *Progress in Planning* 76(4)147–99.

Sager, T. and I.-A. Ravlum (2005): 'From projects to strategies: a transaction cost approach to politicians' problems with strategic transport planning', *Planning Theory and Practice* 6(2)213–32.

Sager, T. and C.H. Sørensen (2011): 'Planning analysis and political steering with New Public Management', *European Planning Studies* 19(2)217–41.

Said, E.W. (1983): *The World, the Text, and the Critic*. Cambridge, Mass.: Harvard University Press.

Saint-Martin, D. (1998): 'The new managerialism and the policy influence of consultants in government: an historical-institutionalist analysis of Britain, Canada and France', *Governance* 11(3)319–56.

Saliba, R. (2001): 'Emerging trends in urbanism: the Beirut post-war experience'. (An essay on a presentation made by Robert Saliba to Diwan al-Mimar on 20 April 2000. Prepared by M. al-Asad and M. Musa in association with R. Saliba). Center for the Study of the Built Environment, Jordan. www.csbe.org/Saliba-Diwan/essay1.htm (accessed 15.01.11).

Salop, S.C. and D.T. Scheffman (1983): 'Raising rivals' costs', *American Economic Association Papers and Proceedings* 73(2)267–71.

——(1987): 'Cost-raising strategies', *Journal of Industrial Economics* 36(1)19–34.

Sandbu, M.E. (2007): 'Valuing processes', *Economics and Philosophy* 23(2)205–35.

Sandercock, L. (1998a): 'The death of modernist planning: radical praxis for a postmodern age', pp 163–84 in M. Douglass and J. Friedmann (Eds): *Cities for Citizens. Planning and the Rise of Civil Society in a Global Age*. New York: John Wiley.

——(1998b): *Towards Cosmopolis*. New York: John Wiley.

——(2000): 'When strangers become neighbours: managing cities of difference', *Planning Theory and Practice* 1(1)13–30.

Santos, B. de S. (1998): 'Participatory budgeting in Porto Alegre: toward a redistributive democracy', *Politics and Society* 26(4)461–510.

Sanyal, B. (2002): 'Globalization, ethical compromise and planning theory', *Planning Theory* 1(2)116–23.

——(2008): 'Critical about criticality', *Critical Planning* 15, 143–60.

Sartre, J.-P. (1982): *Critique of Dialectical Reason*. London: Verso.

Scheyvens, R. (1998): 'Subtle strategies for women's empowerment. Planning for effective grassroots development', *Third World Planning Review* 20(3)235–53.

Schlosberg, D. (1995): 'Communicative action in practice: intersubjectivity and new social movements', *Political Studies* 43(2)291–311.

Schneiderhan, E. and S. Khan (2008): 'Reasons and inclusion: the foundation of deliberation', *Sociological Theory* 26(1)1–24.

Schudson, M. (1997): 'Why conversation is not the soul of democracy', *Critical Studies in Mass Communication* 14(4)297–309.

Schwartz, S.H. and W. Bilsky (1987): 'Toward a universal psychological structure of human values', *Journal of Personality and Social Psychology* 53(3)550–62.

Scott, A.J. and S.T. Roweis (1977): 'Urban planning in theory and practice: a reappraisal', *Environment and Planning A* 9(10)1097–1119.

Scott, E.D. (2002): 'Organizational moral values', *Business Ethics Quarterly* 12(1)33–55.

Scott, J.C. (1997): 'The infrapolitics of subordinate groups', pp 311–28 in M. Rahnema and V. Bawtree (Eds): *The Post-development Reader*. London: Zed Books.

Selle, P. and Ø. Østerud (2006): 'The eroding of representative democracy in Norway', *Journal of European Public Policy* 13(4)551–68.

Sen, A. (1977): 'Rational fools: a critique of the behavioural foundations of economic theory', *Philosophy and Public Affairs* 6(4)317–44.

——(2009): *The Idea of Justice*. London: Allen Lane.

Sengupta, U. and S. Sharma (2009): 'No longer *Sukumbasis*: challenges in grassroots-led squatter resettlement program in Kathmandu with special reference to Kirtipur Housing Project', *Habitat International* 33(1)34–44.

Shaoul, J., A. Stafford and P. Stapleton (2006): 'Highway robbery? A financial analysis of design, build, finance and operate (DBFO) in UK roads', *Transport Reviews* 26(3)257–74.

Shatkin, G. (2002): 'Working with the community: dilemmas in radical planning in Metro Manila, The Philippines', *Planning Theory and Practice* 3(3)301–17.

——(2008): 'The city and the bottom line: urban megaprojects and the privatization of planning in Southeast Asia', *Environment and Planning A* 40(2)383–401.

Shaw, K. (2005): 'The place of alternative culture and the politics of its protection in Berlin, Amsterdam and Melbourne', *Planning Theory and Practice* 6(2)149–69.

Sheikh, K. and S. Rao (2007): 'Participatory city planning in Chhattisgarh: a civil society initiative', *Environment and Urbanization* 19(2)563–81.

Sheppard, E. and H. Leitner (2010): 'Quo vadis neoliberalism? The remaking of global capitalist governance after the Washington consensus', *Geoforum* 41(2)185–94.

Siemiatycki, M. (2005): 'The making of a mega project in the neoliberal city: the case of mass rapid transit infrastructure investment in Vancouver, Canada', *City* 9(1)67–83.

——(2007): 'What's the secret? Confidentiality in planning infrastructure using public/private partnerships', *Journal of the American Planning Association* 73(4)388–403.

——(2010): 'Delivering transportation infrastructure through public-private partnerships: planning concerns', *Journal of the American Planning Association* 76(4)43–58.

Silva, C.N. (2005): 'Urban planning and ethics', pp 311–16 in J. Rabin (Ed.): *Encyclopedia of Public Administration and Public Policy* (First Update Supplement). New York: Facts on File.

Silverman, R.M., H.L. Taylor and C. Crawford (2008): 'The role of citizen participation and action research principles in main street revitalization: an analysis of a local planning project', *Action Research* 6(1)69–93.

Simmons, W. (1999): 'The Third: Levinas' theoretical move from an-archical ethics to the realm of justice and politics', *Philosophy and Social Criticism* 25(6)83–104.

Sintomer, Y., C. Herzberg and A. Röcke (2008): 'Participatory budgeting in Europe: potentials and challenges', *International Journal of Urban and Regional Research* 32(1)164–78.

Sites, W. (2007): 'Beyond trenches and grassroots? Reflections on urban mobilization, fragmentation, and the anti-Wal-Mart campaign in Chicago', *Environment and Planning A* 39(11)2632–51.

Smith, N. (1995): *The New Urban Frontier: Gentrification and the Revanchist City*. London: Routledge.

Smith, N. and S. Low (2006): 'Introduction: the imperative of public space', pp 1–16 in S. Low and N. Smith (Eds): *The Politics of Public Space*. New York: Routledge.

Smithsimon, G. (2008): 'Dispersing the crowd. Bonus plazas and the creation of public space', *Urban Affairs Review* 43(3)325–51.

So, F.S., I. Stollman, F. Beal and D.S. Arnold (Eds) (1979): *The Practice of Local Government Planning*. Washington, D.C.: International City Management Association (in co-operation with the American Planning Association).

Sokoloff, H., H.M. Steinberg and S.N. Pyser (2005): 'Deliberative city planning on the Philadelphia waterfront', pp 185–96 in J. Gaskil and P. Levine (Eds): *The Deliberative Democracy Handbook. Strategies for Effective Civic Engagement in the Twenty-first Century*. New York: Jossey-Bass.

Sokoloff, W.W. (2005): 'Between justice and legality: Derrida on decision', *Political Research Quarterly* 58(2)341–52.

Somin, I. (1998): 'Voter ignorance and the democratic ideal', *Critical Review* 12(4)413–58.

Sørensen, R.J. (2006): 'Local government consolidations: the impact of political transaction costs', *Public Choice* 127(1–2)75–95.

Spivak, G.C. (1988): 'Can the subaltern speak?', pp 271–313 in C. Nelson and L. Grossberg (Eds): *Marxism and the Interpretation of Culture*. Basingstoke, Hampshire: Macmillan Education.

——(1994): 'Responsibility', *boundary 2* 21(3)19–64.

Stahler-Sholk, R. (2007): 'Resisting neoliberal homogenization: the Zapatista autonomy movement', *Latin American Perspectives* 34(2)48–63.

Stein, L. (2009): 'Social movement web use in theory and practice: a content analysis of US movement websites', *New Media and Society* 11(5)749–71.

Stiglitz, J. (1987): 'Principal and agent', pp 966–71 in: *The New Palgrave: A Dictionary of Economics. Volume 3* (Second Edition). New York: Palgrave Macmillan.

Stivers, C. (1994): 'The listening bureaucrat: responsiveness in public administration', *Public Administration Review* 54(4)364–69.

Stocks, E.L., D.A. Lishner and S.K. Decker (2009): 'Altruism or psychological escape: why does empathy promote prosocial behaviour?', *European Journal of Social Psychology* 39(5)649–65.

Street, M.D. (1997): 'Groupthink: an examination of theoretical issues, implications, and future research suggestions', *Small Group Research* 28(1)72–93.

Susskind, L.E. (1999): 'An alternative to Robert's Rules of Order for groups, organizations, and ad hoc assemblies that want to operate by consensus', pp 3–57 in L.E. Susskind, S. McKearnan and J. Thomas-Larmer (Eds): *The Consensus Building Handbook. A Comprehensive Guide to Reaching Agreement*. Thousand Oaks: Sage.

Susskind, L.E. and L. Crump (Eds) (2008): *Multiparty Negotiation. Volume 2: Theory and Practice of Public Dispute Resolution*. Los Angeles: Sage.

Susskind, L.E. and M. Elliott (Eds) (1983): *Paternalism, Conflict, and Coproduction. Learning from Citizen Action and Citizen Participation in Western Europe*. New York: Plenum Press.

Susskind, L.E., S. McKearnan and J. Thomas-Larmer (Eds) (1999): *The Consensus Building Handbook. A Comprehensive Guide to Reaching Agreement*. Thousand Oaks: Sage.

Susskind, L.E. and C.P. Ozawa (1983): 'Mediated negotiation in the public sector', *American Behavioral Scientist* 27(2)255–79.

Svartlamon Housing Foundation (2002): *Annual Report 2002*. Trondheim: Svartlamon Housing Foundation, Trondheim Municipality.

Svartlamon Residents Association (2005): *Miljøplan for Svartlamon* (Environmental Plan for Svartlamon). Trondheim: Svartlamon Residents Association.

Swain, C. and M. Tait (2007): 'The crisis of trust and planning', *Planning Theory and Practice* 8(2)229–47.

Sweet, E.L. and M. Chakars (2010): 'Identity, culture, land, and language: stories of insurgent planning in the Republic of Buryatia, Russia', *Journal of Planning Education and Research* 30(2)198–209.

Swords, A.C.S. (2007): 'Neo-Zapatista network politics: transforming democracy and development', *Latin American Perspectives* 34(2)78–93.

Swyngedouw, E., F. Moulart and A. Rodriguez (2002): 'Neoliberal urbanization in Europe: large-scale urban development projects and the new urban policy', *Antipode* 34(3)542–77.

Tait, M. and O.B. Jensen (2007): 'Travelling ideas, power and place: the cases of urban villages and business improvement districts', *International Planning Studies* 12(2)107–27.

Tamari, D. (2001): 'Military operations in urban environments: the case of Lebanon, 1982', pp 29–55 in M.C. Desch (Ed.): *Soldiers in Cities: Military Operations on Urban Terrain*. Carlisle, Pennsylvania: Strategic Studies Institute of the U.S. Army War College. www.strategicstudiesinstitute.army.mil/pubs/display.cfm?pubID=294 (accessed 13.04.07).

Tarnow, E. (2002): 'Coauthorship in physics', *Science and Engineering Ethics* 8(1)175–90.

Taşan-Kok, T. (2010): 'Entrepreneurial governance: challenges of large-scale property-led urban regeneration projects', *Tijdschrift voor Economische en Sociale Geografie* 101(2)126-49.

Taylor, C. (1994): 'The politics of recognition', pp 25–73 in A. Gutman (Ed.): *Multiculturalism: Examining the Politics of Recognition*. Princeton: Princeton University Press.

Taylor, M., M.L. Kent and W.J. White (2001): 'How activist organizations are using the Internet to build relationships', *Public Relations Review* 27(3)263–84.

Taylor, N. (1998): *Urban Planning Theory since 1945*. London: Sage.

Taylor, P., I. Turok and A. Hastings (2001): 'Competitive bidding in urban regeneration: stimulus or disillusionment for the losers?', *Environment and Planning C: Government and Policy* 19(1)45–63.

Temelova, J. (2007): 'Flagship developments and the physical upgrading of the post-socialist inner city: the Golden Angel project in Prague', *Geografiska Annaler Series B: Human Geography* 89B(2)169–81.

Tewdwr-Jones, M. (2002): 'Personal dynamics, distinctive frames and communicative planning', pp 65–92 in P. Allmendinger and M. Tewdwr-Jones (Eds): *Planning Futures. New Directions for Planning Theory*. London: Routledge.

Tewdwr-Jones, M. and P. Allmendinger (1998): 'Deconstructing communicative rationality: a critique of Habermasian collaborative planning', *Environment and Planning A* 30(11)1975–89.

Thomas, H. (2005): 'Pressures, purpose and collegiality in UK planning education', *Planning Theory and Practice* 6(2)238–47.

Thomas, J.M. and J. Darnton (2006): 'Social diversity and economic development in the metropolis', *Journal of Planning Literature* 21(2)153–68.

Thomas, P.G. (1998): 'The changing nature of accountability', pp 348–93 in B.G. Peters and D.J. Savoie (Eds): *Taking Stock: Assessing Public Sector Reforms*. Montreal: Canadian Centre for Management Development and McGill-Queen's University Press.

Thomassen, L. (Ed.) (2006a): *The Derrida-Habermas Reader*. Edinburgh: Edinburgh University Press.

——(2006b): 'The inclusion of the other? Habermas and the paradox of tolerance', *Political Theory* 34(4)439–62.

Thompson, D.F. (2005): *Restoring Responsibility*. New York: Cambridge University Press.

Thorkildsen, A. (2006): 'Hva kan vi lære av Svartlamon?' (What can we learn from Svartlamon?), *Sosiologisk Årbok* 11(1–2)13–34.

Throgmorton, J.A. (1996): *Planning as Persuasive Storytelling: The Rhetorical Construction of Chicago's Electric Future*. Chicago: University of Chicago Press.

——(2000): 'On the virtues of skilful meandering: acting as a skilled-voice-in-the-flow of persuasive argumentation', *Journal of the American Planning Association* 66(4)367–79.

Tiesdell, S. and P. Allmendinger (2001): 'The New Right and neighbourhood regeneration', *Housing Studies* 16(3)311–34.

Tonn, M.B. (2005): 'Taking conversation, dialogue, and therapy public', *Rhetoric and Public Affairs* 8(3)405–30.

Torfing, J., E. Sørensen and T. Fotel (2009): 'Democratic anchorage of infrastructural governance networks: the case of the Femern Belt forum', *Planning Theory* 8(3)282–308.

Trey, G.A. (1992): 'Communicative ethics in the face of alterity: Habermas, Levinas and the problem of post-conventional universalism', *Praxis International* 11(4)412–27.

Trifonas, P.P. (2000): 'Technologies of reason. Academic responsibility beyond the principle of reason as the metaphysical foundation of the university', pp 89–133 in P.P. Trifonas: *The Ethics of Writing. Derrida, Deconstruction, and Pedagogy*. Oxford: Rowman and Littlefield.

——(2003): 'The ethics of science and/as research: deconstruction and the orientations of a new academic responsibility', *Educational Philosophy and Theory* 35(3)285–95.

Trip, J.J. and A. Romein (2009): 'Beyond the hype: creative city development in Rotterdam', *Journal of Urban Regeneration and Renewal* 2(3)216–31.

Trondheim City Council (2001): *Reguleringsplan med bestemmelser for Svartlamon (Sak 0149/01, Sak 0150/01)* (Development plan with regulations, six pages). Trondheim: Municipality of Trondheim.

Trondheim Municipality (2006): *R 219b. Bestemmelser til endret reguleringsplan for Svartlamoen (Reinaområdet)* (Regulations to revised development plan). Trondheim: City Planning Office, Trondheim Municipality.

Trudeau, D. and M. Cope (2003): 'Labor and housing markets as public spaces: "personal responsibility" and the contradictions of welfare-reform policies', *Environment and Planning A* 35(5)779–98.

Tsivacou, I. (1996): 'The written form of planning', *Scandinavian Journal of Management* 12(1)69–88.

Tuckett, I. (1990): 'Coin Street: there *is* another way…', pp137–49 in J. Montgomery and A. Thornley (Eds): *Radical Planning Initiatives. New Directions for Urban Planning in the 1990s*. Aldershot: Gower.

Turner, R.S. (2002): 'The politics of design and development in the postmodern downtown', *Journal of Urban Affairs* 24(5)533–48.

Turok, I. (2004): 'Cities, regions and competitiveness', *Regional Studies* 38(9)1069–83.

Twight, C. (1988): 'Government manipulation of constitutional-level transaction costs: a general theory of transaction-cost augmentation and the growth of government', *Public Choice* 56(2)131–52.

——(1993): 'Channeling ideological change: the political economy of dependence on government', *Kyklos* 46(4)497–527.

——(1994): 'Political transaction-cost manipulation: an integrated theory', *Journal of Theoretical Politics* 6(2)189–216.

Uhlaner, C.J. (1989): '"Relational goods" and participation: incorporating sociability into a theory of rational action', *Public Choice* 62(3)253–85.

UN (1993): *Agenda 21. The United Nations Programme of Action from Rio (Earth Summit)*. New York: United Nations Department of Economic and Social Affairs.

Veer, D. van de (1986): *Paternalistic Intervention. The Moral Bounds on Benevolence*. Princeton: Princeton University Press.

Verma, N. (Ed.) (2007): *Institutions and Planning*. Amsterdam: Elsevier.

Vernon, R. (1979): 'Unintended consequences', *Political Theory* 7(1)57–73.

Vickers, M.H. and A. Kouzmin (2001): '"Resilience" in organizational actors and rearticulating "voice". Towards a humanistic critique of New Public Management', *Public Management Review* 3(1)95–119.

Vidyarthi, S. (2010): 'Reimagining the American neighbourhood unit for India', pp 73–93 in P. Healey and R. Upton (Eds): *Crossing Borders. International Exchange and Planning Practices*. London: Routledge.

Voogd, H. and J. Woltjer (1999): 'The communicative ideology in spatial planning: some critical reflections based on the Dutch experience', *Environment and Planning B: Planning and Design* 26(6)835–54.

Voyce, M. (2006): 'Shopping malls in Australia. The end of public space and the rise of "consumerist citizenship"', *Journal of Sociology* 42(3)269–86.

Wacquant, L. (2010): 'Crafting the neoliberal state: workfare, prisonfare, and social insecurity', *Sociological Forum* 25(2)197–220.

Wagenaar, H. (2011): '"A beckon to the makings, workings and doings of human beings": the critical pragmatism of John Forester', *Public Administration Review* 71(2)293–98.

Walker, G. and D. Weber (1984): 'A transaction cost approach to make-buy decisions', *Administrative Science Quarterly* 29(3)373–91.

Walks, R.A. (2006): 'Aestheticization and the cultural contradictions of neoliberal (sub) urbanism', *Cultural Geographies* 13(3)466–75.

Wall, M.A. (2007): 'Social movements and email: expressions of online identity in the globalization protests', *New Media and Society* 9(2)258–77.

Wang, H. (2005): 'Aporias, responsibility, and the im/possibility of teaching multicultural education', *Educational Theory* 55(1)45–60.

Warner, M.E. and A. Hefetz (2008): 'Managing markets for public service: the role of mixed public-private delivery of city services', *Public Administration Review* 68(1)155–66.

Warren, M.E. (1993): 'Can participatory democracy produce better selves? Psychological dimensions of Habermas's discursive model of democracy', *Political Psychology* 14(2)209–34.

——(Ed.) (1999): *Democracy and Trust*. Cambridge: Cambridge University Press.

Wart, M. van (1998): *Changing Public Sector Values*. New York: Garland.

Watson, V. (2002): 'The usefulness of normative planning theories in the context of Sub-Saharan Africa', *Planning Theory* 1(1)27–52.

——(2006): 'Deep difference: diversity, planning and ethics', *Planning Theory* 5(1)31–50.

——(2011): 'Planning and conflict – moving on', Paper presented at the 3rd World Planning Schools Congress, Perth, Western Australia, 4–8 July 2011.

Weber, R. (2002): 'Extracting value from the city: neoliberalism and urban redevelopment', pp 172–93 in N. Brenner and N. Theodore (Eds): *Spaces of Neoliberalism. Urban Restructuring in North America and Western Europe*. Oxford: Blackwell.

Webster, C.J. (2005): 'The public assignment of development rights', *Economic Affairs* 25(4)44–47.

Webster, C.J. and L.W.C. Lai (2003): *Property Rights, Planning and Markets: Managing Spontaneous Cities*. Cheltenham: Edward Elgar.

White, W.J. (2008): 'The interlocutor's dilemma: the place of strategy in dialogic theory', *Communication Theory* 18(1)5–26.

Whitzman, C. and J. Perkovic (2010): 'Women's safety audits and walking school buses', pp 219–36 in P. Healey and R. Upton (Eds): *Crossing Borders. International Exchange and Planning Practices*. London: Routledge.

Wilder, M.G. and B.M. Rubin (1996): 'Rhetoric versus reality. A review of studies on state enterprise zone programs', *Journal of the American Planning Association* 62(4)473–91.

Williamson, O.E. (1989): 'Transaction cost economics', pp 135–82 in R. Schmalensee and R. Willig (Eds): *Handbook of Industrial Organization. Volume 1*. Amsterdam: North-Holland.

——(1999): 'Public and private bureaucracies: a transaction cost economics perspective', *Journal of Law, Economics, and Organization* 15(1)306–42.

Willson, R.W., M. Payne and E. Smith (2003): 'Does discussion enhance rationality? A report from transportation planning practice', *Journal of the American Planning Association* 69(4)354–67.

Wilson, P.A. (1997): 'Building social capital: a learning agenda for the twenty-first century', *Urban Studies* 34(5–6)745–60.

Wolf, S. (1982): 'Moral saints', *Journal of Philosophy* 79(8)419–39.

Wolf-Powers, L. (2005): 'Up-zoning New York City's mixed-use neighborhoods. Property-led economic development and the anatomy of a planning dilemma', *Journal of Planning Education and Research* 24(4)379–93.

——(2008): 'Expanding planning's public sphere: STREET Magazine, activist planning, and community development in Brooklyn, New York, 1971–1975', *Journal of Planning Education and Research* 28(2)180–95.

——(2009): 'Keeping counterpublics alive in planning', pp 161–72 in P. Marcuse, J. Connolly, J. Novy, I. Olivo, C. Potter and J. Steil (Eds): *Searching for the Just City. Debates in Urban Theory and Practice.* New York: Routledge.

Woltjer, J. (2000): *Consensus Planning.* Aldershot: Ashgate.

Wu, F. (2005): 'Rediscovering the "gate" under market transition: from work-unit compounds to commodity housing enclaves', *Housing Studies* 20(2)235–54.

Wyly, E.K. and D.J. Hammel (2004): 'Gentrification, segregation, and discrimination in the American urban system', *Environment and Planning* A 36(7)1215–41.

Yang, X., S.K. Tok and F. Su (2008): 'The privatization and commercialization of China's airports', *Journal of Air Transport Management* 14(5)243–51.

Yetano, A., S. Royo and B. Acerete (2010): 'What is driving the increasing presence of citizen participation initiatives?', *Environment and Planning* C: *Government and Policy* 28(5)783–802.

Yiftachel, O. (1995a): 'The dark side of modernism: planning as control of an ethnic minority', pp 216–42 in S. Watson and K. Gibson (Eds): *Postmodern Cities and Spaces.* Oxford: Blackwell.

——(1995b): 'Planning as control: policy and resistance in a deeply divided society', *Progress in Planning* 44(2)115–184.

——(2006): 'Re-engaging planning theory? Towards "South-Eastern" perspectives', *Planning Theory* 5(3)211–22.

——(2009): 'Critical theory and "gray space": mobilization of the colonized', *City* 13(2)246–63.

Yiftachel, O. and H. Yacobi (2002): 'Planning a bi-national capital: should Jerusalem remain united?', *Geoforum* 33(1)137–45.

Young, I.M. (2000): *Inclusionary Democracy.* Oxford: Oxford University Press.

——(2001): 'Activist challenges to deliberative democracy', *Political Theory* 29(5)670–90.

Ysa, T. (2007): 'Governance forms in urban public-private partnerships', *International Public Management Journal* 10(1)35–57.

Zaborowski, H. (2000): 'On freedom and responsibility: remarks on Sartre, Levinas and Derrida', *Heythrop Journal* 41(1)47–65.

Zimmerman, J. (2008): 'From brew town to cool town: neoliberalism and the creative city development strategy in Milwaukee', *Cities* 25(4)230–42.

Zografos, C. and J. Martinez-Alier (2009): 'The politics of landscape value: a case study of wind farm conflict in rural Catalonia', *Environment and Planning* A 41(7)1726–44.

Index